D1523273

The Citizens' Council

Organized Resistance to the Second Reconstruction, 1954–64

THE Citizens' Council

Organized Resistance to the Second Reconstruction, 1954-64

Neil R. McMillen

University of Illinois Press
URBANA / CHICAGO / LONDON

© 1971 by The Board of Trustees of the University of Illinois
Manufactured in the United States of America
Library of Congress Catalog Card No. 75-151999
252 00177 X

HS
2330
.C483
M33

*To Beverly, who always
deserved better*

Preface

THIS is the history of the Citizens' Council and its determined but vain endeavor to resist the implementation of the Supreme Court's school desegregation ruling of 1954. Throughout, the primary objectives have been to describe the movement's rise and decline, to record its thought and action, and to assess its impact on the course of southern history during the first decade of desegregation. Although organized resistance lies at the very heart of this volume, there has been no attempt to record the activity of all groups organized to resist the *Brown* decision and the larger implications of the federal racial policies now generally called the Second Reconstruction. Rather, the focus of this study is on the most "respectable" wing of the resistance movement—more particularly, on those groups most closely identified with that loose confederation of statewide segregation associations known as the Citizens' Councils of America. Thus, for the purposes of this inquiry, not all groups bearing the Council's name have been considered to be Citizens' Councils. For example, both the Citizens' Councils of Kentucky and the Seaboard White Citizens' Councils have been excluded because they more nearly resembled Klans than Councils. Prone to violence and strident anti-Semitism, committed to secrecy and other behavioral patterns associated in the popular mind with hooded night-riders, such groups were condemned, even by Councilors themselves, as "extremist." Conversely, other organizations, such as the Tennessee Federation for Constitutional Government and the Virginia Defenders of State Sovereignty and Individual Liberties, despite their alien nomenclature, have been treated as Council-like groups. Comparatively restrained and dignified, these groups, like others associated with the regional Council organization, sought identification only with the "better class" of southern whites. To be sure, their practices sometimes belied their preachments, but they were ostensibly committed to strictly "legal" avenues of circumvention and defiance of the federal mandate.

Whether respectable or otherwise, resistance groups have left few records of primary value to the historian. To date, there are available few manuscript materials, few financial records, no complete membership lists, and no minutes of closed meetings. Nor does so recent a topic permit the use of census compilations and other "hard" data so highly regarded by the profession's current generation of quantifiers, the "Cliometricians." Thus, altogether innocent of statistical techniques, little touched even by the traditional stuff of history, this volume relies heavily on the Council's own voluminous publications, interviews and correspondence with Council dignitaries and their critics, reports of civil rights and fact-finding agencies, and, most of all, the daily and weekly press. Admittedly, then, it is what Lee Benson has derisively called "impressionistic" history.

It is currently fashionable for writers of books on controversial subjects to acknowledge ruefully their personal prejudices while at the same time assuring the reader of their earnest endeavors to remain dispassionate and straightforward. I, too, would like to employ this worthy convention. Consistently, my sympathies have been with the black struggle to achieve those rights of unimpeded opportunity and free association that white Americans have traditionally taken for granted. But this unwavering commitment to a colorblind constitution has been tempered by years of pleasurable and rewarding association with Deep South segregationists, many of whom, including some relatives by marriage, were members or friends of the Citizens' Council. One of the guidelines used in the preparation of this manuscript is a belief that invective, although more easily mastered, is far less useful to the scholar than empathy. Thus it is my hope that this volume does not ring with condemnation. To be sure, the Council, like any other mass movement, had its miscreants, its mean-spirited and unconscionable demagogues. But it should not be assumed that the people who dominate these pages were necessarily evil or depraved, or even that they were more neurotic or less humane than the population generally. For the most part, they were fully as honest, hard-working, upstanding, and God-fearing as their harshest critics. That they often exhibited the ignoblest prejudices even as they professed the loftiest ideals should surprise only beginning students of human behavior.

In a much-quoted appeal for greater white understanding of the black experience in the United States, W. E. B. DuBois once chided a scholar of the opposite race for his lack of sympathy. One need not, the Negro historian acknowledged, be Japanese to write of Japan, or English to write of Great Britain; but the one who would write of "a group to which he is socially and culturally alien . . . must have some extraordinary gifts." Regrettably, this non-Southerner can claim no such gifts. But I can gratefully acknowledge those patient Southerners, black and white, who generously shared their intimate knowledge of the region I have grown to love.

Dewey W. Grantham, a friend and teacher, not only suggested the topic for this book but expertly guided my efforts through an early draft. Numan V. Bartley offered many valuable suggestions and permitted me to make use of his insightful study of massive resistance well before it was published. James T. Leeson, a wise and gentle native son, shared his broad knowledge of the New South and helped me to accept the region on its own terms. The Southern Education Reporting Service offered me an invaluable collection of material and a convivial environment in which to work. The Anti-Defamation League, the Southern Regional Council, Constantine G. Belissary, Wilson Minor, and at least a score of other agencies and people gave invaluable assistance. Sharon Hannum, Dwight Hoover, John Ray Skates, C. Warren Vander Hill, learned colleagues all, helped rid the manuscript of many embarrassing errors. My wife Beverly and my secretary, Mary Jo Minton, performed admirably the difficult task of typing numerous drafts of a much-revised manuscript. The Woodrow Wilson Foundation and the State of Mississippi underwrote substantial portions of the costs incurred during the research and writing of this study. I am also pleased to acknowledge the help rendered by some of the protagonists in this history. Through letters and conversations of varying degrees of candor, they gave me the kind of immediate contact with history that makes contemporary research, despite its myraid drawbacks, so eminently rewarding. Last, I wish to thank my parents, who, by practicing what they preached, provided my earliest models of forbearance and tolerance.

Table of Contents

Part IV: Action and Decline

Part V: Epilogue

PART I

Prologue

CHAPTER I

Backdrop for Organized Resistance

To a degree unrivaled by any other section, the white South in the middle of the twentieth century retained its peculiar regional awareness. Despite its ever-growing diversity, its cultural, economic, and political heterogeneity, the region clung tenaciously to its sectional self-consciousness. Its traditionally aberrant position within the nation permitted Southerners from Tidewater Virginia to Texas, from the bluegrass region to the piney woods, nearly to overlook the divisive present by focusing on the lost past, and, consequently, to share a sense of solidarity that had little foundation in fact. Indeed, at mid-century there was no static and monolithic South. Beyond a statutory regard for segregated schools, the seventeen widely varying southern and border states which bore the brunt of the Supreme Court's epochal decree of May 17, 1954, had little in common. Their principal bond was the presence of Negroes in relatively high percentages. But even here, wide variations existed.

According to the 1950 census, nearly half of the counties in the South had 10 percent or fewer Negroes, and only about one-fifth had 40 percent or more. Along the border, where nonwhite percentages ranged from West Virginia's scant 6 percent to a high of 17 percent in Maryland, Negroes truly comprised a minority group. But among the eleven former Confederate states, only Texas had a nonwhite population smaller than 13 percent. In the black-belt counties of the Deep South—once so called because of their deep, rich topsoils but now identified as areas where Negro density is highest—whites were frequently outnumbered by blacks. Of the 418 counties and parishes in Alabama, Georgia, Louisiana, Mississippi, and South Carolina, there were 119 in 1950 which had Negro populations of 50 percent or more. There were five counties in Alabama alone whose populations were more than 75 percent black.

When compared with statistics from the remaining six southern states, these black-belt figures become even more significant. Collectively, Arkansas, Florida, North Carolina, Tennessee, Texas, and Virginia could account for only 38 counties where nonwhites either equaled or exceeded the white populations. Of these, only six were to be found in Florida and Texas.[1]

Figures such as these provide compelling evidence of the variety of southern life, and of the existence of what Ralph McGill chose to call the "many Souths."[2] Perhaps more important, they also provide insight into the diverse pattern of white southern resistance to the Supreme Court's desegregation ruling. The best single index to the problem of adjustment required in a given southern community by the decree of May 17, 1954, was the community's own Negro-Caucasian ratio. Almost invariably, racial tensions ran highest and white intransigence was greatest in areas where the Negro population was the most dense. Conversely, in areas where blacks comprised a relatively small minority, white compliance was very often achieved with comparative ease.

But many other factors of no ethnological relevance could and did serve to modify racial attitudes—despite a high proportion of blacks to whites. A community's urbanization, the character of its leadership, its political and economic structure, and its local customs frequently influenced its response to school desegregation. Thus the rapidly industrializing and urbanizing border states, never stigmatized by Confederate affiliations or successfully burdened with large-

[1] Except where otherwise indicated, these and all subsequent population figures are taken from U.S. Bureau of Census, *Seventeenth Census of the United States, 1950, Population.*

[2] Ralph McGill, "The South Has Many Faces," *Atlantic Monthly,* 211 (April, 1963), 83–98.

scale plantation agriculture, retained few tangible links with the South. Oil- and cattle-rich Oklahoma did not become a state until 1907, and in most respects it more closely resembled the plains states than the South. Likewise West Virginia, with its developing complex of industry and mining, shared little with the cotton South; it would become the first in the seventeen-state area to end segregation in all of its biracial school districts. By voting for Theodore Roosevelt in 1904, maverick Missouri demonstrated that the border South, at least, had not been solidly Democratic for half a century. Moreover, if one excludes such obvious exceptions as the eastern counties of West Virginia, Missouri's Bootheel, and Little Dixie along Oklahoma's eastern fringe, the border South had all but outgrown its predominantly agrarian past.

To a lesser degree much the same can be said of the peripheral South—those six southern states which ring Alabama, Georgia, Louisiana, Mississippi, and South Carolina. Here economic, geographic, historical, and social factors combined to weaken sectional and strengthen national ties. Except for its eastern counties, Texas, like Oklahoma, had a distinctly western flavor. On the eve of the Supreme Court's decision, Arkansas, Florida, North Carolina, Tennessee, and Virginia seemed less an integral part of the Confederate South than at any other time. In short, the perimeter of what could be called "the South" had been pushed deeper into Dixie. States which had once been strongly southern now seemed less so.

The quality of state and local leadership was also a factor which profoundly affected the popular response to the desegregation mandate; border state officials generally moved rapidly to establish constructive policies of compliance. By the end of the first week under the new interpretation, Governor J. Caleb Boggs of Delaware declared in a letter to the state board of education that his administration's policy would be "to work toward adjustment to the United States constitutional requirements." In neighboring Maryland, Republican Governor Theodore McKeldin issued a comparable statement. Exhibiting pride in his state's law-abiding tradition, he expressed confidence that Maryland's "citizens and . . . officials will accept readily the United States Supreme Court's interpretation of our fundamental law. . . ." Similarly, the governors of West Virginia and Kentucky immediately indicated the willingness of their states to comply with the law of the land.[3] Only in Oklahoma did upper-echelon state leadership appear to balk. Although Governor Johnston Murray, then chairman of the Southern Governors' Conference, gave assurances that his state would obey the nation's laws, he conceded: "I don't believe in forcing people to do something they don't want to do." His successor, Raymond Gary, acknowledged one year later that some areas of his state did not want desegregated schools. But he sternly warned that Oklahoma school boards which defied the Court's mandate would do so without administrative support.[4]

Under circumstances so salutary, it is not surprising that one liberal research agency, the Southern Regional Council, after observing some 1,100 instances of desegregation occurring in the seventeen-state area between May, 1954, and May, 1956, could report: "There is no longer a solid South of segregation." To be sure, the Southern Regional Council was not inclined to be pessimistic during these early years of the new era. Only a few months after the rendering of the *Brown* decision, it had contended that "the South is moving—not always smoothly, but with seeming inevitability—toward an increasingly integrated society." [5] However naïve it may seem in retrospect, such optimism was not altogether ill conceived. For while Jim Crow had not been routed, he was surely in retreat. The District of Columbia, as well as Maryland, Delaware, West Virginia, and Missouri, had moved almost immediately toward compliance, and (with the notable exception of Milford, Delaware) had done so with a minimum of disorder. In the following school year, 1955–56, some desegregation occurred in Kentucky, Oklahoma, and

[3] *Southern School News,* September 3, 1954, 3, 6, 7, 14.

[4] For a brief account of the gubernatorial mood in the region south of the Potomac, see a chapter entitled "The Governors" in Reed Sarratt, *The Ordeal of Desegregation: The First Decade* (New York: Harper and Row, 1966), 1–27.

[5] Harold C. Fleming, "Integration in the South," *Integration North and South,* by Fleming and David Loth (New York: Fund for the Republic, 1956), 47–49. See also Fleming and John C. Constable, *What's Happening in School Integration?* Public Affairs Pamphlet No. 224 (New York: Public Affairs Committee, 1956), 18–19.

Texas. Although pockets of unyielding segregationist sentiment existed in every border state, school desegregation in some form had begun in each of them by 1955. During the course of that year 70 percent of all the school districts in the border states operated biracial classrooms; by the end of the first decade of desegregation only 10 percent remained totally segregated.[6]

While desegregation of public schools developed at a considerable pace and with a minimum of resistance among the border states, the states of the old Confederacy proved less tractable. Here no politician of stature publicly expressed even tacit approval of the *Brown* interpretation. Here official sentiment ranged from the cautious resignation of Tennessee's liberal Senator Estes Kefauver ("While we may not agree with the decision, we must not let this disrupt our public-school system") to the open defiance of Mississippi's senior senator, James O. Eastland ("The South will not abide by, or [*sic*] obey, this legislative decision by a political court").[7] In marked contrast to the border states, the gubernatorial mood of the eleven-state region was not calculated to encourage hasty compliance. Confident of full popular support, Governor George Bell Timmerman, Jr., of South Carolina informed a national television audience that his state's schools would "not in a thousand years" be integrated. In Georgia, Herman Talmadge's successor, Marvin Griffin, won the Democratic gubernatorial nomination in September, 1954, with a campaign pledge that "come hell or high water, races will not be mixed in Georgia schools." Even such a relatively moderate Deep South governor as Mississippi's James P. Coleman, who was frequently charged with "softness" on the race issue, was willing

[6] As with virtually all other statistics, figures on numbers of desegregated school districts can be misleading. Desegregated districts reflect more the official attitude of a state than the number of Negroes actually enrolled in biracial schools. For example, at the end of the first decade only 55 of the border area's 772 biracial school districts remained segregated, but a full 45 percent of its 514,125 enrolled Negro students still attended segregated schools. ("Ten Years in Review," *Southern School News*, May, 1964, 1–2; U.S. Commission on Civil Rights, *Survey of School Desegregation in the Southern and Border States, 1965–1966* [Washington: Government Printing Office, 1966], 1.)

[7] Quoted in Benjamin Muse, *Ten Years of Prelude: The Story of Integration Since the Supreme Court's 1954 Decision* (New York: Viking Press, 1964), 20.

to promise that "segregation in Mississippi will be permanently preserved so long as the people want it." [8] Clearly, the mood of the ex-Confederacy did not resemble that of the border. At the conclusion of the first decade of desegregation, only about 1 percent of the school-age Negroes residing in these eleven southern states attended biracial classes. And intransigent Mississippi, operating its classrooms throughout the period precisely as it had throughout the century, managed to complete the 1963–64 academic year without so much as a single Negro child to sully its lily-white record of public education.

Unreceptive though the region was to social change, it did not present a solid front. In the six states of the upper South, the states comprising what one observer called "The Token Tier," [9] resistance to the *Brown* ruling was less adamant and collapsed earlier than in Alabama, Georgia, Louisiana, Mississippi, and South Carolina. In the first two years after the decision, only Arkansas, Tennessee, and Texas had any biracial school districts. But in each of the following years, the southern states moved one by one from total defiance to token compliance. North Carolina desegregated some districts during the 1957–58 school year; Virginia followed in 1958–59; and Florida, Louisiana, and Georgia fell into step in 1959–60, 1960–61, and 1961–62, respectively. Two Deep South states, South Carolina and Alabama, resisted even token desegregation until 1963, and not until September, 1964, did a token few Negroes gain admission to Mississippi's all-white schools.

In its most effective and characteristic form, white southern hostility toward the changing pattern of race relations was expressed through the state legislatures. Responding to popular pressures for noncompliance, southern lawmakers enacted a fantastic melange of statutes, ranging from pupil placement acts and compulsory attendance repeal laws to legislation providing for school closure and the establishment of private institutions. Generally content to leave the business of resistance in the hands of their duly elected representatives, the vast majority of white citizens attended to their personal wants and pursued their own pleasures much as they had

[8] *Southern School News,* October 1, 1954, 61; August, 1956, 9; October, 1956, 2.

[9] Sarratt, *The Ordeal of Desegregation,* 352–53.

during the pre-*Brown* period. But a militant minority, the activists among them, were unable or unwilling to sit idly while their legislators, often with considerable success, endeavored to place impediments between the nation's law and the region's schools. In a manner reminiscent of the postbellum period, these disaffected citizens affiliated themselves with some ninety different private groups newly organized to resist the Second Reconstruction.[10] By the second anniversary of the public school decisions, these "protective societies" accounted for a considerable portion of the energies of perhaps as many as 250,000 to 300,000 people from virtually every station of southern life.

In terms of principles and purposes, the organizations varied widely, but in their ultimate goals—the denial of socio-political equality to the black man—they were as one. The variety of their nomenclature is too numerous to list here. Suffice it to say that some of their names, like that of the Southern Gentlemen, smacked of chivalry. Others, such as the White Brotherhood and White Men, Inc., referred to color, and still others—the Christian Civic League and the Association of Catholic Laymen—evoked religion. The names of some were patriotic, including the American States' Rights Association and the Patriots of North Carolina; some, such as the Pond Hollow Segregation Club, were amusing; and others, such as the Society for the Preservation of State Government and Racial Integrity and the Virginia Defenders of State Sovereignty and Individual Liberties, were simply cumbersome. And one, of course, was called the National Association for the Advancement of White People. But none was more powerful than the Citizens' Council, which in the course of a few short years would claim among its members governors, congressmen, judges, physicians, lawyers, industrialists, and bankers, as well as an assortment of lesser men who crowded membership rosters and packed municipal auditoriums to dedicate themselves to the preservation of "states' rights and racial integrity."

[10] See James W. Vander Zanden, "The Southern White Resistance Movement to Integration" (unpublished Ph.D. dissertation, University of North Carolina, 1958), 437–40.

PART II

Organizing for Resistance

CHAPTER II

Mississippi: Mother of the Movement

MISSISSIPPIANS were "shocked and stunned," Governor Hugh L. White informed the state's lawmakers, by the Supreme Court's school desegregation decision. Addressing a joint meeting of the Mississippi legislature convened in special session on September 7, 1954, to consider ways of preserving segregated education, the governor spoke confidently of popular consensus in that moment of crisis. "There were no overt demonstrations [on Black Monday]," he conceded, "but I know I am correct in saying that there was universal resolution not to abide by such an unreasonable decision if lawful means could be found by which to avoid it." [1]

Governor White's assessment of the mood of his fellow Mississippians was essentially correct. Most whites were opposed to a change in the educational status quo; once in session, their elected representatives turned with dispatch to the defense of Jim Crow schools. Indeed, even before the Court's edict, the legislature began to fortify Mississippi's dual system of education. Hoping to show good faith and thereby influence a favorable decision on the school segregation cases pending since December, 1952, the state legislature enacted a public school equalization program late in 1953. Although requiring continued racial separation, the measure pro-

[1] *Journal of the Senate of the State of Mississippi,* Extraordinary Sessions of 1954 and 1955, 8. See also *Southern School News,* October 1, and Jackson *Daily News,* September 7, 1954.

vided for the elimination of many of the most obvious disparities between Negro and white education within the state. It called for equal salaries for Negro teachers and equal educational opportunities for Negro students, as well as equal transportation facilities and equal physical plants for Negro schools. Awaiting a decision favorable to segregation, however, the funds essential for much of the equalization program were not appropriated.[2]

Provisions were also made for an unfavorable ruling. In the regular session of 1954, state legislators established by concurrent resolution a twenty-five-member Legal Educational Advisory Committee "to preserve and promote the best interests of both races" by maintaining separate educational facilities. Composed of the governor, other state officials including the attorney general, and the state's foremost legal talent, the LEAC would serve as the planning agency for Mississippi's defiance of the federal mandate. Its first plan was the so-called "last resort" amendment to the state's sixty-four-year-old constitution, permitting the legislature to abolish Mississippi's public schools. Upon the urging of the governor, the legislature voted overwhelmingly to submit the school closure amendment to the electorate.[3]

Another index to Mississippi's defiant mood was the speed with which organized resistance developed within the state. When Governor White addressed the joint legislative session early in September, 1954, there were already seventeen counties with local Citizens' Council organizations.[4] The first chapters did not emerge until after the *Brown* decisions, but the movement's origins may be traced to the autumn of 1953. For it was in November of that year that Robert B. Patterson, manager of a 1,585 acre Leflore County plantation, learned at a meeting in the Indianola school of cases then pending before the Supreme Court that could radically alter traditional southern social behavior. Describing his reactions in a letter printed for distribution to acquaintances, this former Mississippi State University football star and World War II paratrooper indicated that what he learned that evening had made him "confused, mad and

[2] *Southern School News*, September 3, 1954, 8.

[3] Ibid., September 3, 8; October 1, 1954, 9.

[4] Paul Anthony, "Pro-Segregation Groups' History and Trends," *New South*, 12 (January, 1957), 5.

ashamed." Convinced that national salvation required nothing less than total white solidarity, he urged concerned and patriotic citizens to "stand together forever firm against communism and mongrelization." [5]

The response to Patterson's cry for organized resistance was less enthusiastic than he had hoped. Indeed, not until after a unanimous court nullified "separate-but-equal" public education did the white South come to share his alarm. Then Mississippi Circuit Judge Thomas Pickens Brady, borrowing an epithet used by U.S. Representative John Bell Williams to describe the day of the *Brown* decision,[6] delivered his "Black Monday" address before the Greenwood chapter of the Sons of the American Revolution.

Although educated at Lawrenceville and Yale (class of 1927), Tom P. Brady was every inch a Deep South lawyer. Born in New Orleans in 1903, he studied law at the University of Mississippi and, after graduation in 1930, began his practice in the sleepy southern Mississippi hamlet of Brookhaven. Once the chairman of the speaker's bureau of the States' Rights Democratic Party, this former Dixiecrat believed that the *Brown* ruling, like the Truman administration's civil rights program, was "socialistic." [7]

Primarily, Brady's "Black Monday" speech was an attack on the Court's "disdain" for legal precedent. Encouraged by fellow members of the SAR, he laced it with racial clichés and hastily expanded it to ninety pages. Accorded almost instant success in segregation circles, this crudely printed booklet became the inspiration and first handbook for the Council movement. In 1956 it won for its author

[5] This account of Patterson's pre-*Brown* interest in organizing a resistance movement is recounted in John Bartlow Martin, *The Deep South Says "Never"* (New York: Ballantine Books, 1957), 1–3.

[6] Williams apparently first used the words "Black Monday" in a speech delivered to the House on May 19, 1954. See U.S. *Congressional Record,* 83 Cong., 2 Sess., 1954, 6857.

[7] Interview with Thomas Pickens Brady, June 24, 1970. For details of Brady's life see *Who's Who in the South and Southwest,* 9th ed. (Chicago: Marquis-Who's Who, 1965), 112; Hodding Carter III, *The South Strikes Back* (Garden City: Doubleday, 1959), 26–27; James Graham Cook, *The Segregationists* (New York: Appelton-Century-Crofts, 1962), 13–33; and Phillip Abbot Luce, "The Mississippi White Citizens' Council: 1954–1959" (unpublished M.A. thesis, Department of Political Science, Ohio State University, 1960), 35, 43ff.

the commendation of both houses of the Mississippi legislature.[8] A veritable compendium of segregationist thought, *Black Monday's* central theme was the contention that the *Brown* decision, that "stereotyped psychological opinion," imperiled the nation. Forced to chose between "SEGREGATION OR AMALGAMATION," the United States could be saved only if its responsible white citizenry acted decisively. Among his guidelines for national salvation the Brookhaven lawyer proposed: the popular election of Supreme Court justices, a youth indoctrination program on the "TRUTH ABOUT COMMUNISM" and the "FACTS OF ETHNOLOGY," the creation of a forty-ninth state as the Negro's exclusive domain, and, if necessary, the abolition of public schools. Each of these measures was in turn given more or less serious consideration by the exponents of massive resistance, but the most prescient of Brady's suggestions was his proposal for the formation in each of the southern states of "law abiding" resistance organizations. Open and above-board, in no way resembling the "nefarious Ku Klux Klans," these organizations would be coordinated by a "National Federation of Sovereign States." The Federation's primary task would be to orchestrate a regional concert of defiance, but it would also disseminate "correct information" about the "imminent dangers" confronting the republic. And, should circumstances warrant such action, it could become a third political party, the "National Party of Sovereign States of America." As for individual state organizations, they could select names most suitable for their own purposes; but, for Mississippi, the judge proposed that the group be called the "Sons of the White Magnolia." [9]

Brady's call for organized resistance appealed to many indignant whites, but to none more strongly than to "Tut" Patterson. Years later, he informed the judge that his decision to devote his life to resisting desegregation came after reading *Black Monday*. Fortified by Brady's prose, he gathered the nucleus for the first council: David H. Hawkins, manager of Indianola's cotton compress; Arthur

[8] *Journal of the Senate of the State of Mississippi*, January 3–April 6, 1956, 650, 677; *Journal of the House of Representatives of the State of Mississippi*, January 3–April 6, 1956, 854.

[9] Tom P. Brady, *Black Monday*, 2nd ed. (Winona: Association of Citizens' Councils of Mississippi, 1955), 67–80. A limited first edition, published on the presses of the Brookhaven *Leader*, appeared in June, 1954.

B. Clark, Jr., a Harvard-educated attorney; and Herman Moore, prominent Indianola banker. Then, after a quiet meeting on July 11 with fourteen of the town's substantial civic and business leaders —including its mayor and its city attorney—Patterson and his cadre of activists held a public meeting at the town hall. Attended by seventy-five to one hundred townspeople, this rally resulted in the organization of the Indianola Citizens' Council. Moore was elected president, Clark vice-president, Hawkins treasurer, and Patterson executive secretary.[10] As Patterson later recalled, there were few who suspected on that night in the third week of July that this beginning would soon "expand miraculously into a virile and potent organization." [11]

Situated along the banks of cypress-studded Indian Bayou, Indianola was in most respects a natural birthplace for a white supremacy movement. The seat of Sunflower County, where Senator James O. Eastland maintained his vast plantation, this drowsy trading center lay in the heart of Mississippi's cotton-rich and politically conservative Delta region which arches along the Mississippi River from Vicksburg northward to Memphis. Then, as today, the county was overwhelmingly rural, and most of its 56,031 people earned their livelihood from agriculture. In Sunflower County—where Negroes in 1950 comprised 68 percent of the total population, but accounted for only .03 percent of the registered voters—white resistance to racial equality obscured all other issues. Here organized segregation would flourish nearly as well as premium staple cotton.

The "Indianola Plan," as the procedures used in the organization

[10] There are numerous journalistic accounts of the organziation of the first Citizens' Council, all essentially the same. See Paul Anthony, "Pro-Segregation Groups' History and Trends," 4–10; Carter, *The South Strikes Back*, 31ff.; Martin, *The Deep South Says "Never"*, 3–4; Muse, *Ten Years of Prelude*, 47; and Sarratt, *The Ordeal of Desegregation*, 299. For a detailed and critical account of the July 11 organizational meeting, see Stan Opotowsky, *Dixie Dynamite: The Inside Story of the White Citizens' Councils*, reprinted from the New York *Post*, January 7–20, 1957 (New York: National Association for the Advancement of Colored People, n.d.), 5–6. A more favorable newspaper account of the Council's early development is Thomas R. Waring's second article in a series of three, "Private Citizens Formed Citizens' Councils," Charleston *News and Courier*, September 16, 1955.

[11] *Annual Report: August, 1955* (Winona: Association of Citizens' Councils of Mississippi, 1955), 1.

of the Council in Sunflower County came to be known, served as a model for future Council development. The movement's leaders and sympathizers contended that Councils "start at the grass roots level as a sort of town meeting,"[12] but only the earliest groups were genuinely spontaneous developments initiated by local citizens. To be sure, townspeople at any given organizational meeting did "vote" to form a Citizens' Council, but well beforehand the groundwork was carefully laid by hard-core activists imported for the occasion from previously established Councils. As one early guide for Council organization observed, "the incentive and will to organize a Citizens' Council must come from within the community itself." But because Council organizers also believed that "the more complacency and apathy that the townspeople showed, the greater the need for an organization," they did not hesitate to send in outside representatives to stimulate community "incentive and will." For such purposes service clubs were ideally suited. Not only did they provide readily assembled groups of civic-minded white citizens, but they represented the respectability and contained the "responsible" and "conservative" leadership with which the Council movement so diligently sought identification.[13]

Typically, an organizer such as Patterson or Brady would be invited by a sympathetic member to address a Rotary, Kiwanis, Civitan, or Exchange Club luncheon in an unorganized locality.[14] After explaining the Council's nature and purpose, he met with interested individuals to arrange a second and larger meeting. At this second meeting a temporary chairman and a combination steering-nominating committee were chosen. The committee, in turn, drafted a proposed charter and bylaws and prepared a list of nominees for the board of directors.

[12] Waring, "Mississippi Citizens' Councils Are Protecting Both Races," Charleston *News and Courier*, September 15, 1955.

[13] "How to Organize a Citizens' Council," *The Citizens' Council*, August, 1956, 4; "How to Organize a Citizens' Council," *2nd Annual Report*, August, 1956 (Greenwood: Association of Citizens' Councils of Mississippi, 1956), 1–2; "Citizens' Councils—A Brief History," *The Citizen*, November, 1968, 15.

[14] The Council's use of service clubs for purposes of proselytization was acknowledged by Robert Patterson in *Annual Report: August, 1955*, 1, and *2nd Annual Report: August, 1956*, 1.

The selection of the directors was particularly critical, for they were not only to make organizational policies but to insure "peace and good order in the community." The Council's permanent officers (also proposed by the nominating committee) were drawn from the board of directors, and its president served as board chairman. Moreover, it was from the board's ranks that the president appointed the chairman of the standing committees which performed many of the Council's routine tasks. To insure that directors represented a cross section of the community's "solid" and "respectable" citizenry, every effort was made to recruit "major business, agriculture, labor, and industrial interests, as well as representatives of religious and social groups." [15] By following these procedures, little was left to chance and uniformity was assured. When at last the closed-door sessions were concluded and the nascent "grass roots" organization was revealed to the public, the Council was virtually complete—lacking only a membership to ratify the prefabricated structure.

To supplement this technique of proselytization by personal contact, early Council organizers used form letter campaigns. Among the earliest such efforts was that of former state legislator Fred Jones, a Council stalwart from Inverness and member of Sunflower County's board of supervisors. Addressed to "Dear Friend," Jones's mimeographed letter was designed to arouse apathetic community leaders by raising the specter of a militant and well-organized National Association for the Advancement of Colored People. Declaring it "imperative" that Councils be organized across the state, Jones informed his readers that "Walter White, a Negro from the Society for Advancement of Colored People, will speak in Jackson early in November." "White would not have dared do this ten years ago," he added, "but our complacency has shown the Negro that aggressiveness might pay off." [16]

A second form letter sent in the early stages of the movement's expansion was Robert B. Patterson's controversial circular of Au-

[15] "How to Organize a Citizens' Council," *2nd Annual Report, August, 1956*, 3; "How to Organize a Citizens' Council," *The Citizens' Council*, August, 1956, 4.

[16] Quoted in Jackson *Daily News*, October 24, 1954.

gust 21, 1954, which contained a reading list on desegregation for new and prospective Council members. Most of the recommended material was anti-Negro, but included on the list were items printed by such anti-Semitic organizations as Gerald L. K. Smith's well-organized and well-financed Christian Nationalist Crusade and Gerald Winrod's Defenders, publisher of a vitriolic monthly journal. Admitting that "some of these groups are anti-Semitic," Patterson hastened to indict the liberal racial policies of other religious groups as well, "including all Protestant, Catholic, and Jewish" churches. Then, as if to prove his racial and religious good will, he urged every Southerner, "regardless of . . . race or creed," "to speak out for separation of the black and white races." [17] Several weeks later he strengthened his equivocal attitude toward the Jew still further when he protested in a second circular that "I am not anti-Semitic, but I am against any man or group . . . who aids and abets the NAACP which is trying to destroy our way of life." Again his list of recommended reading matter included blatantly anti-Jewish as well as anti-Negro literature.[18]

In large degree, Patterson's recruitment letters reflected the movement's own ambiguity toward the Jew. From the outset Council leaders, to use Tom Brady's phrase, sought to identify their movement with "the finest and the best intelligence, the best law-abiding group, the most courageous, the most honest" [19] elements in the region. They quickly condemned the hooded night riders of the Klan, as the judge said, "because they hid their faces, because they did things that you and I wouldn't approve of." Having refused on two occasions to join the KKK, Brady believed (as did Patterson and other Council leaders) that "unless we keep and pitch our battle on a high plane, and unless we keep our ranks free from the demagogue, the renegade, the lawless and the violent, we will be branded, as we should be branded, a fearful, underground, lawless

[17] "Segregation and the New Hate Groups," *Facts*, 9 (September, 1954), 21–26; and "The Citizens' Councils and Anti-Semitism, *Facts*, 11 (January, 1956), 67–68.

[18] "The Citizens' Councils and Anti-Semitism," 67–68.

[19] Tom P. Brady, *A Review of Black Monday* (Greenwood: Association of Citizens' Councils of Mississippi, n.d.). This sixteen-page pamphlet is a reprint of an address delivered before the Indianola Citizens' Council, October 28, 1954.

organization." [20] But for all of Brady's insistence that the Council avoid the stigma of anti-Semitism, even his own writing carried a persistent though guarded strain of hostility toward the Jew.[21]

Not remarkably, the ever-vigilant Anti-Defamation League was quick to condemn the fledgling movement. Regarding Patterson's reading list as a stormy petrel heralding the advent of a southern pogrom, the League viewed the growth of Mississippi's "new hate group" with alarm.[22] Yet the Jewish organization's worst fears proved groundless. Negroes, not Jews, were the Council's obsession; and with few exceptions, the movement confined its intolerance to the color line. Unquestionably, many anti-Semites were attracted to the cause of white supremacy, but there was generally a pragmatic awareness among Councilors, as the executive secretary of Alabama's Council expressed it, that "we can't fight everybody." [23] Indeed, a few militant Jew-baiters would later assert, as one upper-South resistance leader did, that Mississippi Council leaders were "suppressing, either through ignorance or fear, the facts concerning the Jewish peril." Similarly, Bill Hendrix, the Imperial Emperor of the Southern Knights of the Ku Klux Klan, contended that Robert Patterson himself was "dominated by the Jews and the Citizens' Councils are full of Jews." [24] These charges are hardly credible, but Council membership was not restricted to Christians. Although Jews were rarely identified with organized racism, there were those in some communities who found it inexpedient not to join the local movement.[25]

Whatever other purposes they may have served, Patterson's circulars helped to bring the heretofore semi-secret movement out from behind the veil of mystery which shrouded its early period

[20] Ibid.; interview with Brady.

[21] See esp. *Black Monday*, 57–58.

[22] "Segregation and the New Hate Groups," 21–26.

[23] Sam Englehardt quoted in Douglas Cater, "Civil War in Alabama's Citizens' Councils," *The Reporter*, 14 (May 17, 1956), 20–21.

[24] Quoted in Luce, "Mississippi White Citizens' Council," 66–67.

[25] That pressure was occasionally applied to force Jews to join the movement is strongly implied in one of the Council's own pamphlets, *A Jewish View on Segregation* (Greenwood: Association of Citizens' Councils of Mississippi, n.d.). Written "voluntarily by a Jewish Southerner who prefers to remain anonymous," the publication asserts that "the Jew who attempts to be neutral [toward organized resistance] is much like the ostrich. And he has no

of expansion. On September 6, one week after the appearance of the Leflore County segregationist's first reading list, Greenville's *Delta Democrat-Times* called upon the Council "to come out into the open." Taking editorial note of these "groups being formed for the purpose of maintaining the status quo," Hodding Carter observed that according to "reliable" reports they were composed of "the most respectable citizens in each community." "If that is true," the veteran Delta editor added, "then the only unresponsible aspect of the organizations is their secrecy." [26]

Three days later, the Associated Press disclosed that Mississippi lawmakers, then convened in extraordinary session, were privately discussing a newly formed organization with a program for stemming the threat of desegregation. One politician, the AP reported, boasted that his constituents in Humphreys County (70 percent black) had organized "the strongest [Council] in the state." "We have about 500 members," he estimated, "and they mean business." He did not specify what that business might be, but other Delta legislators were quoted as having "predicted violence." One reportedly even suggested that "a few killings" would be the best thing for the state, for they might "save a lot of bloodshed later on." [27]

These early press accounts brought the Council's period of clandestine expansion to a close.[28] On September 13, four days after the AP release, Representative Wilma Sledge of Sunflower County interrupted the proceedings of the Mississippi House to deliver a "clarifying statement" about the organizational fever then sweeping

---

right to be surprised or amazed when the target he so readily represents is fired upon." See also Albert Vorspan, "The South, Segregation, and the Jew: A First-Hand Report," *Jewish Frontier,* November, 1956, 18; David Halberstam, "The White Citizens' Councils: Respectable Means for Unrespectable Ends," *Commentary,* 22 (October, 1956), 300–301.

[26] *Delta Democrat-Times,* September 6, 1954.

[27] Jackson *Clarion-Ledger* and *Daily News,* September 10, 1954. Following the AP story, on September 12 Kenneth Toler, a reporter for the Memphis *Commercial Appeal,* interviewed an unnamed Council spokesman—probably Patterson—who reported that for "obvious reasons" the names and connections of the new Councilors would not be revealed.

[28] In September, even some of the national news magazines took note of the Council's emergence. See, for example, "Citizens (White) Unite!" *Time,* 64 (September 20, 1954), 57.

the Delta. Assuring her colleagues of the Council's nonviolent nature, she praised its members as "reliable white male citizens . . . organized for the sole purpose of maintaining segregation. . . ." In her view, the movement's leadership was "composed of the most prominent, well-educated and conservative businessmen"; and, though some of its activities could not be publicized "for obvious reasons," she endorsed its "motives and methods" as "laudable, timely, and impressive." [29]

Representative Sledge's remarks left little doubt that the new movement had friends in high places. Not only were legislators praising it in the capital, but the Council could claim among its circle of influential supporters the powerful Hederman press, which controlled Mississippi's two largest daily newspapers, the morning *Clarion-Ledger* (circulation 47,396) and the evening Jackson *Daily News* (circulation 41,361). Indeed, the *Clarion-Ledger* had anticipated Representative Sledge's remarks with its own front-page statement of September 13. Reassuring Mississippians that the emerging Councils sought primarily to prevent racial disorders, the paper declared that the resistance movement was "growing by leaps and bounds" and "flourishing in both hill and Delta sections of the state." [30]

To be sure, the movement was growing. Within a month of its public appearance, representatives from local organizations in some twenty counties met on October 12 to form the Association of Citizens' Councils of Mississippi.[31] Robert Patterson, the executive secretary—and the only Council official whose name had been made public [32]—set up the ACCM's headquarters in Winona. While not

[29] Quoted in Jackson *Daily News* and *Clarion-Ledger*, September 14, 1954. See also Indianaola *Enterprise* for "home-town" coverage of the Council's birth.

[30] Jackson *Clarion-Ledger*, September 13, 1954.

[31] *Annual Report: August, 1955*, 1; Robert B. Patterson, *The Citizens' Council: A History, an Address to the Annual Leadership Conference of the Citizens' Councils of America, Jackson, Mississippi, October 26, 1963* (Jackson: The Citizens' Councils of America, n.d.), 2.

[32] Although the Council was now openly organizing, a residual aura of secrecy lingered for some months. As late as December 9, 1954, the Kosciusko (Mississippi) *Star-Herald* called it an "apparently . . . mysterious but effective organization."

centrally located in terms of the movement's strength, this small town in the hill farms district east of the Mississippi-Yazoo Delta was a practical choice for the central office of the statewide organization. Despite the presence of Councils within a narrow belt of hill counties stretching eastward from Leflore County to the Alabama line,[33] as well as within three scattered southern counties, the movement's strength lay in the alluvial cotton lands of the Delta. There the nonwhite population in 1950 ranged from a low of 51 percent in Warren County in the south to a high of 82 percent in Tunica County in the northwest, and there, too, most of the counties could boast a Citizens' Council.[34] But by situating its state office in Winona—where more than half a century before James K. Vardaman, champion of the redneck, began his law practice and edited his progressive Winona *Democrat*—the Council could hope to bridge the traditional Mississippi dichotomy between the politically and economically conservative Delta and the more radical hills. Perhaps it might even allay traditional upcountry suspicions of planter organizations.[35]

Winona remained the center of Council activity only one year, but the movement prospered there. In the *Annual Report: August, 1955*, the first of four yearly statements to local organizations, Patterson ebulliently proclaimed that a total of 60,000 members had been enrolled in some 253 Councils distributed throughout each of the state's six congressional districts.[36] His organization's geographic

[33] With the formation of the Lowndes County Citizens' Council in Columbus on October 27, the Associated Press reported that there were thirty-two Councils in Mississippi. (Huntsville *Times*, October 28, 1954.)

[34] Jackson *Clarion-Ledger* and *Daily News*, October 24, 1954. In a statement to the press in October, Patterson indicated that every Delta county except Coahoma was organized, but, according to a map published by the Council's official newspaper, Warren and Issaquena, both Delta counties, had no Council as of January, 1956. (See *The Citizens' Council*, January, 1956, 4.)

[35] Discussing the "animosity of the hills toward the delta," V. O. Key has stated that "Mississippi politics may be regarded, if one keeps alert to the risks of oversimplification, as a battle between the delta planters and the rednecks" (V. O. Key, *Southern Politics in State and Nation* [New York: Alfred A. Knopf, 1949], 230, 236). The Council's motive for establishing its first headquarters in Winona is suggested by Frank E. Smith in *Congressman from Mississippi* (New York: Pantheon Books, 1964), 261.

[36] *Annual Report: August, 1955*, 1.

circumference thus greatly expanded, the executive secretary established permanent headquarters during 1955 in the larger, more prosperous Yazoo River town of Greenwood, a Delta trading center. In Greenwood the Council movement continued to thrive, and in his *2nd Annual Report: August, 1956*, the executive secretary announced that there were 80,000 Councilors scattered throughout sixty-five counties.[37]

The pattern of the Council's development in Mississippi reflected in microcosm the movement's growth throughout the South. Early ACCM-published maps of organizational growth in the Magnolia State reveal that the Council prospered best in counties where Negroes constituted 50 percent or more of the total population. One such map published in January, 1956, showing organizations in fifty-five counties, indicated that Councils were to be found in all six congressional districts. The most thoroughly organized districts, however, were the third and fourth which border the Mississippi River and constitute the western one-third of the state where a majority of its Negroes reside. Conversely, the Council's worst showing was in the sixth district, in the southern portion of the state, where Negro populations in most counties did not exceed 33 percent. Here, the Council's map revealed, only five of sixteen counties had been organized. Likewise, large blocks of unorganized counties were to be found in the first and second districts, located primarily in the hill country and the northeastern and north-central sections of the state. To be sure, unorganized counties in these two districts included black-belt DeSoto and Marshall counties, which had nonwhite populations in 1950 of 67 percent and 71 percent respectively. But the eight remaining counties without Councils had Negro populations considerably smaller than 50 percent, and two, Tishomingo and Itawamba, had 5 percent or fewer each. Significantly, of the twenty-seven counties listed as unorganized, sixteen

[37] *2nd Annual Report: August, 1956*, 1. Like most organizations, the Citizens' Council has not been inclined to underestimate its own strength. But Patterson's estimates seem reasonable and they have been generally accepted. See Ed Townsend, "White Citizens' Councils Flourish in the South," *Christian Science Monitor*, May 11; *New York Times*, February 26; Southern Regional Council, *Special Report: Pro-Segregation Groups in the South*, November 19, 1956.

had Negro populations of one-third or less, and in only five did Negroes exceed whites.[38]

While the most fertile soil for the Council's germination was to be found in black-belt counties, the most salubrious climate for its growth was that created by racial crisis. The story of Council expansion, then, was not one of steady progress. Represented graphically, its growth in Mississippi, and elsewhere in the South, resembled a fever chart with peaks occurring in periods of racial unrest when the white population's perception of the imminence of desegregation was greatest, and slumps coinciding with periods of relative racial calm.[39] The first such growth-producing crisis came with the *Brown* decision in May, 1954. During the following summer and fall the Council rapidly expanded. But later, during the winter and spring of 1955—the period of waiting for the implementation decree of May 31, 1955—Council growth subsided. Then on June 5, six days after the Court called upon the states to desegregate "with all deliberate speed," the National Association for the Advancement of Colored People in Mississippi instructed its branches to petition local boards of education to take "immediate steps" toward compliance with the Supreme Court's edict. During the ensuing month, Negro parents petitioned school boards in Clarksdale, Jackson, Natchez, Vicksburg, and Yazoo City with results more beneficial to Councilors than to black schoolchildren.[40]

38 See "Mississippi Citizens' Council Map," *The Citizens' Council,* January, 1956, 4, and subsequent maps of Mississippi Council growth published in *The Citizens' Council,* March, 1956, 4, and June, 1956, 6. The March map revealed twenty-one unorganized counties and the map for June showed only seventeen such counties—of which fifteen had Negro populations of less than 50 percent.

39 The fever chart–like growth pattern of southern resistance movements is recognized by James W. Vander Zanden in several studies which relate formal sociological theory of social movements to white resistance. Council growth, he observes, represents a countermovement to Negro movement. See his "The Klan Revival," *American Journal of Sociology,* 65 (March, 1960), 456–62; "A Note on the Theory of Social Movements," *Sociology and Social Research,* 44 (September–October, 1959), 3–7; "Resistance and Social Movements," *Social Forces,* 37 (May, 1959), 312–15; and *Race Relations in Transition: The Segregation Crisis in the South* (New York: Random House, 1965), 30.

40 Carter, *The South Strikes Back,* 53; Martin, *The Deep South Says "Never"*, 28–29.

The first of what the NAACP's state president called "not petitions, but ultimatums"[41] was filed with the Vicksburg school board on July 18. Signed by more than one hundred Negroes, it got nowhere. Upon consulting with state Attorney General James P. Coleman, the school board declared that the document "wholly fails to meet the requirements for a petition." Having published the names of the petitioners in a local newspaper, it declared that "the incident is closed."[42] To Council leaders, the NAACP's first challenge to white schools presented an ideal opportunity in Warren County which, despite a heavy concentration of Negroes (51 percent), had proved impervious to the movement's early advances. When the crisis appeared to be passing without the emergence of a Council, Robert Patterson reminded Vicksburgers of the need for "self-defense." "Organized aggression," he remonstrated, "must be met with organized resistance." Moreover, Judge Brady and Jackson Council President Ellis Wright met with anxious whites in a small village outside of Vicksburg and called on the "Gibraltar of the Confederacy" to help school officials maintain segregation by organizing a Citizens' Council.[43] These overtures were in vain, however. For eighty years, the proud city on the bluff chose to ignore Independence Day because it had fallen to Union troops on July 4, 1863. But its white citizens would not answer the mid-twentieth-century call to organized resistance.

Nearby, in the capital city, as whites uneasily observed the first desegregation offensive by Mississippi Negroes, the recently formed Jackson Citizens' Council launched an ambitious drive to enlist 10,000 members.[44] First organized as the Jackson States' Rights Association in late March under the leadership of Ellis Wright, president of the city's chamber of commerce, and William J. Simmons, the son of one of Jackson's most prominent bankers, the group was absorbed by the Council movement. By mid-July, 1955, it had grown from its original nucleus of sixty to more than three hun-

[41] Quoted in *Southern School News,* August, 1955, 17.

[42] Ibid.; Birmingham *World,* July 22, and *Delta Democrat-Times,* July 20, 1955.

[43] *Southern School News,* August, 1955, 17.

[44] Jackson *Daily News,* July 23, 1955.

dred members.[45] When the NAACP's petition, signed by forty-two Negro parents, was filed with the city's board of education on July 26, Council President Wright met with the mayor and board officials, and then charged that the Negroes' ultimate motive for desegregating schools was intermarriage. "If the NAACP thinks that we have the slightest idea of surrendering our Southland to a mulatto race," he warned, "the NAACP had better think again." [46] Generous support for the Council's position was rendered by the city's daily press. Both the *Daily News* and the *State Times* carried long stories of the Council's membership drive, and the *Daily News* admonished those who "believe that segregation provides the only stable arrangement for mutual respect and right conduct between the races . . . to get in touch immediately with the Jackson Citizens' Council. . . ." [47] The Jackson petition was no more successful than had been the one in Vicksburg, but by Simmons's own estimate Council membership in the capital city swelled to over 1,000 in two weeks' time.[48]

In late July, Negroes also petitioned the school board of Natchez, the seat of hitherto unorganized Adams County (50 percent Negro). Seeking outside assistance, concerned whites appealed to the association's executive secretary, Robert Patterson, and to its newly appointed administrator, William J. Simmons. On August 4, Patterson, Simmons, and Brady addressed a capacity crowd at the city auditorium and Natchez formed a Citizens' Council. The NAACP school desegregation petition, like the others, met an early death.[49] Similarly, in Clarksdale, a Delta city of 16,000 in unorganized Coahoma County, Negroes petitioned on August 11. Within a few days, a Council appeared. Describing the mood of Clarksdale, Simmons observed that "the good folks there had said 'we don't need a Citizens Council, our niggers are good niggers, they don't want to in-

[45] Ibid., March 25, July 23, 1955; *Southern School News,* May 4, 1955; Dan Wakefield, "Respectable Racism: Dixie's Citizens Councils," *The Nation,* 181 (October 22, 1955), 340.

[46] Quoted in Chattanooga *Times* and Montgomery *Advertiser,* July 27, 1955.

[47] Jackson *Daily News,* quoted in *Annual Report: August, 1955,* 3.

[48] Wakefield, "Respectable Racism: Dixie's Citizens Councils," 340; Waring, "Mississippi's Citizens' Councils Are Protecting Both Races," Charleston *News and Courier,* September 15, 1955.

[49] Jackson *Daily News,* August 5, 1955.

tegrate, if we organize a Citizens' Council it'll agitate 'em.' But one bright morning they woke up with a school petition with three hundred three signers, including most of their good ones. So they organized a Council." [50]

Throughout much of Mississippi's decade of successful evasion, the Council's pattern of boom-in-crisis continued. Consequently, many of the counties most difficult to organize gained a Citizens' Council in periods of unrest. Such was the case with the Gulf cities of Biloxi and Gulfport in tourist-oriented Harrison County. Like most of the counties in Mississippi's piney woods and coastal regions, where the soil was too thin for cotton and Negroes were a distinct minority, Harrison had shown little interest in forming a Citizens' Council. Of the state's three coastal counties only Jackson, the easternmost, which had organizations in both Moss Point and Pascagoula, had been receptive. But when Gulf Coast Negroes endeavored to gain access to the twenty-six miles of man-made beach stretching from Biloxi westward to Pass Christian, Council organizers were able to capitalize on the slogan "White Solidarity Means White Beaches" and establish a chapter in Harrison County.[51]

The structure of the Association of Citizens' Councils, which presided over the movement's impressive growth in Mississippi, was similar to the structure of the local Councils themselves. In order to coordinate the activities of a growing number of Councils, in September, 1955, the association organized the state by congressional districts.[52] At the base of this administrative unit were the local Councils, which elected a chairman for every organized county within a given district. The county chairmen in turn named a district chairman and a district executive committee of three. There was also a district information and education committee ("to de-

[50] Quoted in Martin, *The Deep South Says "Never"*, 30.

[51] *The Citizens' Council,* May, 1960, 4; *Delta Democrat-Times,* May 30, and Jackson *Daily News,* May 6, June 6, 1960.

[52] At that time, district organizations were completed in only five of Mississippi's six congressional districts. In the sixth district, the slowest area in the state to develop Councils, only one county, Jefferson Davis (the only sixth-district county with a Negro population of more than 50 percent), was organized as of that date. That district's organization was not completed until April, 1956, when seven of its sixteen counties had been organized. See *The Citizens' Council,* May, 1956, 4.

vise means of nullifying the tremendous propaganda assault being waged against the minds of our young people and our citizens") and a district legal advisory committee ("to devise legal means of preventing integration"), each of which was comprised of one member from every organized county within the district.[53] Above the district level was the state executive committee, consisting of the members of the various district executive committees and the officers of the state association. Meeting monthly in Jackson, this committee, at the discretion of the state board of directors, established state association policy. For its part, the board of directors, the highest Council authority in the state, selected the state officers, all of whom, except the full-time executive secretary, served without remuneration. Board members were elected annually by the local Councils, which could elect one director for every 1,000 members or fraction thereof.[54]

Despite appearances, the Council organization in Mississippi was not a rigid hierarchy, and the state association's control over local Council affairs was limited. Dedicated to the principle of local self-government as well as to segregation, the movement boasted that "each Council is a separate autonomous organization." [55] Each was a separate corporation, chartered under its own constitution, possessed of its own bylaws. Each could be dissolved at any time by its own board of directors. Although the state association seldom hesitated to speak for the local membership in matters of general policy, the day-to-day activities of the Councils were largely the concern of local leadership. Indeed, the association never felt pow-

[53] *The Citizens' Council,* October, 1955, 3. In addition to these two standing committees, each of the Councils at the local level had a membership and finance committee which was expected to enlist "all patriotic white citizens for membership," and a political and elections committee to study candidates for local and state elections and advise the electorate on their suitability for public service. (*Annual Report: August, 1955,* 1; [Robert Patterson], *The Citizens' Council* [Greenwood: Association of Citizens' Councils, n.d.], 1–2.)

[54] *Annual Report: August, 1955,* 1; [Robert Patterson], *The Citizens' Council,* 1–2; *4th Annual Report: August, 1958,* 2. See also a sample constitution for a state association in Citizens' Councils of America, "The White Book of Citizens' Council Organization," 2nd ed. (Jackson: Citizens' Council, Inc., 1965), 24–25.

[55] *2nd Annual Report: August, 1956,* 3.

erful enough to standardize the movement's financial arrangements. The state executive committee recommended that members pay annual dues of five dollars, of which only one-fifth would remain in the coffers of the local organization. The remainder, the committee suggested, should be equally divided between the state association and its monthly newspaper, *The Citizens' Council.*[56] Apparently, few Councils were either willing or able to relinquish 80 percent of their yearly revenue, for the association was perennially short of funds.

In his first annual statement to the membership, state Finance Chairman Ellett Lawrence complained in August, 1955, that "left-wing" groups "advocating mongrelization" were all well-heeled, but "a movement like ours has to battle all the way for funds." The state office, he reported, operated on a "day-to-day basis," uncertain whether it would be able to pay salaries and meet routine expenses.[57] Although the finance chairman's report came before the association's district organization had been completed, the new administrative structure could have helped but little. In his report for August, 1956, Lawrence disclosed that incoming funds had been inadequate to meet many budgeted expenses and that a cutback in activities had become necessary.[58] Such was the financial chairman's annual lamentation as he mailed printed letters from his Greenwood office in an appeal for members to pay their dues and local organizations to contribute more generously to the state association.[59] Ultimately it became necessary for the executive committee to revise its suggested distribution of revenues so that 50 percent of local Council dues remained at home. Similarly, *The Citizens' Council,* in an effort to gain a wider audience on the local level, found it

[56] "How to Organize a Citizens' Council," *The Citizens' Council,* August, 1956, 4; *2nd Annual Report: August, 1956,* 3.

[57] *Annual Report: August, 1955,* 2.

[58] *2nd Annual Report: August, 1956,* 4

[59] Typical of these letters was Lawrence's appeal of 1962 in which he suggested that a regular contribution to the Citizens' Council was a sound investment. "If negro political domination comes about in Mississippi," he warned, taxes would double or even triple. A complete collection of Lawrence's annual financial appeals may be seen in Special Collections, Mitchell Memorial Library.

necessary to offer subscription rates at half price ($1 yearly) to those local Councils whose entire membership subscribed.[60]

However uncertain its financial status may have been, there was no lack of industry at the Council's central office. If editor Frederick Sullens of the Jackson *Daily News* was a reliable observer, Patterson was a "veritable fiend for work. He labors from early morning until late at night. He lives, breathes, and eats the work to which he's so deeply consecrated. . . ." [61] The executive secretary was indeed a man of considerable enterprise. With the assistance of two full-time clerks and some borrowed office equipment, he set out to prove his contention that "public sentiment is the law." "History proves," he believed, "that the supreme power in the government of men has always been public opinion." His task, then, was to mobilize white southern opinion and thereby win a reversal of the *Brown* ruling. In his words, "it was the duty of the Citizens' Councils to rally support from the patriotic citizens of the South and then with this support to present the case for the South to the nation." [62]

Toward this end he established contacts and exchanged information during the first year with resistance groups throughout the South, and he corresponded actively with "interested Americans in forty-six states" and with white sympathizers in Alaska, Iceland, Mexico, and South Africa.[63] Moreover, he wrote a pamphlet on the Council's objectives and organizational procedure [64] and, with the assistance of Ellett Lawrence and the Lawrence Printing Com-

[60] *The Citizens' Council*, March, 1957, 1. Because Council records, fiscal or otherwise, are not available at this time, it is possible only to speculate about the status of the organization's annual budget. In 1956, the Southern Regional Council estimated that the Mississippi Council collected $400,000 annually from membership dues. In 1963 William J. Simmons suggested the figure of $200,000. See Southern Regional Council, *Special Report: Pro-Segregation Groups in the South*, November 19, 1956, 13; and Reese Cleghorn, "The Segs," *Esquire*, 61 (January, 1964), 135.

[61] Editorial, Jackson *Daily News*, November 20, 1955.

[62] *Annual Report: August, 1955*, 1; and *2nd Annual Report: August, 1956*, 1; Patterson, *The Citizens' Council: A History*, 2–3.

[63] *Annual Report: August, 1955*, 1.

[64] [Patterson], *The Citizens' Council.* This pamphlet should not be confused with Patterson's *The Citizens' Council: A History*, which was published nearly a decade later.

pany, published and distributed three others.[65] During the association's second year, Patterson published five more handsomely printed pamphlets, including a reprint of an article by former Supreme Court Justice James F. Byrnes of South Carolina, a speech by state Attorney General Eugene Cook of Georgia, and addresses by Senator James O. Eastland and Representative John Bell Williams.[66] Patterson also published a line of single-sheet leaflets which, among other things, purported to prove statistically that crime, illegitimacy, and venereal disease were more prevalent among Negroes than among whites and that, according to the "frank statement" of a South Carolina NAACP official, intermarriage invariably followed integration.[67] Urging members to promote "the case for the South" by passing the movement's literature on to friends and relatives, the executive secretary offered Council publications to local organizations at cut-rate prices.[68]

As the movement matured, Patterson's propaganda barrage mounted. By the end of its second year, he reported that the state association had mailed more than two million pieces of literature into every state,[69] and in his *4th Annual Report* he estimated the

[65] These pamphlets were: G. T. Gillespie, *A Christian View on Segregation, an Address before the Synod of Mississippi of the Presbyterian Church in the U.S., November 4, 1954* (Greenwood: Association of Citizens' Councils of Mississippi, [1955]); D. M. Nelson, *Conflicting Views on Segregation: Letters between Dr. Nelson, President of Mississippi College and Unnamed Alumnus* (Greenwood: Association of Citizens' Councils of Mississippi, [1955]); and Brady, *A Review of Black Monday.*

[66] James F. Byrnes, *The Supreme Court Must Be Curbed* (Greenwood: Association of Citizens' Councils, [1956]); Eugene Cook, *The Ugly Truth about the NAACP: An Address before the 55th Annual Convention of the Peace Officers Association of Georgia* (Greenwood: Association of Citizens' Councils of Mississippi, [1956]); James O. Eastland, *We've Reached Era of Judicial Tyranny: An Address before the State-Wide Convention of the Association of Citizens' Councils of Mississippi, Jackson, December 1, 1955* (Greenwood: Association of Citizens' Councils of Mississippi, [1956]); John Bell Williams, *Where Is the Reign of Terror?* (Greenwood: Association of Citizens' Councils of Mississippi, n.d.); and *Interposition, the Barrier against Tyranny* (Greenwood: Association of Citizens' Councils of Mississippi, [1956]).

[67] *Crime Report* (Greenwood: Association of Citizens' Councils of Mississippi, [1956]); *Prominent Kingstree Negro Makes Frank Statement* (Greenwood: Association of Citizens' Councils of Mississippi, [1956]).

[68] *2nd Annual Report: August, 1956,* 4.

[69] Ibid., 1.

number at five million. By 1958 he believed that the effect was at last beginning to tell. Traditionally, national magazines had offered only slanted coverage of southern news. But "lately, we have noticed a reluctant leakage of truth . . . from even such rabid anti-South publications as *Time* and *Life*."[70]

To supplement the association's printed material, the executive secretary also released in the autumn of 1955 a tape recording that was well designed to serve as a recruitment aid for Council organizers. Purportedly an address delivered in December, 1954, by a "Professor Roosevelt Williams" of Howard University to an NAACP audience in Jackson, the tape was played before Council audiences in Alabama, Arkansas, Georgia, and Mississippi. An Alabama lawmaker played it for the edification of the state senate; and the office of the attorney general of Georgia distributed its text in mimeograph form in its official envelopes.[71] According to the recording the NAACP speaker informed his audience of the near-universal physical dissatisfaction felt by white women with males of their own race and of their secret cravings for Negro men. To one Council newspaper, the speech proved that "the N.A.A.C.P. and their insolent agitators are little concerned with an education for the 'ignorant nigger'; but, rather, are 'demanding' integration in the white bedroom."[72] It was immediately termed "an obvious fake," however, by Roy Wilkins, secretary of the NAACP, who pointed out that his organization has no such "professor" on its staff. The fraud was exposed still further in September, 1956, when the Columbus (Georgia) *Ledger-Enquirer* revealed that Roosevelt Williams, whoever he was, was not on the faculty at Howard.[73] Faced with mounting evidence that his recording was spurious, Patterson said simply "we never claimed it to be authentic," adding that it was up to the NAACP to prove that it was not.[74]

[70] *4th Annual Report: July, 1958*, 3.

[71] See a four-page pamphlet published by the NAACP, "*We Never Claimed It to Be Authentic*" (New York: National Association for the Advancement of Colored People, 1956); Carter, *The South Strikes Back*, 136–40; Carl T. Rowan, *Go South to Sorrow* (New York: Random House, 1957), 157; James W. Silver, *Mississippi: The Closed Society*, 3rd ed. (New York: Harcourt, Brace and World, 1966), 34–35; *Southern School News*, February, 1956, 7.

[72] *Arkansas Faith*, November, 1955.

[73] Editorial, Columbus *Ledger-Enquirer*, September 2, 1956.

[74] Quoted in NAACP, "*We Never Claimed It to Be Authentic.*"

At about the same time that Patterson began distributing his fraudulent tape recording, the state association embarked on a more dignified venture in propaganda. With William J. Simmons as its unpaid editor, the organization began publishing a four-page tabloid newspaper, *The Citizens' Council,* in October, 1955. Its first issue consisted almost entirely of previously published articles by prosegregation journalists, including Thomas R. Waring of the Charleston *News and Courier,* Tom Ethridge, feature writer for the Jackson *Clarion-Ledger,* and John Temple Graves, syndicated Birmingham columnist. In addition to several articles praising the organized resistance movement and condemning Hodding Carter, the first issue carried bits of information about the "tribal instincts" of "NAACP Witch Doctors" who sought "to replace American concepts of justice with those of the African Congo in centuries past" and "the negro 'republic' of Liberia [where] no white man is allowed to vote, own property or hold office."[75] In later issues, Simmons relied less upon borrowed material, but the substance of his paper remained substantially unchanged. Throughout its six years of publication,[76] *The Citizens' Council* in column and cartoon assailed southern apathy and moderation and recounted stories of perfidious white northern liberals and diseased, depraved, and crime-prone Negroes.

From the outset Simmons and Patterson were inclined to be ambitious about the future of the association's newspaper. Even before the first printing, they expressed the hope that it would become the official voice of the entire movement. With this end in view, 125,000 copies of the first issue were printed, and Simmons made an effort to place it in the hands of organized segregationists in virtually every southern state. Printings of subsequent issues were considerably smaller. In November, 1956, when the paper became the official organ of the regional organization, Simmons estimated its average monthly circulation at 40,000, much of which he indicated was outside of Mississippi.[77]

[75] *The Citizens' Council,* October, 1955, 1–4.

[76] In October, 1961, *The Citizens' Council* was replaced by *The Citizen,* a monthly journal.

[77] *The Citizens' Council,* November, 1956, 2. Subsequent circulation figures are not available until September, 1960, when, in compliance with a newly

The audience beyond Mississippi was the target of a substantial portion of the organization's propaganda. To carry more effectively "the light of truth and logic" to that audience, the state association chartered the Education Fund of the Citizens' Councils in December, 1956, to serve as a southern white counterpoise to the NAACP's tax-exempt educational fund.[78] Its founders hoped that the fund would assume the burdensome production and distribution costs of the Council's numerous publications.[79] But more important, it was to seek access to the national information media, including the wire services, television, radio, national periodicals, and the motion picture industry.[80]

The Council's first foray into electronic news media began in April, 1957, with a weekly fifteen-minute telecast, the Citizens' Council "Forum," over WLBT-TV in Jackson. Within a year the program became the radio and television service of the Citizens' Councils of America. Its weekly telecasts were shown by twelve stations in Alabama, Georgia, Louisiana, Mississippi, Texas, and Virginia, and its radio tapes were regularly broadcast over more than fifty stations throughout the South. By the end of its second year, the Forum's producer, William J. Simmons, declared that interviews with more than sixty U.S. senators and representatives had

---

passed act regarding monthly newspapers, Simmons listed the paper's average monthly circulation at 50,000. See *The Citizens' Council,* September, 1960, 4.

[78] See a small pamphlet by the Mississippi Citizens' Councils, *Educational Fund of the Citizens' Councils* (Greenwood: Association of Citizens' Councils of Mississippi, n.d.); and "Why an Educational Fund Is Necessary for Victory," *The Citizens' Council,* April, 1957, 4. The president of this corporation was W. C. Trotter, retired financial secretary of the University of Mississippi and a former member of the Board of Trustees of the State Institutions of Higher Learning. (*Southern School News,* February, 1957, 13.)

[79] Initially the Council declared without equivocation that contributions to its Educational Fund were tax deductible. When the Internal Revenue Service refused to grant it tax exemption status, the organization's approach shifted to: "our auditors advise us that contributions are deductible for income tax purposes." See Charleston *News and Courier,* January 6, 1957, Jackson *Daily News,* January 22, 1961. See also Simmons's editorial, *The Citizens' Council,* September, 1957, 1, for evidence that the Fund, like the association itself, was frequently short of funds.

[80] "Why an Educational Fund Is Necessary for Victory," *The Citizens' Council,* April, 1957, 4.

been either heard or seen by "a vast audience . . . from Alaska to Florida, and from New England to California. . . ."[81]

Because Forum programs were furnished without cost to cooperating stations, the expense of this extensive series could have been beyond the Council's reach had not Mississippi's congressional representatives in Washington assisted in the project. Many of the tapes and films for this "completely non-partisan and non-sectional" enterprise, which by 1962 had featured perhaps as many as one out of every four members of the U.S. Congress, were made in the government recording studios with the compliments of Senator Eastland and Representative Williams. Designed to provide congressmen with an inexpensive means of communicating with their constituencies, these government-supported recording facilities were furnished at cost to senators and representatives. A fifteen-minute Forum film, for example, could be produced in the congressional studio for less than fifty-five dollars, a fraction of the rates charged by a commercial establishment.[82] By cutting its production expenses in this way, the Forum provided a variety of professional-quality programs at minimal costs.

Viewed collectively, the Mississippi Council's propaganda campaign was a highly creditable effort. Although not uniformly so, much of its material was polished, some of it even sophisticated, and virtually all of it fully a cut above the crude productions typical of most segregation groups. Unquestionably this veritable avalanche of propaganda mirrored the great vitality of the movement in its native state. But it also reflected the Council's missionary-like zeal for propagating the faith of organized resistance. From the beginning, stalwarts such as Tom Brady and Robert Patterson envisaged a solid southern front of Citizens' Councils, united in defiance of the desegregation mandate. In his first *Annual Report,* the executive secretary termed it "the duty and responsibility" of all Councilors to encourage the organization of Citizens' Councils throughout the region. "Forty million white Southerners, or a frac-

[81] *The Citizens' Council,* May, 1957, 4; June, 1958, 3; April, 1959, 2.

[82] Cook, *The Segregationists,* 81–83; *Arkansas Gazette,* May 12, 1959. Transcripts of Citizens' Council Forum programs may be seen in the Segregation File, Mitchell Memorial Library.

tion thereof if properly organized, can be a power in this Nation, but they must be thoroughly organized. . . ." [83]

Patterson's thinking was representative of a persistent strain of Council thought identified by a moderate southern journalist as "the dike analogy" [84]—the theory that the region was only as strong as its weakest component. Once a single state gave way before the rising tide of desegregation, this theory posited, all would eventually be swept with it. Recognizing that Mississippi could not stand alone, Magnolia State Councilors hastened to encourage whites in other southern states to reinforce their own dikes.

[83] *Annual Report: August, 1955.*

[84] C. A. McKnight, "The Troubled South: Search for a Middle Ground," *Collier's* 137 (June 22, 1956), 31.

CHAPTER III

Alabama: The Bourbon and the Redneck

WITH characteristic trenchancy V. O. Key observed in his study of southern politics that "Northerners, provincials that they are, regard the South as one large Mississippi. Southerners, with their eye for distinction, place Mississippi in a class by itself." [1] In terms of preparedness for organized resistance to the Supreme Court's mandate of May 17, 1954, white Mississippians were, indeed, in a class by themselves. For not until late in the following November, more than two months after Councilors from twenty-one Mississippi counties met to organize a statewide Association of Citizens' Councils, did whites in Alabama's black belt meet to form the first Council outside Mississippi. By that date Alabama had already weathered its first desegregation crises.

In September, 1954, twenty-three Negroes had been denied admission to an all-white elementary school in Montgomery, and in Anniston, Brewton, and Montgomery, school boards refused to act on desegregation petitions filed by local NAACP chapters. Despite these challenges to the state's segregated schools, Alabama's official demeanor remained calm during the summer and fall following the *Brown* decision. Governor Gordon Persons, resolute in the face of mounting pressure from the state's lawmakers, refused to call an extraordinary session of the legislature to consider a special legis-

[1] Key, *Southern Politics*, 229.

lative committee's proposal for repeal of Alabama's constitutional requirement for public education. Nor was his successor, James E. Folsom, who assumed office in January, 1955, willing to sacrifice the public schools in order to preserve segregated classrooms. Although Folsom had avoided the segregation question when many Deep South politicians were finding it expedient to campaign on the single issue of race, he swept sixty-one of the state's sixty-seven counties in the Democratic primary to amass the largest number of votes ever won by an Alabama gubernatorial candidate. While still governor-elect, he attended a Southern Governors' Conference in Boca Raton, Florida, and refused—along with five governors from border and peripheral states—to sign a statement protesting mandatory desegregation of the region's schools.[2]

Despite what appeared to be an initial reticence, Alabama joined its voice in the rising chorus of southern resistance. In concert with other Deep South states, it sought to maintain separate-but-equal education through open defiance of the nation's fundamental law. During the decade following the school desegregation decision, Alabama legislators passed a resolution of interposition, repealed a compulsory school attendance law, enacted legislation to permit the closure of public schools, inhibited the activities of the NAACP within the state, and pushed through a variety of similar measures which placed the state along with Georgia, Louisiana, Mississippi, and South Carolina in the vanguard of massive resistance. Not until the fall of 1963, when twenty-four Negro children were admitted under federal court orders to previously all-white schools in Birmingham, Huntsville, Mobile, and Tuskegee, did Alabama shift from absolute resistance to tokenism as a means of delaying and restricting public school desegregation.[3]

In Alabama, as elsewhere among the hard-core states of southern

[2] *Southern School News,* November 4, 2; December 1, 1954, 2; February 3, 1955, 2. Folsom's moderate racial views are more fully developed in Numan V. Bartley, *The Rise of Massive Resistance* (Baton Rouge: Louisiana State University Press, 1969), 279ff.

[3] Alabama's initial response to the Supreme Court decision of 1954 has been chronicled by Patrick Earl McCauley, "Political Implications in Alabama of the School Segregation Decisions" (unpublished M.A. thesis, Department of Political Science, Vanderbilt University, 1957). Later developments are summarized in *Southern School News,* May, 1964, 11-B.

resistance, the most persistent champion of continued defiance was the Citizens' Council. Here the movement began, as it did in neighboring Mississippi, in the rich agricultural counties of the black belt. In this cotton-growing area of the state, 1,200 Dallas Countians gathered in Selma on November 29, 1954, to hear two Mississippi legislators exhort them to join an "honor-bound and Christian cause." Told that "there can be no fence-straddling," that whites must be "either for our Council or against it," six hundred men became charter members of the Dallas County Citizens' Council.[4] Within a week some four hundred Marengo Countians formed a second Council at Linden after hearing state Senator Walter C. Givhan promise that if a strong Council movement developed "the whole U.S. Army" would not be sufficient to bring integration to Alabama's public schools.[5] Within a month three more Councils were organized in the black-belt counties of Hale, Macon, and Perry—all of which had Negro populations in excess of 65 percent.[6] But here the movement's initial organizational flurry subsided. Unlike the movement in Mississippi, which had enjoyed considerable success before the Supreme Court's second *Brown* decision of May 31, 1955, organizers in Alabama were able to form only these five Councils prior to the implementation decree. With none of the state's school systems threatened by a court case and with the NAACP's early petition efforts successfully thwarted by local initiative, organized racism was not flourishing in Alabama.

In August, 1955, however, Negroes petitioned educational officials in seven counties to begin immediate steps toward the desegregation of public schools, and by late November there were ten Councils in as many counties.[7] The following month brought an-

[4] *Southern School News,* January 6, 1955, 2; Paul Anthony, "A Survey of the Resistance Groups of Alabama" (unpublished field report, Southern Regional Council, 1956), 1.

[5] For details of the Linden organizational rally, see "How White Citizens' Councils Came to Alabama," *New South,* 10 (December, 1955), 9–11.

[6] *Southern School News,* January 6, 1956, 2.

[7] The seven counties petitioned by Negroes were Bullock, Etowah, Jefferson, Macon, Mobile, Montgomery, and Russell. (Glenn Robinson, "Crusaders for Segregation," *The Nation's Schools,* 58 [December, 1956], 54–55; *Southern School News,* September, 1955, 3; Anthony, "Survey of the Resistance Groups of Alabama," 1.)

other growth-producing crisis. On December 5, in one of the first examples of aggressive, nonviolent action by southern blacks against Jim Crow discrimination, Montgomery Negroes began a protracted boycott of city buses. Again Councils were organized at a feverish rate. By January, 1956, a number of influential Montgomerians, including Mayor W. A. Gayle and the city commissioners, had openly identified themselves with the movement. As one local Negro spokesman acknowledged, prior to the black protest "Montgomerians by and large had decided to keep themselves free of any affiliation with this uprising organization. . . ." Once the boycott began, however, it "took root and became one of the fastest growing councils in the South, with probably more responsible and respectable citizens than any other council of its type." [8]

A third crisis occurred soon thereafter when a twenty-six-year-old Negro, Autherine Lucy, won a three-year court battle to enter the University of Alabama on February 3, 1956. Within two weeks, an Alabama Association of Citizens' Councils was formed with headquarters in Montgomery, and Council officials were claiming that twenty-six Councils in seventeen counties had enlisted 40,000 members.[9] Although the organization's estimates of its own strength can seldom be relied upon, there is little doubt that organized resistance had profited greatly from Negro challenges to the status quo in Montgomery and Tuscaloosa. The Council in Montgomery, for example, which probably had no more than 200 members in early November, attracted a crowd of nearly 15,000 to a public segregation rally protesting the admission of Miss Lucy to the state university.[10] Throughout 1956 the movement continued to boom. By

[8] Uriah J. Fields, *The Montgomery Story: The Unhappy Effects of the Montgomery Bus Boycott* (New York: Exposition Press, 1959), 50–51. See also *Southern School News*, February, 1956, 6, and "The Montgomery Boycott," *Nation*, 182 (February 11, 1956), 102.

[9] New York *Times*, February 7; Birmingham *News*, February 12, 19, 1956. On March 4 the Birmingham *News* noted that the number of Councils "has grown from about 40 to more than 60 in Alabama in the last eight weeks."

[10] St. Louis *Post-Dispatch*, February 28; New York *Times*, March 13, 1956. The Council in Alabama, like those elsewhere in the region, capitalized on racial crisis without as well as within the state. When federal troops entered Little Rock in the fall of 1957, the AACC ran a large advertisement in the Montgomery *Advertiser* headlined: "IT COULD HAPPEN HERE." "Like in Little Rock," it warned, "the monster of integration can creep upon us before we

fall, state Senator Samuel Martin Engelhardt, the executive secretary of the AACC, declared that there were more than one hundred Councils in Alabama and more than 80,000 Councilors. During May, 1957, the state association boasted that it was an "organization of 100,000 white families . . . united to maintain segregation." [11]

Primarily, the movement's strength in Alabama, as elsewhere in the Deep South, lay in the black belt, a band of rural, densely Negro-populated counties stretching across the south-central portion of the state. A secondary center of Council strength and activity was to be found in Jefferson County in and around Birmingham or, as that industrial and financial center is known to Alabamians, the "Big Mule" area.[12] Indeed, the pattern of Council development conformed remarkably well to the sectional cleavage that frequently characterized the Alabama political scene. In this sectional pattern of political alignment, as Key described it in *Southern Politics*, "north Alabama and southeastern Alabama are usually allied against the black belt. . . . The black belt . . . tends to ally itself with the 'big mules' of Birmingham and the lesser 'big mules' of Mobile." [13] Certainly Council organizers did not fare well in north Alabama, amid what Key has called "a strident radical agrarian[ism]," where attitudes were generally more progressive and the Negro population comparatively smaller than in the black belt. As late as June, 1957, when the movement was at or near its peak, the Alabama Council on Human Relations reported the "little

---

know it has hit." The advertisement launched a membership drive which, according to Sam Engelhardt, brought "a tremendous response throughout the state." See Montgomery *Advertiser*, September 29; and Arkansas *Gazette*, October 3, 1957.

[11] Montgomery *Advertiser*, October 23, 1956, May 16, 1957. On July 25, 1956, the *Advertiser* estimated the movement's strength at 100,000. But in an August 21, 1970, interview with the author, Engelhardt returned to 80,000 as the maximum membership figure.

[12] The black belt–"Big Mule" pattern of Council development became apparent during the Council's first year of growth in Alabama. Ten Councils were organized in as many countries during the period from November, 1954, to November, 1955, and all except one were confined to nine contiguous, south-central cotton counties where the nonwhite population in 1950 ranged from 44 percent in Montgomery County to 84 percent in Macon County. The tenth Council was organized in Tarrant City, a suburb of Birmingham.

[13] Key, *Southern Politics*, 42.

known fact" that Citizens' Council organizers had been unable to establish a single Council north of Gadsden, Birmingham, or Tuscaloosa, an area of fifteen counties comprising fully one-quarter of the state.[14] Moreover, Council strength was hardly greater in southern Alabama. Despite repeated efforts, the movement never successfully penetrated the Gulf coastal plain or the wire-grass region of the southeast.

In order to coordinate organizational activity, Alabama Councilors began to structure their local groups into sectional units in October, 1955. By early 1956 this procedure was completed, and, theoretically at least, the movement's activity within the state was directed from four regional organizations centered in Montgomery (the Central Alabama Citizens' Council), Birmingham (the North Alabama Citizens' Council), Tuscaloosa (the West Alabama Citizens' Council), and Mobile (the South Alabama Citizens' Council). Developed before the emergence of a statewide Council and designed primarily for purposes of expansion, the regional approach to organization never developed into an effective vehicle for administration. Soon after the formation of the Alabama Association of Citizens' Councils, the four subdivisions rapidly became inoperative.[15]

The most successful of these four entities, the Central Alabama Citizens' Council, was organized in October, 1955, and, though dominated by the Councils of Dallas and Montgomery counties, it eventually embraced seven other adjacent counties.[16] Strategically located and ably led, the CACC became the center of Alabama's Council movement, and when the statewide association was formed in February, 1956, it was largely the product of the CACC's efforts. Much of the Central Alabama Council's vigor is attributable to its organizers, all of whom were drawn from the hard core of Alabama's resistance leadership. Among them were Alston Keith, a Selma attorney who organized the first Council in Alabama; Walter

[14] *Alabama Council* [on Human Relations] *Newsletter,* 3 (June, 1957), 4.

[15] Interview with Sam Engelhardt; Anthony, "Survey of the Resistance Groups of Alabama," 1–2, 11–34; Birmingham *News,* February 29, 1956.

[16] *Southern School News,* January, 1956, 13; Anthony, "Survey of the Resistance Groups of Alabama," 11–12.

Coats Givhan of Safford, a state senator and an active Council speaker; and Luther Ingalls, a lawyer and one of the earliest leaders of the Montgomery Council.[17] But the most important leader of the CACC was Sam Engelhardt, a young, bespectacled, balding planter-legislator from Shorter. The co-owner of 6,500 acres of rich cotton land possessed by his mother's family for four generations, a locally prominent merchant and cotton ginner, Engelhardt first entered politics in 1950 as a state representative from Macon County. Largely on the strength of his reputation as an outspoken white supremacist, he was elected in 1954 to the state senate, where he became one of the most effective obstacles to desegregation in the Deep South.[18] Financially independent, the legislative spokesman for a county with the highest ratio of Negroes to whites in the United States, and an unyielding segregationist, the Shorter planter was a natural leader for an organized resistance movement.[19] When the Association of Citizens' Councils was formed in February, 1956, he became its paid executive secretary. Perhaps more than anyone else, he was responsible for the respectability which the movement achieved in Alabama.

Quite another kind of man was Asa Earl Carter, executive secretary of the North Alabama Citizens' Council. "Ace" Carter's bailiwick was primarily the industrial suburbs of Birmingham, and unlike that of the Central Alabama Citizens' Council, his membership was comprised almost entirely of laborers, many of whom were union men. Neither well-born nor wealthy, his career prior to becoming a professional segregationist was at best checkered. During World War II he received radio training in a Navy program at the University of Colorado in Boulder. After the war he returned to study journalism briefly at Boulder, worked for a time for profes-

[17] See brief biographical sketches of Givhan and Ingalls in Anthony, "Survey of the Resistance Groups of Alabama," 41, 44.

[18] By the time the Supreme Court handed down its implementation decree in late May, 1955, Engelhardt had already introduced three bills to maintain segregation in the schools. See Birmingham *News*, May 31, 1955.

[19] The details of Engelhardt's biography were drawn from the personal scrapbook of Sam Engelhardt; Anthony, "Survey of the Resistance Groups of Alabama," 39–40; Bob Ingram, "Man with a Mission," Montgomery *Advertiser*, July 25, 1956; and Martin, *The Deep South Says "Never"*, 105ff.

sional anti-Semite Gerald L. K. Smith, and held numerous broadcasting jobs in Denver, Colorado, Yazoo City, Mississippi, and Anniston and Birmingham, Alabama. Immediately prior to entering full-time Council work, Carter was employed as a commentator for a series of broadcasts over a Birmingham radio station (WILD) sponsored by the American States' Rights Association, a Birmingham-based resistance organization founded soon after the Supreme Court's desegregation edict. His career in radio ended abruptly in 1955, when he was fired by station WILD after a Brotherhood Week broadcast in which he linked the National Conference of Christians and Jews with what he believed to be an international communist conspiracy.[20] At this point in his career Carter turned to the organized resistance movement, and in October, 1955, he formed the North Alabama Citizens' Council.

Somewhat later in formation, the West Alabama Citizens' Council was organized in Tuscaloosa during February, 1956, by a former student at the University of Alabama. A product of the crisis precipitated at the state university by the admission of Autherine Lucy, the WACC, like its counterpart in northern Alabama, was confined to a single county. Prior to the Lucy disorders, Tuscaloosa County had no Council. Indeed, even after the black coed's admission, reputation-minded Council leaders in Montgomery were initially opposed to the expansion of the movement there, fearing that it might be linked with campus violence. But by mid-1956 there were five groups, all affiliated with the WACC, and, according to "conservative estimates" given by the state Council on Human Relations, there were 3,000 Councilors. Behind this remarkable growth was Leonard Wilson, a twenty-year-old former student who had played a leading part in the campus riots and was subsequently expelled for his attack on the University's administration. Despite his role as rabble-rouser during the rioting and his reputation as "Flagpole" Wilson (at one point during the melee he climbed a flagpole in order to exhort the mob), he proved to be an able organizer and administrator, and in time he became the executive secretary of the

20 Both Engelhardt and Givhan were on the original board of governors of the American States' Rights Association, Inc. (Anthony, "Survey of Resistance Groups of Alabama," 5, 29ff.; Martin, *The Deep South Says "Never"*, 107ff.)

state association and a principal figure in the movement throughout the South.[21]

The South Alabama Citizens' Council was of considerably less significance. Formed early in February, 1956, largely through the efforts of black-belt organizers, the SACC did not develop significant leadership of its own, and it was never more than a paper organization. The first Council to be developed in this portion of the state appeared in Escambia County soon after the Lucy incident. A second Council appeared shortly thereafter in Mobile County, where the SACC's headquarters were located. The Mobile Council did not survive, however, and the South Alabama Council faded with it.[22]

The experience of organized resistance in Mississippi clearly demonstrated the worth of a central agency as a means of coordinating and directing the Council's expansionist efforts. With the success of the movement's mother state in view and with Robert Patterson there to guide the proceedings, the Alabama Association of Citizens' Councils was formed in Montgomery on February 17, 1956. Senator Engelhardt, the black-belt planter, became the executive secretary, and, in order to give the association an appearance of greater geographical balance, John Whitley, a Tarrant City druggist, was named president. "Dedicated to the maintenance of peace, good order, and domestic tranquility in our communities and in our State and to the preservation of our States' Rights under the 10th Amendment," the AACC was closely modeled after the Association of Citizens' Councils of Mississippi. Like its Mississippi counterpart, the association's primary objective was "to organize new Citizens' Councils and to promote expansion of the membership of existing Councils." [23]

[21] *Southern School News*, April, 1956, 5; September, 1956, 15; New York *Times*, February 18, 1956, and editorial, February 19, 1959; Anthony, "Survey of the Resistance Groups of Alabama," 42–43; Birmingham *Post-Herald*, March 12, 1955.

[22] Brief details of the activities of the South Alabama Citizens' Council appear in Anthony, "Survey of the Resistance Groups of Alabama," 2, 22–23. The Mobile Citizens' Council was reorganized in 1963. See Mobile *Register*, August 29, 1963.

[23] "Constitution of the Citizens' Council of Alabama" (unpublished document in the files of the Southern Office, Anti-Defamation League); Montgomery *Advertiser*, February 18, 1956.

In mid-February, 1956, there was indeed ample reason for optimism about the future of the movement in Alabama. In the backwash of desegregation petitions in August, a major bus boycott in December, and an attempt to desegregate the state university in February, local Councils in a period scarcely longer than six months had multiplied from five to more than twenty-five, and their membership rolls had swollen to an estimated 40,000. Although assisted somewhat by the four regional Councils, this growth had been accomplished without benefit of a central office. A well-coordinated program of expansion, Engelhardt believed, could net 160,000 new members by January 1, 1957.[24] To achieve this goal, he established an office in a motel on the Jefferson Davis Highway outside of Montgomery, and equipped it with a duplicator, a postage meter, and other paraphernalia for a propaganda campaign to mobilize white public opinion. But the flow of leaflets and pamphlets—some of them borrowed from the Mississippi Council[25]—had hardly begun before the unity of the movement suffered a major setback with the expulsion of the North Alabama Citizens' Council from the ranks of the state association.

The rift within the organization came into the open on February 29, 1956, just twelve days after the formation of the AACC, when three officers of the North Alabama Council resigned after Carter demanded the retirement of the president of the University of Alabama for permitting even the temporary desegregation of that institution. These resignations were only the first public manifestations of a fissure in the Alabama movement which began forming even before the appearance of the state association. From many quarters of the state—including some Council leaders—considerable criticism was leveled against the exclusion of Jews from the North Alabama Council's membership. Earlier in February, Alston Keith cautioned against the incursions of anti-Semitism into the Council. With unconscious irony, he declared: "There is no place for prejudice . . . in this movement." Warning against the "meth-

[24] See Montgomery *Advertiser,* February 5; *Dixie-American,* March 1; Birmingham *News,* February 19; Mobile *Press Register,* March 18, 1956.

[25] See, for example, *The Citizens' Council: The South's Only Answer* (Montgomery: Citizens' Council of Alabama, n.d.), an unacknowledged reprint in slightly altered form of Robert Patterson's pamphlet, *The Citizens' Council.*

ods" and "systems of operation" employed by Carter, Keith expressed regret that the northern Alabama leader had an "organization with the name Citizens' Council." More pointedly still, Engelhardt branded Carter a "fascist" and declared that "the Citizens' Council of Alabama has no room for Ace and his kind."[26]

Without question, Carter's presence within the resistance movement became increasingly uncomfortable to the leaders of the AACC. Soon after the break with the northern Alabama group, the Montgomery office apologetically announced to the press that "inevitably, from time to time, perhaps in all organizations that mushroom so swiftly from the grass roots, demagogic rabble rousers temporarily capture segments of such a group and harangue them into overt acts against the best interests of the whole community."[27] Yet there was more involved than Carter's well-known anti-Semitism and his ill-conceived attacks on a university president. By March it was apparent that the schism in Alabama's Citizens' Council possessed many of the overtones of what one observer called "the old feud between the Bourbon and the Redneck."[28]

Born on a small farm in Calhoun County in the northeastern corner of the state where the spurs of the Appalachians jut down from Tennessee and Georgia, "Ace" Carter identified himself and his organization, not with the partrician cotton South of the black belt, where the preponderance of Council strength lay, but with the poorer, upcountry red hills region, where agricultural holdings were smaller and less fertile and Negroes fewer. Graphically conveying this identification in the March issue of *The Southerner,* the North Alabama Council's crudely edited magazine, he described his kind of Councilor:

> Through his veins flow the fire, the initiative, the stalwartness of the Anglo Saxon. Proof of his enviable reputation is the attack upon him. For such has been coined the words "red neck" and "wool

[26] Birmingham *Post-Herald,* March 1, April 14, 1956; Anthony, "Survey of the Resistance Groups of Alabama," 3–4.

[27] This statement was prepared by the AACC for the Birmingham *Dixie-American,* as quoted in Louisville *Courier-Journal,* March 11, 1956. See also "Special Citizens' Council Section," *Dixie-American,* April 14, 1956, and an editorial, "For the Record," *The Citizens' Council,* February, 1957, 1.

[28] Douglas Cater, "Civil War in Alabama's Citizens' Councils," *The Reporter,* 14 (May 17, 1956), 20.

> hatter" . . . "cracker," and "hill billy." He has accepted the words rather than fought them . . . accepted them for what they are: For "red neck," takes mind of the toil beneath God's Sun and with His good earth, of that he feels no shame; the "wool hat" has been his way, with little money, of wearing something "special" to God's house on Sunday morning: the "cracker" he adopts as his calling card of delicate cocksureness; and if "hilly billy" he be, then he exults in the high whine of the fiddle's bow that calls up the sound of the fierce Scot blood that sounded the bagpipe of battle and lamented in the ballads of yore.[29]

Another divisive issue between Carter's faction and the state association was a fundamental disagreement over the kind of organization that the Citizens' Council should be and the course of action that it should pursue. The AACC, like its Mississippi counterpart, sought the support of the responsible white citizen who believed in segregation but who would avoid open affiliation with any organization that advocated violence. Through its monthly newspaper *The Alabamian* and its successor, the *States' Rights Advocate*, the organization condemned the extralegal procedures of the Klan and endeavored to confine the activities of its constituent organizations within a framework of law and order. Directing its program against a single minority, the Negro, it welcomed others, including Jews and Catholics, into its ranks.[30] Perhaps most important, it believed that the well-established procedures of politics and propaganda could be employed to preserve the racial status quo. Toward this end it strived to enlist politicians and other dignitaries from the state and local power structure, and it actively encouraged the election of candidates whose views were similar to its own. Carter,

[29] *The Southerner: News of the Citizens' Council*, 1 (March, 1956). The first issue of this "monthly" magazine appeared in February, 1956. Thereafter, it appeared sporadically for about one year. Carter told John Bartlow Martin that he printed 15,000 copies of each issue. (Martin, *The Deep South Says "Never"*, 117.)

[30] *The Alabamian* was published during Engelhardt's tenure as executive secretary of the Alabama Council. After his retirement in 1958 the *States' Rights Advocate* appeared. The AACC's position in the feud with the northern Alabama faction is covered by "Repudiated," *South*, 21 (March 19, 1956), 14. See also McCauley, "Political Implications in Alabama of the School Segregation Decisions," 69–71.

at Birmingham's Municipal Auditorium.[36] Undismayed by the popular outcry against such violence, the man who believed that "Bebop Promotes Communism" refused to repudiate the offenders. Calling Cole "a vicious agitator for integration," Carter sponsored a White People's Defense Fund for the six assailants who had been arrested immediately after the attack.[37]

By 1957, it became increasingly difficult to distinguish between the activities of Carter's North Alabama Council and the Birmingham area Original Ku Klux Klan of the Confederacy with which he became identified. In that year members of his following were arrested and eventually convicted of the initiation-rite castration of an elderly Negro man in a local Klan meeting house. Also during 1957 the executive secretary himself was charged with attempted murder when a hooded and robed Klansman who had complained of Carter's "one-man rule" of the klavern was shot during a Klan rally at Carter's Birmingham headquarters in a ramshackle former movie house. Although identified by the victim as his assailant, Carter professed his innocence, and the charges were later dropped for lack of evidence.[38] But Carter's continued involvement with violence undermined his status within the movement and he could no longer be considered a serious challenge to the state association's dominion over Alabama Councilors.[39]

[36] *The Southerner: News of the Citizens' Council,* 1 (March, 1956); Cater, "Civil War in Alabama's Citizens' Councils," 19–20.

[37] Typical of the southern press reaction to the attack was that expressed by the editor of the Richmond *News Leader,* April 14, 1956: "*The good South is sorry.*" Councils across the region were also critical. The Georgia States' Rights Council, the South Carolina Association of Citizens' Councils, and a Council in New Orleans expressed revulsion for the acts of the North Alabama Councilors. See Atlanta *Journal,* April 24; Richmond *Times-Dispatch,* April 13; Chattanooga *Times,* April 26, 1956.

[38] David M. Chalmers, *Hooded Americanism: The First Century of the Ku Klux Klan, 1865–1965* (New York: Doubleday, 1965), 344–45; "Klans and Councils," *The New Republic,* 137 (September 23, 1957), 6; "Carter and the KKK," *The New Republic,* 136 (February 4, 1957), 6; James Vander Zanden, "The Klan Revival," *American Journal of Sociology,* 65 (March, 1960), 456.

[39] From time to time it was necessary to repudiate local Councils which became involved in "side issues." This was the case with the Elmore County Citizens' Council, which was disavowed by the Citizens' Councils of Alabama

73223

The triumph of the Citizens' Councils of Alabama was pyrrhic at best. No sooner was Carter's threat quashed than the organization's popular appeal began to wane. The rancorous infighting and the adverse publicity which it engendered exacted a heavy toll. As its spokesmen well understood, "the chief danger [to "respectable" resistance groups] comes from the zealots who happen to be opposed to integration, hence their affinity for the Councils, but who are consumed with assorted hatreds, bitterness, and warped ideas. . . ."[40] But decry as it would the "anti-Jewish agitators" and the "fanatics," the Council's reputation for respectability, a reputation for which it strived so ardently, had been blemished by the taint of extremism. More than a decade after the fact, Engelhardt bitterly declared that "Ace killed it. He killed the Council dead." Once the Council's "good name" had been besmirched by Carter's antics, Engelhardt averred, the state's "respectable element" lost interest in organized resistance.[41]

Contributing still further to the evanescence of the CCA was the very nature of the organized resistance movement itself. Its fate in Alabama, as elsewhere in the region, was closely linked with developments on the racial front. Because its programs were essentially negative, designed primarily to bar the Negro from full citizenship, the Council tended to attract and lose support in an erratic fashion. As has been noted, the organization's membership soared as Negroes boycotted Montgomery buses. But after white indignation cooled and the crises passed, popular interest sagged. It is probably true also, as bus boycott leader Martin Luther King, Jr., asserted, that the successful desegregation of the city's transit system tended to undermine white faith in the Council's ability to preserve Jim Crow. In his first major book, *Stride toward Freedom,* the

---

in 1961 after it circulated anti-Semitic literature (Montgomery *Advertiser,* May 21, 1961). Typical of the Elmore Council's propaganda leaflets was one entitled, "The Biggest 'Big-Lie' of All." According to this broadside, the biggest lie was the "ridiculous *myth* that the modern American jew is a Whiteman." The next biggest lie was "the propaganda fraud that Adolph Hitler killed six million jews. . . ." Most of that number, the leaflet stated, were in the United States attempting to destroy the "Great White Christian Race." See "The Biggest 'Big-Lie' of All," Files of the Southern Office, A-DL.

40 Editorial, *States' Rights Advocate,* April, 1958.

41 Interview with Sam Engelhardt.

future Nobel Prize winner observed: "That such organizations could not prevent this [desegregation] from happening was evidence to many of the dues-paying members that they could best use their own dollars elsewhere." [42]

At most the Citizens' Councils of Alabama could fight only a delaying action. As traditional racial walls continued to crumble in the face of federally supported Negro pressure, all but the most intransigent white segregationists became aware of the inevitability of at least token desegregation in the public schools. When in June, 1963, two Negro students registered at the Tuscaloosa campus once again to desegregate the state university, the Council in Alabama no longer had a mass following. Unlike the earlier crisis, the incident was followed by no sudden surge of popular interest. Its ranks badly depleted, the Council wisely chose to accept the situation with greater grace than it had demonstrated during Autherine Lucy's brief campus appearance in 1956. In striking contrast to that performance, it urged its members and the public in general to stay away from the university. Although encouraging Governor George C. Wallace to keep his campaign pledge and "stand in the schoolhouse door," the organization's executive committee bowed to the unavoidable, declaring "we must not have violence." [43]

The erosion of Council strength in Alabama became apparent as early as 1958. In that year Executive Secretary Sam Engelhardt resigned to campaign unsuccessfully for the Democratic nomination for lieutenant governor.[44] Soon thereafter, CCA headquarters were transferred to Selma, where state Senator Walter C. Givhan, head of the Dallas County Council and newly elected chairman of the state association, directed its affairs. Under Givhan's leadership the organization's popular strength declined still further. By 1962, when he retired, even the sympathetic Alabama Foundation (an organiza-

[42] Martin Luther King, *Stride toward Freedom: The Montgomery Story* (New York: Harper, 1958), 187. See also Abel Plenn, "Report on Montgomery a Year After," *New York Times Magazine*, December 29, 1957, 36.

[43] Quoted in Montgomery *Advertiser*, June 7, and Birmingham *News*, June 14, 1963. For his stand at the university, the Houston County Council presented the governor with a "red badge of courage." See Montgomery *Advertiser*, June 16, 1963.

[44] Engelhardt was defeated in the May primary by a fellow Councilor, state Senator Albert Boutwell.

tion of ultraconservative businessmen identified with the Alabama Council) acknowledged, "the Citizens' Council on a state basis, has declined steadily in all but three or four counties in the last five years and is at a low ebb financially and in total membership." [45] Givhan's successor as state president, C. E. Hornsby, Jr., a prominent Bibb County lumberman, managed no better. Even the appointment of former state Vice-Chairman Leonard Wilson as full-time executive secretary, a post unoccupied since Engelhardt's resignation, brought no noticeable resurgence.[46]

Numerical strength, however, is not always the best index of an organization's influence. Long after the Council's mass membership began to dwindle, it enjoyed the continued favor of high public officials. Although many older and more responsible Alabama politicians (notably Senators Lister Hill and John Sparkman) remained aloof, and although Governors Gordon Persons and James E. Folsom were never supporters, subsequent administrations proved more friendly. Close working relationships with the administrations of both Governors John Patterson and George C. Wallace gave the organization a visible presence and a potent voice after those in many other states were all but eclipsed from public view.

45 Letter from Alabama Foundation to selected supporters, February, 1961, as quoted in interoffice memorandum, January, 1962, Southern Office, A-DL. A-DL policy forbids more specific attribution. All such memoranda will be cited hereafter as Report, A-DL, Southern Office, date.

46 Presidents of the Citizens' Councils of Alabama, in order of their service, were: John Whitely, Verdo Wilson Elmore, Walter C. Givhan, C. E. Hornsby, Jr., and W. H. Garner, Sr.

CHAPTER IV

Louisiana: And Catholics Too

LOUISIANA moved with a rapidity second to none in establishing an official attitude of defiance to the Supreme Court decision of May 17, 1954. Almost alone among southern states, its legislature was in session on "Black Monday," and it wasted little time in responding to the threat posed by the *Brown* doctrine to the state's system of segregated schools. On May 20, lawmakers introduced in the lower house a resolution censuring the nation's highest tribunal for its "unwarranted and unprecedented abuse of power." Passing that body with only three dissenting votes, the measure carried every vote but one in the Senate.[1] On this note of recalcitrance, the legislature proceeded to build a legal barricade against desegregation in the public schools which by 1964 included more than 131 acts and resolutions—more than twice the number enacted by any other state.[2]

Rapid though it was in effecting a defiant public posture, the Pelican State was surprisingly slow in developing a viable private resistance movement. Not until April, 1955, did the first Citizens' Council spill over from Mississippi into the northern part of the

[1] All four dissenting votes were cast by southern Louisiana legislators. See Earleen Mary McCarrick, "Louisiana's Official Resistance to Desegregation" (unpublished Ph.D. dissertation, Department of Political Science, Vanderbilt University, 1964), 27–31; and *Southern School News*, September 3, 1954.

[2] *Southern School News*, May, 1964, special section, "Ten Years in Review," 11-B.

state. In view of numerous attempts by Negroes to breach the state's traditional color line, this apparent reluctance to imitate organization-minded segregationists in Alabama and Mississippi seems all the more remarkable. Even before the *Brown* decision, NAACP lawyers had initiated desegregation suits in Orleans and St. Helena parishes, and when school opened in the fall of 1954, forty Baton Rouge Negro students sought and were denied entrance to an all-white school in Dixie, a predominantly Negro suburb. That same September school authorities in Gretna, a village directly across the Mississippi River from New Orleans, also refused to enroll Negro applicants in an all-white school.

More successful were Negro efforts to bring down racial barriers for institutions of higher learning. Loyola University of the South in New Orleans, a pioneer in desegregated higher education in the Deep South, opened its doors to students of all races in September, 1954, as it had each September since 1950. Similarly, Negro ministerial students enrolled in the Baptist Seminary in New Orleans, and Negro coeds were admitted to the College of the Sacred Heart at Grand Coteau for the 1954–55 academic year. Even among state-supported colleges some progress toward compliance was made prior to the Supreme Court's implementation decree of May, 1955. Louisiana State University in Baton Rouge, while excluding Negro undergraduates, had no racial obstructions to its graduate school, and in Lafayette, perhaps as many as eighty Negroes were admitted to Southwestern Louisiana Institute.[3]

A large majority of the registered voters in Louisiana, however, took little apparent pride in the remarkable adjustments made by many of the state's colleges to the ruling of the Court. Early in November, 1954, the electorate approved by nearly five to one an amendment permitting the state to employ its police powers to preserve segregated public schools in the interests of "public health, morals, better education, peace, and good order." Favored in all sixty-four parishes, Amendment Number 16, as this segregation measure was known, received its greatest support upstate, where the ratio of Negroes to whites was the greatest. In Claiborne, a north-central parish on the Arkansas border, an incredible 99.04

[3] Ibid., October 1, 1954.

percent of those voting approved the amendment.[4] Not remarkably, the first Council in Louisiana was formed in this parish.

Claiborne Parish was in most respects a likely setting for the origin of Louisiana's Council movement. Except for the obvious presence of rich gas and oil fields, the parish, which had one of the highest percentages (52 percent) of nonwhites in the state, was not unlike Sunflower County, Mississippi. An important center for cotton production, Claiborne was preponderantly rural. Its largest population center was its parish seat, Homer, a town of about 4,500. The parish also produced some of the state's most ardent spokesmen for white supremacy, most notably state Senator William M. Rainach, chairman of the Joint Legislative Committee to Maintain Segregation which sponsored Amendment 16.[5] Regarded by one authority on the politics of massive resistance as "Louisiana's most powerful legislator" during the later half of the 1950's,[6] Rainach was largely responsible for the consistently defiant stand assumed by a state long considered racially moderate by Deep South standards. Although Louisiana had had its share of demagogues, it had never spawned a Negro-baiter of the magnitude of Mississippi's

[4] Altogether, a total of 264,921 Louisianians voted on the amendment, of whom 82 percent favored it. See W. D. Workman, Jr., "The Deep South," in Don Shoemaker, ed., *With All Deliberate Speed* (New York: Harper, 1957), 98; and *Southern School News*, December 1, 1954.

[5] The Joint Legislative Committee on Segregation was established by joint resolution soon after the Supreme Court decision. It operated until 1960, serving as the official voice of evasion, defiance, and delay in Louisiana. During the campaign for the popular ratification of Amendment Number 16, it produced and distributed to television stations throughout the state a fifteen-minute film, moderated by Senator Rainach, which linked "the arrogant, alien NAACP" and the struggle for civil rights with the communist conspiracy. See McCarrick, "Louisiana's Official Resistance to Desegregation," 32, 40–41; *Southern School News*, November 4, 1954.

[6] Bartley, *The Rise of Massive Resistance*, 90–91. For additional evidence of Rainach's great power, see McCarrick, "Louisiana's Official Resistance to Desegregation," 26–90; and Edward L. Pinney and Robert S. Friedman, *Political Leadership in Louisiana*, Eagleton Institute Case Studies in Practical Politics (New Brunswick: Rutgers University Press, 1963), passim. Journalistic accounts on the same subject include A. J. Liebling, *The Earl of Louisiana* (New York: Simon and Schuster, 1961), 29–30, passim; and Stan Opotowsky, *The Longs of Louisiana* (New York: E. P. Dutton, 1960), 169–70, 175.

Theodore G. Bilbo, South Carolina's Benjamin R. Tillman, or Georgia's Thomas E. Watson. During the years of Louisiana's massive resistance, however, this Claiborne politico, frequently wearing a colorful Confederate flag-embossed cravat, led a legislature which became increasingly preoccupied with the issue of race. In addition to his status as the chief spokesman for white supremacy in the state, he became president of the Association of Citizens' Councils of Louisiana (ACCL) upon its formation early in 1956. The following April, when the Citizens' Councils of America was organized, he became its first president.[7]

Rainach's counterpart in the state House of Representatives was John S. Garrett, also of Claiborne Parish, and also a dedicated segregationist. During Rainach's tenure, Garrett served as vice-chairman of the Joint Committee on Segregation, and in 1959, when Rainach resigned as president of the ACCL to run for governor, Garrett became his successor.[8] Claiborne Parish's third major contribution to the Louisiana Council hierarchy was William M. Shaw, a Homer attorney who served as chief counsel for Rainach's Joint Committee on Segregation. Shaw was instrumental in the formation of the Homer Council on April 19, 1955, and in 1956 he became executive secretary of the ACCL.[9]

During the months following the formation of the Council in Homer, three other Louisiana resistance groups made their presence known: the Southern Gentlemen, Inc., a semi-secret organization founded by J. B. Easterly in Baton Rouge several months before the Council's appearance in Claiborne Parish; the Knights of White Christians, a short-lived Klan-like group founded by Alvin A. Cobb in New Orleans; and the Society for the Preservation of State Government and Racial Integrity, organized in New Orleans by Harry P. Gamble, Sr., who later became identified with the Citizens' Councils.[10] None of these groups attracted significant grass-roots

[7] Birmingham *News,* January 30; New Orleans *Times-Picayune,* January 31, 1956, April 20, 1955.

[8] *Southern School News,* May 1959, 5; New York *Times,* November 27, 1960.

[9] New Orleans *Times-Picayune,* January 31, 1956.

[10] *Southern School News,* September, 1955, 7; August, 1955, 5; Southern Regional Council, *Special Report: Pro-Segregation Groups in the South,* November, 1956, 7. In this, the first of several similar reports, the Southern Re-

support, however, and the organized resistance movement in the state languished until September, 1955, when a second Citizens' Council was formed in the wake of a desegregation petition campaign. Then, in rapid succession, a number of Councils began to appear in the northern part of the state. In late January, 1956, when the Association of Citizens' Councils was formed in Baton Rouge, Senator Rainach reported to the press that Councils operated in thirteen parishes, and that their combined membership exceeded 8,000.[11] By the following April, the first anniversary of the movement in Louisiana, there were Councils in twenty-eight of the state's sixty-four parishes, and the ACCL was claiming a combined membership of from 75,000 to 100,000.[12] In June the authoritative *Southern School News* estimated Council strength at 100,000 to 125,000 in thirty parishes.[13] Virtually all of these organized parishes were in the so-called Anglo-Saxon and Protestant portion of the state north of Alexandria.[14] Situated in the upland cotton districts along the Arkansas border and the fertile lowlands of the Red River and upper Mississippi River deltas, the Councils formed a solid bloc of twenty-two parishes in the large-plantation area of the state, where Negro concentration was heaviest and resistance to social change greatest.[15]

---

gional Council noted that by November, 1956, both the Knights of the White Christians and the Society for the Preservation of State Government were inactive.

[11] Birmingham *News,* January 30; New Orleans *Times-Picayune,* January 31, 1956.

[12] "Louisiana Reports Rapid Growth: Groups Functioning in Every Section as Membership Climbs," *The Citizens' Council,* June, 1956, 7. In this, the first article about the Council movement in Louisiana to appear in *The Citizens' Council,* organized parishes listed were: Bienville, Bossier, Caddo, Calcasieu, Claiborne, Concordia, De Soto, East Baton Rouge, East Carroll, West Carroll, Franklin, Jackson, Lincoln, Livingston, Madison, Morehouse, Natchitoches, Orleans, Ouachita, Plaquemines, Rapides, Red River, Richland, St. Bernard, Tensas, Union, Webster, and Winn.

[13] *Southern School News,* June, 1956, 3.

[14] The most perceptive study of Louisiana's ethno-religious diversity is Homer L. Hitt and T. Lynn Smith, *The People of Louisiana* (Baton Rouge: Louisiana State University Press, 1952). See also Alvin L. Bertrand, *The Many Louisianas: Rural Social Areas and Cultural Islands,* Bulletin No. 496, Louisiana State University, June, 1955.

[15] "Louisiana Citizens' Council Map," *The Citizens' Council,* June, 1956, 7.

A second center of Council activity, curiously enough, was in southern Louisiana's cosmopolitan and urbane port city, New Orleans, and its environs. French Catholic Louisiana is a vast and irregular triangle of some twenty-five parishes running from the mouth of the Sabine River in the southwest and the mouth of the Mississippi River in the southeast to a vertex at the junction of the Mississippi and Red rivers near the center of the state. Unlike northern Louisiana, which in terms of ethno-religious factors is not dissimilar from other Deep South states, this region has traditionally steered a course of relative racial moderation. While it cannot be said that southern Louisiana in the 1950's was a hotbed of desegregationist sentiment, the section did demonstrate throughout the state's period of massive defiance a generally more permissive attitude toward civil rights than did northern Louisiana. In the French Catholic parishes, for example, more than half of all potential Negro voters were registered in 1956, whereas in the remainder of the state only 20 percent were.[16] Similarly, a striking majority of the desegregated colleges were located in southern Louisiana. In brief, as one student of public opinion expressed it, "Catholic Louisiana took race much less seriously than did Protestant Louisiana." [17]

There were enclaves in French Catholic Louisiana, however, which did take race very seriously. For it was in New Orleans, threatened since 1952 by an NAACP school desegregation suit, that the second Council in the state was organized. The immediate impetus for a Council's appearance in the Crescent City was a petition signed by 180 New Orleanians in mid-September, 1955, requesting that school officials terminate segregated education in Orleans Parish. Reflecting its potential strength, the newly formed Council in a matter of two weeks gathered 15,000 signatures on a counterpetition encouraging parish authorities to uphold "separate but equal fa-

[16] The difference in Negro registration between Catholic and Protestant areas of Louisiana is explored in detail in John H. Fenton and Kenneth N. Vines, "Negro Registration in Louisiana," *American Political Science Review*, 51 (September, 1957), 704–13. See also John H. Fenton, *The Catholic Vote* (New Orleans: Hauser Press, 1960), 111; and Margaret Price, *The Negro Voter in the South* (Atlanta: Southern Regional Council, 1957), 25.

[17] Fenton, *The Catholic Vote*, 111–12.

cilities."[18] So well did the Council flourish in this southeastern corner of Louisiana that by January, 1956, eight individual groups were functioning in Orleans and its surrounding parishes—Jefferson, Plaquemines, and St. Bernard—and a central Council, the Greater New Orleans Citizens' Council, had been formed.[19]

The rapid pace that marked the Council's organizational activity during the fall and early winter was accelerated still further in February, 1956, when it became apparent that both the public (78,000 pupils) and the parochial (75,000 pupils) school systems in Orleans Parish faced the immediate possibility of desegregation. On February 11, Archbishop Joseph Francis Rummel, in a pastoral letter read in Catholic churches throughout the archdiocese of New Orleans, placed the weight of his influential office on the side of the Constitution. Declaring that "racial segregation is morally wrong and sinful," he hinted that integration would soon come to the Catholic schools under his jurisdiction. Only four days later, on February 15, a federal district court in a sweeping decision struck down Louisiana's legislative program to maintain separate-but-equal public education, and ordered officials in Orleans Parish to proceed with plans to end segregation in the parish's schools.[20] The Council's response was a public meeting at the New Orleans Municipal Auditorium on March 20, featuring an hour-long Dixieland jazz concert and anti–Supreme Court oratory by Georgia's roving ambassadors of segregation, former state Speaker of the House Roy V. Harris and state Attorney General Eugene Cook. Attended by an estimated 6,500 white citizens, many of whom waved miniature

[18] *Southern School News,* October, 1955, 11; New Orleans *Times-Picayune,* September 14, 27, 1955.

[19] Five of these eight Councils were located in Orleans Parish, and one each in the other three. (New Orleans *Times-Picayune,* January 13, 1956.)

[20] *Southern School News,* March, 1956, 5. The several statutes and the constitutional amendment passed in Louisiana during the summer and fall of 1954, requiring segregation in exercise of the state's police powers, represented the first southern legal attempts to evade and delay. They were also the first pieces of segregation legislation specifically designed to defy the *Brown* decision to be declared invalid by a federal court. See Louisiana State Advisory Committee to the U.S. Commission on Civil Rights, *The New Orleans School Crisis* (Washington: Government Printing Office, 1961), 51–52.

Confederate flags, the rally launched a house-to-house Orleans Parish canvass in a drive to enlist 50,000 people.[21]

Apparently the canvass met with considerable success. Before the month of March had passed, the membership chairman reported to the local press that new members were joining more rapidly than anticipated and that the early goal of 50,000 could well be exceeded. Nevertheless, it seems unlikely that the GNOCC ever enlisted 50,000 members, though such a claim was frequently made during the ensuing years.[22] But it cannot be denied that organized resistance prospered in the Crescent City. Simply in raw statistical terms, *The Citizens' Council* may well have been correct when it asserted that the movement "is as strong in the predominantly Catholic portions of South Louisiana as in the Protestant northern parts of the Pelican State." Indeed, William J. Simmons informed a northern audience in 1958 that the Greater New Orleans Council was the largest Citizens' Council in the nation.[23] Even the ACCL, dominated though it was by officers from the northern parishes, readily acknowledged that the Council in the New Orleans area had more than half of the state's total members. With some pride, then, CCA spokesmen could boast that "Catholics are active in Citizens' Councils all over the South, especially in Southern Louisiana where the movement is predominantly Catholic." [24]

Much of the vitality enjoyed by the Council in this sophisticated city of the Deep South was attributable to the protracted New Orleans school desegregation crisis. Beginning in September, 1952, when *Bush* v. *Orleans Parish School Board* was filed, it continued

21 New Orleans *Times-Picayune*, March 14, 22; Jackson *Daily News*, March 21, 1956. A higher estimate of attendance was given by the Southern Education Reporting Service, which listed the number at 8,000. See *Southern School News*, April, 1956, 14.

22 New Orleans *Times-Picayune*, March 22, 1956; New York *Times*, November 27, 1960.

23 *The Citizens' Council*, January, 1958, 4; William J. Simmons, *The Mid-West Hears the South's Story: An Address before the Oakland Farmers-Merchants Annual Banquet, Oakland, Iowa, February 3, 1958* (Greenwood: Association of Citizens' Councils of Mississippi, n.d.).

24 Southern Regional Council, *Pro-Segregation Groups in the South*, November 19, 1956; *The Citizens' Council*, April, 1957, 4.

until November, 1960, when actual desegregation began in the Orleans Parish public schools. The high quality of its leadership, which included many locally prominent Catholic lay people, also contributed to the strength of the Greater New Orleans Citizens' Council. Louis Porterie, one of the founders and early leaders of the movement in this metropolis, was the son of Gaston Porterie, former state attorney general and federal judge. Another was Dr. Emmett Lee Irwin, past president of the Louisiana Medical Association, former head of the department of surgery at the Louisiana State University Medical School, and perennial president of the GNOCC until his death in 1965.[25] Jackson Ricau, the first executive director of the organization, was a graduate of Loyola University and one-time editor of its alumni association's monthly publication. A public school teacher who resigned his position to become a full-time employee of the Greater New Orleans Council movement, Ricau was also a founder, board member, and executive secretary of the Association of Catholic Laymen, "a group of Catholics devoted to Holy Mother Church," organized in March, 1956, to oppose the liberal racial policies of Archbishop Rummel.[26] Emile A. Wagner, Jr., another Loyola graduate active in Council circles, was an attorney who served as president of the Association of Catholic Laymen. The only unswerving segregationist on the five-member Orleans Parish board of education, Wagner, who preferred no schools to desegregated schools, proved to be an indefatigable advocate of lily-white classrooms. The most influential spokesman for the movement in the New Orleans area, however, was Leander H. Perez, powerful district attorney and political boss of St. Bernard and Plaquemines parishes. Although an officer in neither the GNOCC nor the state association, Judge Perez was one of seventeen charter members of the Association of Citizens' Councils of Louisiana and

[25] Irwin was also a vice-president of the ACCL. (*Southern School News*, October, 1955, 11; New Orleans *Times-Picayune*, January 31, 1956.)

[26] According to Ricau, the Association suspended its activities on May 1, 1956, after Archbishop Rummel threatened to excommunicate its directors. (Jackson Ricau, *The Tragic Truth about the Catholic Race-Mixing Program in New Orleans: Address to Parents and Friends of Catholic Children, New Orleans, Louisiana, July 25, 1962* [Jackson: Citizens' Councils of America, n.d.], 7, 10. See also *The Councilor Newsletter*, November, 1957.)

was considered by many in the movement as "a national Citizens' Council leader." [27]

The vigor of the Council in the greater New Orleans area was unmatched elsewhere in Louisiana south of Alexandria. In June, 1956, very nearly the heyday of the movement's strength, the only other Councils in the southern portion of the state were to be found in Calcasieu, East Baton Rouge, and Livingston parishes. Of these three, Calcasieu alone was predominantly French Catholic in ethnoreligious composition. Both East Baton Rouge and Livingston were heavily Protestant.[28] Senator Rainach's goal of a Council in every parish, announced upon the birth of the ACCL in January, 1956, was never realized. In early 1960, soon after he resigned his Council post, *The Councilor Newsletter,* official monthly publication of the state association, could claim organizations in only thirty-four of the state's sixty-four parishes. Although optimistic about the future, the *Newsletter* conceded that "the French Country of South Central Louisiana"—"that large area, between Baton Rouge and Lake Charles"—had remained unresponsive to the ACCL's plea for a solid front against desegregation.[29]

Rainach's resignation to run unsuccessfully for the Democratic gubernatorial nomination in 1959 was followed by the rapid disintegration of the already debilitated Louisiana Council movement. Having reached its meridian late in 1956, Council strength in the Pelican State, like that in virtually every other southern state, began a gradual erosion as popular ardor for organized resistance cooled. In its heyday the ACCL claimed more than 100,000 dues-paying members and organizations in thirty-four parishes.[30] Like most of the movement's membership claims, this one seems highly inflated. Because state Council records are not available, and according to

[27] Jackson Ricau, "The Revealing Story of My Excommunication—An Act of Desperation by the Race Mixers," *The Citizen,* 6 (April, 1962), 6; "Articles of Incorporation of the Association of Citizens' Councils of Louisiana," Article 8, reprinted in U.S. Commission on Civil Rights, *Hearings Held in New Orleans, Louisiana, September 27–28, 1960, May 5–6, 1961* (Washington: Government Printing Office, 1961), 528.

[28] See "Louisiana Citizens' Council Map," *The Citizens' Council,* June, 1957, 7; Hitt and Smith, *The People of Louisiana,* 136.

[29] *The Councilor Newsletter,* February, 1960. 3.

[30] *Southern School News,* June, 1956, 3; Southern Regional Council, *Spe-*

Rainach may no longer exist,[31] any estimate of the organization's strength is hazardous. Nevertheless, at its peak the Council probably had more than 50,000 members, and perhaps substantially more.

But during 1957 membership began to drop; by 1958 even Greater New Orleans Council officials were complaining that popular interest was "very low," despite the recent desegregation of the city's public transit system. Typical was the lament of Cullen E. Vetters, Gentilly chapter chairman, who believed that "the whiteness God put in me is the supreme thing in me." In July, 1958, soon after a federal judge labeled the Orleans Parish pupil assignment law a "legal artifice," "unconstitutional on its face," Vetters surveyed his shrinking flock at a public rally and inquired: "What's the matter with you white people? Aren't you interested in the preservation of the white race?"[32] Although Orleans schools managed to avoid desegregation for another two years, all but a few of the Crescent City's Caucasian population apparently recognized that, if indeed the preservation of the white race were in question, the negative programs of the Citizens' Council offered scant hope for its salvation.

Troubling though it was to ardent segregationists, local apathy was perhaps the least of the Council's problems in New Orleans during the summer of 1958. Divisive forces, already at work, soon sundered badly depleted Council ranks. In November, 1958, a faction led by Executive Secretary Jackson Ricau and Joseph E. Viguerie, charter member and one of five incorporators of the state association, withdrew from the Greater New Orleans Citizens' Council to organize the South Louisiana Citizens' Council. Although ostensibly formed "to meet a growing need for expansion of the Citizens' Council movement in the area,"[33] the emergence of the splinter group was the first public indication of a growing cleavage within the statewide organization. While it was not fully apparent for more than a year, at the heart of this internecine rift lay

---

cial Report: Pro-Segregation Groups in the South, May 23, 1957; New Orleans *Times-Picayune,* March 7, 1960.

[31] William M. Rainach to the author, January 12, 1967.

[32] Quoted in *Southern School News,* September, 1958, 5.

[33] "News from the Local Councils," *The Citizens' Council,* November, 1958, 4.

essentially the same vexatious issue that had roiled Council waters in Alabama. Representing the more "respectable" wing of the New Orleans area movement, the Ricau-Viguerie faction feared the increasingly strident anti-Semitism of such GNOCC stalwarts as Leander Perez. Aware that the intrusion of Jew-baiting could only tarnish the Council's reputation, the South Louisiana Council endeavored to remain free of the stigma of anti-Semitism. Like principal organized resistance groups throughout the region, Ricau's Council, which by 1960 claimed a membership of 2,000, sought the support of the "better class" of segregationists, and that necessitated a more selective approach to racial exclusion.[34]

The Greater New Orleans Council, on the other hand, was little troubled by such refinements. In order to "educate" the public to what it believed to be the realities of the racial crisis, the organization sponsored the "Voice of Truth," a telephone recording project. By simply dialing their telephones, citizens of the seaport city could learn that "Some Jews—not all—but some are in favor of complete integration. . . . Why do some Jews want the Negro and the Gentile to mix? Can it be that a segment of our Jewish brethren want to destroy the Gentile?"[35] In similar tones, Judge Perez, the most influential spokesman for the GNOCC, propounded his theory that "an unseen web," a "Communist Zionist web," exercised "an unnatural influence . . . over the course of our government in Washington." At Council rallies and public gatherings in the Crescent City and across the South, he affirmed that "international Jews" were exploiting the Negro issue in order to destroy America, and that "the most dangerous people in this country are Zionist Jews."[36]

Fortunately for organizational unity in Louisiana, this side of the Greater New Orleans Council's ideology remained largely sub-

[34] The official posture of the South Louisiana Citizens' Council, Inc., was best reflected by its bulletin, *The Citizens' Report*, published monthly in Metairie. Scattered copies of this publication, which by 1961 claimed a circulation of 60,000, may be seen in the files of the Southern Office, A-DL. See also New Orleans *Times-Picayune*, March 1, 1961.

[35] See unpublished transcripts of "The Voice of Truth" recordings, January 11, 27, 1964, and n.d., Southern Office, A-DL. See also Baton Rouge *State Times*, February 15, 1964.

[36] Quoted in Cleghorn, "The Segs," 72; New Orleans *Times-Picayune*, August 30, 31, September 2, 1960.

merged until after 1960. Despite their basic differences, both factions remained within the statewide association, and both were represented among its officers and directors. But after the resignation of Willie Rainach, their paths diverged.

Rainach's successor, Representative John Garrett, proved unable to shore up the weakening structure of the statewide Council. Even a March, 1960, "revitalization" meeting in Alexandria, called "to bring the Council movement in Louisiana back to life," failed to buoy the foundering organization. Although such regional Council dignitaries as Robert B. Patterson and William J. Simmons delivered speeches calculated to inspire enthusiasm for the cause, the gloomy reports of the state officers clearly marked this meeting in Rapides Parish as more a wake than a rally. "We're going to have to have some money or fold up," declared ACCL Treasurer T. B. McKeithen. "The state organization has $300 in its treasury and by the end of the month will be $600 in the hole." [37]

The following November, Garrett, too, resigned. Under his successor, Charles L. Barnett, state headquarters were shifted temporarily to Baton Rouge and then early in 1961 to Shreveport.[38] Following its relocation in that northwestern Louisiana city on the Red River, the organization rapidly began to move out of what might be called the mainstream of the region's Council movement. Its raucous Negrophobia, excessive even by Deep South standards, its apparent obsession with the "internal Red menace," and its unblushing anti-Semitism marked it as an extremist organization akin to the Ku Klux Klan.[39] Stripped of whatever respectability it had enjoyed under Rainach's tenure, the Citizens' Councils of Louisiana, under the leadership of Executive Director William H. Rutledge, maintained few contacts with the larger Council movement, which quietly repudiated it.[40] With only a small body of supporters in

[37] Quoted in New Orleans *Times-Picayune,* March 7, 1960.

[38] F. A. Wallis, "Report from Louisiana," *The Citizens' Council,* August, 1960, 3.

[39] On some occasions officials of the organization even addressed Klan rallies. See Biloxi-Gulfport *Daily Herald,* October 28, 1965. For examples of its extremism, see any issue of *The Councilor,* official journal of the Citizens' Councils of Louisiana, Inc.

[40] According to W. M. Rainach, "The Citizens' Councils of America and the Citizens' Councils of Louisiana, Inc. share certain common objectives. The

the Shreveport area and a working relationship with the increasingly ineffective Greater New Orleans Council, the reconstituted Citizens' Council of Louisiana never achieved a significant following. To date its principal achievement has been the publication since 1962 of a fortnightly tabloid, *The Councilor.* Under the acerbic editorship of Ned Touchstone, this self-styled "unfettered truth medium" has consistently supplemented its more conventional prosegregation fare with sensational headlines and lurid exposés ("KILLERS OF JOHN KENNEDY ARE STILL ALIVE AND ROAMING U.S.") to attract an unusually large circulation for a newspaper of its type.[41]

The South Louisiana Council discreetly avoided any formal relationship with Rutledge's group, and in early 1960, as proof of its allegiance to the purposes and ideals of the Mississippi-based regional Council movement, it named both Patterson and Simmons as honorary lifetime members.[42]

---

structural differences between the two organizations is due, I think, to certain differences as to methods, policies and somewhat as to objectives. I do not think it would contribute to our common cause for me to elaborate upon these differences." (Rainach to the author, June 30, 1967.) These basic "differences" were also acknowledged by Citizens' Councils of America Executive Director Louis Hollis, and by Citizens' Councils of Louisiana Secretary Courtney Smith. (Interview with Louis Hollis, May 26, 1967; Courtney Smith to the author, January 15, 1967).

41 *The Councilor,* November 15, 1966; February 20, 1967. As of the latter issue, the tabloid claimed it was "Now Read by More Than 254,000 in 50 States and 8 Nations."

42 *The Citizens' Council,* February, 1960, 4; interview with Medford Evans, May 26, 1967.

CHAPTER V

South Carolina and Georgia: Weak Sisters of the Deep South

In Georgia and South Carolina the foundations for massive resistance were laid several years before the Supreme Court nullified segregated public schools. Endeavoring to render the separate-but-equal fiction more credible, both states took steps in 1951 to diminish many of the more obvious disparities between educational opportunities for black and white children. As a second line of defense of the educational status quo, both established agencies—the Georgia Commission on Education and the South Carolina School Committee—to prepare blueprints for state action in the event of an unfavorable ruling in the school segregation cases. Similarly, both made advance preparations to abandon public schools should the *Plessey* formula be reversed. When the ruling finally came, the universally damnatory statements of the elected officials in these Atlantic seaboard states clearly indicated that both would figure prominantly in the Deep South's hard core of massive resistance.[1]

[1] *Southern School News*, September 3–December 1, 1954; Howard H. Quint, *Profile in Black and White: A Frank Portrait of South Carolina* (Washington: Public Affairs Press, 1958), 13–15; Ernest McPherson Lander, Jr., *A History of South Carolina, 1865–1960* (Chapel Hill: University of North Carolina Press, 1960), 201–2; Cullen B. Gosnell and C. David Anderson, *The Government and Administration of Georgia* (New York: Thomas Y. Crowell, 1956), 194ff.

Most white South Carolinians, like their Attorney General T. C. Callison, could find "no constitutional authority, no statutory authority, no judicial precedent, no reason and no justice in that decision." With their junior Senator J. Strom Thurmond, they agreed that it was "one of the worst decisions ever handed down by any court. . . ."[2] Seeking ways to express their own defiance, the most indignant among them joined the state's all-white "protective societies," as Thomas R. Waring, the tradition-minded editor of the Charleston *News and Courier,* chose to call the more respectable groups of the organized resistance movement.[3] Bearing such names as the Association for the Preservation of Southern Traditions, the Grass Roots League, the National Association for the Advancement of White People, and the States' Rights League, these organizations were the ineffectual vehicles of local protest against social change. None of them achieved what could even vaguely be construed as a statewide following, and all of them either lapsed rapidly into inactivity or were absorbed by the more dynamic Council movement.[4]

Although it was among the last of the resistance groups to appear in South Carolina, the Citizens' Council was not long in establishing its dominance. Under the leadership of S. Emory Rogers, an obscure country lawyer who, as counsel for the Summerton school board, had defended segregation in the Supreme Court case of *Briggs* v. *Elliott,* the movement began in the Orangeburg County hamlet of Elloree. Spurred by a rash of NAACP desegregation petitions filed with local boards of education in low-country counties, four additional Orangeburg County towns were organized.[5] By late September, the Columbia *State* reported that in "sprawling Orangeburg County . . . Councils have been organized in every community

[2] Quoted in Quint, *Profile in Black and White,* 22.

[3] Thomas R. Waring, "The Southern Case against Desegregation," *Harper's,* 212 (January, 1956), 44.

[4] Southern Regional Council, "The Resistance Groups of South Carolina" (unpublished field report, 1956), 4; Quint, *Profile in Black and White,* 38, 43–45.

[5] Julian Scheer, "The White Folks Fight Back," *The New Republic,* 133 (October 31, 1955), 9–10; *The Citizens' Council,* June, 1956, 5; *The Orangeburg Citizens' Council,* February 13, 1956; Columbia *State,* August 31, 1956; Charleston *News and Courier,* September 13, 1955; *Southern School News,* September, 1955, 6; Anthony, "Pro-Segregation Groups' History and Trends," 7.

of any consequence."[6] Meanwhile, Councils were prospering elsewhere in the low country as new groups formed and such older resistance organizations as the States' Rights League and the Association for the Preservation of Southern Traditions changed their names in several counties to be absorbed by the advancing Council movement.[7] By the end of September, there were no fewer than twenty Councils operating in Orangeburg and ten surrounding counties, and preparations were being made for the organization of a state association.

The initial plans for the South Carolina Association of Citizens' Councils were made at a September 20 meeting in Summerton, where S. Emory Rogers met with fifteen black-belt county leaders of various local resistance groups. Included in that group was Farley Smith, son of the late U.S. Senator Ellison D. ("Cotton Ed") Smith, who represented the informally structured but influential Committee of Fifty-two. Composed of prominent white South Carolinians, Smith's committee had sponsored a resolution soon after the appearance of the first NAACP petitions urging, among other things, that the legislature "interpose the sovereignty of the state of South Carolina between federal courts and local school officials. . . ."[8] While it never functioned as a formal organization, the committee lent to the cause of organized resistance the considerable prestige of its membership, which according to the Charleston *News and Courier* comprised "a cross section of the better-class moderate, white people," the state's "leaders in law, clergy, business, farming, education, and politics."[9] Following the initial meeting at Summerton with Rogers, the Committee, acting at the Summerton lawyer's request, invited seventy representatives from thirty-eight local Councils to meet in Columbia. There, on October 10, 1955, the Association of Citizens' Councils of South Carolina was formed. Modeled closely after the Mississippi Association, the new organization chose Rogers as its full-time executive secretary and Micah

[6] Columbia *State*, September 21, 1955.

[7] Charleston *News and Courier*, September 22, 1955.

[8] "South Carolina Girds for Action," *The Citizens' Council*, June, 1956, 5. See also W.D. Workman, *The Case for the South* (New York: Devin-Adair, 1960), 279–81; and Southern Regional Council, "Resistance Groups of South Carolina," 7–9.

[9] Charleston *News and Courier*, August 19, 1955.

Jenkins, a Charleston businessman who had led a local Grass Roots League, as its chairman. Having played midwife at the birth of the statewide organization, the Committee of Fifty-two drifted into obscurity.[10]

During his brief tenure as executive secretary, Rogers proved to be an able and energetic organizer. Prior to his involvement with the *Briggs* case, his duties as a school board lawyer were the routine legal chores of approving building and faculty contracts and in other ways advising the education officials of a largely rural school district. He took readily to the more stimulating task of forging a mass movement. During the first six months, he traveled more than 5,000 miles, delivered more than fifty speeches, wrote several pamphlets, and mailed thousands of pieces of propaganda to local chairmen for distribution to the membership.[11] Growing at a rate of one a week, there were fifty-five Councils by July 1, 1956; according to the estimate of William D. Workman, a prominent South Carolina journalist and one of the Council's most outspoken allies, there were from 25,000 to 40,000 members concentrated predominately in the low-country counties in the eastern portion of the state.[12]

Like other states in the Deep South, South Carolina had its subregions marked by intrastate economic and social cleavages. Running northeast from Aiken County on the Georgia border to the boundary of Chesterfield and Marlboro counties on the North Carolina border, a fall line divided the Piedmont, with its rolling hills, developing industries, small farms, and relatively sparse Negro population, from the flat and once-fertile coastal plain, where large-

[10] M. H. Sass, "Report on Citizens' Council Movement in South Carolina," *The Citizens' Council,* November, 1955, 3; "South Carolina Girds for Action," *The Citizens' Council,* June, 1956, 5; Charleston *News and Courier,* October 11, 1955.

[11] Sass, "Report on Citizens' Council Movement in South Carolina," *The Citizens' Council,* November, 1955, 3. Sass reported that as of late October "there are some thirty-odd councils," of which "Rogers has personally helped to organize twenty or more." See also Martin, *The Deep South Says "Never"*, 68–70.

[12] Charleston *News and Courier,* July 1, 1956. Similar figures were reported by S. Emory Rogers, the Southen Regional Council, and Southern Education Reporting Service. See "Resistance Groups of South Carolina," 2; SERS, *Statistical Summary,* April 15, 1957; New York *Times,* March 13, 1956; Columbia *State,* March 18, 1956.

scale cotton and tobacco agriculture dominated economic life and the disproportionately high ratio of Negroes to whites in some counties exceeded 70 percent. Here, in the counties of the eastern plain, the Citizens' Council flourished. From its beginning in Orangeburg, a black-belt county in the heart of the low country, the movement within two months spread to ten adjoining counties, in all but four of which Negroes outnumbered whites.[13] This pattern, established during the early developmental stages, remained essentially unchanged throughout the Council's history in South Carolina. Even during the summer of 1956, the period of its greatest strength, the state organization's only upcountry affiliate was to be found in Spartanburg, a busy mill town in the foothills of the Blue Ridge Mountains, which had organized after local school officials received an NAACP desegregation petition.[14] Not until early in the next decade were additional Councils formed beyond the fall line. In 1960 and 1961, after Negroes staged "sit-in" demonstations at segregated lunch counters in several upcountry towns, small and relatively ineffectual groups appeared in the three western hill counties of Greenville, Greenwood, and York.[15] By that time, however, the Council's influence in the state had been seriously eroded.

Contributing to the Council's decline in South Carolina was its rapidly changing leadership. Unlike other Deep South states, where key positions in the Council hierarchy rarely changed hands, the ACCSC was beset with frequent and disruptive turnovers. S. Emory Rogers, the first executive secretary, was an energetic promoter of organized resistance; under his direction the movement expanded and the state office was fairly active. But after his retirement in December, 1956, the executive secretariat remained vacant for more than two years. Meanwhile, the day-to-day conduct of the association's business was left to the state chairman, who held an unpaid

13 These ten counties and their nonwhite population percentages in 1950 were as follows: Bamberg (58 percent), Calhoun (71 percent), Charleston (42 percent), Clarendon (71 percent), Darlington (46 percent), Fairfield (59 percent), Florence (45 percent), Kershaw (49 percent), Lee (67 percent), Williamsburg (68 percent).

14 See "South Carolina Citizens' Council Map," *The Citizens' Council*, June, 1956, 5.

15 Columbia *State*, March 5, 1959; Charlotte (N.C.) *Observer*, February 17, 1960; *Southern School News*, March, 1960, 4, August, 1961, 13.

office which changed hands almost yearly. Micah Jenkins, the first chairman, served only until 1957; he was then replaced by Thomas D. Keels of Sumter, a do-nothing executive who was succeeded in 1958 by Baxter A. Graham. Under Graham, a Florence County farmer and businessman, the state office virtually ceased all operations, and the movement's membership dropped off markedly. During this interlude the Charleston *News and Courier,* a tireless supporter of organized resistance, lamented editorially that "the citizens council movement in South Carolina has been taking a siesta." [16]

While the Council's central office slumbered, charges were aired from several quarters that the movement, once prideful of the "top grade leadership in the local Councils," [17] was being subverted by the Ku Klux Klan. In this vein, William D. Workman, one of the Council's earliest champions, warned that Klansmen, concealing their identity with the hooded order and outwardly subscribing to the principles of "legal" defiance and nonviolence, were waging a determined campaign to infiltrate the movement in some parts of the state in order to use it for their own "cowardly, secretive" ends.[18] Responding to Workman's allegations, Graham asserted that his consistent policy had been to obtain "the highest type of conservative leadership" for both state and local organizations. Although denying that the Klan had made significant inroads into the movement, he announced that "in view of the possibilities of radical activities being fostered under the name of Citizens' Councils," the accredited organizations of the state would be issued charters by the state association. By this method, he believed, the movement could be assured that only those "willing to work under the [Council's] constitution and by-laws" would be recognized by the state organization.[19]

The decision to issue charters to the association's constituent

[16] Charleston *News and Courier,* July 14, 1958.

[17] "South Carolina Girds for Action," *The Citizens' Council,* June, 1956, 5.

[18] *Southern School News,* January, 1959, 11; W. D. Workman, "Councils Must Be Alert to Keep out Klansmen," Charleston *News and Courier,* December 7, 1958; William D. Workman, Jr. (editor, Columbia *State*), to the author, February 28, 1967.

[19] Quoted in *Southern School News,* January, 1959, 11.

Councils as a safeguard against Klan subversion was among Baxter Graham's last acts as chairman. A lackluster leader unable to revitalize a declining movement, he retired from office amidst considerable controversy early in February, 1959. After an all-day closed session of forty-one state officers and executive committeemen in Orangeburg—a meeting marked by the temporary walkout of seventeen representatives from Aiken, Florence, and Sumter counties—Graham and the association's treasurer, H. L. Bowling of Elloree, one of the state's original Councilors, resigned. Although no official explanation was ever given, it was generally acknowledged that for several months dissatisfaction with Graham's leadership had been mounting and that the South Carolina Council had been threatened by an open split over the "policies and personnel of his administration." [20] The interim leadership of Dr. W. M. Crosswell of Timmonsville gave the organization a semblance of unity until mid-February, when John Adger Manning, a Columbia realtor and the son of former Governor Richard I. Manning, was elected chairman. At the same time, the long-vacant office of executive secretary was filled by Farley Smith, one of the movement's ablest leaders.[21]

Under the leadership of this Lynchburg planter, the association began a campaign to revive the flagging movement. A special objective of Smith's administration was the extension of the Councils into "every county and community" of the hitherto virtually unorganized Piedmont region.[22] In support of this ambitious policy the executive committee selected as treasurer William Lowndes, a leader of the newly organized Council in Greenville County. Although this wealthy textile executive came from an old and prominent Charleston family, he was the first representative of the Piedmont to serve as an officer of the low-country–dominated state association.[23] Yet,

[20] Ibid., March, 1959, 9; Charleston *News and Courier*, February 7, 1959.

[21] "South Carolina: Fulfill, Not Destroy," *South*, 24 (March 9, 1959), 7–8; *The Citizens' Council*, March, 1959, 2; Charleston *News and Courier*, February 21; Columbia *State*, March 5, 1959.

[22] Columbia *State*, March 5; Charleston *News and Courier*, March 19, 1959.

[23] "South Carolina: Fulfill, Not Destroy," 7–8; Charleston *News and Courier*, February 21, 1959.

despite this apparent attempt to give the movement a geographical balance which it so obviously lacked, the western hills remained unmoved by Smith's expansionist endeavors.

In time, Smith himself came to question the wisdom of a mass movement. As he remarked in 1962, "a large membership can be unwieldy." "If an objective can be accomplished with 1,000 members," he reasoned, "it's foolish to have 10,000." At the end of his second full year as executive secretary, he retired from office and apparently lost interest in the movement. The Council, he believed, had suceeded in its purpose. By mobilizing public opinion, it had demonstrated to the politicians and officeholders that "the people of South Carolina were not going to accept integration." Once having alerted county and state governments to the necessity of resisting social change, there was no longer a need for a "third agency." William Lowndes, who succeeded Manning as chairman in February, 1961, and the new executive secretary, the Reverend L. B. McCord, were essentially in accord with Smith on these issues. Lowndes, president of the Southern Weaving Company, expressed the mood of the association's leadership by the maxim: "the least said, the easiest mended." It was not essential that the Council have a large membership; for, as he believed, "it's often not worth the price." [24]

Not remarkably, the Citizens' Council in the Palmetto State was never again a thriving concern. By January, 1963, when Harvey B. Gantt, a Negro architecture student, breached the state's educational color line by enrolling in Clemson College, grass-roots Council activity was virtually nonexistent in South Carolina.

Although comparatively small and inactive by Deep South standards, the South Carolina Council was considerably more vibrant than its counterpart in Georgia. To be sure, the Peach State stands apart in the history of southern resistance for it alone among the five states of the lower South failed to develop a viable organized segregation movement. At its peak, the States' Rights Council of Georgia, Inc., the only prosegregation organization in the state with a significant following, had fewer than 10,000 members.[25] The

24 Quoted in Charleston *News and Courier,* July 1, 1962.

25 Estimate of William A. Lufburrow, executive secretary of the States' Rights Council. See Atlanta *Constitution,* August 20, 1958.

absence of popular support for the States' Rights Council, however, cannot be attributed to a diminishing vitality of the Negro question in this state. To be sure, Georgia enjoyed an enviable record of industrial and urban growth among states of the Deep South.[26] But, though thrust at last into the present century, its white citizens had not, for the most part, softened their views on race. Nor does the evidence suggest that here in the cradle of the twentieth-century Klan, the political habitat of such symbols of racial bigotry as Tom Watson and Eugene Talmadge, whites were more tolerant in the decade of the 1950's than in Alabama or Mississippi. Rather, the explanation for the signal failure of organized racism lies with the leaders of the movement themselves and with the political nature of the organization they fostered.

The first States' Rights Council appeared in Augusta, "the Industrial Giant on the Savannah," late in December, 1954. Dedicated to the use of "every legal means" in "the preservation of the social, political, and economic institutions of our beloved Southland," its organizers were Hugh Gladney Grant, a distinguished journalist and statesman who served as President Franklin D. Roosevelt's minister to Albania (1935–39) and Thailand (1940–41), and Roy V. Harris, attorney, four-time speaker of Georgia's lower house, and one of the state's most successful campaign managers.[27] Despite the renown of its organizers, the Augusta Council was seldom active and it apparently attracted few supporters. Its most notable achievement came in July, 1955, when it frustrated an "attack on our white civilization" by having canceled Augusta's thirteenth annual soapbox derby in order to prevent a pair of Negro boys from competing against a field of more than eighty.[28] Little more was heard of the Council until the next September, when, following a series of con-

[26] In 1960, Georgia was second only to Louisiana among the five Deep South states in terms of the percentage of its total population which lived in cities. See Rembert W. Patrick, "The Deep South, Past and Present," in *The Deep South in Transformation: A Symposium,* ed. Robert B. Highsaw (University, Ala.: University of Alabama Press, 1964), 114–15.

[27] *States' Rights Council of Georgia, Inc.* (Augusta: States' Rights Council of Georgia, n.d.); *A Brief History of the States' Rights Council of Georgia, Inc.* (Atlanta: States' Rights Council of Georgia, n.d.); Augusta *Courier,* August 29; *Southern School News,* February 3, 1955.

[28] St. Louis *Post-Dispatch,* August 8, 1955.

ferences between Grant, Harris, and such influential political spokesmen as former Governor Herman Talmadge and Governor Marvin Griffin, the Augusta Council's charter became the basis for a statewide organization.

Although it had only a single constituent Council and virtually no membership, the States' Rights Council of Georgia had a most imposing body of organizers. At the invitation of cosponsors Griffin and Harris, two hundred prominant Georgians active in public affairs attended the organizational dinner at Atlanta's aging Biltmore Hotel on September 23, 1955. Speakers for the occasion included former Governor Herman Talmadge, Lieutenant Governor Ernest Vandiver, and two of the state's better-known legal minds—Charles J. Bloch, former president of the Georgia Bar Association and chairman of the education committee of the state Board of Regents, and R. Carter Pittman, prominent constitutional lawyer and member of the Georgia Board of Bar Examiners.[29] Among the assembled luminaries were most of the state's political elite—its most eminent elective and appointive officials,[30] its top Democratic party leaders, and members of both of its school boards (the Board of Regents and the Board of Education), as well as several judges and numerous county sheriffs. Although a majority of those present were political allies of either Griffin or Talmadge, representatives from a variety of factions were in attendance, notably several of the governor's archrivals from the last gubernatorial campaign. Indeed, the nonfactional spirit of the GSRC was demonstrated by the close cooperation of Griffin and Harris, who in the primary of 1954 had been bitter political foes. In that contest, Harris's usually unerring instinct for backing the winner failed, and he supported Fred B. Hand. In a similar display of good will, Hand himself accepted

29 *Brief History of the States' Rights Council of Georgia, Inc.;* Augusta *Courier,* October 3; Atlanta *Constitution* and Atlanta *Journal,* September 24, 1955.

30 In addition to the governor and lieutenant governor, state officials who participated in the organizational rally included Attorney General Eugene Cook, the assistant attorney general, the comptroller general, the state revenue commissioner, the directors of correction and welfare, three members of the state highway board, and top legislative spokesmen, including the floor leaders of both houses. See Atlanta *Constitution* and Atlanta *Journal,* September 24, 1955.

the governor's invitation to participate in the organizational rally. So did James L. Gillis, the wealthy boss of Treutlen County, who was forced by Griffin to resign as chairman of the state highway board for having supported one of the governor's rivals in 1954.[31] Thus Georgia's warring politicos thrust aside mutual grievances to join in founding a "non-partisan, non-factional organization dedicated to principles which transcend personalities and individual ambition and/or differences." [32]

Before adjourning the Biltmore assembly approved recommendations by Harris and Talmadge for an administrative structure patterned closely after that of the Association of Citizens' Councils of Mississippi and adopted by resolution a slate of officers for the newly formed Council. George D. Stewart and Freeman Strickland, secretary and treasurer respectively for the state Democratic party, were named to corresponding posts for the Council. Hugh Grant and Charles J. Bloch of Macon were elected vice-presidents. For its president the assembly chose the son of a Confederate soldier (and grandson of a Union army captain), R. Carter Pittman of Dalton. An adamant segregationist and anti-Communist, the new president was well known in legal circles throughout the state for his attacks on the Warren court's use of "non-legal, illegal, and inadmissible sociological materials to sustain judicial legislation based on false Marxist propaganda secretly supplied to the court by the NAACP." In his view, as he expressed it to the Georgia Institute of City and County Attorneys only a few weeks after his election as Council president, "the South has no racial problem and has had none for a half century. Its racial problems were solved by segregation." [33] A professional patriot of sorts, Pittman served as Council president until 1958, after which time he became identified with numerous

[31] For additional examples illustrating the same point, see Atlanta *Constitution*, September 24, 1955.

[32] States' Rights Council of Georgia, "Resolutions Adopted at Organizational Meeting of the States' Rights Council of Georgia, Inc." (unpublished manuscript, SERS). See also copies of two unpublished and undated manuscripts at the Southern Regional Council: States' Rights Council of Georgia, "Charter of the States' Rights Council of Georgia, Inc.," and "The Constitution of the States' Rights Council of Georgia, Inc."

[33] Quoted in Atlanta *Constitution*, October 22, 1955.

right-wing organizations, including the Liberty Lobby, the John Birch Society, the Council for Individual Freedom, and Billy Hargis's Christian Crusade.[34]

At a series of meetings in October and early November, 1955, the remaining organizational details were completed. Permanent headquarters were established in Atlanta, a full-time clerical staff was hired, and an executive director was appointed. For this position the Council's executive committee selected William T. Bodenhamer of Tift County, a fifty-year-old preacher-legislator with various interests and impressive credentials. The grandson of two Confederate soldiers, Representative Bodenhamer was a second-term member of the General Assembly, the full-time pastor of the Ty Ty Baptist Church, a member of the Georgia Baptist Convention, and a champion of temperance legislation. Moreover, as a past president of the Georgia Association of Junior Colleges, former president of Norman Park Junior College, a member of the state Board of Education, and a former superintendent of Tift County schools, this graduate of Mercer University was a man of considerable educational experience. He was also an active civic leader, a Rotarian, a Civitan, a thirty-second degree Mason, a Shriner, and a member of both the Knights Templar and the Sons of Confederate Veterans.[35] In short, he was a man of stature and much influence, a man apparently well suited to accomplish the executive committee's goal of a States' Rights Council in every county and a membership of at least 150,000.[36]

Despite such ambitions, the Council began its program of expansion at a leisurely pace, not staging its first "grass-roots meeting" until January 11, 1956. On that date, Bodenhamer launched a membership drive at Americus, a prosperous black-belt county seat (Sumter County) of more than 11,000 inhabitants. As segregation rallies go, it was an impressive affair, featuring a parade of dig-

34 For details on Pittman's right-wing activities, see "R. Carter Pittman," *Group Research Report,* Sec. 2-IND (November 14, 1963).

35 For details of Bodenhamer's biography, see Atlanta *Journal,* November 6, 1955, and "Biography of William T. Bodenhamer" (unpublished manuscript, SERS, 1958). The latter was probably prepared as a news release during Bodenhamer's 1959 campaign for the Democratic gubernatorial nomination in Georgia.

36 Augusta *Journal,* November 21, 1955.

nitaries including Herman Talmadge, Governor Griffin, Lieutenant Governor Vandiver, and Attorney General Cook, as well as such Council stalwarts as Harris and Pittman. In keeping with the expansive mood of the occasion, the Governor urged that Councils be organized in every town and at every crossroads. "The rest of the nation," he declared, "is looking to Georgia for the lead in segregation." Not yet officially campaigning for Senator Walter F. George's seat in Congress, Herman Talmadge similarly assured the gathering that it was witnessing "the beginning of a great crusade which will sweep the state and southern regions." [37]

Whether or not the rest of the nation awaited Georgia's lead, the rally at Americus signaled no great crusade. During the ensuing months a few additional groups were formed. But by mid-summer —despite Bodenhamer's claim of twenty-eight organizational rallies for the month of March alone—there were probably fewer than a dozen organizations affiliated with the central Council in Atlanta.[38] Nor did things improve significantly later in the year. In November, the Southern Regional Council in Atlanta tersely observed in its first survey of southern resistance groups: "Since its formation the group has enjoyed the unqualified support of the Governor, the state Attorney General, Senator-elect Herman Talmadge, and most of the other significant political leaders of the state. It has not, however, developed into a grass roots movement." [39]

The ineffectiveness of the Georgia States' Rights Council was given a public airing during the gubernatorial race of 1958, which demonstrated, as only a political campaign could, the uneasy coalition upon which the organization was constructed. In April of that year, executive director Bodenhamer resigned his position to enter the Democratic primary against Lieutenant Governor Ernest Vandiver. With Governor Griffin, who could not succeed himself, and

[37] Quoted in Atlanta *Journal,* January 12, and Columbia *State,* January 11, 1956.

[38] Press accounts reveal that by July, organizations had been formed in at least the following counties: Harris, Gordon, Sumter, and Walker. See Chattanooga *Times,* February 18, March 13; Atlanta *Journal,* July 14, 1956; *Southern School News,* April, 1956, 7.

[39] Southern Regional Council, *Special Report: Pro-Segregation Groups in the South,* November 19, 1956. Essentially the same statement was made in the revised report of May 23, 1957.

Vandiver openly at political odds, it appeared to many—and certainly to Bodenhamer—that the preacher-legislator would run with the administration's approval, and perhaps with at least the tacit endorsement of the organization he led for more than two years. But Griffin remained publicly neutral, Vandiver won the support of both Senator Richard B. Russell and Senator Talmadge, and the States' Rights Council rendered no aid to its former executive director. Both Roy Harris, newly elected president, and R. Carter Pittman, past president, lent full public support to the lieutenant governor, whose campaign was managed by Council executive committeeman James L. Gillis. The favorite from the outset, Vandiver swept 156 of the state's 159 counties, defeating Bodenhamer, his nearest opponent, by a popular vote margin of more than four to one.[40]

For the most part, it was a campaign without meaningful issues and without popular interest. Stumping the state in shirt sleeves and bright red elastic arm bands, Bodenhamer based his entire campaign on the patent absurdity that the lieutenant governor was "soft" on segregation, and that he was in fact the NAACP's candidate.[41] The strategy backfired, however. By interjecting race into a campaign in which all of the candidates were sworn champions of white supremacy, Bodenhamer succeeded only in bringing into focus his own ineffectiveness as director of the Council. Responding to these "smear" tactics, the Council's executive committee made public in mid-August a correspondence between Bodenhamer's successor W. A. Lufburrow and R. Carter Pittman, which cast doubts on the Tift County preacher's abilities as a segregation leader. Written during the previous spring, these letters revealed that the States' Rights Council under Bodenhamer had been a "dismal failure," that it had never organized "a strong home defense" through "a large and active membership." "Our director was a member of the Legislature, a minister, and a member of the State School Board," Pittman informed Lufburrow. "In my opinion he did not

[40] Atlanta *Constitution,* August 26, September 11; Atlanta *Journal,* April 21, August 17, September 3; Augusta *Courier,* August 25, 1958; *Southern School News,* October, 1958, 18.

[41] Atlanta *Journal,* July 27, August 17; Atlanta *Constitution,* September 3, 1958; *Southern School News,* August, 1958, 16, September, 1958, 12, October, 1958, 18.

average more than twelve hours a week in our Atlanta office and when he spent that time in our office, he was doing nothing toward serving our membership." Lamentably, he concluded, "we are exactly where we were in the spring of 1955, we must start from there."[42]

A few days later Roy Harris followed the release of the Lufburrow-Pittman correspondence with charges of his own. In the September 1 issue of his Augusta *Courier,* the new States' Rights Council president ran a front-page headline in red type: "STATES' RIGHTS COUNCIL OF GEORGIA SABOTAGED BY CANDIDATE BODENHAMER." "The preacher candidate," he asserted, "sabotaged it by simply failing to do his duty. He did as little of nothing as a man could do when he held the office of Executive Director of the council." Worse, "he used the office in Atlanta for his own personal and political benefit and for no other purpose."[43]

The timing of the attack on the former executive director suggests that, in part at least, it was motivated by the exigencies of a political campaign. Moreover, it should be noted that there were members high in Council officialdom who objected to the use of Bodenhamer as a whipping boy in an effort to explain away the organization's chronic inertia. In a joint statement issued soon after the appearance of the Pittman-Lufburrow correspondence, the Council's founder and vice-president Hugh Gladney Grant and John T. Haines, president of the Richmond County (Augusta) States' Rights Council, asserted that the responsibility for the Council's failure at the grass roots rested not with Bodenhamer, but with the politicians who controlled it. From the outset, they charged, the SRCG had been a "political rather than a grass roots organization."[44]

Again in August, 1960, Grant publicly blamed the personal ambitions of Roy Harris, then in his third year as Council president, for

[42] Quoted in William M. Bates, "Bodenhamer Called 'Ineffective' in States' Rights Council Post," Atlanta *Constitution,* August 20, 1958. See also Augusta *Herald,* July 12; Macon *News,* July 15, July 31, 1958. Herman Talmadge, in an interview with John Bartlow Martin, also attributed the Council's small membership to Bodenhamer, who had "too many irons in the fire." See Martin, *The Deep South Says "Never"*, 180.

[43] Augusta *Courier,* September 1, 1958.

[44] Quoted in *Southern School News,* September, 1958, 12.

the movement's impotence. The organization, he argued, was little more than a machine for in-power Democratic politicians whose interests were primarily reelection, and only incidentally segregation. Harris, Grant declared, had given only "lip service to the organization of the rank and file." Overriding the opposition of many members and leaders, Harris's consistent policy had been to "leave the solution of the segregation issue to the political leadership of the state, in which he has played a leading role as a shrewd politician and as editor of the Augusta *Courier*." [45]

These charges and countercharges were not altogether devoid of substance. Bodenhamer had been an indifferent and irresponsible executive director. Despite an annual salary of $10,000, he devoted little time to the affairs of his office. Alone among the states of the Deep South, the Council under his leadership did not publish its own newspaper, or even a regular bulletin for its members.[46] Although the organization produced what one civil rights agency called "an unusually expensive collection of publications" during his tenure, the executive director never managed to establish adequate means for their distribution.[47] Complaining that Bodenhamer was never able even to set up a mailing system for the Council's "educational materials," R. Carter Pittman wrote an Atlanta member

[45] Quoted in Atlanta *Journal,* August 23, 1960.

[46] In a general way the Augusta *Courier* served this purpose. Moreover, it seems likely that Harris would have resisted any effort to publish another such paper.

[47] Southern Regional Council, *Pro-Segregation Groups in the South,* November 19, 1956. Examples of this literature include J. Paul Barrett, *The Church and Segregation* (Atlanta: States' Rights Council, n.d.); Charles J. Bloch, *The Need for States' Rights Councils and Citizens' Councils* (Atlanta: States' Rights Council, [1957]); Bloch, *We Need Not Integrate to Educate* (Atlanta: States' Rights Council, n.d.); William T. Bodenhamer, *The Aims and Purposes of the States' Rights Council of Georgia, Inc.* (Atlanta: States' Rights Council, n.d.); Bodenhamer, *Who Started Segregated Schools in Georgia* (Atlanta: States' Rights Council, n.d.); Roy V. Harris, *To the School Teachers and School Officials of Georgia* (Atlanta: States' Rights Council, n.d.); John R. Leatherbury, *The National Council of Churches of Christ—Activities Revealed* (Atlanta: States' Rights Council, n.d.); R. Carter Pittman, *The Supreme Court, the Broken Constitution, and the Shattered Bill of Rights* (Atlanta: States' Rights Council, [1956]); Herman E. Talmadge, *Great Masses of People Leaderless, Confused by Slogans of Highly Organized Minorities* (Atlanta: States' Rights Council, n.d.).

in July, 1958, recalling an occasion when "a Mississippi organization agreed to mail out 5,000 pieces of our literature if we would merely ship these pieces to that organization." The shipment was never made.[48] Furthermore, the Tift County pastor was something less than frugal with the organization's funds—so much so that the executive committee removed a large part of the Council's revenue from his control, fearing that it would be dwindled away on nonessentials.[49]

Bodenhamer's departure did not bring a sudden burst of organizational energy. Until its collapse in 1962, the Council's spokesmen made occasional gestures in the direction of the grass roots, but no membership drive ever materialized. Although Roy Harris from time to time assured Georgia militants of his intentions to launch an ambitious campaign to organize local chapters in every county in the state,[50] it seems unlikely that he had an abiding interest in recruiting a mass movement. The power base of his organizational scheme rested upon the state's political leadership, not on a popular following. As Grant had charged, the Augustan built a "political rather than a grass roots organization." Having served in both houses of the General Assembly and as a close adviser to several successive governors, Harris was generally regarded as "Georgia's most prominent and energetic political manager." Adroitly migrating from one camp to another, he managed successful gubernatorial campaigns for Eurith Dickinson (Ed) Rivers (1936), Ellis G. Arnall (1942), Eugene Talmadge (1946), and Herman Talmadge (1948 and 1950).[51] In 1954, however, for the first time in two decades, he backed a losing candidate and found himself temporarily at odds with the occupant of the statehouse. But, though his

[48] Letter from R. Carter Pittman, quoted in Augusta *Courier*, September 1, 1958.

[49] The installation of a dictaphone in Bodenhamer's private automobile at the Council's expense was an example of this quality. Upon Pittman's insistence, the executive director promised to repay this expenditure. (Ibid.; Atlanta *Constitution*, August 20, 1958.)

[50] Augusta *Courier*, February 23, 1959.

[51] Key, *Southern Politics*, 124; Joseph L. Bernd, *Grass Roots Politics in Georgia: The County Unit System and the Importance of the Individual Voting Community in Bi-Factional Elections, 1942–1954* (Atlanta: Emory University Research Committee, 1960), 55.

reputation as "kingmaker" was somewhat tarnished, his politically powerful days were far from over. Using the States' Rights Council for leverage, he worked his way into a position of considerable influence with Governor Griffin. In the 1958 primary he backed the successful candidacy of Ernest Vandiver and once again managed to tie his organization to the state administration.[52] In this manner, by working almost from within the administration, he remained close to the seat of power and retained much of his former political influence.

One measure of Harris's political acumen was his ability to persuade Griffin to preside over the Council's organizational dinner in the fall of 1955. Also indicative of his continuing influence was the fact that each year thereafter the governor presided over the Council's annual fund-raising dinner, its only significant source of revenue and one of its few activities. At these twenty-five-dollar-per-plate occasions, speakers, most frequently Senators Russell and Talmadge, vied with each other in offering ritualistic praise for the States' Rights Council and its officers, and pledged anew their allegiance to white supremacy.[53]

But following the admission under court order of two Negro undergraduates to the University of Georgia in early 1961, Georgia shifted from a policy of massive resistance to token compliance. Thereafter, its governors proved less willing to use their influence to swell attendance at Harris's annual banquets. Undoubtedly irritated by the head Councilor's encouragement of disruptive student protests at the Athens campus and by his intemperate criticism of the administration's policy of "capitulation," Vandiver presided over the 1961 banquet with apparent reluctance.[54] The following autumn, additional racial barriers fell, and Negroes were admitted to four previously all-white Atlanta public schools. Then in September, 1962, Griffin, campaigning on a promise to "restore sovereignty" to Georgia, was defeated in the Democratic primary by a relative

52 See, for example, Atlanta *Journal,* November 9, 1961.

53 See, for example, Atlanta *Constitution,* October 8, 1957, July 20, 1961; Atlanta *Journal,* October 9, 1957, December 17, 1962.

54 "Georgia Abandons Laws of Massive Resistance: A Report on University of Georgia Desegregation," *New South,* 16 (February, 1961), 3–7; Atlanta *Journal,* January 12, May 7, 1961, December 17, 1962; Atlanta *Constitution,* January 25, July 20, 1961.

moderate, state Senator Carl Sanders, despite heavy support from Harris. The new governor was even less disposed than Vandiver to lend official cooperation to the old Augusta politician's favorite project.[55] Deprived of its quasi-official status and lacking adequate grass-roots support, the States' Rights Council did not long survive.

[55] *Southern School News*, September, 1962, 5; October, 1962, 9; Atlanta *Constitution*, December 19; Atlanta *Journal*, December 17, 1962.

CHAPTER VI

On the Periphery: Councils and Council-like Groups in the Upper South

THE states of the peripheral South faced the era of desegregation with far greater equanimity than was evidenced in the Deep South.[1] Beginning in Arkansas and Texas in 1954 and culminating in Florida and Virginia in 1959, racial barriers in each of the six outer states of the old Confederacy were breached before the first public classrooms were desegregated in the Deep South during the fall of 1960. With the notable exception of Virginia, the desegregation process began in each of these six states voluntarily, and continued with increasing tempo throughout the first decade after the *Brown* decision. By 1964, the states of Arkansas, Florida, North Carolina, Tennessee, Texas, and Virginia accounted for more than 90 percent of all Negroes enrolled in biracial classes in the eleven-state area.

Although the battlements of segregation were more easily scaled in the peripheral South than in the hard-core states of Alabama, Georgia, Louisiana, Mississippi, and South Carolina, considerable hostility to change and no little racial animus were to be found in

[1] For a more complete chronicle of the formation of organized resistance groups in the six states of the peripheral South, see Neil R. McMillen, "The Citizens' Council: A History of Organized Southern White Resistance to the Second Reconstruction," (unpublished Ph.D. dissertation, Department of History, Vanderbilt University, 1969), 138–204.

the six states which ring the Deep South. Here, as elsewhere in the region, violence was the frequent companion of school desegregation. Not insignificantly, it was in Texas, and not Mississippi or Alabama, where the first incidence of violence occurred in what was to become a recurring pattern of desegregation-related lawlessness.[2] It was in Hoxie, Arkansas, that southern school officials first clashed with organized white racists over the admission of Negro children to previously all-white classrooms. Moreover, the road to Little Rock—scene of the first major showdown between state and federal authorities on the issue of segregated schools—was bestrewn with the racial turmoil of such peripheral cities as Mansfield, Texas, where rangers were employed to disperse angry mobs of segregationists, and Clinton, Tennessee, where Governor Frank G. Clement restored order only after National Guardsmen used tanks and tear gas to quell unruly whites.[3]

This juxtaposition of adamant defiance with comparatively swift compliance in the peripheral South dramatized the great variety of the region. For not only did the reaction to school desegregation vary from subregion to subregion and from state to state, but it varied from one locality to another within a given state. Superficially, at least, a relatively low proportion of blacks to whites and a consistently moderate racial climate seemed to presage an easy adjustment to the new order. But in each of the six upper states there were areas where geographic and demographic conditions combined to forge cultural patterns not unlike those of the Deep South. Thus Arkansas, divided by a remarkably regular mountain-plains line running northeast from Little River County, in the southwestern corner of the state, to Mississippi County on the Missouri-Tennessee border, lies in two nearly equal sections. West of this line, the Ozarks and Ouchitas, the only mountains between the Appalachians and the Rockies, rise abruptly. Here in the uplands,

[2] "Violence Chronology: Public Protest and Violence Accompany Desegregation Moves," *Southern School News*, May, 1964, 12–13.

[3] See the following Anti-Defamation League field reports: John Howard Griffin and Theodore Freedman, *Mansfield, Texas: Report on the Crisis Situation Resulting from Efforts to Desegregate the School System* (New York: Anti-Defamation League, n.d.); and Anna Halden et al., *Clinton, Tennessee: A Tentative Description and Analysis of the School Desegregation Crisis* (New York: Anti-Defamation League, n.d.)

far removed from the state's cotton-belt counties which border the Mississippi River, Negroes are few and overt race prejudice minimal; here Arkansans adjusted to the school decision with relative ease.[4] Such was not the case, however, east of the fall line, in the lowlands which sweep flat in an alluvial plain toward the Delta counties along the river. In this low-country section of the state, cotton flourished on vast tracts of rich land, much as it did on the opposite shore in Mississippi; and here, in concentrated density, were to be found the great majority of Arkansas's Negro population and many of its Deep South racial attitudes. But given even the predictably intractable mood of the low country, there was little reason for alarm. As the first decade of desegregation began, only the most gloomy of prophets would have foretold that in the troubled years ahead Arkansas would become a symbol of white defiance. A pioneer among southern states in biracial higher learning, the first of the former Confederate states to begin compliance with the Court's writ, the "Land of Opportunity" was, as one optimistic NAACP field secretary phrased it, "the bright spot of the south."[5] Neither retiring Governor Francis A. Cherry nor his January, 1955, successor, Orval E. Faubus, had exhibited a taste for massive resistance. And the state legislature which convened in its regular sixty-day biennial session during the winter following the *Brown* ruling refused to enact a pupil assignment bill designed to preserve segregated public schools.[6]

Equally encouraging to racial moderates was the feeble beginning of the state's resistance movement. Appearing first in the black-belt community of Pine Bluff early in 1955,[7] organized segregationists

[4] In September, 1954, there were two school districts operating on a desegregated basis in the state, and both were to be found in western Arkansas. (*Southern School News*, October 1, 1954.)

[5] Quoted in "Has Arkansas Gone Liberal," Chicago *Defender*, May 7, 1955. The tone of this article in a Negro daily reflects the general optimism expressed by many on the course of desegregation in Arkansas. See also "Integration Is Right in Arkansas," Charleston *News and Courier*, June 2, and "Integration Working in Arkansas School," Birmingham *News*, June 17, 1955.

[6] *Southern School News*, April 7, 1955.

[7] See Neil R. McMillen, "White Citizens' Councils and Resistance to School Desegregation in Arkansas," *Arkansas Historical Quarterly*, 30 (Summer, 1971), 95–122.

waged a noisy but ineffective campaign the following summer and fall to block desegregation in Hoxie, a rural trading center in the northeastern portion of the state. Aided by a federal restraining order, determined school officials of District 46 overcame a concert of opposition by the White Citizens' Councils of Arkansas, White America, Inc., and the Citizens' Committee Representing Segregation in Hoxie to integrate the village's twenty-six black schoolchildren with more than 800 whites.[8]

That same autumn militants received yet another setback in the southeastern county of Lincoln, where 53 percent of the population was Negro. In Star City, the county seat, White Citizens' Council organizers were prevented from holding a rally in October, 1955, after white residents petitioned against it. Expressing the view of many residents of the county, the sheriff declared, "we're getting along fine without anybody stirring up trouble."

Clearly, such incidents demonstrated that organized racism in the upper South would not enjoy the same successes it was then experiencing deep in Dixie. But ineffective though it was, the movement persevered. During the following year its more vigorous representatives, including the White Citizens' Council, White America, and the Citizens' Committee, merged to form the Association of Citizens' Councils of Arkansas. Organized in Pine Bluff by segregationists from some twenty-one counties, the association was formed under the leadership of state Senator James Johnson of Crossett, founder of the White Citizens' Council and recently defeated Democratic gubernatorial candidate. L. D. Poynter, a local railroad official and founder of White America, became its president and acting executive secretary.[9] Although well into his sixties, Poynter's new responsibilities could not have been burdensome, for the activities of the ACCA were never more than limited. Unlike

[8] For thorough coverage of the early stages of the Hoxie story, see "Hoxie Schools Desegregate in Arkansas without Incident," ibid., August, 1955, 15; and Cabell Phillips, "Integration: Battle of Hoxie, Arkansas," *New York Times Magazine,* September 25, 1955. Compare an account by the White Citizens' Council of Arkansas, "The Hoxie Story," *Arkansas Faith,* November, 1955, 9–10.

[9] Eventually Robert Ewing Brown was retained as executive secretary. (*Southern School News,* November, 1956, 12; *Arkansas Gazette,* September 2, 1956.)

many state associations, it was never vital enough to sustain a regular publication for its membership. Even the *Arkansas Faith*, published during 1955 by the White Citizens' Council of Arkansas, did not survive the merger.

The most viable of the local affiliates was the Capital Citizens' Council of Little Rock. Originally organized in 1955 as the Capital City Chapter of White America, it became one of the largest and most vocal segregation groups in the upper South. But it too was small by Deep South standards. At peak strength the organization could boast of only some five hundred dues-paying members, and fewer than three hundred of these actually resided in the capital city.[10] Moreover, its public rallies rarely attracted large crowds. Nor did it enjoy the support of the city's "substantial" middle class; and, unlike those of many another southern city, the organization's officers were not drawn from the city's traditional civic leadership. Indeed, on the eve of the Little Rock school desegregation crisis the organization's limited standing in the community was underscored during a school board election when the city's voters rejected a pair of Council-endorsed candidates—one of whom was the CCC president—in favor of two others pledged to uphold the board's desegregation plan. To make matters worse, Council membership was seriously fragmented in September, 1958, when Robert E. Brown, a former CCC president and onetime executive secretary, led a group of dissidents out of the organization to form the States' Rights Council of Little Rock.[11]

But though hardly formidable when compared to its counterparts in Birmingham, Jackson, Montgomery, and New Orleans, the Council in Little Rock was a disruptive force of no small consequence. In truth, its strength may probably be better measured by

[10] Forced to make public its records in November, 1957, under the city's so-called Bennett ordinance, the CCC revealed that of its 510 members, 295 lived in Little Rock, 86 in North Little Rock, 121 elsewhere in the state, and 8 outside the state. Proposed by state Attorney General Bruce Bennett as a weapon to be used against the NAACP, Bennett ordinances were adopted by Little Rock, North Little Rock, and Crossett. They required that the records of "extremist groups" be made public. See *Arkansas Gazette*, October 27, 31, November 1, 1957; and *Southern School News*, November 1957, 7.

[11] All but two of the States' Right Council's twelve incorporators were former members of the CCC. (*Arkansas Gazette*, September 5, 18, 1958).

its considerable contributions to the bipolarization of public sentiment in Little Rock than by the number of its members. Given the troubled course of public school desegregation in the capital city, it seems apparent that the CCC's extreme segregationist sentiments appealed to a far greater audience than its comparatively small membership would indicate.

In time the state association acquired more or less active local affiliates in such counties as Arkansas, Crittenden, Drew, Lonoke, and Jefferson, as well as in the western cities of Texarkana and Van Buren.[12] Generally, however, the movement possessed little strength in these localities. Groups were formed to meet the needs of a local desegregation crisis, but once racial tensions subsided popular interest in organized racism faded. Because membership lists have never been released, it is difficult to estimate Council strength in any state; in Arkansas it is particularly hazardous. Unlike many state associations, the ACCA seldom quoted membership figures to the press. But in August, 1957, it did report that there were organizations in thirty-two of the state's seventy-five counties, a figure that appears to be exaggerated.[13] Similarly, the Southern Regional Council, an Atlanta-based civil rights agency that frequently overestimated resistance group strength, suggested 20,000 as "the maximum realistic figure" for the association's total membership.[14] In light of the available evidence, this too seems inflated.

Whatever its peak size, there can be no doubt that by 1960 the organization's strength had diminished significantly. After a noisy and often unseemly year-long battle to block the court-ordered desegregation of the Dollarway school district, even Council leaders betrayed some recognition of the futility of their task. Variously described by segregationists as the last redoubt in Arkansas's battle for race purity and the key to the doors of every white school in the state, Dollarway was unquestionably a community of strategic importance in the Council's defense of the status quo. But in August, 1960, when district school officials admitted

[12] *Southern School News,* April 7, 1955, November, 1958, 8, September, 1959, 1–2, 15; *Arkansas Gazette* and Memphis *Commercial Appeal,* June 29, 1957; Pine Bluff *Commercial,* January 31, February 1, 1962.

[13] Memphis *Commercial Appeal,* September 1, 1957.

[14] Southern Regional Council, *Pro-Segregation Groups,* November 19, 1956, May 23, 1957.

six-year-old Delores Jean York to an all-white elementary school, state and local Council leaders united in an appeal for popular acceptance of the action. As L. D. Poynter conceded, the board had exhausted its every resource for delay; no other avenue of nonviolent resistance remained open. When school convened on September 7, Arkansas enjoyed its first peaceful school opening in four years. What the ACCA had repeatedly called the gateway to southeast Arkansas was thrown open, and, when a single black girl marched in, the organization retreated.[15] Two years later, the school board in Pine Bluff itself admitted five Negro children to three previously segregated schools. It did so without court order, and without significant opposition from the Citizens' Council. To be sure, by that date, the voice of organized resistance in Arkansas was scarcely audible.

To a greater degree than Arkansas, that "bright spot of the South," Florida in the mid-1950's was abundantly blessed with conditions which augured well for early compliance with the desegregation ruling. Despite its common boundaries with Alabama and Georgia, its traditionally Democratic politics, and its occasional resort to what Key has called "a faintly tropical rebel yell," Florida shared little with the Deep South.[16] Penetrated only in its northern extremity by antebellum plantation agriculture, suffering little from such lingering sectional afflictions as a one-crop economy and sharecropping, the region's most urbanized state was characterized by a comparatively small black population (20 percent in 1950), a diversified economy, the highest per capita income in the South, a ready flow of northern immigrants, and a never-ending invasion of affluent and cosmopolitan tourists. In combination, these were conditions which discouraged the strident Negrophobia that so often characterized southern politics. Although not strangers to the tradition-honored art of race-baiting, Floridians generally demanded something more from their political aspirants than mere promises to keep the Negro in his place.[17]

15 *Arkansas Gazette,* August 15, 21, 1959, September 7, 1960; Nashville *Tennessean,* August 21, 22, 1959; *Southern School News,* September, 1959, 1–2, October, 1960, 11.

16 Key, *Southern Politics,* 83.

17 H. D. Price, *The Negro and Southern Politics: A Chapter of Florida History* (New York: New York University Press, 1957), 60.

Nevertheless, Florida was caught unprepared for the new epoch in race relations. Flirting with massive resistance until 1959, it delayed until the toppling of racial barriers in every other peripheral state before admitting the first Negro pupils to two previously all-white Dade County schools. The explanation for this apparent paradox lies in the peculiar regional dichotomy which geography, history, and an antiquated system of legislative apportionment imposed upon the state. As one of the state's ubiquitous guidebook writers aptly expressed it, "Florida has its own North and South, but its northern area is strictly southern and its southern area definitely northern." [18] South Florida, or Peninsular Florida as the area below Marion County is frequently called, was virtually unsettled in the nineteenth century. But so rapid was its growth during the present century that by 1950 nearly three-fourths of all Florida's citizens lived there, and most of them were found in the urban agglomerations along the east and west coasts [19]—far removed from the historic experiences which combined to form the basis of southern one-party, race dominated politics.

The state's system of legislative apportionment, however, failed to keep pace with this pattern of demographic change. During the critical first decade following the *Brown* decision, Florida's legislature was the nation's least representative. Although in gubernatorial elections the urban majority spoke with authority, rural overrepresentation rendered it all but voiceless in the selection of the state's lawmakers.[20] The legislative dominance of the rural, tradition-bound northern Florida minority was reflected in the increasing rigidity of the state's official attitude of resistance following the court-ordered admission of Virgil Hawkins to the University of Florida in 1956. Shifting the state from a policy of reluctant resignation to one of unrelenting defiance, resistance-minded lawmakers adopted a five-point segregation program during a special session

[18] Florida Federal Writers' Project, *Florida: A Guide to the Southernmost State* (New York: Oxford University Press, 1939), 3.

[19] William C. Havard and Loren P. Beth, *The Politics of Mis-Representation: Rural-Urban Conflict in the Florida Legislature* (Baton Rouge: Louisiana State University Press, 1962), 3–4; Kathryn Abbey Hanna, *Florida: Land of Change* (Chapel Hill: University of North Carolina Press, 1948), 380–99.

[20] Havard and Beth, *The Politics of Mis-Representation*, 41–81; Price, *The Negro and Southern Politics*, 103ff.

in 1956. Throughout the regular biennial sessions of both 1957 and 1959, the preservation of Jim Crow schools remained the overridding issue.[21]

Upstate intransigence was reflected also in Florida's resistance movement. In addition to numerous and often mutually hostile Ku Klux Klans, there were several prosegregation groups operating in Florida by mid-1956. Drawing their support primarily from the rural northern counties, they included the Association of Citizens' Councils of Florida; the Florida Federation for Constitutional Government, a branch of the Federation for Constitutional Government founded in New Orleans; the National Association for the Protection of White People and Fair Treatment of Negroes, a Fort Lauderdale–based group open to segregationists of both races; the Pro-Southerners of Fort Pierce, an organization founded in Georgia by an ex-Klansman from Memphis; and the States' Rights Council, organized by a former state legislator in Dade County.[22] None would ever attract wide popular support, and only the Citizens' Council and the Federation for Constitutional Government could be considered significant.

Although the Council appeared first in Florida during the summer of 1955, its activities attracted little attention before June, 1956, when some two hundred delegates from eleven counties (mostly northern) met in Tallahassee to form a "statewide" organization. Managing to declare its formation, and little else, the Association of Citizens' Councils of Florida disappeared from view until the following February.[23] Then, under the experienced direction of Mississippi's Robert Patterson, a second Tallahassee assemblage adopted the Mississippi plan of Council administration and elected permanent officers and the nucleus of a projected twenty-four-member executive committee. Homer T. Barrs, manager of a lunch counter in a Tallahassee drugstore and one of the state's original Councilors, was named administrator. The Reverend George Downs of Orlando, a retired Baptist evangelist who edited the *Gospel*

21 *Southern School News,* April, 1956, 1, August, 1956, 10, July, 1957, 12, July, 1959, 6.

22 Ibid., January, 1956, 15, August, 1956, 11, October, 1956, 11; Southern Regional Council, *Pro-Segregation Groups,* November 19, 1956; New York *Times,* March 13, 1956.

23 Miami *Herald* and Richmond *Times-Dispatch,* June 26, 1956.

Times, an anti-Communist, anti-United Nations, and anti-Negro monthly publication, became the association's paid executive secretary and organizer.[24]

Like its counterparts elsewhere in the region, the ACCF aspired to co-ordinate a truly statewide network of local Councils. But if the variegated geography of the Deep South—reflected as it was in the broad social and economic cleavages of Delta versus hills or Tidewater versus Piedmont—made the achievement of this objective difficult in such states as Mississippi or South Carolina, it was made doubly so by the even more apparent intrastate differences of Florida. The experiences of other southern states had demonstrated that the movement was likely to thrive best in the black belt, and Florida proved to be no exception. Its black belt, if such it may be called, was situated in the long-settled, rural northern counties of the Apalachicola and Suwannee rivers area. In this old plantation region, where in antebellum days cotton, tobacco, and slaves were mainstays of the economy, vestiges of the Old South were still discernible. Although long-range population trends significantly reduced the nineteenth-century concentration of Negroes in "Middle Florida," as this region was called in territorial and pre–Civil War days, its ratio of blacks to whites remained the highest in the state.[25] Measurably more race conscious than Peninsular Floridians, most whites from rural northern Florida confronted the prospect of social change with the same hostility experienced by their white neighbors in Alabama and Georgia.[26]

Not remarkably, then, the area from Marion County north was the center for Council activity in the state. But central Florida was also represented, as the appointment of an executive secretary from Orlando and four of the ACCF's first eleven executive committee-

[24] The only other officer announced at this time was the state treasurer, Charles Creel, a banker from Bunnell in Flagler County. See "Florida Moves to Organize Councils," *The Citizens' Council,* March, 1957, 4; Miami *Herald* and St. Petersburg *Times,* February 4, 1957; *Southern School News,* March, 1957, 16; editorial, Tampa *Tribune,* February 11, 1957.

[25] Key, *Southern Politics,* 86–92; Price, *The Negro and Southern Politics,* 36–37.

[26] Price has analyzed a series of three elections and legislative roll-call votes occurring between 1947 and 1952 as determinants of the location of white supremacy sentiment in Florida. (*The Negro and Southern Politics,* 48–54.)

men from Hernando, Pinellas, and Volusia counties would seem to indicate. In St. Petersburg (Pinellas County), a bustling winter resort city on the western coast, one of the state's earliest Councils was organized during the summer of 1955. Under the leadership of the Reverend C. Lewis Fowler, head of Kingdom Bible Seminary, this group claimed more than 1,500 members as early as November, 1955.[27] More typical of the Council's fortunes in Peninsular Florida, however, was the experience of Council organizers in Clearwater, another Pinellas County resort town. The efforts to hold an organizational rally there were initially frustrated when the city manager denied segregationists the use of a public meeting place in October, 1955. Although a later organizational effort proved more successful, the group voted in March, 1956, to leave the ACCF and affiliate with the Federation for Constitutional Government. As its president observed, segregation in the schools was not a consuming interest of the membership. Its focus was on the more elemental constitutional questions of states' rights.[28] Similarly, the ACCF's only active affiliate in the southern portion of the state—the Dade County Property Owners Association—was, as its name implied, not primarily interested in school segregation. Like property owners' groups in several border and western states, the threat of deflated property values, far more than the specter of miscegenation, accounted for the existence of this Miami organization.[29]

Membership figures for Florida are not available, but the movement's rank and file was never large. As the Southern Regional Council observed in 1957, the Council had "little success" in this state; resistance groups here generally enjoyed less influence than in anywhere else in the region.[30] Foundering along with little popular support, the association survived until the Reverend Mr. Downs retired as executive secretary to run for governor in 1960. For all

[27] St. Petersburg *Times,* September 29, 30, October 14, 19, 1955. This organization encountered difficulties during 1957 when one of the original leaders led an extremist faction out of the fold and established a rival group, the Citizens' Council, Inc. It was not recognized by the state association. (St. Petersburg *Times,* October 1, 1957.)

[28] Ibid., October 27, 1955; *Southern School News,* April, 1956, 9.

[29] *Southern School News,* October, 1957, 11, March, 1958, 5.

[30] Southern Regional Council, *Pro-Segregation Groups,* May 23, 1957. See also an earlier report of the same title dated November 19, 1956, 3.

practical purposes, his resignation marked the end of the movement in Florida.[31]

Texas, unlike Florida, turned to token compliance soon after the *Brown* ruling. In September, 1954, months before the rendering of the implementation decree, the state's first Negro children were enrolled in a previously all-white school in Friona, a northwestern farming village.[32] The following September sixty additional school districts abandoned segregated classes. Before the first decade of desegregation had passed, progress-minded Texans could boast of some 60 percent of the region's desegregated school districts and more than half of its blacks attending biracial schools. Moreover, Negroes were attending nineteen state-supported and ten church-supported colleges and universities that once were restricted to whites.[33]

So rapidly and peacefully had Texas begun its adjustment to the new order that not a few observers were ready to classify it among the border states in terms of the apparent ease of its compliance. But comparatively numerous though they were, the Lone Star State's desegregated districts involved few Negroes. With minor exceptions, its biracial classrooms were to be found in southern and western counties, in the recently settled portions of the state where nonwhites frequently constituted 1 percent or less of the total population. Although the Negro population of Texas was the smallest anywhere in the former Confederacy (13 percent), approximately 90 percent of it was concentrated in the northeast portion of the state. There the ratio of blacks to whites, and consequently racial sentiment, most closely approximated that found in the lower South.

[31] In a letter to the author, Lola Lee Bruington, onetime secretary of the Association of Citizen's Councils of Florida, stated: "In one of our heated Florida elections, 1960, the organizer ran for governor, was not elected, and the organization became so split over his actions that it has never recovered. . . ." (Mrs. Lola Lee Bruington, Pensacola, to the author, March 10, 1967.) See also Mrs. J. C. Bruington, "Report from Florida," *The Citizens' Council*, March, 1960, 3.

[32] The desegregation of Friona was not disclosed until May, 1955. (*Southern School News*, June, 1955, 15.)

[33] Harry K. Wright, *Civil Rights U.S.A. Public Schools, Southern States, 1963: Texas* (Washington: Government Printing Office, n.d.), 4, 6; *Southern School News*, October, 1956, 14.

The generally less acquiescent attitude of this area of the state was made obvious in September, 1956, when federally ordered desegregation yielded to local white hostility in two eastern Texas towns within a single week. In Mansfield, a small community near Fort Worth, where the state's first public school district faced a court desegregation decree, Governor Allan Shivers quieted local hostility by blocking the federal order. That same week Texas Rangers were ordered into Texarkana to resore tranquility at Texarkana Junior College, a white institution under court order to admit two Negroes. Again violence was averted, and again defiant whites prevented the execution of a federal order.[34]

Clearly, the compliant attitude of southern and western Texas found no parallel in the Negro-dense counties of the east—a fact which small but voluble Citizens' Councils had been emphasizing since 1955. During the summer of that year, one of the first Councils in the state was organized at Kilgore, a town of some 9,500 inhabitants near the Louisiana border. In this Gregg County community, Dr. B. E. Masters, president emeritus of Kilgore Junior College, enlisted more than 300 members at an organizational meeting in July. Before the month was over, the fledgling Council not only claimed a membership of some 1,500 but was predicting that, when Kilgore's segregated schools convened in the fall, it would be 2,500 strong.[35]

The formation of the Kilgore Council was followed by the emergence of Councils in numerous other eastern Texas towns and cities, including Arlington, Beaumont, Dallas, Fort Worth, Galena Park, Houston, La Grange, Mansfield, Marshall, Orange, and Texarkana. In November, 250 Councilors from some ten eastern counties met in Dallas to form the Associated Citizens' Council of Texas. Officially designated as an "educational" corporation chartered for the purposes of assembling and disseminating "facts of history, science, and experience," the ACCT chose Ross Carlton, a middle-aged attorney and stalwart of the Dallas Council, as its president. When Carlton resigned in May, 1956, to run unsuccessfully for state attorney general, his post was filled by Dr. Masters, chief or-

34 Griffin and Freedman, *Mansfield, Texas: Report on the Crisis Situation; Southern School News*, September, 1956, 12, October, 1956, 14.

35 Dallas *Morning Star*, July 23, 29, 1955.

ganizer of many of the local Councils and the statewide association as well.[36]

Although the ACCT coordinated one of the least effective networks of Councils in the South, it never underestimated its own strength. In November, 1955, its spokesmen boasted that the movement had 20,000 members and was growing rapidly. Within six months, they reported a figure of 25,000 members in thirty counties.[37] Clearly, such numbers are inflated. Altogether there may have been as many as twenty-five chapters, but the movement in the Lone Star State never possessed great vitality. Although Councils were organized in such western Texas communities as Big Spring and Midland,[38] there was never a truly statewide membership. From the outset, the ACCT's rather minimal grass-roots support was almost exclusively confined to the northeastern quarter of the state.

In the three remaining states of the peripheral South—North Carolina, Tennessee, and Virginia—the resistance movement took forms other than that of the Citizens' Council. Although resembling Councils in most respects these groups were comparatively dignified and respectable. To be sure, their numbers, like those of Councils in Arkansas, Florida, and Texas, were never substantial, but the quality of their leadership clearly set them apart. A case in point is the Virginia Defenders of State Sovereignty and Individual

[36] Augusta *Courier,* September 5, 1955; *Southern School News,* September, 1955, 9, June, 1956, 4; Dallas *Morning News,* November 12, 1955; Warren Breed, *Beaumont, Texas: College Desegregation without Popular Support,* No. 4, Field Report on Desegregation in the South (New York: Anti-Defamation League, n.d.), 5; Southern Regional Council, *Pro-Segregation Groups,* November 19, 1956. The Citizens' Council in Dallas should not be confused with the Dallas Citizens' Council, a conservative businessmen's group whose primary purpose was to prepare the city of Dallas for peaceful adjustment to school desegregation in 1961.

[37] Dallas *Morning News,* November 12, 1955; *Southern School News,* December, 1955, 1, May 1956, 13; New York *Times,* March 13, 1956. During the summer of 1957, Masters declared that "we now have Citizens' Councils in all of the larger cities of East Texas except three. . . ." See *Southern School News,* May, 1956, 13; B. E. Masters, "Texas Council Makes Report of Operations," *The Citizens' Council,* August, 1957, 2.

[38] See Washington *Post,* August 27, 1955, and Candy Patterson, "New Citizens' Council in Midland, Texas," *The Citizens' Council,* October, 1960, 3.

Liberties, founded in the autumn of 1954 by eighty-five prominent representatives from eighteen black-belt counties—including three state senators, two state delegates, members of several county boards of supervisors, county clerks, county treasurers, physicians, and businessmen. Sharing the field at first with such groups as National Protective Individual Rights, Inc., the Virginia League, the Crusaders for Constitutional Government, and the Seaboard White Citizens' Council, the Defenders quickly asserted its dominance.[39] Although preferring a small and decorous membership to a large and boistrous one, it may have enrolled as many as 12,000 members in some thirty-seven chapters.[40] In order to screen out undesirables, the organization required each proselyte to have the sponsorship of an established Defender; each new chapter had to await the careful scrutiny of headquarters in Richmond before receiving its charter. Occasionally this process proved ineffective, and irresponsible, rowdy chapters appeared.[41] But for the most part, as one scholar has observed, "the Defenders were as different from the stereotyped white citizens' councils of the Deep South as Harry Flood Byrd was from the late Theodore Francis [*sic*] Bilbo."[42]

The Defenders typically pitched their propaganda campaign on a relatively sophisticated plane, avoiding to a considerable degree the irresponsible Negrophobia that characterized the expressions of many resistance organizations. From the outset, its leaders sought to dignify the movement's defense of segregation by identifying it with a broader conservatism.[43] Pamphlets published by the De-

[39] Richmond *Times-Dispatch,* October 7; Richmond *Leader,* October 8, 1954; *Southern School News,* January 6, June 6, 1955; Benjamin Muse, *Virginia's Massive Resistance* (Bloomington: Indiana University Press, 1961), 9.

[40] J. Barrye Wall, editor and publisher, Farmville *Herald,* to the author, August 4, 1967; *Defenders News and Views,* April, 1956, June, July, 1957; Southern Regional Council, *Pro-Segregation Groups,* November 19, 1956; Frederick B. Routh and Paul Anthony, "Southern Resistance Forces," *Phylon,* 18 (1957), 57.

[41] Particularly in northern Virginia. See Benjamin Muse, "When and How the South Will Integrate," *Harper's,* 214 (April, 1957), 53; Roanoke *World News,* May 3, 1955.

[42] Robbins L. Gates, *The Making of Massive Resistance: Virginia's Politics of Public School Desegregation, 1954–1956* (Chapel Hill: University of North Carolina Press, 1964), 48–49.

[43] See excerpts from several interviews with Robert B. Crawford, Defender president, ibid., 158–63; Bob Smith, *They Closed Their Schools: Prince Ed-*

fenders tended to focus on such issues as the evils of centralized government—"one of the greatest internal dangers facing this nation"—and the virtues of that "cornerstone of our Republic," the tenth amendment.[44] The organization's newspaper, the *Defenders News and Views*, frequently engaged in near-hysterical Communist-baiting, but it seldom resorted to the crude racial demagoguery that was the stock in trade of many similar publications.

In other important respects, however, the Defenders scarcely differed from counterparts elsewhere in the South. Pledged to defend the state's "domestic arrangements" "by all honorable and lawful means," [45] the organization, no less than the Citizens' Councils, was an intractable foe of school desegregation. Moreover, it too was a black-belt organization. Founded in Prince Edward County under the leadership of J. Barrye Wall, editor and publisher of the Farmville *Herald*, and Robert B. Crawford, a businessman who for fifteen years had served on the county school board (1932–47), the Defenders drew the great bulk of its strength from a narrow band of rural southeastern counties known to Virginians as the Southside. Once the cultural center for the Old Dominion, this bleak area of marginal worked-out farms, scrub pine, red clay, and somnolent villages had seen history and tragedy in abundance. Here Nat Turner's band of insurrectionists cut a wide swath of death in August, 1831, and here scarcely three decades later General Robert E. Lee surrendered at Appomatox Courthouse. By 1950, in a state where nearly eight out of every ten inhabitants were white, Southside had a black population approaching 50 percent.[46] Such a setting proved most congenial for the resistance movement. Elsewhere in the state, however, the response to organized segregation was minimal and unenthusiastic.

Much the same may be said of the Tennessee Federation for Constitutional Government, the only Volunteer State resistance group with a significant following. Comparatively dignified and restrained,

ward County, Virginia, 1951–1964 (Chapel Hill: University of North Carolina Press, 1965), 99–100; and Haldore Hanson, "No Surrender in Farmville, Virginia," *New Republic*, 133 (October 10, 1955), 15.

[44] See, for example, the Defenders' pamphlet, *Principles for Which We Stand* (Richmond, [1958]).

[45] Ibid.

[46] See Gates, *The Making of Massive Resistance*, 1–12.

the Federation styled itself as "the only statewide organization devoted exclusively to legal and peaceful opposition to the insidious whittling away of the rights of Tennessee and its people."[47] It denounced violence and disclaimed the insincere "interloper" and the "outside agitator,"[48] who only hampered the endeavors of genuine patriots to "preserve the traditions, beliefs, customs and the constitution and laws and the public policies of Tennessee and the United States of America."[49] Emphasizing primarily states' rights, including the right of every state to maintain separate-but-equal schools, the organization generally eschewed the less seemly activities in which many prosegregation groups engaged. Disapproving of the tactics used by Tennessee's other resistance groups—the Pro-Southerners, the White Citizens' Council, and the Society to Maintain Segregation—it did not join a January, 1956, automobile caravan of segregationists that converged on the state capitol to demand gubernatorial leadership in "the fight for state's rights."[50] In September, 1956, when the Cumberland Mountain village of Clinton was engulfed by rioters protesting court-ordered desegregation, it urged peace and nonviolence as "the only way we can achieve our ends." The Federation was also a bitter critic of Frederick John Kasper, the itinerant New Jersey demagogue who used Tennessee as a base for his far-flung operations in the region's racial trouble spots.[51]

Much of the credit for the Federation's apparent restraint belongs to its president and founder, Donald Davidson, professor of English at Vanderbilt University. One of the twelve Southerners who wrote *I'll Take My Stand,* Davidson was a leading poet of the

[47] Donald Davidson, as quoted in Richard Burrows, "Report from Tennessee," *The Citizens' Council,* July, 1958, 2.

[48] Quoted in "Embattled White South Digs In," *Life,* 43 (July 22, 1957), 28.

[49] Charter of the Tennessee Federation for Constitutional Government, as quoted in *Southern School News,* August, 1955, 1, 17.

[50] See Neil R. McMillen, "Organized Resistance to School Desegregation in Tennessee," *Tennessee Historical Quarterly,* Fall, 1971.

[51] Kasper's career as race-baiter-at-large for the central South has been recounted, ibid.; James Rorty, "Hate-Monger with Literary Trimmings: From Avant-Garde Poetry to Rear-Guard Politics," *Commentary,* 22 (December, 1956), 533–42; Wilma Dykeman and James Stokely, "Failure of a Hate Mission," *Nation,* 184 (April 20, 1957), 342–44.

"fugutive school" whose most recent works, no less than those of the 1930's, were remarkable for their agrarian ardor.[52] Unlike most of the fugitive writers who made peace with the twentieth-century South,[53] Davidson, as an admiring Russell Kirk has written, remained one of the "unmachined," who with "a high disdain for nearly the whole tendency of things in this country since 1865" was "still carrying on the fight against the triumph of technology."[54] In Davidson's view, one of the most disturbing phases of this "whole tendency of things" was the manner in which the nine justices of the Warren Court "violated the constitutional principle of the separation of powers by attempting to declare, not what the law is, but what they thought it ought to be." In so doing, they "usurped" state and federal legistative prerogative, abandoned "established precedent and judicial procedure in favor of mere sociological and psychological opinionating," and did "gross and possibly irreparable injury" to American judicial procedure.[55]

Endeavoring to organize a responsible protest against what he believed to be judicial irresponsibilities, Davidson and a small group of like-minded Nashvillians incorporated the Tennessee Federation for Constitutional Government late in June, 1955. Described by one historian as "a Snopesian perversion of the aristocratic agrarian tradition,"[56] the organization's officers included several business executives, an attorney, a locally prominent artist, the chairman of the Romance language department, and an instructor in English

[52] Compare Donald Davidson's *Still Rebels, Still Yankees* (Baton Rouge: Louisiana State University Press, 1957), esp. 159–278, with his *The Attack on Leviathan: Regionalism and Nationalism in the United States* (Chapel Hill: University of North Carolina Press, 1938).

[53] Compare, for example, Robert Penn Warren's *Segregation, the Inner Conflict in the South* (New York: Random House, 1956) and his *Who Speaks for the Negro?* (New York: Random House, 1965) with Davidson's "The New South and the Conservative Tradition," *National Review*, 9 (September 10, 1960), 141–46.

[54] Russell Kirk, "A Professor of Genius," *National Review*, 3 (June 8, 1957), 555. In a less complimentary vein, Ralph McGill has written that among the writers of *I'll Take My Stand* only Donald Davidson "put on armor and rode out to challenge the snorting bulldozer dragon" in the post-*Brown* period. See Ralph McGill, *The South and the Southerner* (Boston: Little, Brown, 1964), 208.

[55] Quoted in *Southern School News*, August, 1955, 1, 17.

[56] Bartley, *The Rise of Massive Resistance*, 99–100.

at Vanderbilt University.[57] Unquestionably it was true, as Richard Burrow, Jr., a member of the Federation's board of advisers, asserted, that the TFCG was "the most respected and influential [resistance] organization in the state."[58] Nevertheless, in a report to the membership in the summer of 1957, Davidson could claim chapters in only fourteen of the state's ninety-five counties. Although releasing no figures, the president noted further that during the past year the organization had doubled in size and that its members could now be found in fully seventy-five counties and 230 towns and cities throughout the state. The following year, the organization was vaunting the paid allegiance of "patriots from Bristol to Memphis."[59]

Despite such claims, the Federation was never able to enlist a substantial popular following. Although it produced and distributed a variety of attractively published pamphlets,[60] held frequent rallies, and in other ways sought to make itself "a dominant force in the struggle to retain and regain our Constitutional rights,"[61] it failed to generate significant grass-roots enthusiasm for its program. Along with the Citizens' Council of Florida, it ranks as the least effective of the region's major resistance organizations. For all its pretensions of statewide support, a large majority of its membership and all but a few of its chapters were found to be in western Tennessee—where the bulk of the state's relatively sparse Negro population

57 Davidson provided "a kind of 'Who's Who' list of our officers" in a letter to James P. Williams, December 9, 1955. (Photocopy, Southern Regional Council; see also Nashville *Tennessean* and Nashville *Banner*, July 12, 1955.)

58 Richard Burrow, "Report from Tennessee," *The Citizens' Council*, August, 1957, 4.

59 Donald Davidson, *Report of the State Chairman, Tennessee Federation for Constitutional Government* (Nashville: Tennessee Federation for Constitutional Government, 1957); Nashville *Tennessean*, June 16, 1957; Burrow, "Report from Tennessee," *The Citizens' Council*, July, 1958, 2.

60 See, for example, Morris Cunningham, *Red Espionage, Increase Warned by F.B.I.'s Hoover* (Jackson, Tenn., 1961); Donald Davidson, *Tyranny at Oak Ridge* (Nashville, 1956); *A Message to the People of Tennessee from the Tennesseee Federation for Constitutional Government* (n.p., 1956); Billy James Hargis, *Integration by Force Is Not a Christian Crusade* (Jackson, Tenn., n.d.); *Why Segregation* (Jackson, Tenn., n.d.); Marvin Brooks Norfleet, *Forced Racial Integration* (Jackson, Tenn., [1961]).

61 Lambeth Mayes, secretary of the Federation, as quoted in *The Citizens' Council*, August, 1959, 2.

(16 percent in 1950) was concentrated, and where white attitudes on race most nearly approximated those of the Deep South.[62] With the exception of trouble-plagued Anderson County, scene of the state's first and most chaotic desegregation incident, the Federation possessed virtually no strength in Republican and Unionist eastern Tennessee, which had traditionally demonstrated its independence from those portions of the state that constituted slave-holding and Confederate Tennessee in 1861.[63]

The Patriots of North Carolina, Inc., like the Tennessee Federation and the Virginia Defenders, was a sedate version of the Citizens' Council. Among its incorporators were to be found three former speakers of the state house of representatives, a trustee of the University of North Carolina, a state senator, two state representatives, and a number of well-known civic and religious leaders.[64] "All in all," commented the moderate Winston-Salem *Journal*, "few North Carolina Corporations can boast a more impressive list of charter members. . . . The group represents something more than a scrubbed-face revival of the Ku Klux Klan." [65] Similarly, the Charlotte *Observer* could report: "Some of the most respected men in North Carolina became charter members of the Patriots." [66]

Additional proof of the organization's respectability came soon after its formation, in September, 1955, when its officers were announced. Heading a list of five Piedmont professional men [67] and

[62] The Federation's most active chapters were those in Gibson County (Milan), Madison County (Jackson), and Shelby County (Memphis).

[63] One of the earliest to be formed, the Anderson County chapter appeared in September, 1955. It grew out of the Oak Ridgers for Segregation, an organization formed earlier in the summer to resist the desegregation of the Atomic City. See Davidson, *Tyranny at Oak Ridge*, 9–10, and Nashville *Banner*, September 21, 1955.

[64] Southern Regional Council, "Patriots of North Carolina, Inc.," unpublished field report, 1956; "Certificate of Incorporation of Patriots of North Carolina, Inc." (unpublished manuscript, SERS, August 22, 1955); Greensboro *Daily News*, August 23; Atlanta *Journal*, August 28, 1955.

[65] Winston-Salem *Journal*, June 3, 1956.

[66] Charlotte *Observer*, May 18, 1956.

[67] A sixth officer, Vice-President Robert E. Stevens, was from Wayne County, east of the fall line. Patriot officialdom, like the organization's charter members, was predominantly from upcountry counties. Twenty-two of the group's sixty-member board of directors and five of its fifteen-member ex-

business executives elected to lead the Patriots was Dr. Wesley Critz George, a retired University of North Carolina Medical School professor and one of the nation's foremost scientific racists. Although his dubious theories on innate racial characteristics were roundly criticized by fellow scientists and academicians, the career of this former president of the North Carolina Academy of Science was distinguished and his name was widely respected in scientific circles. Other Patriot leaders of note included the organization's founder, C. L. Shuping, an attorney and former Democratic national committeeman whose early antipathy to the New Deal led him into the American Liberty League,[68] as well as its full-time executive secretary, A. Allison James, a civic-minded Winston-Salem pharmacist who was once head of the U.S. savings bond sales in North Carolina.[69]

Although similar in most respects to its black-belt counterparts elsewhere in the region, the Patriots differed in one very significant way. Deviating from a well-established pattern of segregation group formation, it was born in the Piedmont, west of the fall line, west of the old plantation counties of the Tidewater where the majority of the state's Negroes were concentrated. Quite unlike any other resistance group, its natural habitat was the upcountry.

Partially, at least, the explanation for the apparent geographic novelty of North Carolina's resistance movement lies in the comparative impotence of the state's black belt itself. Although (with the obvious exception of Virginia's Southside) this irregular block of northeastern counties constituted the largest black belt in the peripheral South,[70] it had not been an area of preeminent political and economic significance in the state for some decades. The powerful position once enjoyed by the agricultural counties of the coastal plain and Tidewater shifted upcountry, beyond the fall line

---

ecutive committee were from Greensboro alone; fully ninety-one of its 356 charter members were from Guilford County.

68 See George Wolfskill, *The Revolt of the Conservatives: A History of the American Liberty League, 1934–1940* (Boston: Houghton Mifflin, 1962), 181; editorial, Raleigh *News and Observer*, August 24, 1955.

69 Southern Regional Council, "Patriots of North Carolina, Inc."

70 In 1950 North Carolina had ten counties with Negro populations of 50 percent or more. In Virginia there were sixteen, in Arkansas six, in Texas four, and in Florida and Tennessee there were only two each.

that runs from Anson County on the South Carolina border northeast to Northampton County along the Virginia border. The bulk of the state's population, its financial and business energy, and its political leadership were now to be found centered around the four major Piedmont industrial cities of Charlotte, Durham, Greensboro, and Winston-Salem. Unlike a Deep South state, such as Mississippi, where the agricultural counties of the black belt still exercised considerable influence, North Carolina was dominated, politically as well as economically, by what V. O. Key has called "an economic oligarchy," "an aggressive [upcountry] aristocracy of manufacturing and banking." [71] It was perhaps not unnatural, then, that the state's resistance movement should derive its impetus from sources other than the planter–merchant–county-seat elite of the low country—the sources whence the Deep South Councils had sprung.

The nucleus for the Patriots was formed early in the summer of 1955 in Greensboro, a manufacturing center for cigars, chemicals, cotton textiles, hosiery, and a variety of machinery. Late in November, its first local affiliate appeared in Sanford, seat of Lee County, on the eastern edge of the Piedmont.[72] From there the movement spread fairly rapidly into a number of Piedmont counties, including Alamance, Caswell, Forsyth, Mecklenburg, Richmond, and Rockingham.[73] Just how large it actually became is a matter of some doubt. Unquestionably, its claim of 20,000 members and a growth rate of 1,500 to 2,000 per week by late December, 1955, is exaggerated. Hardly more useful are the figures suggested by the Southern Regional Council. After completing its survey of resistance groups across the South during the summer of 1956, this agency could only report that "membership wise the group has been estimated to be from 20,000 to 200,000 strong, though it probably has no more than the minimum figure at best." [74] If durability is any

[71] Key, *Southern Politics*, 211–23. See also two essays by Hugh Talmadge Lefler and Albert Ray Newsom, "A Quarter Century of Economic Growth" and "The Modern Industrial Revolution after 1930," *North Carolina* (Chapel Hill: University of North Carolina Press, 1963), 543–54, 596–609.

[72] Sanford *Herald* and Raleigh *News and Observer*, December 1, 1955.

[73] Greensboro *Daily News*, December 7, 1955, March 25, April 21, 1956; Charlotte *Observer*, December 14, 1955; Raleigh *News and Observer*, July 21, 1956.

[74] Greensboro *Daily News*, December 7; Charlotte *Observer*, December 14, 1955; Southern Regional Council, "Patriots of North Carolina, Inc."

index, it is doubtful that the Patriots' membership roster ever approached the 20,000 mark. For despite an impressive beginning, the Patriots never demonstrated significant mass appeal. To it belongs the dubious distinction of being the most short-lived of the major resistance groups in the eleven-state area. Even before North Carolina's first public schools began desegregating in three Piedmont cities during September, 1957, the group had started to wane.[75] By the summer of 1958, its third anniversary, the Patriots had passed from the scene.

Organized racism, however, did not depart with it. With almost indecent haste, Tarheel white supremacists chartered a second organization in November, 1958. The successor group, the North Carolina Defenders of States' Rights, like the Patriots, was essentially a Piedmont organization, and among its ranks were to be found many of the old faces. Six of its fifteen officers and directors were Patriot charter members, including A. Allison James and Wesley Critz George.[76] Its president and most effective spokesman was the Reverend James P. Dees, a militant white supremacist who believed that the *Brown* decision had been the harbinger of "the most critical time in the history of the human race." [77] Although he was the rector of the Trinity Episcopal Church of Statesville, Dee's racial views were openly at variance with the official policy of the Episcopal Church. Charging it with fostering "socialism," "pseudo-brotherhood," and "appeasement of the Communists," he resigned from the diocese of North Carolina in 1963 and established an independent congregation, the Anglican Orthodox Church.[78]

For all of the segregationist ardor of its leader, the Defenders was even less effective at recruiting a mass following than had been the Patriots. By January, 1959, it could claim only "several hundred" followers. It seems unlikely that the organization's membership ever numbered more than a few hundred, for not until the spring of 1961 was it able to employ a retired Presbyterian minister from Morehead City, the Reverend Joseph S. Jones, as its first executive

[75] See Southern Regional Council, *Pro-Segregation Groups,* May 23, 1957.

[76] "North Carolina Defenders Seek Members," *The Citizens' Council,* April, 1959, 1.

[77] Quoted in Raleigh *News and Observer,* January 11, 1959.

[78] New York *Times,* November 22, 1963; "Segregationist Preacher Leaves Protestant Episcopal Ministry," *Alabama Baptist,* December 5, 1963.

secretary.[79] Under Jones's leadership the group succeeded no better. During 1963, it passed from the scene.

The indifferent record of both Patriots and Defenders was indicative of the problems encountered by organized segregationists in states where the atmosphere was one of comparative racial moderation. Reluctant though it was to abandon its Jim Crow schools, the Old North State avoided much of the disorder accompanying desegregation in many southern states. From the outset its leadership shied from what Governor William B. Umstead chose to call "rash statements" and "impossible schemes."[80] Steering a middle course between prompt acquiesence and protracted defiance, the state enacted no resolution of interposition, it closed no public schools, and the concept of massive resistance was never seriously considered as official policy.[81] Preceded only by Arkansas, Texas, and Tennessee, desegregation began voluntarily and quietly in North Carolina during the fall of 1957, when the state's three largest cities—Charlotte, Greensboro, and Winston-Salem—admitted twelve Negroes to hitherto all-white schools. By the end of the first decade after the *Brown* ruling, 41 of the state's 171 school districts had begun at least token desegregation, and more than 1,800 of its 346,000 Negroes were attending biracial schools.[82]

Measured against a Deep South backdrop, this was indeed the "prompt and reasonable start" required by the implementation decree of May 31, 1955. Amid such a climate of moderation, organized segregation could hardly flourish. Such was the fate of the movement throughout the peripheral South.

[79] Raleigh *News and Observer*, January 11, 1959; *The Citizens' Council*, March, 1961, 4; Greensboro *Daily News*, January 10, 1963.

[80] Quoted in *Southern School News*, September 3, 1954.

[81] Richard E. Day, "North Carolina," *Civil Rights U.S.A. Public Schools: Southern States, 1962*, ed., U.S. Commission on Civil Rights (Washington: Government Printing Office, n.d.); Lefler and Newsome, *North Carolina*; Muse, *Ten Years of Prelude*, 147ff.

[82] Desegregation in North Carolina occurred under the so-called Pearsall Plan, or Pupil Assignment Law, enacted in 1956. In contrast to the massive resistance legislation of Virginia and the Deep South states, this law was designed to limit, not preclude, racial mixing in the public schools. Capus M. Waynick et al., eds., *North Carolina and the Negro* (Raleigh: North Carolina Mayors' Co-operating Committee, 1964), 236–38; Sarratt, *Ordeal of Desegregation*, 353.

CHAPTER VII

The Citizens' Councils of America: Solidifying the South

To many an advocate of massive resistance, the solution to most of the problems confronting the post-*Brown* South lay in the formation of a regional confederation of organizations welded together by common dedication to the principles of white supremacy. Even before the first Citizens' Council appeared in Sunflower County, Mississippi, Judge Tom P. Brady suggested the need for a network of statewide segregation organizations throughout the South under the general direction of a National Federation of Sovereign States of America.[1] During the summer of 1955, Senator James O. Eastland pronounced it "essential that a nation-wide organization be set up" to "mobilize and organize public opinion" throughout the United States in order to combat school desegregation. It must be, he declared, a "great crusade," a "people's organization," an organization not controlled by "fawning politicians who cater to organized racial groups," an "organization to fight the C.I.O., to fight the N.A.A.C.P., and to fight all the conscienceless pressure groups who are attempting our destruction." [2] Again the following December, in an address to the first statewide convention of the Mississippi Citizens' Council, the Delta politician declared it

1 Brady, *Black Monday*, 72–80. See also *A Review of Black Monday*, a Council reprint of an October, 1954, speech by Brady on the same topic.

2 Quoted in "Segregation and Southern Politics," *Facts*, 10 (October–November, 1955), 1.

"urgently imperative" that a regional organization be formed to counter "the illegal, immoral and sinful doctrine" of school desegregation. Supported by public funds and patterned after the Citizens' Council, the commission proposed by the senator would present the case for segregation to "fair-minded Americans in other regions . . . who are being hoodwinked, misled and deceived." [3]

Within the month, as if in response to Eastland's call, the Federation for Constitutional Government was formed in Memphis by representatives from twelve southern states who invited "all patriotic organizations" to join them in "a united movement for the preservation of America under a constitutional form of government." [4] The Federation enjoyed the support of a distinguished body of state and national political figures, including Senator Eastland, Senator J. Strom Thurmond of South Carolina, Governor Marvin Griffin of Georgia, former Governors Fielding Wright of Mississippi and Herman Talmadge of Georgia, and U.S. Representatives John Bell Williams of Mississippi and L. Mendel Rivers of South Carolina—all of whom accepted positions on the Federation's hundred-member board of advisers.[5] State and local resistance group leaders also figured prominently in its formation, as well as in its power structure. Such stalwarts of the movement as Judge Brady, Donald Davidson, Roy Harris, Robert Patterson, Willie Rainach, and William J. Simmons were elected to a majority of the positions on the Federation's fifteen-member executive committee and to numerous seats on its advisory board.[6] As if to clearly indicate its political orientation, the

[3] Eastland, *We've Reached Era of Judicial Tyranny,* 10–11. Eastland repeated the call in February, 1956, to a crowd of some 15,000 cheering whites gathered in the Coliseum in Montgomery, Alabama. Termed a gathering of "the largest political crowd in the recent history of the state," the rally was called at the height of the Lucy crisis at the University of Alabama by the Central Alabama Citizens' Councils. See Montgomery *Advertiser,* February 11; Birmingham *News,* February 12, 1956; "Who Incites Southern Race Mobs and Why," *The Christian Century,* 72 (February 22, 1956), 228.

[4] Quoted in Weldon James, "The South's Own Civil War," in *With All Deliberate Speed,* 18.

[5] Among the 115 members of the Federation's executive and advisory boards 49 held either state or national offices. Six of these were U.S. representatives and 9 were former governors. See Memphis *Commercial Appeal,* December 29, 30, 1955, and *Southern School News,* February, 1956, 8–9.

[6] Among other Council notables serving on either the executive board or

organization selected as its president John U. Barr, a retired New Orleans industrialist who had stood in the vanguard of the Dixiecrat movement of 1948 and who would lead a third party movement to elect T. Coleman Andrews president in 1956.[7]

It was Barr's intention that the Federation would "co-ordinate the work of such groups as the Citizens' Councils and the States' Rights Council of Georgia and the Committee for Individual Rights in Virginia."[8] It soon became apparent, however, that many Councilors, particularly those from Mississippi, did not share Barr's ambitious view of the Federation's role in the organized resistance movement. Proof of that fact came early in April, 1956, when a second interstate organization was created in New Orleans. Under a shroud of secrecy, sixty-five representatives from Councils or Council-like groups in eleven southern states met at the Roosevelt Hotel to form the Citizens' Councils of America. With state Senator Willie M. Rainach, head of the Association of Citizens' Councils of Louisiana, presiding, the delegates pledged to defend such "natural rights" as "the separation of the races in our schools and all institutions involving personal and social relations. . . ." After a committee was appointed to draft a charter and bylaws acceptable to each of the several statewide associations, the group extended an invitation for affiliation to "all organizations dedicated to these purposes."[9]

At a second meeting in Jackson, Mississippi, the following October, the CCA completed the remainder of its organizational details. Rainach was elected president and Robert Patterson sec-

---

the advisory board were John Garrett, Walter C. Givhan, Micah Jenkins, James D. Johnson, Fred Jones, Alston Keith, Ellett Lawrence, William Manning, B. E. Masters, Leander Perez, S. Emory Rogers, William M. Shaw, and Farley Smith. Notables from other resistance organizations included Charles Bloch, Richard Burrow, Robert Crawford, and Hugh Grant. See Mitchell, "Report on the Rise of the White Citizens' Council"; Charleston *News and Courier*, December 30, 1955; *Southern School News*, February, 1956, 8–9.

[7] See Martin, *The Deep South Says "Never"*, 140; "Conservative Leader John U. Barr Is Dead," *The Citizens' Council*, July–August, 1961, 3.

[8] Quoted in Charleston *News and Courier* and Memphis *Commercial Appeal*, December 30, 1955.

[9] *The Citizens' Council*, May, 1956, 1; New Orleans *Times-Picayune*, April 8, 1956.

retary, temporary headquarters were established in Patterson's Greenwood office, and *The Citizens' Council*, organ of the Mississippi Council, became the official publication. The organization's charter, as William J. Simmons interpreted it, provided for "an association of associations," "a slightly more formalized arrangement of an informal but practical working relationship that has developed between the several established state associations." As merely a coordinating and planning agency, the CCA was nothing more than "the logical extension of the state associations." [10]

The organization's structure, like most of its affiliates, was closely patterned after the Mississippi Council. Policy-making and the overall direction were vested in a board of directors elected by the executive committees of the several state associations. Designed to ally the fears of the smaller, less effective groups of the peripheral South, this arrangement gave each state association (ostensibly at least) an equal voice in the conduct of CCA affairs. Even before the charter was drafted, the Deep South promoters of regional unity, eager to extend assurances of good intentions, carefully defined the limited relationship between the central Council and the state associations. Simmons, then rapidly becoming the most influential individual in the entire movement, stressed in the news columns and editorials of *The Citizens' Council* that the CCA would serve only as an "information center and co-ordinating agency." Assuringly, he wrote that "It does not have and may not assume power or control of any kind over . . . local groups or members." It would accomplish its objectives by "combining the strength of these groups as one, but at the same time maintaining that degree of local autonomy and independence which is such a fundamental characteristic of the Citizens' Council philosophy." Similarly, Willie Rainach, perhaps expressing the apprehensions of many Councilors who must have feared that the CCA would become the tool of the powerful Mississippi Council, reported that the organization throughout the South "will have no plenary power over any state or local council, inasmuch as each is independent." The organized resistance movement, Rainach reminded the wary, was opposed to

[10] "Our Scope and Purpose," *The Citizens' Council*, November, 1956, 2. See also Jackson *Daily News*, October 13, 1956; *Southern School News*, November, 1956, 3.

political centralization, whether in the Federal government or in its own ranks.[11]

Despite such early attempts to assuage peripheral-South misgivings, it seems clear that many did not eagerly embrace the opportunity of forming a united front under the banner of the Citizens' Councils of America. Indeed, even the question of exactly which organizations were eventually drawn into the informal orbit of the CCA is open to debate. At one time or another spokesmen for the Council, primarily Simmons and executive director Louis Hollis, directly linked their organization with each of the major resistance groups in the eleven-state area, the Georgia States' Rights Council, the North Carolina Patriots, the Tennessee Federation for Constitutional Government, and the Virginia Defenders of State Sovereignty and Individual Liberties, as well as the more numerous associations of Citizens' Councils.[12] Perhaps this was true, but only in a most informal manner. For while the Councils in Alabama, Arkansas, Florida, Louisiana, Mississippi, South Carolina, and Texas can be linked more or less directly with the regional Council, the relationships of the other organizations were more tenuous. Jealous of their independent identities, and reluctant to surrender their operations to the coordination of a regional organization which would in all likelihood fall under the domination of the more vigorous Citizens' Councils of the Deep South whose name it bore, these four organizations were inclined to resist the CCA's program for regional unity.

Most adamant of all in the assertion of its independent status was the Defenders. Although willing to cooperate on a limited basis with the organization throughout the South, the Virginians refused to become directly identified with it, preferring, as one of the group's founders later recalled, "state control and state autonomy—one of the purposes of the organization." [13] Not until 1958, when the

[11] *The Citizens' Council,* May, 1956, 1, June, 1956, 6. See also the issues for August and November, 1956.

[12] Interview with Louis W. Hollis, Jackson, Mississippi, May 26, 1967. See also Hollis, "We Have a Plan for Victory," *The Citizen,* 8 (March, 1964), 4–8; Simmons, *The Mid-West Hears the South's Story,* 12ff.; *The Citizens' Council,* September, 1961, 1.

[13] J. Barrye Wall, editor and publisher, Farmville *Herald,* to the author, August 4, 1967. After April, 1959, the Virginia Defenders were represented on

much smaller and less influential Association of Citizens' Councils of Virginia was formed, could the CCA justly claim the Old Dominion among its chain of affiliated states.[14] Somewhat less resolute was the Georgia States' Rights Council. As late as October, 1957, fully a year after Simmons first identified it as a CCA affiliate, Roy V. Harris, president of the Georgia organization, expressed doubt that a truly regional segregation group would ever be possible. Varying "laws, customs and conditions," Harris indicated, stood in the way of interstate unity. The old Augustan's reluctance, however, was overcome in 1958, when he was named president of the CCA, a position he holds to the present day.[15] Thereafter, the SRC, until its demise early in the 1960's, was an affiliate of the regional Council.

Similar were the relationships of the Tennessee Federation and the short-lived North Carolina Patriots. But even in the case of those seven states which had associations of Citizens' Councils, the CCA was hardly more than a paper organization. Although segregation leaders from as many as nine states met annually, and sometimes twice annually, under the banner of the regional Council to exchange views, and though a representative from each state association served on the editorial advisory board of the CCA's official publication, there was in fact little coordination of effort and in actuality no united front. From his vantage point within the regional headquarters in Greenwood, Phillip A. Luce, secretary to Robert Patterson, observed that "there is little contact between the various men who lead the different [Council] groups. . . ." Occasionally leaders of the state organizations met to discuss issues, and they corresponded from time to time. But there was no united front.[16] Thus not until after the grass-roots resistance movement

the editorial board of *The Citizens' Council*, the CCA's official publication, through its director, James R. Orgain. But Orgain, who was also a member of the Citizens' Councils of Virginia, served independently, according to Wall, and not as an official representative of the Defenders.

[14] *The Citizens' Council*, September, 1958, 4.

[15] Atlanta *Constitution*, October 26; Atlanta *Journal*, October 26, 27, 1957; *The Citizens' Council*, September, 1958, 4. See also Harris's comments on the States' Rights Council's affiliation with the "loose association of . . . state groups." Augusta *Courier*, September 1, 1958.

[16] Luce, "The Mississippi White Citizens' Council," 40.

had perished—indeed, not until early in the 1960's when the indigenous segregation groups in most of the southern states were either dead or dying—did the Citizens' Councils of America begin effectively to coordinate organized racism in the South.

The man most responsible for this emergence of the CCA as segregation's aggressive central agency was William J. Simmons, the tall, mustachioed bellwether of the Jackson Citizens' Council, the largest and most influential group in Mississippi. A suave and articulate man of good education and dignified demeanor, Simmons projected the image of respectability that the movement so ardently sought. Unlike the parochial former football captain, "Tut" Patterson, this son of one of the state's most successful bankers represented Mississippi's "better class" of people. As a young man, he traveled widely in South America and Europe, and in 1939 he went to France to study French literature at the Sorbonne. When the outbreak of World War II disrupted his plans, he went to the British West Indies, where he was employed by the Royal Engineers. After the Japanese attack on Pearl Harbor, he returned to the United States and served briefly in the Navy until his release in August, 1942, on a special order discharge.[17] After the war, he established several short-lived enterprises, including a chartered airline service and a fruit and food brokerage house, worked briefly as an accountant for a Lake Charles, Louisiana, oil company, and returned to Jackson just as the resistance movement was being organized.[18]

It has been darkly rumored, though never substantiated, that the future Citizens' Council chief was a Nazi sympathizer during his college years and that he actually affiliated with fascist organizations while in Europe on the eve of the war. Some observers have even suggested that his discharge from the service came after it was discovered that he was "a security risk because of his association with

17 Unpublished press dispatches of Wilson Minor (n.d.), and Minor, "The Citizens' Council."

18 Interview with William J. Simmons, May 26, 1967. Particularly useful for the personal details of Simmons's life is Martin, *The Deep South Says "Never"*, 137–39. See also a summary of Simmons's life and background prepared by the liberal agency, Group Research, Inc., "William James Simmons," *Group Research Reports*, Sec. 2-IND (May 13, 1964), 1–2.

Nazi groups."[19] These assertions Simmons attributes to liberals and race-mixers who wish to discredit the segregation movement he leads by associating it with "the lunatic fringe of the far right" and, thereby, "pin[ning] the anti-Semitic label on the Citizens' Councils." In fact, the charges do appear to be without foundation. An investigation conducted by the Anti-Defamation League—an agency which may hardly be judged sympathetic to organized racism—did turn up a W. J. Simmons among the disciples of Sir Oswald Moseley, leader of the British Union of Fascists. That particular Simmons, however, first entered the British armed forces in 1914, two years before the Mississippi Councilor was born.[20]

Personally disconcerting though it may have been, the cloud of suspicion hovering over Simmons's past had little effect on his rapid rise within the Council's hierarchy. First in the obscure capacity of secretary for the Jackson Council and then in the decidedly more influential position of editor of *The Citizens' Council*, Simmons employed his considerable talents to become what one journalist has chosen to call "Dixieland apartheid's number-one organization man."[21] Although the headquarters of the state and regional Councils were still officially found in Patterson's Greenwood office, the center of both organizations had actually shifted by 1960 to Simmons's offices in downtown Jackson. Soon even the headquarters of the Citizens' Councils of America were moved to the capital city and Simmons, now called the administrator, became de jure as well as de facto head of the regional association. Patterson continued to serve as the executive secretary of the Mississippi Council and he retained his title as secretary of the CCA, but his position within the movement was one of subordination to his more astute former lieutenant.

The transition, made without fanfare and without public acrimony, occurred gradually and in recognition of the changing nature of the organization itself. By the early 1960's the Council, as one student

[19] J. Francis Pohlhaus, counsel, Washington Bureau of the NAACP to Federal Bureau of Investigation, September 12, 1955. Copy in the files of the Southern Office, A-DL.

[20] Report, Southern Office, A-DL, 1960.

[21] Cook, *The Segregationists,* 84.

of the movement observed, had "changed from a 'grass roots' rural movement to a Madison Avenue–type operation manned by city folks."[22] What began as a localized and largely spontaneous popular protest had become a systemized and businesslike operation, skillfully managed by a staff of professionals who had found careers in the defense of white supremacy. No more graphic illustration of this transformation can be found than the relocation of the movement's "national" headquarters from Patterson's dingy, one-room, Confederate flag–cluttered office in a lazy Delta town to Simmons's handsome quarters in a modern office building near the heart of the state's largest population center.

Next to Simmons in the Council hierarchy was Louis W. Hollis, business manager of *The Citizen,* executive director of the Citizens' Councils of America, and, above all, the right-hand man to the administrator. The proud great-grandson of "a hero of the war for Southern Independence" who assisted General Nathan B. Forrest in the formation of the original Ku Klux Klan,[23] Hollis attributed his militant segregation attitudes not to his youth in Arkansas and Tennessee but to a brief business experience in Harlem during World War II. Although he managed the S. H. Kress Company store in that Negro ghetto for only ten months, the plague of labor problems and the lingering shadow of a recent race riot combined to make the experience the least pleasant of his many years with the company. In 1946, after managing Kress stores for twenty-one years in seven states, he retired to Mississippi to operate his own wholesale appliance and investment counseling business. When the Jackson Citizens' Council was formed in 1955, he was among the first to join, and two years later he became a full-time member of Simmons's staff.

By applying to the crusade for white supremacy the same administrative and public relations skills that he had found effective in business, the portly, gray-haired former dime-store executive rapidly became one of the movement's more successful recruiters.

[22] Ibid., 62.

[23] See Louis W. Hollis, *John H. Wisdom, the Man Who Saved Rome [Georgia]: An Address to the Jackson Civil War Round Table, Jackson Mississippi, October 18, 1963* (n.p., n.d.).

In his first major assignment he conducted a block-by-block canvass in the capital city to enlist new members and determine the "expected conduct" of "every white resident of the Jackson . . . metropolitan area."[24] Completed during the summer of 1958, this so-called "Freedom of Choice" survey was a notable success in the view of the Council's press. Not only had new members joined by the hundreds, but, according to Council statistics, the canvass revealed that "99 per cent of Jackson's white residents will look to the Council for guidance if trouble comes."[25] Reflecting pridefully on this early membership drive, Hollis recalled in 1962 that "when I first came up with Bill, we had 2,200 members in Jackson. Now we have between 5,000 and 6,000."[26]

Even as Hollis was recalling the canvass of 1958, he was again directing a recruiting drive, this one on a regional scale. With the movement on the wane throughout much of the eleven-state area, the executive director—"the Roy Wilkins of the Citizens' Council movement,"[27] as he has jocosely called himself—led the campaign to extend the CCA's influence.

Assisting Hollis in the job of membership recruitment was Richard Morphew, the Council's youthful public relations director and perhaps the most widely known member of Simmons's staff. A graduate of the University of Missouri School of Journalism and an experienced television news reporter, Morphew entered full-time Council employment in 1958. Until his death in an Alabama automobile accident in 1966 (en route to interview George and Lurleen Wallace), he served capably as moderator and executive producer of the Citizens' Council "Forum," and as managing editor of *The Citizen*.[28]

Last on the list of what Simmons has facetiously called the CCA's "chain of seniority" was Medford Evans, a graduate of Yale with a doctorate in English literature. A super-patriot who liked to boast of

[24] *The Citizens' Council*, April, 1958, 1. See also *Delta Democrat-Times*, April 25, June 3, 1958.

[25] *The Citizens' Council*, April, 1958, 2.

[26] Quoted in Cook, *The Segregationists*, 78.

[27] Quoted in Houston *Post*, May 28, 1965.

[28] Cook, *The Segregationists*, 83–84. See also Richard D. Morphew, "Operation Information," *The Citizen*, 8 (January, 1964), 17–23.

his "certified right-wing extremism," Evans tried many occupations before finding a career in organized racism. For several years before 1952 he had been employed by the Atomic Energy Commission. Then, in rapid succession, he edited the *Facts Forum News*, monthly bulletin of H. L. Hunt's "Facts Forum," taught social sciences at Northwestern Louisiana College, worked as an organizer and coordinator for the John Birch Society, and served as a special aid to Major General Edwin Walker during the hearings of the Senate Special Preparedness Subcommittee in 1962. In that year he entered the full-time employ of the CCA, first in the capacities of organizer and staff consultant, and then, after 1966, as managing editor of its monthly journal.[29]

Whatever their official capacities, the organization men of segregation found themselves increasingly preoccupied after 1961 with the problem of expanding the perimeter of the Council's influence. By that date, with some degree of desegregation a reality in every state but Alabama, Mississippi, and South Carolina, the organized resistance movement was at its nadir. In Louisiana, the first of the Deep South states to begin admitting Negroes to white public schools, the Association of Citizens' Councils had disintegrated; and in still-segregated South Carolina, the once-powerful state organization atrophied for want of popular interest and dynamic leadership. In Georgia, where public officials abandoned the state's official policy of massive resistance early in 1961, the never-vigorous States' Rights Council trembled on the brink of dissolution. The associations of Citizens' Councils of Arkansas, Florida, and Texas, always the weakest links in the Council's chain, were inactive. Perhaps in even more critical decline were the principal Council-like organizations. The North Carolina Defenders, frail successor to the equally weak Patriots, and the Tennessee Federation had all but ceased to function. Even the Virginia Defenders, once the most vital of the peripheral groups, though still nominally operating, grew increasingly ineffective.

Simmons and his associates did not fail to recognize that the vacuum thus created provided an auspicious opportunity for greater

29 Interview with Medford Evans, May 26, 1967. See also Jackson *Daily News*, June 10, 1962; *Human Events*, 8 (September 15, 1956), 4.

regional unity under Citizens' Council leadership. There were, as they professed to believe, "40 million white Southerners . . . whose attitude towards racial integration is exactly like ours."[30] With such troublesome impedimenta as rival organizations and jealous local leaders now conveniently minimized, all that remained was for each community in the South to begin "a steady and sustained buildup of Citizens' Council membership to a point where city government and other elements of the local power structure become a part of the mass effort to preserve racial integrity." Spurred on by the tantalizing vision of a defiant Caucasian South, united at last under the banner of the Citizens' Councils of America, the professionals in the Plaza Building began a far-ranging campaign during the fall of 1961 to remobilize southern resistance "from the town and county level up." By 1965, this ambitious endeavor carried the CCA's pitchmen the length and breadth of the region—as well as to several states considerably beyond Dixie's frontiers. But initially they focused on those states where the original segregation groups had assumed forms other than that of the Citizens' Council, such as Tennessee.[31]

The CCA's campaign to organize the Volunteer State began in the autumn of 1961, soon after several all-white Memphis schools admitted thirteen Negro children. Deploring this "shameful surrender on the very borders of unyielding Mississippi," Simmons used an editorial in *The Citizen* to urge Memphians to "organize to the hilt." Then, in November, he personally supervised the formation of a small Memphis Citizens' Council. Led locally by Richard T. Ely, a community-minded lawyer who served as president of the influential Memphis and Shelby County Council of Civic Clubs, the fledgling group claimed a membership of two hundred by late

[30] Patterson, *The Citizens' Council: A History*, 5.

[31] William J. Simmons, "Organization: The Key to Victory," *The Citizen*, 6 (February, 1962), 7; Patterson, *The Citizens' Council: A History*, 5; interview with Louis W. Hollis, May 26, 1967. In 1964, Hollis wrote that "various state organizations began to 'die on the vine' so to speak, and many states were without a functioning group of local organizations. . . . [So] in late 1961, we began an ambitious program to bring together under the Citizens' Council name, the citizens in local communities in several states. . . ." Hollis, "We Have a Plan for Victory!" *The Citizen*, 8 (March, 1964), 4.

December.[32] The following March, it launched a recruitment campaign with a goal of 10,000 members determined to "resegregate the city." Although state and local dignitaries turned down invitations to attend the opening rally,[33] the drive began auspiciously enough with a rousing key-note address by Governor Ross Barnett of Mississippi. After recounting his own experience as a Council recruiter and ward leader during the Jackson "Freedom of Choice" survey in 1958, the governor assured a responsive crowd of some 650 that by building a stronger organization they were "saving Memphis from the race mixers."[34]

If white Memphians were concerned about this kind of salvation, they gave little indication of it. So tepid was the popular response to the Council's plea for members, and so easily did this community appear to be adjusting to desegregated schools, that Robert Patterson was moved to write the editor of the *Commercial Appeal* about his dismay "at the lack of organized resistance to integration in Memphis."[35]

A second more systematic recruiting drive undertaken in June, 1963, brought greater success. Throughout the summer Council workers, armed with questionnaires and membership blanks, employed Hollis's house-to-house technique to canvass the city. Although no membership figures were released, state field secretary Jack Kershaw, former executive secretary of the Tennessee Federation for Constitutional Government, awkwardly informed the CCA's Annual Leadership Conference in October, 1963, that "the city of

[32] See *The Citizen,* 6 (October, 1961), 2, and (February, 1962), 6; Memphis *Commercial Appeal,* November 8, December 29, 1961; Richard T. Ely, "We Have a Plan and It Works," *The Citizen,* 6 (February, 1962), 5–6; *Southern School News,* January, 1962, 12.

[33] Amid what the press called "catcalls" from the audience, Ely read letters from U.S. Senators Estes Kefauver and Albert Gore and Police Commissioner Claude A. Armour declining the Council's invitation to the rally. Soon after the Council's appearance in Memphis, Commissioner Armour warned that if its members attempted to hamper the city's peaceful adjustment to desegregation, "we will deal with them as strongly as we know how." Quoted in Memphis *Commercial Appeal,* December 28, 1961, March 17, 1962; *Southern School News,* April, 1962, 12.

[34] Jackson *Daily News,* March 18; Memphis *Commercial Appeal,* March 17, 1962; *Southern School News,* April, 1962, 12.

[35] Letter to the editor, Memphis *Commercial Appeal,* April 8, 1962.

Memphis [now] has more members than before had been in any similar organization over the entire state." [36]

The organization of the Memphis Council in November, 1961, was followed by similar efforts in other Tennessee cities, usually those where earlier resistance groups had been most successful. In Chattanooga, where the Tennessee Society to Maintain Segregation had been formed soon after the *Brown* decision, Simmons and Hollis assisted TSMS founder Arthur A. Canada in the formation of a Citizens' Council in July, 1962. The following September they organized yet another unit in Jackson, a western Tennessee city which had been the center for one of the most active chapters of the Tennessee Federation for Constitutional Government. In December, with local Councils operating more or less effectively in such additional cities as Knoxville, Murfreesboro, and Nashville, Louis Hollis assisted some fifty local Councilors in the formation of the Association of Citizens' Councils of Tennessee. Prominent among those organizing the statewide Council were segregationists formerly identified with the old Federation, including Richard Burrow and Jack Kershaw.[37]

The Council in Tennessee fell heir to the Federation's pattern of limited grass-roots support as well as to its leadership. By 1965, it could claim only from two to three thousand members, and even these figures, supplied by a spokesman for the Mississippi office, may well have been padded.[38] Even the following which it did enjoy was concentrated, as had been the Federation's, in those areas of the state where Deep South ties were strongest. Try as it could, it was never able to establish an effective beachhead in Nashville—the key, many Councilors believed, to the successful organization of the Volunteer State. Because Nashville was "the very citadel of carpetbag liberalism," and "because more leftwing and integration propaganda emanates from this city than from any other city in the South," the capital was a high-priority target for Council activity. Consequently, it received the early attention of the Mississippi

[36] See a reprint of Kershaw's address, "Here's How We Are Winning the Fight!" *The Citizen*, 8 (March, 1964), 16.

[37] Chattanooga *News Free-Press*, July 25, 1962; *Southern School News*, August, 1962, 10, September, 1962, 10, January 1963, 5; Nashville *Banner*, August 21; Memphis *Commercial Appeal*, December 16, 1962.

[38] Nashville *Tennessean*, June 20, 1965.

professionals. At an April, 1962, rally in the Noel Hotel, Hollis and Simmons formed a small unit with local assistance from such Federation stalwarts as Lambeth Mayes, secretary of the older organization, and John M. Aden, an associate professor of English at Vanderbilt University and a friend and colleague of Federation founder Donald Davidson. Never very active, the group probably had fewer than twenty-five members by June, 1965. At that time, a spokesman from the CCA headquarters in Mississippi, recalling the difficulties the movement had encountered there, could report with not a little bitterness: "Nashville is the worst city in the world."[39]

Frustrating though the Council's experience may have been in the Volunteer State, Tennesseans generally responded to its solicitations with greater alacrity than did Georgians and North Carolinians. In both states, grass-roots support for organized segregation was limited during the 1950's, and the passage of a decade did nothing to increase that support. Beginning the systematic formation of the Tarheel contingent of the CCA in Charlotte in September, 1962, Simmons's organizers managed to establish only about twenty local groups by August, 1964, when the state association was formed.[40] Usually small (seldom more than one hundred members each), and, like the state's original resistance groups, almost exclusively confined to the Piedmont, these organizations were seldom remarkable for their great activity. Indeed, a few never met after their organizational rallies, and others suffered embarrassing reversals. Durham Councilors, for example, while making last-minute preparations for a 1963 mass meeting featuring Governor George Wallace of Alabama, discovered on their roster of members in good standing a Negro student from the University of North Carolina.[41] Perhaps more disturbing was a fiasco in Winston-Salem, where the Forsyth County Citizens' Council died aborning after the CCA-appointed temporary chairman publicly confessed to grave doubts

39 Kershaw, "Here's How We Are Winning the Fight!" *The Citizen*, 8 (March, 1964), 15; Nashville *Banner*, October 3, 1962; Nashville *Tennessean*, April 6, 7, 1962, June 20, 1965.

40 Charlotte *News*, September 10; Charlotte *Observer*, September 14, 15, 17, 1962; Winston-Salem *Journal*, August 31, 1964; *Southern School News*, September, 1964.

41 Winston-Salem *Journal*, October 18, 1963.

about the morality of segregation and suggested that perhaps even interracial marriage, although undesirable, was a matter of concern only to the personal conscience. One year later, Hollis managed to regroup Forsyth County segregationists and form a Council, but this time he discreetly avoided inhospitable Winston-Salem and bypassed local leadership entirely. To insure success, he called in Donald Poteat, full-time CCA field director for North and South Carolina, to serve as temporary chairman.[42]

Local initiative in Georgia, too, was often lacking. The campaign there began in May, 1962, in Atlanta, which Simmons believed to be the integration "nerve center" of the Deep South. Proclaiming the moment "the turning point in the [city's] modern history," Simmons and Hollis officiated at an organizational rally attended by more than two hundred people. During the next several years, similar activities occurred in Macon, Savannah, and a few other cities, and in late February, 1964, a state association was formed.[43] Just how many groups were functioning at that time is not now known, but there is no evidence to suggest that there were many. Indeed, so limited was the movement's success in the Peach State that the executive secretary, J. K. (Jack) Calloway, found it necessary to append a telling reminder to letters soliciting members and funds: "Membership in the Citizens' Council is confidential. Anyone can belong to it without their [*sic*] employer or the public knowing it." [44]

Although the results of the campaigns in Georgia, North Caro-

[42] Ibid., September 8, 17, 1963, August 21, 28, 29, 1964; Norfolk *Journal and Guide*, September 28, 1963. See also a brochure, *Why Must Winston-Salem Organize?* ([Jackson: Citizens' Councils of America, 1964]).

[43] *Southern School News*, December, 1960, 7; William J. Simmons, *The Road to Victory: An Address to the Organizational Meeting of the Atlanta Citizens' Council, May 14, 1962* (n.p., n.d.); Atlanta *Journal* and Jackson *Daily News*, May 15, 1962; Charleston *News and Courier*, March 3, 1964.

[44] J. K. Calloway to members of the Association of Citizens' Councils of Georgia, September 21, 1964, Southern Regional Council. The executive secretary expressed the urgency of the organization's need for popular support during the following summer when he informed the membership that "the main thing for members of the Citizens' Councils to do is to sign up as many members as they can as quickly as possible." (Association of Citizens' Councils of Georgia's *Bulletin*, July–August, 1965.)

lina, and Tennessee were not inspiring, these three states served as proving grounds for the Council's expansionist techniques. Procedures found most effective there were adopted as the modus operandi wherever resistance organizers plied their trade. These field-tested methods were first compiled in 1962 in the "White Book of Citizens' Council Organization," a semisecret guidebook for Council leaders and organizational committees. Expanded and revised in 1965, the "White Book" contained the "plan for victory," a somewhat rigid formula recommended by the Council's organization men for use in the formation of new groups.[45] In mature form, the "plan for victory" dictated that the overall responsibility for the development of a given state be vested in a field director, a paid employee of the Jackson office, whose job it was to oversee the development of new Councils.[46] (In 1968 field secretaries were added in some localities to conduct continuing recruitment campaigns.) According to the plan, the field director, once having selected a locality for organization, appointed an organizational committee and a rudimentary slate of temporary officers (usually only a chairman and a secretary-treasurer) from among the community's segregationists. These local citizens in turn compiled lists of potential members and made all preparations for the organizational rally. One week before the rally, the secretary mailed to prospective members a confidential form letter, furnished by CCA headquarters, inviting them to join in the formation of a Citizens' Council.[47] About three days later, each person so invited also received a brochure (also furnished by the Plaza Building) explaining, for example, *Why*

[45] See "White Book of Citizens' Council Organization" (unpublished volume, Citizens' Councils of America, Jackson, Mississippi, 1965). Hereafter cited as "White Book." For an example of the purpose of the "White Book," see Louis W. Hollis, "We Have a Plan for Victory!" *The Citizen*, 8 (March, 1964), 6–7. This article is a reprint of an address to the Annual Leadership Conference in October, 1963, in Jackson, Mississippi.

[46] In the spring of 1967, Simmons listed the Councils' field men and their areas of responsibility as follows: Frank Bain, West Coast; R. C. Bradshaw, Mississippi; William D. Lord, Arkansas and Tennessee; Donald W. Poteat, North Carolina, South Carolina, and Virginia; William K. Shearer, West Coast; and Leonard Wilson, Alabama, Georgia, and Florida.

[47] See, for example, J. H. Norman III, temporary chairman, organization committee, Halifax County Citizens' Council, to "Dear Fellow Citizen," October, 1966, Southern Office, A-DL.

Must Memphis Organize? [48] Following the mailing of the brochures, a telephone committee completed the process by reminding all persons on the lists yet another time.[49]

Even with all of this promotional work, Councilors learned to expect only a partial response. As one seasoned field director suggested, for a new Council to succeed, a minimum of three thousand people had to be invited to the organizational rally. "From experience," he reported to a gathering of Council leaders, "we know that about 10 per cent of those whom we invite will actually attend . . . you must invite many to get a few." [50]

Following the enlistment of new members at the initial meeting, a second meeting followed within a month to permit the election of the group's local leadership. This was at best a perfunctory task, for the local membership seldom did more than endorse a slate of directors presented by the organizing committee and approved in advance by representatives of the Mississippi office. One CCA organizer observed candidly that each local Council was a self-governing unit—"but we're very careful who controls it." [51] To be sure, local self-government was emphasized by the Council's regional leadership in the 1960's no less than in the 1950's. "The fundamental principle of our plan for organization," executive director Hollis often said, "is the local, antonomous groups." [52] Similarly, recruitment literature distributed by the CCA to prospective

[48] Like the form letters, these brochures were tailored somewhat to fit local conditions, but each carried essentially the same message—unless the community's "patriots" organized a Citizens' Council, a "well organized group of liberals . . . [will] eventually destroy the way of life we have known." See for example: *Why Must Brinkley [Arkansas] Organize?* ([Jackson, 1966]); *Why Must Denver Organize?* ([Jackson, 1965]); *Why Must Humboldt [Tennessee] Organize?* ([Jackson, 1963]); *Why Must San Diego County [California] Organize?* ([Jackson, 1965]); *Why Must Webster County [Mississippi] Organize?* ([Jackson, 1967]); *Why Must Windsor [Virginia] Organize?* ([Jackson, 1964]).

[49] "White Book," 22–25. See also Donald W. Poteat, "How to Organize a Citizens' Council," *The Citizen*, 8 (March, 1964), 9–13.

[50] Poteat, "How to Organize a Citizens' Council," *The Citizen*, 8 (March, 1964), 12.

[51] Joseph McDowell Mitchell, as quoted in Atlanta *Constitution*, August 23, 1964. See also "White Book," 22–25; Poteat, "How to Organize a Citizens' Council," 13.

[52] See, for example, Hollis, *Integrity*.

members asserted that each Council was "an autonomous organization with power of decision at the local level."[53] But such expressions must be balanced against Simmons's much-quoted slogan, "Organization: The Key to Victory." Only through "organization and more organization," the editor-administrator believed, could the Council's objectives be achieved.[54] In the light of subsequent developments, it seems obvious that when Simmons wrote these words in 1962 he had something more in mind than merely the formation of new groups. No one knew better than he that effective leadership of the resistance movement throughout the South required greater centralization than had originally been vested in the regional headquarters. And centralization, however one defined it, could be achieved only at the expense of full autonomy at the local level. Just as experience had shown that local initiative was inadequate to sustain a protracted resistance movement, it also demonstrated that, if the rising tide of desegregation were to be checked, something in addition to spiritual guidance would be demanded of the Citizens' Councils of America.

The CCA's consistent policy in the 1960's, then, was the assumption of greater coordination and control of state and local Council affairs. Perhaps no better evidence may be found of this increased centralization under Simmons's leadership than the fiscal system the Jackson office imposed on the groups it organized. In order to relieve local leaders of the "time consuming and arduous" task of collecting and distributing dues, the CCA assumed the responsibility. Under its "central billing plan," the Jackson office collected monthly dues (a minimum of $2.00) directly from the members of each local Council, retaining 10 percent for its own operational expenses and an additional 20 percent for the production costs of its monthly publication, *The Citizen*, and its weekly radio and television series, the Citizens' Council Forum. Fifty percent of the balance was returned to the local Council whence the dues originated,

[53] Typical of this kind of literature was that prepared for Chattanooga. See a brochure, *Why Must Chattanoogans Organize?* ([Jackson: Citizens' Councils of America, 1962]), and the form letter, John P. Hoover to "Dear Fellow Citizen" [July, 1962], Southern Regional Council.

[54] Simmons, "Organization: The Key to Victory," *The Citizen*, 6 (February, 1962), 7–8.

and the remaining 20 percent went to the appropriate state associations.[55]

Further to consolidate its position in the region, the organization also endeavored to remobilize ineffective or inactive Citizens' Councils in at least five other states. This phase of its expansion program began during the fall of 1963, when the CCA announced through Donald W. Poteat, its field director for the Carolinas, plans for the statewide reorganization of the Councils of the Palmetto State. The original movement in South Carolina, Poteat explained, had staggered under the weight of its own provincial and defensive policies. Establishing only minimal contacts with its stronger sisters in other Deep South states, and advancing no positive and aggressive program for resistance, the ACCSC had been unable to forestall a developing sense of the inevitability of desegregation among South Carolinians. The new association, he asserted, would assume the offensive in racial struggles across the state; unlike its predecessor, it would cooperate to the fullest with the regional organization. In September, assisted by Simmons himself, the Sumter County Citizens' Council became the first group in the state to reorganize. Throughout the winter and spring of 1963–64 the remobilization continued as Councilors in Charleston, Columbia, Florence, Greenville, Kingstree, Manning, Orangeburg, and Walterboro responded to the CCA's call for a renewal of organized resistance. In March, with Evans and Hollis serving as midwives, the state association was reborn under a new constitution.[56]

Concurrently, similar operations were under way in Arkansas, Florida, Texas, and Virginia, where Evans and Hollis, with occasional assistance from Patterson, Morphew, and even Roy Harris, endeavored to revive popular interest. In each state, scattered Councils were reorganized and, in a few cases, organized for the first time, but nowhere did the movement regain anything like its

[55] "White Book," 31–32. See also a four-page pamphlet, *Over Dues: A Dialogue by and for Concerned Citizens* (Jackson: Citizens' Councils of America, n.d.). All Councils were urged to adopt the "central billing plan," but only those organized or reorganized directly by the CCA after 1961 were required to do so.

[56] Columbia *State*, September 17, 1963, March 2, April 6, 1964; Charleston *News and Courier*, October 11, 1963, March 3, 1964.

original vitality. In Little Rock, for example, home of the once-aggressive Capital Citizens' Council, only about 60 people turned out for a December 2, 1963, "remobilization rally." In Monticello, Arkansas, where 2,000 persons were requested to assist in the reorganization of the Drew County Citizens' Council in May, 1965, only 55 persons attended—and of these, only 15 answered Medford Evans's invitation to membership, bringing the county's total to 17. Indeed, for all of this "remobilization," nowhere in Arkansas was there to be found a Council with as many as 100 members by 1965.[57] In all likelihood, the Association of Citizens' Councils of Arkansas in that year had substantially fewer than 1,000 dues-paying members.

The CCA's achievements in Florida,[58] Texas,[59] and Virginia[60]

[57] *Southern School News,* January, 1964, 6; *Arkansas Gazette,* May 14, 1965; *Southern School News,* June, 1965, 6. Other "remobilization" efforts in Arkansas included one at Texarkana, where the local membership was boosted to thirty-five, and one at Stuttgart, where the membership was increased to perhaps a total of sixty. See *Southern School News,* January, 1965, 6; *Arkansas Gazette,* December 10, 11, 1964, June 15, 17, 1965; *The Citizen,* March, 1966, 35–36; Report, July, 1965, Southern Office, A-DL.

[58] "Remobilization" in Florida began during August, 1964, when Hollis assisted in the reorganization of a local Council in St. Augustine. By September, 1967, Council leaders in Florida were also claiming organizations in Bradenton, Chattahoochee, Clearwater, Jacksonville, Madison, Marianna, Monticello, Orlando, Perry, and Sarasota. There were also several independent Councils, such as the Marion County Citizens' Council, which were not affiliates of the CCA. (*Florida Times-Union,* August 27, 1964; J. L. Harrison, Jr., president, Manatee County Citizens' Council, to the author, September 14, 1967.)

[59] Most of the Council activity in Texas occurred in Houston, where a Council was reorganized by Roy Harris and Louis Hollis in May, 1965. The Houston Citizens' Council succeeded the Citizens' Council of America in Texas, Inc., which was organized in Houston late in the 1950's only to die out by the turn of the decade. An unsuccessful attempt was made by Ross Barnett to revive the latter organization in 1964. (Houston *Post,* July 22, 1964, May 28, 1965; Houston *Tribune,* June 3, 1965; Report, June 3, 1965, Southern Office, A-DL.)

[60] In a progress report to the Annual Leadership Conference of 1965, Joseph McD. Mitchell, then field director for Maryland, Virginia, and Washington, D.C., indicated that weak and ineffectual Councils functioned in only four cities in the Old Dominion—Hampton, Norfolk, Richmond, and Windsor. See notes taken by Norman Kilpatrick, "Report on D.C., Virginia, and Mary-

were even less impressive. Despite the concerted effort of the movement's ablest evangelists, new life was infused into only a few organizations. Failing to stimulate sufficient popular support, the Jackson office postponed indefinitely its plan for the reestablishment of state associations in these three states.[61]

At mid-decade, regional unity remained as illusory as ever. If there were in fact forty million white Southerners who shared the Council's alarm over desegregation, they were more than a little hesitant to step forward and be counted. Nevertheless, the Mississippi professionals were entitled to some satisfaction with their achievements. For the first time, they could claim for the CCA—with only a little exaggeration—the allegiance of a network of local groups throughout the eleven-state area. That many of these were scarcely more than paper organizations was a fact which they were inclined to gloss over.

---

land Work Given by Joe Mitchell," unpublished (1965), Southern Regional Council.

[61] Early in 1967 an Association of Citizens' Councils of Florida was formed. (J. L. Harrison, Jr., to the author, September 14, 1967.)

CHAPTER VIII

Beyond Dixie's Borders

While the immediate thrust of the Council's energy since 1961 has been focused on expanding and strengthening the movement within the South, its long-range objective was the forging of a nationwide organization. As early as 1956, William Simmons expressed visions of a segregation movement so vast in its appeal that it would transcend regional boundaries. Announcing the formation of the Citizens' Councils of America in the May, 1956, issue of *The Citizens' Council,* the editor observed that, while its "impelling spirit and sustenance . . . arose in the South, the very name chosen indicates the profound hope that those embattled Southerners will be joined by their Northern brothers across sectional lines and work as one for the racial integrity which has made America great." [1] Within a very few months, the Council's monthly newspaper reported astonishing progress toward the realization of that ambitious dream. In August, 1956, the tabloid disclosed that "the movement has spread across the United States, from the Atlantic to the Pacific and from Canada to the Gulf," and that Citizens' Councils or their imitators functioned in "at least 30 states." Although vague on just which nonsouthern states had Councils, the newspaper indicated that Councils had been "reported" in Chicago, Cleveland, Detroit, Los Angeles, St. Louis and Washington, D.C. And in Newark, an organization of 5,000 Councilors had a year-end goal of 40,000 members.[2]

1 "Our Movement Expands," *The Citizens' Council,* May, 1956, 1.

2 Ibid., July, 1956, 1, August, 1956, 1.

Whatever else it may have indicated about the CCA, this extravagant claim did accurately reflect the organization's overweening ambition for nationwide influence. It also reflected a certain pragmatic awareness on the part of the Council's leaders of the enormity of their self-assigned task of reversing the "Black Monday" decision, a task that loomed ever larger as the number of wholly segregated states diminished. Increasingly, CCA spokesmen became conscious, as Roy V. Harris expressed it, that "we in the South can't win this fight by ourselves. We need the support of decent white people everywhere. . . ."[3] To encourage that support, professional Councilors sought and filled speaking engagements outside of the region. On these occasions, the hard line on race was frequently muted in deference to broader issues of concern to conservatives generally. Thus in San Francisco in October, 1957, Judge Tom Brady, in an address to the conservative Commonwealth Club of California, could reduce the threat of desegregation in the South to merely "a small segment in the over-all plan to first socialize and then communize America." Optimistically, he awaited the day when "all conservative Americans . . . all constitutional, liberty loving citizens in this country will rise up in our defense and join hands with us in waging our lonely fight to protect and preserve America from Godless Communism!"[4] Similarly, in an Oakland, Iowa, address to the Farmers-Merchants Annual Banquet during February, 1958, Simmons chose to emphasize the conservative side of Council ideology. Paying only brief homage to "our bi-racial system," the administrator sketched a fearful portrait of encroaching federalism and creeping collectivism in which the *Brown* decision was but one of many portentous deviations from constitutionalism effected by New Dealers, Fair Dealers, and other "totalitarian 'liberals.'"[5]

This phase of CCA activity was stepped up during the summer of 1963, when the organization launched its "Operation Information" to present its views to nonsouthern audiences. Under this project, the Council managed to place official spokesmen on several network

[3] Roy V. Harris, "How We Can Win the Fight!" *The Citizen*, 8 (December, 1963), 22.

[4] Tom P. Brady, *Segregation and the South: An Address Delivered to the Commonwealth Club of California at San Francisco on October 4, 1957* (Greenwood: Citizens' Councils of Mississippi, n.d.).

[5] Simmons, *The Mid-West Hears the South's Story.*

telecasts and provided speakers for local television programs in numerous northern and western cities, notably Boston, Chicago, Denver, Indianapolis, Las Vegas, and New York. Council speakers also addressed student and faculty assemblies at the California Institute of Technology, Elmira College, the University of Notre Dame, and Yale University. Combined with the Citizens' Council "Forum," the CCA's radio and television series which was then being used (or so the organization claimed) by 1,500 stations in fifty states, "Operation Information" provided broad exposure of the Council's message to points outside the region. Surveying the summer's activities from the vantage point of October, 1963, public relations director Richard Morphew reported expansively that "since July, the Citizens' Council message has been placed before every American who has access to a television set or a radio or a newspaper!" For the first time, he asserted, "enough people have absorbed enough of our message to make a big difference." Consequently, "during the past several months . . . national opinion has undergone an about face." "Slowly but surely we are now on the road to victory." [6]

Having introduced itself and its program to the nation at large through "Operation Information," the CCA announced early in the summer of 1964 that it was planning to place a full-time organizer in every northern and western state. The first such position went to Kent H. Steffgen, a thirty-four-year-old former John Birch Society recruiter.[7] An early convert to Robert Welch's anti-Communism crusade, Steffgen joined the Society's professional staff in 1958, soon after graduating from the University of California at Berkeley. First in the capacity of organizer and coordinator for the Los Angeles area, and then as chief coordinator for Kansas, Nebraska, and Missouri, the native Pasadenian supervised Birch activity for five years before entering the employ of the Citizens' Councils of

[6] Morphew, "Operation Information," *The Citizen,* 8 (January, 1964), 17–23. See also Charleston *News and Courier,* September 25, 1963.

[7] Los Angeles *Times,* June 25, 1964, quoted a West Coast John Birch Society official as saying that Steffgen had been fired "for a variety of reasons." For Steffgen's racial views, see his *The Bondage of the Free* (Berkeley: Vanguard Books, 1966).

America.[8] As the field director for California, his first assignment was to form a Greater Los Angeles Citizens' Council. After some difficulty, occasioned by his inability to secure a meeting hall in Los Angeles, Steffgen, assisted personally by both Hollis and Simmons, managed to organize a Council in nearby Pasadena on June 30, 1964. Although the occasion was marred somewhat by the presence of a massive picket line of approximately six hundred civil rights enthusiasts, the Pasadena organizational rally was moderately successful. Nearly five hundred potential Councilors were present to hear Simmons explain "Why California Is Organizing," and if (as is rarely the case) the Council's figures may be relied upon, nearly three hundred of them became dues-paying members.[9] Within a month, the Los Angeles Council was claiming a membership of one thousand, comprised of "a vast cross section of all America," even "quite a few liberals."[10] The professionals in Mississippi, jubilant over "the recent upsurge of interest by Californians in the Citizens' Council movement," proclaimed that in this, the nation's most populous state, white citizens had at last been "awakened" to the dangers posed by "irresponsible and lawless . . . racial agitators and Negro pressure groups."[11]

Despite the early euphoria, California was not swept headlong into the Council's orbit, and Kent Steffgen, for all of his experience as an organizer of extremist activity, was unable to form additional groups. In February, 1965, amid a storm of local discontent,[12] he was replaced by Walter White, a retired radio actor and a tireless

8 "Citizens' Councils Expand Activities in California!" *The Citizen,* 8 (June, 1964), 10–11; Los Angeles *Times,* June 26, 1964.

9 Los Angeles *Times,* July 1, 2, 1964. See also a form letter from Kent Steffgen, temporary chairman, organizing committee, Los Angeles Citizens' Council, to "Dear Patriot," June, 1964, Southern Regional Council.

10 Clyde Reynolds, president of the Greater Los Angeles Citizens' Council, as quoted in Atlanta *Constitution,* August 23, 1964.

11 Louis Hollis, as quoted in New York *Times,* August 5, 1964. For Hollis's early optimism on the Council's future in California, see also "Citizens' Councils Expand Activities in California!" *The Citizen,* 8 (June, 1964), 10–11.

12 Although unable to identify the reasons, an Anti-Defamation League observer of the West Coast Council noted that "a severe internal conflict" had resulted in "the expulsion of the whole of the leadership . . . from Kent Steffgen down." (Report, March 4, 1965, Southern Office, A-DL.)

foe of "Communist influence within the entertainment industry." The new field director, whose career in show business dated back to the early years of radio when he played "The Count of Monte Cristo,"[13] fared little better, and he too was supplanted. For its third representative in less than two years, the Council chose Frank E. Bain, a thirty-nine-year-old, college-educated businessman from San Diego who has continued in that position to the present day. Under his supervision a state association was formed at Burbank in August, 1966. By that date there were Councils operating in at least five southern California counties.[14]

From the outset, the operation in California proved to be a financial drain on the treasury of the Citizens' Councils of America. Having underwritten the organizational costs of its far-western outpost during its first two years of operation, the national office found it necessary—even after the formation of the statewide association—to provide the California Council with a monthly subsidy of $250.[15]

No less disconcerting to Mississippi professionals were the numerous difficulties encountered by the movement's western recruiters. More often than not liberal picketers at Council rallies outnumbered the segregationists, and to add further confusion, small but bellicose bands of swastika-wearing American Nazi Party members occasionally counterpicketed the picketers.[16] On several occasions Council-sponsored public gatherings were disrupted by disorderly and hostile Negro and white civil rights workers. At one such rally in San Diego during November, 1965, a crowd of nearly seven hundred hecklers so frequently interrupted an address by James G. Clark, Jr., sheriff of Dallas County, Alabama, that he was moved to threaten

13 "Californians Organize Local Citizens' Councils," *California Statesman,* February, 1965. Although not charging White himself with anti-Semitism, the Anti-Defamation League has noted that his wife, Opel Tanner White, once was the secretary of Gerald L. K. Smith. (Report, March 5, 1965, Southern Office, A-DL.)

14 The five counties were Kern, Los Angeles, Orange, Santa Clara, and San Diego. See Bakersfield *Californian,* March 12, 1966; *California Statesman,* February, 1966; *The California Councilman,* 3, No. 1, n.d.; Santa Ana *Register,* October 7, 1965; San Diego *Evening Tribune,* November 17, 1965.

15 *The California Councilman,* 3, No. 1, n.d.

16 See, for example, Los Angeles *Times,* July 1, 1964, March 5, 1965.

that he would "deliver this speech if it takes all night." [17] In Pasadena, where the Greater Los Angeles Council presented him with a black pistol-belt engraved with the words "Courage, Strength, Wisdom," Clark was unable to deliver his speech on "Sex and Civil Rights." Confronted by a noisy throng of civil rights demonstrators numbering nearly six hundred, he left the stage after fifteen futile minutes, angrily declaring that "this thing wouldn't happen in Selma." [18]

The Council's attempts to form new organizations, as well as its public meetings, were sometimes delayed and on several occasions permanently foiled by the work of liberal Californians. Perhaps the most notable failure occurred in the capital city where Meredith Crown, a civic-minded housewife who actively supported the state's open housing legislation, was appointed by Walter White as temporary secretary of the Sacramento Citizens' Council. Although alerting Mrs. Crown to the possibilities of "sabotage"—"we could be infiltrated during the early organizational meetings"—he entrusted her with the responsibility of inviting prospective members to the initial rally. Whereupon Mrs. Crown packed the audience with civil rights advocates who formed a Council, proceeded to endorse the Civil Rights Act of 1964, and opened their ranks to all persons "regardless of race, creed, or nationality." [19] Much embarrassed by this turn of events, White was soon forced to abandon altogether his efforts to organize the capital city when Clarence Edmund Patton, the man he had appointed as temporary chairman of the Sacramento organizational committee, was arrested and charged with interstate transportation of stolen securities, forgery, and possession of stolen property.[20]

Despite numerous setbacks and distressing failures, the movement in California survived. Ineffective though it was, by 1967 it possessed the strongest network of Councils to be found anywhere

[17] Quoted in San Diego *Evening Tribune,* November 17, 1965.

[18] Quoted in Los Angeles *Times,* November 16, 1965. See also Report, November 23, 1965, Southern Office, A-DL.

[19] Telephone interview with Meredith Crown, August, 1967; Walter White to Meredith Crown, April 13, 1965 (Copy in author's possession); Meredith Crown to the author, October 1, 1967; Sacramento *Union,* April 21, 1965.

[20] Patton, an advertising salesman for local radio stations, moved to Sacramento from Chicago in 1964. (Sacramento *Union,* June 21, 1965.)

outside the eleven states of the former Confederacy.[21] In part, this relative vitality may be attributed to the flexibility of the Council's approach. "We have no intention of incorporating southern social mores into California," Steffgen assured news reporters soon after his appointment as field director. "Our focus will be on state legislation." [22] Simmons, too, indicated that in its bid for a truly national organization, the Citizens' Councils of America was ready to suppress its regional bias in favor of a more national appeal. In an address to the first Council gathering in the state, he judiciously chose to identify the nascent movement on the West Coast, not with the embattled South but with what he called "the mainstream of American attitudes and values today." By forming a Citizens' Council, he declared, white Los Angelenos were simply joining "white majorities" in states across the nation who were girding themselves to resist federal "tyranny." "You are not alone in this fight," he informed California's charter Councilors. "There are millions who agree with you. They are ready to follow when you show the way." [23]

Perhaps even more skillful than Simmons at linking the Council with the "American mainstream" was William K. Shearer, a Republican political consultant and publisher of an ultraconservative San Franciso monthly newspaper, the *California Statesman.* Although only thirty-one years old in the summer of 1964, Shearer's reputation among California conservatives was already such that he served as administrative assistant to Republican Assemblyman E. Richard Barnes. And, when the California Real Estate Association launched its successful campaign that year to nullify the state's fair housing statutes, he was chosen to direct the attack.[24] He was also a frequent contributor to *The Citizen* and a vigorous Council recruiter. In 1966, when the statewide association was formed, he

[21] Interview with Louis Hollis, May 26, 1967.

[22] Quoted in Los Angeles *Times,* June 26, 1964. For amplification of this point, see *Action,* the monthly bulletin of the Greater Los Angeles Citizens' Council, April, 1966.

[23] Simmons, *Why California Is Organizing.*

[24] See Los Angeles *Times,* January 23, 1964; Norman Kilpatrick, "California to Maryland with the White Citizens' Councils" (unpublished paper, Southern Regional Council, [1965]), 1.

became both a member of its executive committee and its secretary-treasurer.[25] But it was as a propagandist that he was most useful to the organization. Although an avowed white supremacist who openly advocated that the Republican party forsake the Negro in order to win the votes of southern segregationists,[26] Shearer preferred the subtleties of innuendo to head-on assault. In his newspaper columns, pamphlets, and public speeches, he employed a submerged kind of racism to identify the Citizens' Council program in California with the needs of the state's "majority community." Articulated in numerous variations, the essence of the Republican publisher's argument was simple enough: "The 'liberal' political power structure which now dominates California government, and which has effectively denied representation to the majority community is built upon the fragile mechanics of combining—for control purposes—a number of economic, ethnic, and racial minority voting blocs." To rid the state of this "liberal-leftist power bloc," it was simply necessary to create "an effective majority community consensus." As a full decade of Deep South experience amply demonstrated, such a consensus could best be achieved through the medium of the Citizens' Council.[27]

When the CCA launched its drive in the summer of 1964 to organize California, the state was already in the midst of creating what Shearer called the first great example of a "majority community consensus."[28] Since January, the so-called Committee for Home Protection, supported by the California Real Estate Association and the Apartment Owner's Association of California, had been boosting

[25] *California Councilman*, 3, No. 1, n.d. See also Shearer's "Use of Federal Force Heralds Dictatorship," *The Citizen*, 7 (November, 1962), 19–22, and "Can Conservatives Unite to Save Our Nation?" *The Citizen*, 7 (February, 1963), 4–6.

[26] See esp. William K. Shearer, "Can Conservatives Unite to Save Our Nation?" *The Citizen*, 7 (February, 1963), 4–6; Kilpatrick, "California to Maryland with the White Citizens' Councils," 1.

[27] William K. Shearer, *The Majority Consensus: An Address to the Los Angeles Citizens' Councils, March 4, 1965* (Jackson: Citizens' Councils of America, n.d.). For similar statements, see also *Why Must San Diego County Organize?*, and editorial, *California Statesman*, February, 1966.

[28] William K. Shearer, "California Voters Win Big Victory in Battle against Mixed Housing!" *The Citizen*, 9 (November, 1964), 9–10.

an initiative campaign to repeal by constitutional amendment the state's Unruh and Rumford acts, which banned racial discrimination in the sale or rental of most privately owned real property. Upon its arrival in June, the Council joined the effort, endeavoring to exploit the wide popular support for Proposition 14, as the proposed amendment was called. Summarizing the organization's position with considerably more candor than syntax, the president of the newly formed Greater Los Angeles Citizens' Council observed: "There are a lot of people who are liberals who are worried about their private property. They may have certain general liberal views, but when it comes down to a man's house, to a man's apartment, to who do I live next door to, those people agree with us." [29] As the verdict at the polls demonstrated in November, 1964, this assessment was not altogether incorrect. Proposition 14 carried every county in the state except one, winning a majority of more than 65 percent.[30] Whether or not the amendment can be viewed as an expression of the white majority's revulsion for open housing, as *The Citizen* proclaimed, there can be little question that segregation, when draped in the raiment of private ownership rights, possessed broad appeal outside of the South.

Encouraged by the response of conservatives in the Golden State, the Council divulged plans for membership drives in "all 50 states, including Alaska and Hawaii." [31] Moving next to the border state of Maryland, it launched a recruiting campaign in the midsummer of 1964 with promises to liberate the state's white majority from left-wing dominated, bloc-voting minority groups. In its bid for popular support, the organization joined indigenous segregationist groups, notably the Maryland Petition Committee and the Dorchester County Businessmen's and Citizens' Association, in an unsuccessful endeavor to repeal a recently enacted public accommodations

[29] Quoted in Atlanta *Constitution,* August 23, 1964.

[30] "Right Turn in California?" *New Republic,* 152 (January 16, 1965), 18; "The Backlashers," *The Citizen,* 9 (November, 1964), 23. Proposition 14, which became Section 26 of the California constitution, was found unconstitutional by the state Supreme Court in 1966. In June, 1967, The U.S. Supreme Court upheld the California decision. See "Saying No to Proposition 14," *Time,* 89 (June 9, 1967), 75.

[31] Louis Hollis, as quoted by Ben A. Franklin, "Race Group Opens Maryland Drive," New York *Times,* September 13, 1964.

law.[32] In January, 1965, it assumed the lead in a campaign to ban a state open occupancy law by constitutional amendment.[33]

Leading the Council's expansionist drive into Maryland was field director Joseph McDowell Mitchell, a native son who as city manager of Newburgh, New York, won wide respect in conservative circles, both North and South, for his austere welfare policies.[34] Mitchell was a veteran of both World War II and the Korean War, a college graduate, and an archsegregationist who had only recently rejected a position on the professional staff of the John Birch Society because of that organization's equivocal posture on race.[35] Optimistic about the future of organized racism in Maryland, Mitchell predicted soon after his appointment in July that by election day in November, Maryland's white majority would be sufficiently organized to make its presence known at the polls. Furthermore, he anticipated that before the new year arrived a state association with a paid full-time director based in Annapolis would be effectively neutralizing the previously dominant influence of "brainwashed" equalitarianism on state and local government.[36] But despite his apparent aptitude for the job, and his roseate hopes, Mitchell's record as a Council organizer was not lustrous. Within a year the Council in Maryland was something of a laughingstock in the nation's press, and Mitchell himself was drummed out of the organization.

[32] Maryland's limited public accommodations law, passed by the state General Assembly in March, 1964, received sufficient popular support at the polls in November to have its coverage extended to eleven additional counties previously not covered. See New York *Times,* November 4, 5, 1964.

[33] See Kilpatrick, "California to Maryland with the White Citizens' Councils," 3, and his "The White Citizens' Councils Move North" (unpublished paper, Southern Regional Council, [1965]); Baltimore *Sun,* January 28, 1965.

[34] In 1961, Mitchell was named "Man of the Year" by the New York State Taxpayers' Party. ("New Field Men Join Citizens' Council Staff," *The Citizen,* 8 [July–August, 1964], 10–11.) See also A. H. Raskin, "Newburgh's Lesson for the Nation," *New York Times Magazine,* December 17, 1961; George Fowler, "The Newburgh Question—Who's Being 'Inhuman'?" *Human Events,* 18 (August 4, 1961), 500.

[35] See Norman Kilpatrick, "Councils Divided over John Birch Society" (unpublished paper, Southern Regional Council, [1965]).

[36] New York *Times,* July 25; Baltimore *Sun,* September 15, 1964.

The first recruiting rally in the state occurred late in September, 1964, in Glen Burnie. Although perhaps as many as 25,000 Ann Arundel Countians were invited to join, only about 200 appeared at the organizational meeting at the Glen Burnie armory—and a disappointingly large percentage of these were nuisance-minded liberals, including several District of Columbia NAACP officials.[37] From this point forward, Mitchell's problems in Maryland were only to be compounded. A second rally, held in the wealthy Washington suburb of Bethesda, where the field director hoped to organize a Montgomery County Council on September 29, was broken up when Negro and white civil rights sympathizers staged a sit-in demonstration. Later in the fall, a Montgomery group was formed, but a small membership and local indifference held out little promise for its survival.[38]

Still another organizational effort in Prince Georges County suffered numerous setbacks throughout the months of October, November, and December, and it was only after the local leadership had been changed three times that a small organization was formed.[39] Despite a membership of only twenty, the Prince Georges County Citizens' Council was a promising group. Among its members were two attorneys, a pair of journalists, a museum curator, a college professor, a Catholic priest, and several federal employees. Not only was it Mitchell's "model Maryland chapter," but it was also, in his opinion, one of the "finest, most active, intelligent Councils I've ever seen."[40] Indeed, so pleased was he with Norman Kilpatrick, the resourceful twenty-seven-year-old president of the group, that he invited him to come along when he attended the annual leadership conference at Montgomery, Alabama, in January, 1965. At the conference, Kilpatrick reported briefly on his work in

[37] Baltimore *Sun,* September 23; Baltimore *Afro-American,* October 3, 1964.

[38] Kilpatrick, "Report on D.C., Virginia, and Maryland Work Given by Joe Mitchell"; Washington *Post,* October 9, 1964, June 10, 1965.

[39] See a single-page sketch by Norman Kilpatrick, "Short History of the Citizens' Councils in Maryland" (unpublished paper, Southern Regional Council, [1965]).

[40] Quoted in Baltimore *Sun,* January 27, 1965. See also New York *Times,* January 28, 1965; Tom Kelley, "Catch a Bigot by the Toe," *Nation,* 200 (February 15, 1965), 169–70.

Maryland, posed eagerly for pictures with such heroes of segregation as George Wallace and Leander Perez, and even offered the suggestion, apparently in all seriousness, that the Citizens' Councils of America adopt "We Shall Overcome" as its theme song.[41]

The Council's leadership did not adopt this proposal, although Robert Patterson considered it a good idea. But it was obviously impressed by the dynamic, youthful Marylander. This opinion was rapidly revised. Soon after returning from Montgomery, Kilpatrick, with the support of fully eighteen of his twenty-member Council, merged the model Maryland chapter with the local chapter of the Congress of Racial Equality.[42] After releasing the story to the press and turning over to the Federal Bureau of Investigation all confidential records,[43] Kilpatrick and his civil rights–minded Councilors announced a scheme to infiltrate and expose the plans of Councils in other Maryland cities as well as in neighboring Virginia by April Fool's Day.[44]

Mitchell did not long survive the fiasco of Prince Georges County. Out of favor with the CCA, he returned to city management, this time in Holidaysburg, Pennsylvania.[45] But the problems in Maryland were not solved simply by changing field directors. Mitchell's successor, Lee A. Dodson, a Rockville carpenter and stalwart of both the Montgomery County Citizens' Council and the Maryland

[41] See Norman Kilpatrick, "Impressions from a White Citizens' Council Conference," (unpublished paper, Southern Regional Council, [1965]); and his "I Was a Member of the Citizens' Council," Baltimore *Afro-American*, February 20, 1965.

[42] Kelley, "Catch a Bigot by the Toe," 169–70; Carlyle Rivers, "Reporters Help to Turn Racial Group into Farce," *Editor and Publisher*, 98 (February 6, 1965), 55.

[43] Copies of all of the records turned over by Kilpatrick to the FBI may be seen at the Southern Regional Council—including one bearing the following note: "Norm, this list would be valuable to the liberals, and would seriously embarrass me if it gets in the wrong hands. Please take care." It was signed by Mitchell. Regarding this material, see Joseph McD. Mitchell to Norman Kilpatrick, January 24, 1965, copy in files of the Southern Regional Council.

[44] In all, Kilpatrick named fifteen cities, including St. Louis, Los Angeles, and San Diego, as well as Baltimore and Annapolis, Maryland, and Norfolk, Hampton, and Windsor, Virginia. (New York *Times*, Februray 19, 1965.)

[45] Mitchell was fired in July, 1965. See Report, August 5, 1965, Southern Office, A-DL; Washington *Post*, May 18, 1966.

Petition Committee, did manage to organize an Association of Citizens' Councils of Maryland. But as late as 1966 it had only four constituent Councils. With the exception of the Baltimore chapter, which may have had at one time as many as two hundred members, none of these could boast anything but a tiny membership.[46] To be sure, the organization continued to fare so poorly that the Washington *Post* caustically reported in May, 1966, that "the white Citizens Councils may be doing all right in Alabama, but in Maryland, where they have been trying for [two] years to get a toehold, they have turned into a standing joke." "The problem faced by the Citizens Councils in Maryland," the *Post* observed, "is that they have been so infiltrated that the infiltrators are tripping over one another." [47]

Poorer still was the Council's recruiting record in major cities in such scattered states as Colorado, Missouri, and New York. In New York City, once described by a CCA mogul as the very "fountainhead and intellectual source of the whole collectivist revolution in our nation," [48] a 1965 organizational rally failed to materialize when Louis Hollis was unable to secure a meeting place.[49] Only slightly more hospitable were St. Louis [50] and Denver,[51] where Council organizers did manage to form small but noisy groups during the summers of 1964 and 1965, respectively. Con-

[46] Kilpatrick, "Report on D.C., Virginia, and Maryland Work Given by Joe Mitchell."

[47] Peter A. Jay, "Infiltrators Tripping up Rights Foes," Washington *Post,* May 18, 1966.

[48] Simmons, *Why California Is Organizing.*

[49] New York *Times,* June 18; Jackson *Daily News,* June 19, 1965.

[50] The St. Louis Metropolitan Area Citizens' Council was organized under the direction of Medford Evans and Joseph Mitchell on October 10, 1965. During the fall of 1965, the president of that organization, the Reverend W. C. Barlow, announced plans for the formation of future groups in Cape Girardeau, Jefferson City, Kansas City, St. Joseph, and Springfield. Apparently none of these materialized, and the St. Louis Council itself required remobilization in December, 1968. (St. Louis *Post-Dispatch,* September 29, October 12, 15, 1964, November 29, 1965; *The Citizen,* May, 1969, 18–21.)

[51] The Denver Council was organized by William K. Shearer and Louis Hollis on August 5, 1965. By October, its president, Lyman E. Steel, a native of Memphis, boasted that the group had 1,000 members. See a reprint of Shearer's address, "The Majority Must Mobilize," *The Citizen,* 9 (September, 1965), 7–17; *Why Must Denver Organize?* [Jackson, 1965]; Denver *Post,* November 29, 1965.

fronted as they were by hostile community officials and an unresponsive citizenry,[52] neither organization enjoyed a promising future.

The numerous reversals occasioned by the Council's endeavors to extend its influence beyond the former Confederacy made necessary a revision in the tactical procedures it employed in organizing northern and western communities. As late as March, 1964, only a few months before the formation of the first nonsouthern Council, *The Citizen* carried a treatise on proper recruiting techniques which advised that careful screening of prospective members before an organizational rally was unnecessary: "All you need to know about those receiving invitations [to join in forming a new Council] is that they are white. Don't worry about those with white skins and black hearts. The overwhelming sentiment of the American people is on our side. The few scalawags receiving your invitation will not cause trouble. Most of them are yellow anyway, and if they do attend your meeting they will keep their mouths shut." [53] Only a few embarrassing episodes such as that in St. Georges County, Maryland, exploded this naïve supposition. Very soon the CCA was recommending less open tactics in order to avoid what the "White Book" referred to as "unfortunate experiences and unfriendly troublemakers." In 1965, the official handbook admonished pointedly that "experience has shown that it is usually best to give no publicity to the organizational rally." [54]

In some areas, the Councilors were so harried by hostile forces that even relatively routine gatherings occasionally assumed something of a cloak-and-dagger aura. One such meeting in Los Angeles in March, 1965, was observed by an anonymous agent of the Anti-Defamation League. According to his hastily recorded impressions, there were about sixty-five persons present, most of whom were "middle aged couples," and "flanking the meeting hall were scores

[52] In December, 1964, the community relations director of the St. Louis Police Department linked the Citizens' Council in that city with the States' Rights Party as a potential threat to the city's welfare. (St. Louis *Post-Dispatch,* December 11, 1964.) For an account of official hostility to the Councils' presence in Denver, see Report, November 23, 1965, Southern Office, A-DL.

[53] Poteat, "How to Organize a Citizens' Council," *The Citizen,* 8 (March, 1964), 13.

[54] "White Book," 14.

of men, dressed in business suits with 'usher' cards pined [*sic*] on their jackets. These were the omnipresent 'security detail,' the most distinctive feature of the Council [in California]. They cordoned off the hall, roamed through the parklots equipted with walkie-talkies reporting on any suspicious movements and surveyed closely the meeting itself." [55]

Secret meetings and tighter security, however, were not enough. Beyond Dixie's frontiers, the Council's greatest successes remained minor, its failures almost legion. While the CCA may have been, as its Mississippi leadership unabashedly asserted, "the most powerful and largest white supremacy organization in the nation" by the mid-1960's,[56] it was such only because it had so little competition. Even within the former Confederacy, there was no longer a mass Council movement by that time—nor had there been for half a decade or more. Having reached a zenith by 1957, resistance groups throughout the South began a steady decline, and by the end of the decade grassroots support for organized racism had either vanished or was greatly diminished in every southern state. Despite a vigorous remobilization effort by some of segregation's most accomplished spokesmen, the organization never regained the broad popular base it enjoyed within the region during the early post-*Brown* period.

Beset as they were by disinterest from within the region and discomfiture from without, Council spokesmen grew hesitant in discussing the organization's numerical strength. State associations, probably as a matter of official policy, became increasingly taciturn on the topic of membership. Local leaders tended to demur when pressed for figures. Even the Mississippi professionals were close-lipped on the subject, professing inability to estimate accurately Council strength. Membership in the Citizens' Council, one Jackson official insisted, was comparable to church membership: many Councilors, not unlike many Baptists and Methodists, drifted in and out of active participation. While they may have fallen behind in their monthly contributions, they nevertheless continued to regard themselves as loyal members.[57] In times of crisis, most official spokesmen professed to believe that all Councilors, whether dues-

[55] Report, March 4, 1965, Southern Office, A–DL.
[56] Kilpatrick, "The White Citizens' Councils Move North," 1.
[57] Interview with William J. Simmons, May 26, 1967.

paying or otherwise, would stand united behind the Citizens' Councils of America and the defense of white supremacy.

This reticence was, of course, a departure from previous behavior. In earlier, more palmy days, leaders on every level boasted readily of burgeoning membership rosters. As early as August, 1956, only a few months after the formation of the CCA, the movement's official newspaper vaunted a membership of 500,000 white southern citizens.[58] Early in 1958, William J. Simmons offered a revised but still unrealistic figure of 350,000.[59] No reliable figures are available, and until Council records are opened to the researcher (and it does not appear that they will ever be), there can be no precise means of gauging the organization's maximum strength. Nevertheless, it seems unlikely that membership in all southern resistance groups combined ever exceeded 300,000. In all probability, the Council in its heyday never had as many as 250,000 members.[60]

In more recent years, federal legislation requiring an annual statement of average monthly circulation figures by most periodicals has provided a fairly accurate index for measuring Council membership. The earliest such statement published by the CCA's official organ appeared in September, 1960, and it revealed that monthly circulation to paid subscribers averaged 50,000 during the previous year.[61]

58 "Council Movement Spreads as Nation Reacts to Danger," *The Citizens' Council,* August, 1956, 1.

59 Simmons, *The Mid-West Hears the South's Story,* 12.

60 Estimates of the Council's strength have been as varied as the estimators themselves. One of the highest figures was suggested by the Gale Research Company, which placed the Council's membership at 750,000. See *Encyclopedia of Associations, Volume 1: National Organizations of the United States* (Detroit: Gale Research Company, 1964), 621. In 1956, a spokesman for the United Press stated that "conservative estimates" of the Council's membership put the total well over 500,000—"but no one can say for sure because it swells by the hundreds daily." (*Delta Democrat-Times,* March 15, 1956.) Paul Anthony of the Southern Regional Council, who observed the Council's early development more closely than perhaps any other person, suggested in 1957 that 325,000 was a "conservative estimate" for all resistance organizations. (Routh and Anthony, "Southern Resistance Forces," 50.) See also Southern Regional Council, *Special Report: Pro-Segregation Groups in the South,* 13. James Vander Zanden has fixed the Council's maximum strength at 250,000. ("The Citizens' Councils," *Alpha Kappa Deltan,* 29 [Spring, 1959], 3–9.)

61 *The Citizens' Council,* September, 1960, 4.

Quite possibly, paid membership in 1960 exceeded that figure, for at that time subscription to *The Citizens' Council* was optional in most states. But subsequently, under the so-called "central billing plan" prescribed by the "White Book," a subscription to the monthly magazine became a condition of membership. It is true that the compulsory subscription plan applied only to those Councils organized or reorganized by the Citizens' Councils of America after 1961. But it is also true that such a condition included almost every active Citizens' Council in the country, except, of course, many of those found in the three Deep South states of Alabama, Louisiana and Mississippi. Furthermore, the constitution of the Alabama state association required that each membership include a subscription, as did the constitutions of most local Mississippi Councils.[62] It is quite possible, therefore, that by 1966—the year of the CCA's tenth anniversary—the Council's total dues-paying membership did not greatly exceed the circulation of its journal, *The Citizen,* which averaged only 21,844 subscriptions per month.[63]

But if the organization men in Mississippi were troubled by the shrinking appeal of the Citizens' Council or apprehensive about what lay ahead, their public expressions gave no indication. Although unwilling to provide information on current membership, they were seldom reluctant to discuss the movement's future. In the spring of 1967, the national executive director, Louis Hollis, spoke enthusiastically of the Council's continued growth, and he indicated that if present-day expansions were maintained the organization would enjoy the allegiance of no fewer than 750,000 Councilors by late 1968.[64] As if to prove that Hollis's prediction was no idle boast, *The Citizen* for October, 1967, announced the commencement of construction of a new national office building in Jackson to provide staff headquarters for "the expanding organizational activities of the Councils from coast to coast." Completed during the summer of 1968

62 Leonard R. Wilson, "Some Helpful Tools," *The Citizen,* 8 (March, 1964), 20.

63 Sworn annual statements published in *The Citizen* provide the following average monthly subscription figures for the years 1961–67: 45,000, 1961; 50,000, 1962; 23,056, 1963; 26,896, 1964; 25,543, 1965; 21,844, 1966; 21,688, 1967; 20,062, 1968; 24,478, 1969.

64 Interview with Louis Hollis, May 26, 1967.

at a cost of $162,000, the handsome, modern, two-story "shrine and fortress" of glass and stone was constructed near the state capitol on property once owned by a Confederate general.[65]

[65] *The Citizen,* 12 (October, 1967), 19; 13 (November, 1968), 5–9, 10–11, 12.

PART III

Ideology

CHAPTER IX

The Prosegregation Argument

"SELDOM have so few been accepted by so many as the voice of all," declared Wilma Dykeman and James Stokely. After traveling through thirteen southern and border states to sample the region's mood, this husband and wife team from Tennessee concluded in their award-winning book *Neither Black nor White* (1957) that "North and South, the W[hite] C[itizens'] C[ouncil]'s defiant pronouncements have been heeded as 'the' voice of 'the' South."[1] Indeed, although always a numerical minority, the organization did become the mouthpiece of southern defiance. Its affirmations on race and states' rights were quoted in the nation's congressional chambers and in state legislative halls. From pulpits, editorial columns, political hustings, and schoolhouse lecterns, the assumptions of the movement were approvingly reiterated. Its propaganda films and tape recordings were used weekly by sympathetic television and radio stations in many parts of the region, and its pamphlets, many of which were superbly printed, were distributed either free or at a nominal fee to defiant whites across the South.

Yet despite the wide exposure of its views on race and government, the Council movement as a whole did not develop a systematic intellectual framework in which to operate. For Council attitudes, like the subregions in which they evolved, frequently varied from one locality to the next. The Citizens' Councils of Florida dif-

[1] Wilma Dykeman and James Stokely, *Neither Black nor White* (New York: Rinehart, 1957), 109.

fered from the Citizens' Councils of Mississippi, just as the peripheral South differed from the Deep South. Nor was the regional organization, the Citizens' Councils of America, able to overcome this intra-organization heterogeneity. Although seldom hesitating to speak for state and local Councils on matters of general policy, CCA headquarters in Jackson never managed to dominate fully the entire movement. Unlike such authoritarian-structured organizations as the John Birch Society and the Nation of Islam, there emerged within the Council movement no authority figure—no Robert Welch, no Elijah Muhammad—possessed of sufficient power to dictate policy. The CCA's president, Roy V. Harris, was little more than a figurehead whose frequently embarrassing extremist utterances were endured but not always adhered to. Even William J. Simmons, the most powerful member of the Council's professional staff, never presumed to speak in anything but general terms for the organization's rank and file. True to the original design, the Council associations of the various states remained largely autonomous. Although the several state Councils, through their publications and public professions, exercised considerable influence over local Council organizations, ultimate authority over a wide range of actions rested with the local leadership itself.

The results of this decentralization were confusing, as the status of the Jew within the movement's racial construct well illustrated. Although the CCA from the outset endeavored to dissociate the Council from the onus of anti-Semitism, an anti-Jewish undercurrent persisted within the ranks of the movement. Despite its repeated disavowals, the organization's headquarters never managed to refute effectively the charge that it was anti-Jew as well as anti-Negro.[2] Periodic professions of innocence by William J. Simmons and other CCA professionals were not sufficient to offset the blatant Jew-baiting of state and local Councils in Louisiana and Arkansas,[3] for example, nor to obscure the occasional anti-

2 See esp. Southern Regional Council, "Partial Description of Anti-Semitic Activities, and of Literature Recommended and Distributed by White Citizens' Councils and Other Groups in the South" (unpublished manuscript, Southern Regional Council, February 27, 1956); interoffice memoranda, 1960–62, Southern Office, A-DL.

3 The newspapers published by both the Citizens' Councils of Arkansas

Semitic outbursts of the organization's own president, Roy Harris.[4]

But though much of Citizens' Council thought may have been fraught with contradictions and incongruities, there was a common body of assumptions generally acceptable to the entire movement. Though disagreement existed on many issues, all Councilors could agree with the CCA's executive director, Louis W. Hollis, when he declared the United States to be "a white man's government, conceived by white men and maintained by them through every year of its history." Like Hollis, they were united in their determination that "by the God of our fathers, it shall be ruled by the white man until the end of time." [5]

Primarily the ideology of the Citizens' Council was the ideology of white supremacy. Like Negrophobes of an earlier age the Councilors rested their case for white dominance on the postulate that Negroes were inherently different from Caucasians and that this difference, this hereditary inferiority, rendered them unsuitable for free association with white society.[6] In the Council's view the black man's presence could be tolerated only so long as the range of his economic, political, and social interaction with the white man's world could be systematically defined. In the Council's syllogism of white supremacy, then, segregation was the conclusion that necessarily followed the premise that human worth is calculable in terms of apparent physical characteristics.

The color-caste notion of social structure in mid-twentieth century

---

and the Citizens' Councils of Louisiana are replete with anti-Semitic suggestions.

4 Harris's latent anti-Semitism emerged occasionally, as it did in the Augusta *Courier,* December 7, 1959. Although insisting that he was not "prejudiced against the Jews, or the members of any other race," Harris, the arch-Negrophobe, stated that "Jewish money and Jewish influence" must be directed away from "race-mixing" or the Jewish "race" may suffer "the wrath of the Anglo-Saxon people in this nation."

5 Louis W. Hollis, *Integrity: An Address to the Annual Conference of the Citizens' Councils of America, Montgomery, Alabama, January 16, 1965* (Jackson: Citizens' Councils of America, n.d.), 5.

6 See Guion Griffis Johnson, "The Ideology of White Supremacy, 1876–1910," *Essays in Southern History,* ed. Fletcher Melvin Green (Chapel Hill: University of North Carolina Press, 1949), 124–56; and James W. Vander Zanden, "The Ideology of White Supremacy," *Journal of the History of Ideas,* 20 (June–September, 1959), 385–402.

America, as in earlier periods, thrived on the expression of racial differences. Councilors, like white supremacists before them, indulged their most imaginative fancies in delineating these differences. In order to demonstrate to southern school children that the black was not simply "a sun-burned white man," the CCA enumerated in an official handbook for fifth- and sixth-graders what it believed to be the eleven most essential differences between the two races:

1. The Negro's arm is about two inches longer than the white man's.
2. The jaw is shaped differently.
3. The weight of the brains differ.
4. The eyes are different.
5. The noses are different.
6. The lips are different.
7. The cheek bones are different.
8. The skulls are different.
9. The ears are different.
10. The hair is different.
11. The voices are different.[7]

Many of the Council's publications for adult consumption were hardly more sophisticated. Typical of this genre of propaganda was a Mississippi association brochure, *Racial Facts,* which listed such standard racist "facts" as "the Negro IQ is from 15 to 20 points below the average white IQ" and the "characteristic odor of the Negro's skin . . . is inherent and not caused by uncleanliness."[8]

One of the most intemperate expressions of racial differences may be found in Judge Brady's *Black Monday.* Throughout the movement's first decade, this hastily written, unabashedly racist manifesto of white southern resistance was widely regarded as the most systematic expression of Council thought. A spiritual descendant of such best-selling historical romances of an earlier generation as Thomas Dixon's *The Leopard's Spots* (1902) and *The Clansman* (1905), *Black Monday* contained a portrait of the Negro which recalled a description given by one of Dixon's characters.[9] Speaking

[7] "A Manual for Southerners," *The Citizens' Council,* June, 1957, 3.

[8] Association of Citizens' Councils of Mississippi, *Racial Facts* (n.p., n.d.), 5.

[9] Despite his ties with the Ku Klux Klan, which the more respectable

through a Clansman, the novelist had described a "creature, half-child, half-animal . . . a being who left to his will, roams at night and sleeps in the day, whose speech knows no word of love, whose passions, once aroused, are the fury of the tiger. . . ."[10] In faithful paraphrase, Brady echoed: "You can dress a chimpanzee, house-break him, and teach him to use a knife and fork, but it will take countless generations of evolutionary development, if ever, before you can convince him that a caterpillar or a cockroach is not a delicacy. Likewise the social, political, economic, and religious preferences of the Negro remain close to the caterpillar and the cockroach. . . ."[11]

But the venomous Negro-baiting that served Thomas Dixon so well early in the twentieth century could have little appeal to more sophisticated modern Americans. Since the days of the silent cinema when Dixon's glorification of white supremacy in its film version, *The Birth of a Nation,* had been seen by an estimated one hundred million people,[12] the burden of proof of Negro inferiority had gradually shifted from the black man to the white racists themselves. Well before World War I, new-school social scientists, led by anthropologist Franz Boas, began to challenge not only misguided popular notions on race but the ill-founded theories of older generations of sociologists, anthropologists, and psychologists, whose speculations about innate racial traits had long dignified the illogic of prejudice.[13] Indeed, by 1944 scientific thought in the United

---

Citizens' Councils held in contempt, Councilors often felt a kinship with Dixon. See untitled, undated Citizens' Councils of America broadside, Southern Education Reporting Service, which contains excerpts from *The Leopard's Spots* and *The Clansman.* See also *The Councilor,* March 6, 1967, and the Kansas City, Missouri, Citizens' Council, *The Greater Citizen,* August 15, 1969.

[10] Quoted in Muse, *Ten Years of Prelude,* 41–42. Muse suggests "one might suspect that Judge Brady had just put down an old copy of *The Leopard's Spots.*"

[11] Brady, *Black Monday,* 12. In retrospect, Brady informed the author that this passage of his book was "unfortunate," the "product of too much haste." Nevertheless, he insisted that the analogy was valid: "It's all true. I wouldn't change a word of it."

[12] *Variety,* January 8, 1958, as cited by Muse, *Ten Years of Prelude,* 41.

[13] Standard studies of scientific racism in the United States include: William Stanton, *The Leopard's Spots: Scientific Attitudes toward Race in America,*

States had progressed to a point where Gunnar Myrdal could approvingly observe that *"it is now difficult for even popular writers to express other views than the ones of racial equalitarianism and still retain intellectual respect."* [14]

Yet the race theories so prominent in an earlier age had not capitulated; they were merely in retreat. On May 17, 1954, when the Supreme Court at last guaranteed equal educational opportunities, scientists of the old school began dusting off their outmoded conceptions in preparation for the campaign against what William J. Simmons liked to call "the equalitarian dogma" of modern science.[15] Once again the authority of science, that perennial handmaiden of race bigotry, was invoked by those who sought to negate the Negro's constitutional right to full citizenship. But the "new racism," as Oscar Handlin has called it,[16] differed markedly in several respects from the old. Most noticeably, it abandoned the widely inclusive discriminatory pattern of the past

---

1815–1859 (Chicago: University of Chicago Press, 1960); William Sumner Jenkins, *Pro-Slavery Thought in the Old South* (Chapel Hill: University of North Carolina Press, 1935); Thomas F. Gossett, *Race: The History of an Idea in America* (New York: Schocken Books, 1965); John Higham, *Strangers in the Land: Patterns of American Nativism, 1866–1925* (New Brunswick: Rutgers University Press, 1955); Oscar Handlin, *Race and Nationality in American Life* (Boston: Little, Brown, 1957); Idus A. Newby, *Jim Crow's Defense: Anti-Negro Thought in America, 1900–1930* (Baton Rouge: Louisiana State University Press, 1965).

14 Gunner Myrdal, *An American Dilemma: The Negro Problem and Modern Democracy* (New York: Harper and Brothers, 1944), Vol. 1, 96. See also Newby, *Jim Crow's Defense*, viii.

15 Simmons's fondness for this expression can be seen in much of his writing and speech-making. For example, see the following addresses: *Race Relations and Civil Rights: An Address to the Yale Political Union, New Haven, Connecticut, February 28, 1963* (n.p., n.d.); *Why Segregation Is Right: An Address Presented at Notre Dame University, South Bend, March 7, 1963* (n.p., n.d.); *Civil Rights and the Second Reconstruction: An Address to the Jefferson Society, University of Virginia, Charlottesville, March 22, 1963* (n.p., n.d.).

16 For a brief but suggestive analysis of the post-*Brown* genre of scientific racism, see Handlin, *Fire Bell in the Night: The Crisis in Civil Rights* (Boston: Little, Brown, 1964), 73–85. A much fuller statement on the same subject is Idus A. Newby, *Challenge to the Court: Social Scientists and the Defense of Segregation, 1954–1966* (Baton Rouge: Louisiana State University Press, 1967).

and identified only one inferior human type. An older generation of scientific racists, including Anglo-Saxon nativists like Madison Grant and Theodore Lothrop Stoddard, had created a veritable pyramid of human worth with "Nordics" representing the apex, other members of the "races" of Europe—the "Alpines" and the "Mediterraneans"—enjoying lesser though still exalted status, and the "dregs" of humanity, the Negro among them, situated at the base. The white supremacists of the new racist persuasion, however, resorted to the shibboleths of Anglo-Saxonism only infrequently; rather, their focus was the black man. Second, and far more important, neoracism could not hide beneath the protective canopy of intellectual respectability. Although an earlier age had seldom questioned biological interpretations of history and civilization, the newly refurbished scientific racism had limited appeal to the American public of the mid-twentieth century.

Not remarkably, then, Carleton Putnam, the most influential spokesman of the new racism, was not a scientist at all, but a retired airline executive. When he turned to ethnology in 1958, Putnam had a baccalaureate degree in history and politics from Princeton and a degree in law from Columbia; he had pioneered in commercial aviation and been chairman of the board of Delta Air Lines;[17] he had written an interesting and highly readable memoir about his career, and he was the author of an impressive history of Theodore Roosevelt's early years.[18] By any standard, this was a commendable record; but it could hardly qualify him as an authority on cultural anthropology. Yet despite his lack of formal credentials in the biological and natural sciences, Putnam had qualities that would well serve the cause of segregation. Possessed of an impeccable pedigree stretching back in American history to

17 William D. McCain, "Who Is Carleton Putnam?" *The Citizen,* 6 (November, 1961), 9–11.

18 Carleton Putnam, *High Journey: A Decade in the Pilgrimage of an Air Lines Pioneer* (New York: Charles Scribner's Sons, 1945); *Theodore Roosevelt: A Biography,* Vol. 1: *The Formative Years, 1858–1886* (New York: Scribner's, 1958). Although only the first of a projected four-volume effort has appeared, Putnam's life of Roosevelt has been well received. In the words of Howard K. Beale, "Putnam has written an interesting and important book that any professionally trained historian could be proud of." See *American Historical Review,* 64 (October, 1958), 124–26.

the French and Indian Wars, he was clearly of Yankee stock and therefore not subject to accusations of regional bias. An impassioned social and economic conservative who viewed race as the key to civilization, this descendent of a Revolutionary War hero[19] fancied himself a kind of latter-day ethnological Paul Revere riding to alarm a sleeping people of the perils of racial miscegenations.

Setting forth his ethnological assumption in an influential and widely circulated book, *Race and Reason* (1961), Putnam asserted that one need not have advanced scientific training to dispute theories of racial equalitarianism: "Any man with two eyes in his head can observe a Negro settlement in the Congo . . . can compare this settlement with London or Paris, and can draw his own conclusions regarding relative levels of character and intelligence. . . ." That so few informed Americans saw things so clearly was compelling proof to Putnam that the nation had been victimized by a "pseudo-scientific hoax" popularized by such early exponents of racial equipotentiality as Franz Boas and several subsequent generations of like-minded anthropologists more devoted to "the demi-Goddess of Equalitarianism" than to "the Goddess of Truth."[20]

A veritable white supremacist's catechism consisting largely of refutations of desegregation arguments, *Race and Reason* reportedly sold 60,000 copies in its first six months; by 1969 its publisher indicated that sales totaled 150,000.[21] Taking early note of this reception, the Council of the American Anthropological Association denounced Putnam's position. Similarly critical were the Committee

19 William D. McCain observes that Putnam "is directly descended from the grandfather of Israel Putnam . . . and from the brother of General Rufus Putnam. . . ." ("Who Is Carleton Putnam?" *The Citizen*, 6 [November, 1961], 9.)

20 *Race and Reason: A Yankee View* (Washington: Public Affairs Press, 1961). Putnam's more recent *Race and Reality* is a similar, though enlarged, treatment of the same subject. For Putnam's defense of his "scientific" views on race, see his *These Are the Guilty: Address Delivered before the Washington Putnam Letters Club, February 12, 1963* (Richmond: National Putnam Letters Committee, n.d.).

21 M. B. Schnapper, editor, Public Affairs Press, to the author, March 24, 1970.

on Science in the Promotion of Human Welfare (an affiliate of the American Association for the Advancement of Science), the American Association of Physical Anthropologists, and a host of leading scientists, including the geneticist Theodosius Dobzhansky, all of whom issued statements condemning the work as unscientific.[22] But the disapprobation of distinguished scholars and learned societies had little effect, either on Putnam or the prosegregation South.

Senators J. Strom Thurmond of South Carolina, Harry Flood Byrd of Virginia, Richard B. Russell of Georgia, and a host of lesser southern statesmen gave *Race and Reason* their unqualified endorsement. So too did leading southern journalists like Thomas R. Waring, editor of the Charleston *News and Courier,* Virginius Dabney, editor of the Richmond *Times-Dispatch,* and John Temple Graves, regionally syndicated columnist.[23] The Louisiana State Board of Education purchased 5,000 copies for distribution to public schools. The Virginia House of Delegates entertained a resolution calling upon the board of education to consider the book as required reading in the commonwealth's schools.[24] By concurrent resolution, both houses of the Mississippi legislature urged the creation of a special course so that the state's school children might study *Race and Reason,* "a book that exposes the flagrant distortion and perversion of scientific truth by so-called social anthropologists and socialistically oriented sociologists." Governor

[22] See *American Anthropologist,* 64 (June, 1962), 616–17, and Newby, *Challenge to the Court,* 167–69. For Putnam's view of the "pseudo-scientists" who attacked *Race and Reason,* see his *The Road to Reversal: An Address Delivered before the Fifth Annual Attorney General's Conference for District Attorneys, State of Louisiana, New Orleans, February 16, 1962* (Washington: National Putnam Letters Committee, n.d.).

[23] See the Washington *Post,* December 2, 1969; C. Lawson Crowe, "Race and Reason: A Study in Frustration," *Christianity and Crisis,* July 9, 1962, 122; and Putnam, *Race and Reason,* iii–v, 1–14. In the foreword to Putnam's book, Waring called it "a succinct reply to every sophistry advanced by the propagandists."

[24] Crowe, "Race and Reason: A Study in Frustration," 122; Baton Rouge *State Times,* July 26, 1961; New York *Times,* February 18; Norfolk *Journal and Guide,* February 24; Washington *Post,* March 2, 1962. The Virginia resolution died in committee after the Virginia Teachers' Association testified against it.

Ross Barnett declared October 26, 1961, to be "Race and Reason Day in Mississippi," and called upon Magnolia State citizens to observe the occasion by reading and discussing Putnam's volume.[25]

Leading the Putnam bandwagon, of course, was the Citizens' Councils of America from its offices adjacent to the governor's mansion in Jackson. The Council's chief executive, William J. Simmons, one of Governor Barnett's close advisers, had been largely instrumental in the declaration of Race and Reason Day. One of Simmons's lieutenants, Louis W. Hollis, executive director of the Jackson Citizens' Council and business manager of the Council's official journal, played a key role in the planning of the Race and Reason Day Dinner.[26] The lead editorial of the November, 1961, issue of *The Citizen*—an issue devoted entirely to Carleton Putnam and his book—hailed Putnam's Race and Reason Day address as "the turning point" in the region's struggle to preserve segregation.[27] Through *The Citizen,* the CCA offered the paperback edition of *Race and Reason* to subscribers at half price and announced the release of a fifty-minute long-playing record album of "highlights" of the festivities. In order to exploit fully the entire range of the communications media, the Citizens' Council Forum produced and distributed to sympathetic radio and television stations of thirty-minute documentary film and a sixty-minute tape recording of the occasion.[28]

Plaudits for Putnam were not exclusively confined to the segregationist laity of the South. Treading the perimeter of academic respectability were a few elder scientists who certified the "inescapable scientific validity" of *Race and Reason.* Among them, one of the most notable of the American scholars was Wesley Critz George (born 1888), professor emeritus of histology and embryology and

25 *Southern School News,* May, 1962, 9, 12; Jackson *Daily News,* October 26, 1961. Barnett's proclamation was reprinted in *The Citizen,* 6 (November, 1961), 4.

26 Louis W. Hollis, "Here's How We Did It," *The Citizen,* 6 (November, 1961), 39–41. For a list of civic leaders, headed by U.S. Representative John Bell Williams, serving on the Carleton Putnam Dinner Committee, see "Distinguished Community Leaders," *The Citizen,* 6 (November, 1961), 42–45.

27 "The Turning Point," ibid., 2. A subsequent issue of *The Citizen* was also devoted wholly to Putnam's work. This issue Simmons entitled "A Southern Survival Kit," *The Citizen,* 7 (March, 1963), 2.

28 *The Citizen,* 6 (November, 1961), 11, 38, 47.

former head of the department of anatomy at the University of North Carolina Medical School, who would soon become a Citizens' Council hero in his own right. Indeed, even before endorsing the Putnam study, Dr. George emerged from retirement to write his own tract on innate racial characteristics. Entitled *The Biology of the Race Problem,* it resembled, in both content and motivation, a work by Thomas R. Dew, the antebellum professor of history and metaphysics at the College of William and Mary who was asked in 1831 by the Virginia legislature to produce a summary of the controversy over the abolition of slavery. Like Dew's *Review of the Debate* in the Virginia legislature of 1831–32, George contended that as an inferior being the Negro's subjugation to the white man was morally justifiable. Like Dew again, George was retained by a southern state expressly to arrive at these conclusions. Paid $3,000 by the Alabama Governor's Emergency Fund, George surveyed the findings of "the most credible scientists" [29] and concluded that desegregation and its inevitable result, intermarriage, could result only in evil. And "doing evil," he concluded, "is not Christian."

Not remarkably, the impresarios of massive resistance delighted in the George Report. With the desegregation crisis at the University of Mississippi raging about them, Council leaders in Jackson jubilantly proclaimed that "another major scientific report has shattered the equalitarian myth." [30] The October, 1962, issue of *The Citizen* offered it in booklet form at fifty cents a copy, and in lots of ten for $3.50. Council administrator William J. Simmons, lecturing on "the scientific aspect of race differences," recommended it to university audiences at Yale, Notre Dame, and Virginia as an

[29] *Southern School News,* December, 1961, 3; New York *Times,* March 13, 1956; and Wesley Critz George, *The Biology of the Race Problem* (Richmond: Patrick Henry Press, [1962]), 1–2. George's list of "the most credible scientists" differed not at all from Putnam's. George cites R. Ruggles Gates, Robert Gayre, Henry E. Garrett, Henry Pratt Fairchild, Carleton S. Coon, and R. M. Yerkes, among others, as his "authorities." (See iv–vii.)

[30] William J. Simmons, "The Truth about Racial Differences," *The Citizen,* 7 (October, 1962), 7. For an example of the coverage the George Report got among Councils on the local level, see a tract by Herbert C. Sanborn, professor emeritus and former chairman of the department of philosophy and psychology, Vanderbilt University: *Dr. W. C. George's* The Biology of the Race Problem: *A Review* (Nashville: Nashville Citizens' Councils, [1962]).

antidote to the "false science" and "equalitarian dogma" which "has been disseminated so widely in academic circles during recent years. . . ."[31]

Similarly well regarded were the controversial works of Carleton S. Coon. The president of the American Association of Physical Anthropologists and curator of ethnology and professor of anthropology at the University Museum in Philadelphia, Coon speculated—largely on the basis of fossil skulls and fire remains—that the evolutionary development of the Negroid was some 200,000 years behind that of the Caucasoid race.[32] But, unlike George and Putnam, he did not attempt to relate his theories to the debate over segregation. Moreover, the anthropologist pointed out that although the use of fire in Europe could be traced back 250,000 years as compared to a mere 40,000 in Africa, its first use in China occurred fully 360,000 years ago. Untroubled by such details, *The Citizen* proclaimed Coon's work to be "a major breakthrough in anthropology" which "should put an end once and for all to the bogus equalitarian propaganda now parading as 'science.'"[33] In a later issue of the same journal, Carleton Putnam offered further interpretations of Coon's findings as "new evidence" of Negroid

[31] William J. Simmons, *Race Relations and Civil Rights and the Second Reconstruction*. The great faith which the Council possessed in the intellectual appeal of George's work can also be seen in the example of the state association of South Carolina, which distributed his *Race, Heredity and Civilization: Human Progress and the Race Problem* (New York: Alliance, 1963) to students at Clemson University.

[32] See his *The Story of Man* (New York: Alfred A. Knopf, 1954), and *The Origin of Races* (New York: Alfred A. Knopf, 1962). Representative attitudes of American scientists on Coon's research are: F. S. Hulse, *American Anthropologist*, 65 (June, 1963), 685; Margaret Mead, *Saturday Review*, 46 (June 22, 1963), 41; and Theodosius Dobzhansky, *The Scientific American*, 208 (February, 1963), 172. Dobzhansky noted that, in *The Origin of Races*, Coon committed "some unfortunate misstatements that are susceptible to such misinterpretation." "[But] there are absolutely no findings in Coon's book that even suggest that some human races are superior or inferior to others in their capacity for culture or civilization."

[33] "A Meeting of the Minds," *The Citizen*, 6 (June, 1962), 2. See also William J. Simmons's endorsement of "the most eminent of living American physical anthropologists" in *Why California Is Organizing*, 8–9.

inferiority.[34] Understandably, he failed to apply a similar kind of logic to the Caucasoids' sluggish 110,000-year lag behind precocious Mongoloid fire-builders.

Psychology, too, could be employed in the defense of Jim Crow customs. In Henry E. Garrett (born 1894), professor emeritus of psychology at Columbia and past president of the American Psychological Association, segregationists found an old-style devotee of the World War I Army's alpha intelligence test unhesitatingly willing to attribute intelligence quotients of "average" Negro children and "average" white children to inborn racial differences.[35] For sociological justification they invoked the name of Harvard's late Pitirim Sorokin, in whose *Contemporary Sociological Theories* (1928) Councilors found compelling evidence that heredity, not environment, explained why "American negroes have not up to this time produced a single genius of great caliber." [36]

The prosegregation argument invoked God as readily as it did science. "The races of man are the handiwork of God, as is everything in nature," a Mississippi Citizens' Council tract declared. "If He had wanted only one type of man, He would have created only one." [37] It was, then, the duty of the godly to keep the races as He had made them—distinct.

There was ample precedent for the Council's use of providential judgment as justification for its racial attitudes. Indeed, a most

[34] Carleton Putnam, "Evolution and Race: New Evidence," *The Citizen*, 6 (July–August, 1962), 7–11.

[35] For a summary of Garrett's views on the results of intelligence testing, see John J. Synon, "White IQ vs. Negro IQ," *The Citizen*, 10 (September, 1966), 11–12. See also the following examples of Garrett's work: *Race: 11 Questions and 11 Answers* (Washington: National Putnam Letters Committee, n.d.); *The South and the Second Reconstruction* (n.p., n.d.); and *How Classroom Desegregation Will Work* (Richmond: Patrick Henry Press, n.d.). The last was first published in *The Citizen*, 9 (October, 1965). All of these pamphlets have been distributed by the Council through *The Citizen*. A more detailed account of Dr. Garrett's contribution to scientific racism may be found in Newby, *Challenge to the Court*, 99–105.

[36] *The Citizens' Council*, January, 1957, 2. See also William J. Simmons, "Race in America: The Conservative Stand," *The Search for America*, ed. Huston Smith (Englewood Cliffs, N.J.: Prentice-Hall, 1959), 54–64.

[37] *Racial Facts*, 6.

pervasive theme in the history of white supremacy in America has been the readiness of its advocates to swaddle their beliefs in the holy writ. The scriptural defense of bondage was a mainstay of the antebellum proslavery argument. Nor did the theological defense of human subordination atrophy with the advent of abolition. To be sure, the language of subjugation shifted during the postbellum period in recognition of the Negro's free status, but the tenets of religion were still used to defend his inferior position in society. Both the original Klan and its twentieth-century successors, as well as turn-of-the-century Anglo-Saxon expansionists, practiced their own peculiar version of the Ten Commandments, secure in the knowledge of divine approval. Against such a backdrop, it is not remarkable that the Citizens' Council, which drew the bulk of its membership from Bible-belt fundamentalists, should have enlisted providence in the campaign to keep the Negro in his place. But the Council's effort to preempt the religious argument for the prosegregation position was greatly complicated by the readiness with which the South's major denominational bodies embraced the Court's decision.[38]

Scarcely a month after the rendering of the school desegregation decree of May 17, 1954, the Southern Baptist Convention met in St. Louis to approve overwhelmingly the report of its Christian Life Commission: "the Supreme Court decision is in harmony with the constitutional guarantee of equal freedom to all citizens, and with the Christian principles of equal justice and love for all men." After expressing confidence in the nation's public schools, the Convention called upon political and religious leaders of the South to act responsibly in order that "this crisis in our national history

[38] For insightful overviews of the three dominant Protestant sects during this period, see Kenneth K. Bailey, *Southern White Protestantism in the Twentieth Century* (New York: Harper and Row, 1964), 130–59, and David M. Reimers, *White Protestantism and the Negro* (New York: Oxford University Press, 1965), 109–33. See also C. Vann Woodward, "The 'New Reconstruction' in the South: Desegregation in Historical Perspective," *Commentary*, 21 (June, 1956), 507. In this article Woodward compares the post-*Brown* period, the "New Reconstruction," with the "Old Reconstruction" and notes that one of the striking ways in which the new differed from the old has been the unanimity of organizational policy of the major churches North and South on the race question.

shall not be made the occasion for new and bitter prejudices, but a movement toward a united nation."[39]

Following the example of the Baptists, the region's largest and perhaps most conservative church, the general convocations of the other major denominations of the Protestant South issued similarly positive affirmations of Christian brotherhood.[40] Thus, at least in terms of official policy, the overwhelming majority of southern church members belonged to denominations which had endorsed the school desegregation decision. But all too frequently the policies adopted by church hierarchies did not reflect the attitudes of the local congregations from which came the rank and file of the organized resistance movement. The readiness with which individual Baptists, Methodists, Presbyterians, and Episcopalians rallied to defend traditional southern racial customs was one very valid index to the growing cleavage between denominational leaders in the South and their communicants.[41] This estrangement from high church councils became increasingly apparent during the first decade of desegregation. But it was not indicative of diminishing piety among southern churchgoers. Indeed, prosegregation gatherings frequently exhibited all of the religiosity of old-fashioned re-

[39] Quoted in "The Churches Speak," *New South,* 9 (August, 1954), 1–6.

[40] See ibid. and "Answers for Action: Schools in the South," *New South,* 9 (June–July, 1954), 6ff.; Bailey, *Southern White Protestantism,* 142ff.; Ernest Campbell and Thomas Pettigrew, *Christians in Racial Crisis: A Study of Little Rock's Ministers* (Washington: Public Affairs Press, 1959), 157ff.; Thomas D. Clark, *The Emerging South* (New York: Oxford University Press, 1961), 261–62; Reimers, *White Protestantism and the Negro,* 116ff.

[41] State conferences of the upper South generally found it more expedient to endorse the positions adopted by general denominational convocations than did those of the lower South. When conferences in the states of the Deep South did endorse the high court ruling, they very often encountered opposition from ministers and laymen at the local level. The Methodist Men's Club of Asbury Memorial Methodist Church in Charleston, for example, repudiated the liberal position adopted by the Annual Conference of the Methodist Church in South Carolina in 1955 and urged "all Christians to actively engage in these [Citizens'] councils." Similarly, the Florence Methodist Church went on record as "being 100 per cent in accord with the Citizens' Council" following the statement by the Annual Conference in South Carolina. (Charleston *News and Courier,* October 21, 23, 1955.) See also Bailey, *Southern White Protestantism,* 144–45; Quint, *Profile in Black and White,* 55–70.

vival meetings. Typical was a Jackson Citizens' Council rally of June, 1958, commemorating the third anniversary of the movement's birth. Following the invocation ("Thou didst keep men apart in their differences and their habitations"), the pastor of the Highland Baptist Church of Montgomery, Dr. Henry L. Lyon, who had twice served as state president of Alabama's more than 600,000 Baptists, spoke on the topic "Why Integration is Un-Christian." Using as his text Matthew 7:12 ("Whatsoever ye would that men should do to you, do ye even so to them . . ."), Dr. Lyon advised Council members that "separation of the races is the commandment and the law of God." With appropriate Sunday morning responsiveness, a portion of the crowd was moved to say, "Amen." [42]

Not every Council rally ended with a chorus of amens, but virtually every Council had its chaplain and most meetings did begin with a prayer for God's blessings.[43] Moreover, a sizable portion of the movement's leadership came from the Protestant clergy. On the twelve-member editorial board of *The Citizens' Council* and its successor, *The Citizen*, official organs of the Citizens' Councils of America, there were three clergymen—the Reverend Henry J. Davis, of Dundas, Virginia; the Reverend James P. Dees, rector of Trinity Episcopal Church, Statesville, North Carolina; and the Reverend L. B. McCord, an ordained Presbyterian minister who had the unenviable responsibility of serving as superintendent of schools in Clarendon County, South Carolina, in 1954. In addition to his ministerial and editorial duties, Dees was president of the statewide Council movement in North Carolina, the Defenders of States' Rights. Similarly, Davis headed the Association of Citizens' Councils of Virginia, and McCord served as executive secretary of the statewide Council association in South Carolina.[44] William T. Bodenhamer, the executive secretary of the Georgia States' Rights

[42] Quoted in Jackson *Daily News*, June 11, 1958.

[43] To quote an editorial in *The Citizens' Council*, May, 1956, 2, "The Citizens' Council not only believes that God is on its side . . . but it also believes it is on God's side. Every session is opened with fervent prayer to God for guidance, leadership, and protection in these times when the devil is shaking the very foundations of our land."

[44] See *The Citizens' Council*, March, 1961, 2, and *The Citizen*, 6 (October, 1961), p. 14.

Council, was also the pastor of the Baptist Church in Ty Ty.[45] In Arkansas, the Reverend Wesley Pruden, who rose from the post of chaplain to become president of Little Rock's Capital Citizens' Council, was one of the most powerful Council spokesmen in the state.[46] The first executive secretary of the Council's statewide association in Florida was the Reverend George H. Downs, a Baptist minister.[47]

Like its leadership, much of the Council's literature bore an ecclesiastical impress that possessed remarkable appeal to religious Southerners, torn in the seemingly irreconcilable conflict between their own deep-seated racial attitudes and the liberal statements of their churches. Among the most widely circulated of the Council's many propaganda pieces were those that sought to establish the moral justice of segregation by reference to divine revelation. In format these materials varied from crudely mimeographed throw-aways to more sophisticated pamphlet-length expositions, but in substance they differed very little. Bearing such titles as *Christianity and Segregation, God the Original Segregationist, Is Segregation Un-Christian?, The Church and Segregation,* and *Christian Love and Segregation,* the great bulk of this propaganda had but a single theme: "segregation—God's own plan for the races." [48] Typical of this genre of literature was a tract by a Presbyterian minister, the Reverend G. T. Gillespie, president emeritus of Belhaven Col-

[45] *Atlanta Journal,* November 6, 1955; "Biography of William T. Bodenhamer" (unpublished manuscript, Southern Education Reporting Service, 1958).

[46] *The Citizens' Council,* January, 1958, 3. In announcing Pruden's election as the successor to Robert Ewing Brown as president of the Little Rock Council, *The Citizens' Council* said: "A Southern Baptist Convention minister, Reverend Pruden is symbolic of the churches of the South who are standing firm on America's traditional ways of life and freedom."

[47] Miami *Herald,* June 26, 1956; St. Petersburg *Times,* January 1, 1957.

[48] Quotation from J. Paul Barrett, *The Church and Segregation.* See also W. A. Criswell, *Christianity and Segregation: An Address by Dr. W. A. Criswell, Pastor, First Baptist Church, Dallas, Texas, to the Sovereign State of South Carolina* (n.p., n.d.); Carey Daniel, *God the Original Segregationist* (Dallas: By the Author, [1957]); *Is Segregation Un-Christian?* (Montgomery: Citizens' Councils of Alabama, n.d.); and S. Emory Rogers, *Christian Love and Segregation* (Summerton: Association of Citizens' Councils of South Carolina, n.d.).

lege, Jackson. Published by the Mississippi Association of Citizens' Councils, and given regional distribution by the Citizens' Councils of America, Gillespie's *A Christian View on Segregation* was remarkably similar to works published by proslavery advocates during the decade before the Civil War. In the spirit of the *Pro-Slavery Argument* (1853), that massive collaboration in propaganda by Thomas R. Dew, Chancellor William Harper, Governor James H. Hammond, and William Gilmore Simms, Gillespie's defense of segregation invoked historical and scriptural justifications, focused on the ruinous effects of abolishing the institution, and ultimately concluded that it was not merely a social necessity but a positive good.[49]

Less dogmatic than proslavery militants, Gillespie would admit that the scriptures contained no precise mandate for or against segregation. Nevertheless, he argued, they do contain considerable evidence from which "valid inferences" may be derived in support of segregation as a development of divine purpose. Supporting his exegesis on providential will, Gillespie cited passages in Genesis, Leviticus, Ezra, the Gospels, Acts, Epistles, and Revelation to demonstrate that segregation was sanctioned by divine authority during the patriarchal age, vested with legal status in the Mosaic period, and wholly in harmony with the spirit and the teachings of Christ and the Apostles.[50] In effect, Gillespie's study of the Bible brought him in 1954 to the same conclusions reached in 1845 by the eminent Baptist divine, Dr. Richard Fuller: "WHAT GOD SANCTIONED IN THE OLD TESTAMENT AND PERMITTED IN THE NEW, CANNOT BE SIN." [51]

49 G. T. Gillespie, *A Christian View on Segregation*. For a critical analysis of Gillespie's biblical defense of segregation, see Everett Tilson, *Segregation and the Bible* (New York: Abingdon Press, 1958). For the moral aspects of the proslavery argument, see especially studies by Jenkins, *Pro-Slavery Thought in the Old South*, 200–241, and Arthur Young Lloyd, *The Slavery Controversy, 1831–1860* (Chapel Hill: University of North Carolina Press, 1939), 162–93, as well as William Harper et al., *The Pro-Slavery Argument as Maintained by the Most Distinguished Writers of the Southern States* (Philadelphia: Lippincott, Grambo, and Co., 1853).

50 Gillespie, *A Christian View on Segregation*, 1–13.

51 Richard Fuller and Francis Wayland, *Domestic Slavery Considered as a Scriptural Institution* (New York, 1845), as quoted in Lloyd, *The Slavery Controversy*, 188.

Willing to concede that Jesus had taught not only the love of God for all mankind but the essential oneness of all Christian believers, Gillespie proved more hesitant in stamping Jim Crow with the unqualified endorsement of Christ than were many writers of subsequent Citizens' Council tracts. For example, the Reverend T. Robert Ingram, rector of St. Thomas Episcopal Church of Houston and one of the foremost exponents of the morality of compulsory social separation,[52] believed that race discrimination was simply applied Christianity: "The most complete and devastating discriminatory practices that can ever be exercised," he asserted in the Council journal, "are those of Jesus Christ." To embrace human equality, the minister warned, was to judge "Jesus, the great discriminator, accursed." Had not He damned some and saved others?[53]

Biblical interpretations such as these reinforced the Council's view, as expressed by Judge Brady at a New Orleans segregation rally in 1955, that "segregation is a holy thing."[54] If segregation had the sanction of the providentially inspired writings and the approval of the Son of God, then integration could only be sinful, the work of either Satan or (as Council propaganda came increasingly to assert) his blood brother, Karl Marx. Indeed, the whole "myth of equality" could be traced to those nefarious "-isms" —socialism, communism, and one-worldism—which threatened the ultimate annihilation of all Christendom. By accepting this myth, and declaring segregation un-Christian, the general assemblies of the region's major denominations became the dupes of "false prophets."[55] Moreover, Council spokesmen believed that the organization which represented most of American Protestantism, the National Council of Churches of Christ in America, had become so

[52] See T. Roger Ingram, ed., *Essays on Segregation* (Houston: St. Thomas Press, 1960).

[53] T. Robert Ingram, " 'Civil Rights' Proposals Are Anti-Christian." *The Citizen*, 8 (November, 1963), 4–5. See also "Courage, Christian Soldiers!" *The Citizen*, 6 (December, 1961), 20–23, and "Why Integration Is Un-Christian," *The Citizen*, 6 (June, 1962), 6–16. Ingram also appeared on the Citizens' Council "Forum" television and radio series.

[54] Jackson *Daily News*, November 2, 1955.

[55] "The Myth of 'Equality,' " *The Citizen*, 8 (November, 1963), 2, 15. See also Rogers, *Christian Love and Segregation*, 1–4, and Ingram, *Essays on Segregation*, 1–14.

infused by "multi-racial, collectivist theorists" and "ecclesiastical bureaucrats" that it had been reduced to a "propaganda tool" for "left wing movements of every kind." [56]

Believing as it did that the proper role of the church was to teach racial harmony through separation, the Council focused the brunt of its attack on liberal theology, upon the "pinkos in the pulpit." Having decided that "racial preference" is un-Christian, these ministers of "socialized Christianity" had also declared that "private enterprise, rugged individualism, and conservatism in politics are equally un-Christian." This "pharisaical concern" with social reform, this meddling in race relations and other purely social, economic, and political affairs, Council literature asserted, so preoccupied the "Social Gospel left winger" that he had neglected individual religious experience—the church's only legitimate sphere of interest.[57]

The Council's offensive against liberal clergy was in some ways reminiscent of Bible-belt attitudes during the Scopes trial. Yet it was less a reflection of the suspicions of Deep South fundamentalism toward intellectually oriented theology than it was of Deep South racial mores. The "Social Gospelers," as the Councils were wont to call all but the most ardently prosegregation clergymen, embodied a threat to the white supremacists' resolute conviction that the Negro, by the will of God and the testimony of science, occupied a status considerably lower than the white man.

The corollary to the Citizens' Council contention that segregation was the law of God is the assertion that it was also the law of nature. In the Reverend Gillespie's view racial separation was not

[56] Council literature is replete with attacks on the National Council of Churches. For some of the more representative examples, see Thomas R. Waring, "Aroused Churchmen Are Studying Leftist Trends," *The Citizen*, 6 (April, 1962), 11–12; "Pinkos in the Pulpit," *The Citizens' Council*, December, 1956, 2; "Church Council Is Propaganda Tool," *The Citizens' Council*, November, 1957, 1; "Church Group Names Left President Again," *The Citizens' Council*, January, 1958, 1. Similar in tone is John R. Leatherbury, *The National Council of Churches of Christ—Activities Revealed*, which suggests that the N.C.C. is pro-Communist. See also a news bulletin published by the Citizen's Council of Atmore, Alabama, *The Southern Defender*, July, 1965.

[57] See the literature listed in the footnote above as well as the cartoons in *The Citizens' Council*, June, 1957, 1, 4; August, 1957, 2; September, 1957, 4.

only commanded by nature, but it was "one of nature's universal laws."[58] Conversely, the Reverend James P. Dees affirmed that racial mixing was a "violation of God's natural law in creation," was "contrary to the moral law revealed in nature," and was in fact a "crime against nature." "Do black birds," he inquired, "intermingle with the blue birds? Does the redwing fly with the crows? Would it make sense for my Senior Warden to mix Black Angus cattle with his pure-bred Herefords?" Such would be "abhorrent to the natural created order."[59]

Thus the elementary laws of the universe taught that black-skinned people, like Black Angus cattle, could be crossed with white-faced creatures, Caucasian or Hereford, only by violating one of nature's most fundamental precepts. History taught that segregation was not simply natural, it was beneficial. Much more than a social necessity, it was an unqualified good. For where else, ran the Council's argument, had the Negro progressed so rapidly in so few years as he had in the segregated South?[60] Had he not, as Judge Brady insisted, been "saved from savagery," been "compelled to lay aside cannibalism, [and] his barbaric savage customs," and had he not been transported from aboriginal ignorance and superstition and been "introduced to God?"[61]

Believing that Negroes had failed to develop even the rudiments of civilization in their "natural habitat," Councilors could only conclude that whatever culture blacks had acquired they owed to the white society in which it had been their good fortune to dwell.[62] Recurring throughout segregation literature, this view was

[58] Gillespie, *A Christian View on Segregation*, 2.

[59] *The Citizens' Council*, April–May, 1961, 1, 4; James P. Dees, "Should Christians Support Integration?" *Essays on Segregation*, 35–51.

[60] See, for example, James O. Eastland, *We've Reached Era of Judicial Tyranny, an Address before the State-Wide Convention of the Association of Citizens' Councils of Mississippi, Jackson, December 1, 1955*, 9.

[61] Brady, *Black Monday*, 11.

[62] In an editorial ("Lesson from the Congo," *The Citizens' Council*, July, 1960, 1–2), William Simmons pointed to the Congo as evidence that the Negro remains even today a "howling savage": "Once the discipline of white control was removed, the innate savagery of Congolese Negroes burst through the thin veneer acquired by several generations of exposure to Caucasian civilizations." For additional examples of the Council's equation of the American Negro with Africian savagery, see *The Citizens' Council*, December, 1958, January, 1959, February, 1959, and *The Citizen*, 8 (March, 1964), 2.

given characteristic expression in CCA president Roy V. Harris's weekly tabloid, the Augusta *Courier:* "in the land of the Nile both the Negro and the white man started. No race of people in antiquity developed and made progress as did the Egyptians. . . . Yet during all this development, the Negro contributed two things to the history of mankind: 1. Human slavery. 2. Cannibalism."[63] Brady, too, juxtaposed the pyramids against the cannibals in order to demonstrate the Negro's innate incapacity for civilization. While Caucasoid man in Egypt, Greece, and Rome was creating the intellectual and technological foundations of western civilization, while Mongoloid man during the Chow and Ming dynasties formulated the art, literature, and high standards of eastern morality, Negroid man, Brady averred, "like the modern lizard," had not evolved. While the culture of the modern world had found its matrix in the white and the yellow races, the black race had spawned no elemental idea, given birth to no fundamental innovation. Instead, "although both the other races of mankind had for some time tabooed it, cannibalism was an expected risk in the life of the Negro of this period."[64]

From the Council's historical perspective, the presence of the Negro was a threat to more than just the flesh of his neighboring tribesman. For despite the white man's superior capacity for civilization, he could not withstand the infusion of the black man's blood. The "facts" of history, Council spokesmen believed, revealed that whenever and wherever the white man drank "the cup of black hemlock," whenever and wherever he infused his blood with that of the Negro, white intellect and white culture perished. This was the tragic story of Egypt and Babylon, Greece and Rome; and it was the story of India, Spain, and Portugal—"negroid blood like the jungle, steadily and completely swallowing up everything."[65]

A careful study of the past, then, revealed that the Negro carried in his very blood a destructive force that could pull down the

63 Augusta *Courier,* January 9, 1956. See also Amos R. Koontz, "'Uhuru' Does Not Confer 'Equality,'" *The Citizen,* 8 (November, 1963), 6–10; and Louis W. Hollis, *A Five Point Action Program: An Address to the Reorganization Rally, Savannah Citizens' Council, Savannah, Georgia* [*July* 22, 1963] (n.p.. n.d.), 15.

64 Brady, *Black Monday,* 2.

65 Ibid., 5, 7; *Racial Facts,* 4.

mightiest of civilizations. But history had other lessons from which its modern students could profit. In the papers of the nation's most revered heroes, segregationists discovered some of their most effective parries for the thrusts of the desegregationists. "If we are bigoted, prejudiced, un-American . . ." Councilors argued, "so were George Washington, Thomas Jefferson, Abraham Lincoln, and our other illustrious forebears who believed in segregation."[66]

Theodore G. Bilbo, the Magnolia State's loquacious Negro-baiting progressive, was an obvious choice as a source of authority on racial questions for the Mississippi-dominated Citizens' Councils of America. His speeches were colorful, quotable, and virtually always couched in the argot of white supremacy. Particularly useful was his statement on miscegenation. If all of the tangible evidence of American civilization—its buildings, its highways, its cities, and even its army—were destroyed, he had said, the nation could survive and would ultimately recover. "But if the blood of our white race should become corrupted and mingled with the blood of Africa, then the present greatness of the United States of America would be destroyed and all hope for the future would be forever gone."[67]

This quotation was repeated in Council speeches, cited in its pamphlets, and distributed by it on ink blotters and leaflets.[68] But a statement by Bilbo had only limited value for the prosegregation argument. Although his memory was much revered by a broad segment of Deep South society, particularly by poor whites of the rural, red clay hills, his popular reputation outside the region was scarcely that of wisdom.

The same could hardly be said of Thomas Jefferson. His writings, too, when submitted to the selective mining of the organized resistance movement, bore a rich ore capable of being hammered into a flimsy armor for white supremacy. In his autobiography, the third president alluded to certain unbridgeable racial differences which required the colonization of the Negro, once emancipated, in another land: "Nothing is more certainly written in the book of

66 *The Citizens' Council: The South's Only Answer* (Montgomery: Citizens' Council of Alabama, n.d.).

67 Typical of the Council's pamphlets in which this Bilbo statement appears are: Louis W. Hollis, *Integrity*, 5, and *Racial Facts*, 7.

68 Southern Education Reporting Service, Citizens' Council materials.

fate, than that these people are to be free; nor is it less certain that the two races, equally free, cannot live in the same government. Nature, habit, opinion have drawn indelible lines of distinction between them."[69] Lifted from the context of Jefferson's voluminous papers, this statement made effective propaganda for the segregationist's cause. Like the one from Bilbo, it too became a part of the CCA's "Famous Quotations" series of blotters and leaflets. It too, was cited in speech and pamphlet as evidence of the "fact" of Negro inferiority.[70]

Even more useful to the prosegregation argument were Abraham Lincoln's numerous statements on race.[71] Claimed as he has been by the advocates of Negro rights, the Great Emancipator's darker side was not universally recognized. Lamenting what he termed "the big lie about Lincoln," William J. Simmons charged that "dishonest integrationists in a brazen historical theft" had appropriated the prestigious name and memory of the sixteenth president for their own "devious ends." If Lincoln were alive today, Simmons assured his fellow Councilors, "his position would be regarded not merely as that of a segregationist, but of an out-and-out white

69 Thomas Jefferson, *Autobiography,* Vol. 1 of *The Writings of Thomas Jefferson,* Andrew A. Lipscomb and Albert Ellery Bergh, eds. (Washington: Thomas Jefferson Memorial Association, 1903–4), 72–73.

70 *Racial Facts,* 7; Southern Education Reporting Service, Miscellaneous Files. See also Workman, *The Case for the South,* 142, and Herman Talmadge, *You and Segregation* (Birmingham: Vulcan Press, 1955), 48–49. Other Jeffersonian quotations on Negro-white relations were overlooked by segregationists—particularly those demonstrating the Sage of Monticello's misgivings about his own views on innate racial characteristics. For Jefferson's views on environment as a possible explanation for apparent racial differences, see Thomas Jefferson to General Chevalier de Chastellux, June 7, 1785, and Jefferson to M. Henri Gregoire, February 25, 1809, *Writings of Thomas Jefferson,* Lipscomb and Bergh, eds., Vol. 5, 6; Vol. 12, 254–55.

71 For analyses of the uses to which the segregationists have put Lincoln, see Paul Anthony, "An Analysis of the Hate Literature of Resistance Groups of the South" (unpublished manuscript, Southern Regional Council, 1956), and Shepherd Raymond, "Lincoln and the White Supremacists," *Fact* (May–June, 1964), 49–52. For other examples of the Council's uses of Lincoln quotations, see "Abe Said: More Words of Lincoln That the Race-Mixers Never Quote," *The Citizens' Council,* May, 1956, 3; December, 1957, 3, 4; March, 1958, 3, and Robert B. Patterson, *The Truth Cries Out: Speech to Annual Leadership Conference, Chattanooga, Tennessee, January 8, 1966* (Greenwood: Association of Citizens' Councils of Mississippi, [1966]), 6.

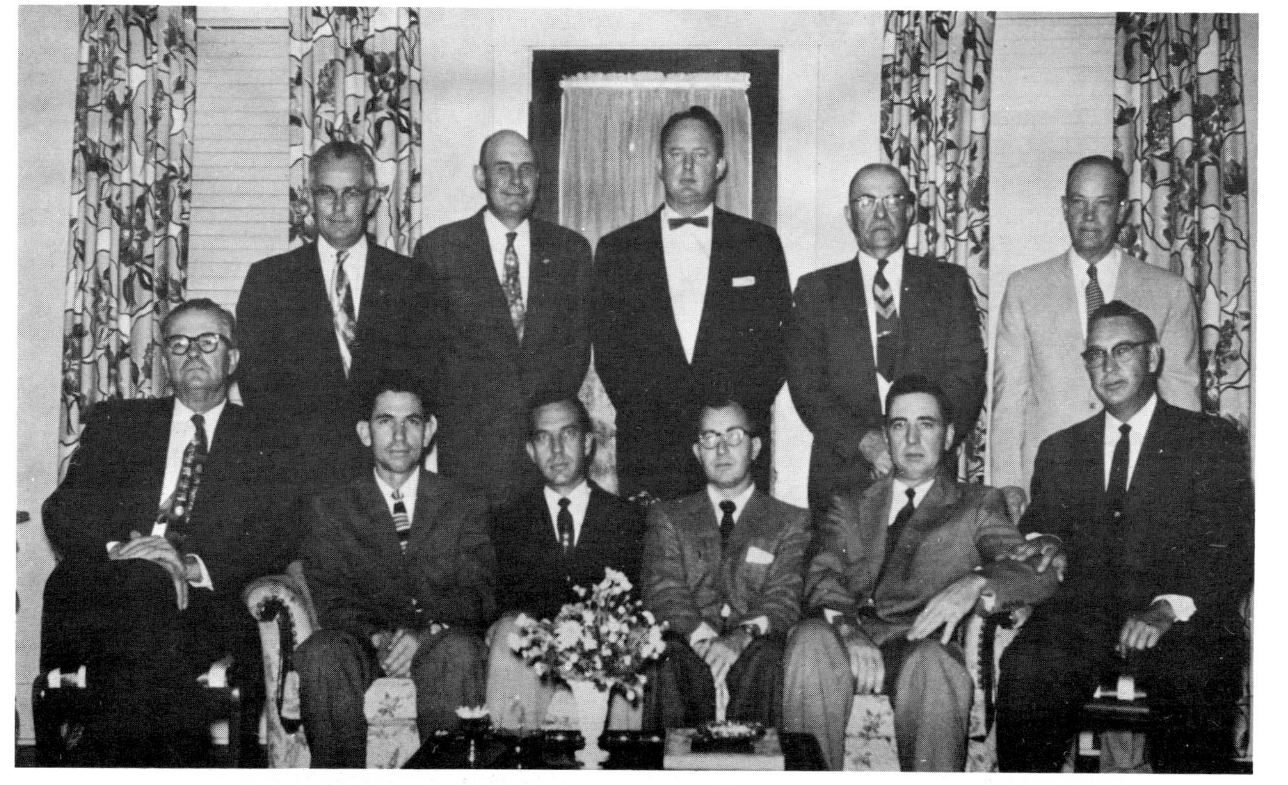

Eleven of the Council's fourteen charter members. *Seated, L to R:* Dink Gibson (farmer), Frank Tindall (farmer), J. C. Shirley (dentist), Arthur Clark, Jr. (lawyer), Ed Britt (farmer), Billy Gist (farmer-implement dealer). *Standing, L to R:* Alton East (undertaker), W. D. Hemphill (automobile dealer), Robert B. Patterson (farmer), Dave Hawkins (compress manager), Tom Pitts (mayor of Indianola and scrap iron dealer).

Part of the crowd at the Mississippi Citizens' Council's White Monday Rally, May 17, 1965.

Louisiana Council leader Leander Perez flanked by George C. Wallace (left) and Roy V. Harris, president of the Citizens' Councils of America.

Governors Wallace and Barnett upstage an applauding William J. Simmons on the speaker's platform at the White Monday Rally.

Representative of the St. Louis area Council presenting recent Council hero Lester Maddox, governor of Georgia, with a commemorative ax handle.

The original Council school, September, 1964.

Change of classes at Council School No. 3 (1,500 students, grades 1–12), one of the CCA's five modern educational facilities in Jackson, Mississippi.

Built in the shadow of the Mississippi state capitol (upper right), the new CCA headquarters is a tasteful and beautifully appointed modern structure.

Roy V. Harris, founder of the States' Rights Council of Georgia and president of the Citizens' Councils of America.

Judge Tom P. Brady speaking at a Council leadership conference.

State Senator Sam Engelhardt, executive secretary of the Citizens' Councils of Alabama.

Wearing his Confederate flag necktie, state Senator Willie Rainach, president of the Association of Citizens' Councils of Louisiana, is shown with New Orleans Council leader Cullen E. Vetter.

William J. Simmons, administrator and chief spokesman of the Citizens' Councils of America.

Medford Evans, managing editor of *The Citizen*.

Louis W. Hollis, director of the Citizens' Councils of America.

Robert B. Patterson, secretary of the CCA and founder of the first Citizens' Council.

Suh,

Here's Sweet MUSIC!

Yes, YOU too, can be

SUPERIOR

Join The Glorious Citizens Clan

Next Thursday Night!

What? Worried about being socially acceptable?

Learning to play the piano by ear? Taking dancing lessons? Using the right toothpaste?

Possibly taking a course in public speaking? Want to be the life of the party? No need to worry anymore! The grand opportunity now awaits you!

Join The CITIZENS CLAN and BE SAFE From SOCIAL WORRIES

(Absolutely No Coupons Are Needed)

BE SUPER-SUPERIOR

Compare These 10 Freedoms with other Old Fashioned Offers

- Freedom to interprete the Constitution of the United States to your own personal advantage!
- Freedom to hunt "Blackbirds" with no bag limit, and without fear of prosecution! (To date no member of the Clan has been convicted for killing a nigger)
- Freedom to sit on a jury in behalf of your fellow members!
- Freedom from worry and fear if you happen to sit before a jury!
- Freedom to exercise a great Southern privilege: TO EXERT ECONOMIC PRESSURE!
- Freedom from fear of having economic pressure exerted against you!
- Freedom to yell "Nigger" as much as you please without your conscience bothering you!
- Freedom to wonder who is pocketing the five dollars you pay to join!
- Freedom to take a profitable part in the South's fastest growing business: Bigtory!
- FREEDOM TO BE SUPERIOR WITHOUT BRAIN, CHARACTER, OR PRINCIPLE!

(Many Other Freedoms, Too . . . Only A Few Listed Above)

- - This Wonderful Offer Open To White Folk Only - -

Other Items To Keep In Mind

Remember:	No Niggers allowed! (Not even "good" Niggers can join this SUPERIOR Clan.)	**Remember:**	Not to join could mean you're a Nigger Lover!
Remember:	You, too, can be SUPER SUPERIOR!	**Remember:**	The Time: 7:30 P. M., Thursday, March 22nd
Remember:	For only five dollars, GUARANTEED SUPERIORITY!	**Remember:**	The Clan needs YOU—But most of all, YOU may need the Clan!

This Page in Behalf of Liberalism, Fairness and Progress Donated By: . .

The Petal Paper

P. D. East's famous "Jack Ass Ad" hailing the formation of the Forrest County, Mississippi, Citizens' Council.

Catching the NAACP with its trousers down. Cartoon by Jackson *Daily News* cartoonist Bob Howie for *The Citizens' Council,* October, 1956.

It's Later Than You Think!

The call to organize. Cartoon by Bob Howie for *The Citizens' Council,* May, 1956.

The NAACP's assault on segregated public schools, as portrayed by Bob Howie for *The Citizens' Council*, March, 1956.

Negro Surplus Or Deficit For Each State

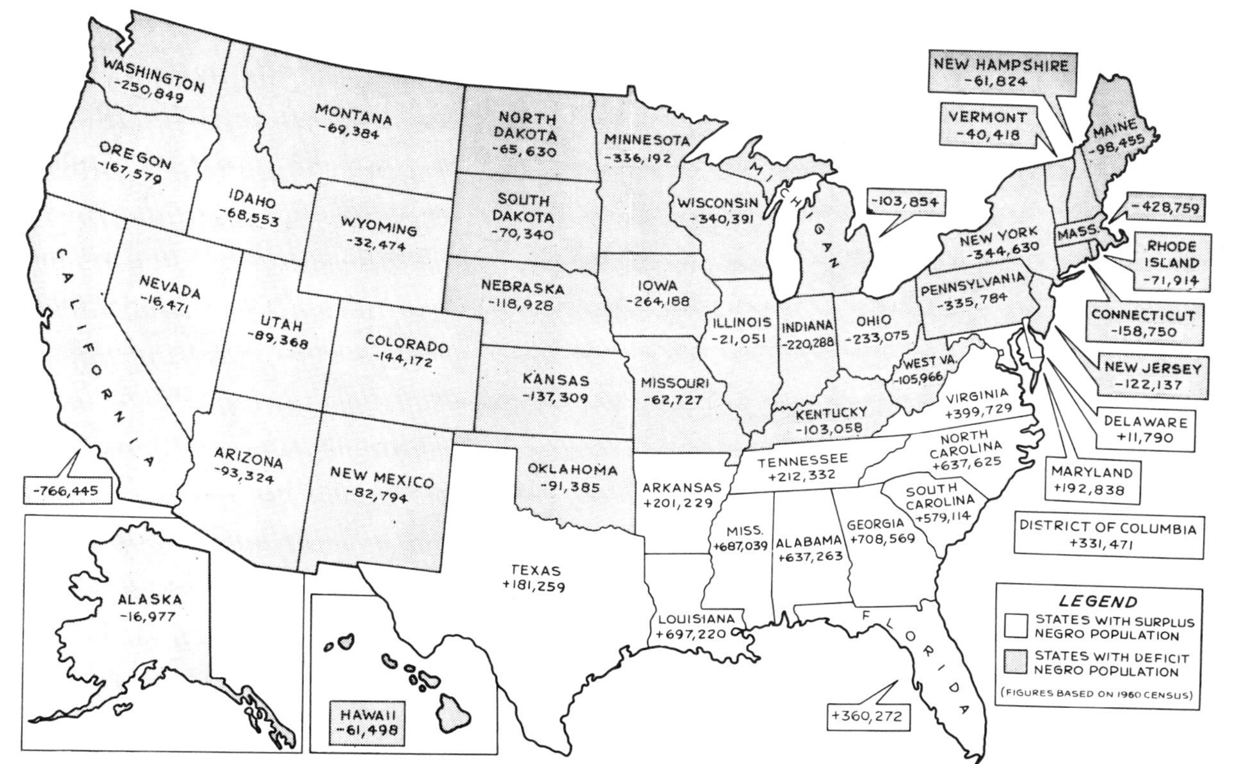

Map from a Mississippi Council brochure urging "voluntary migration" and resettlement of Negroes.

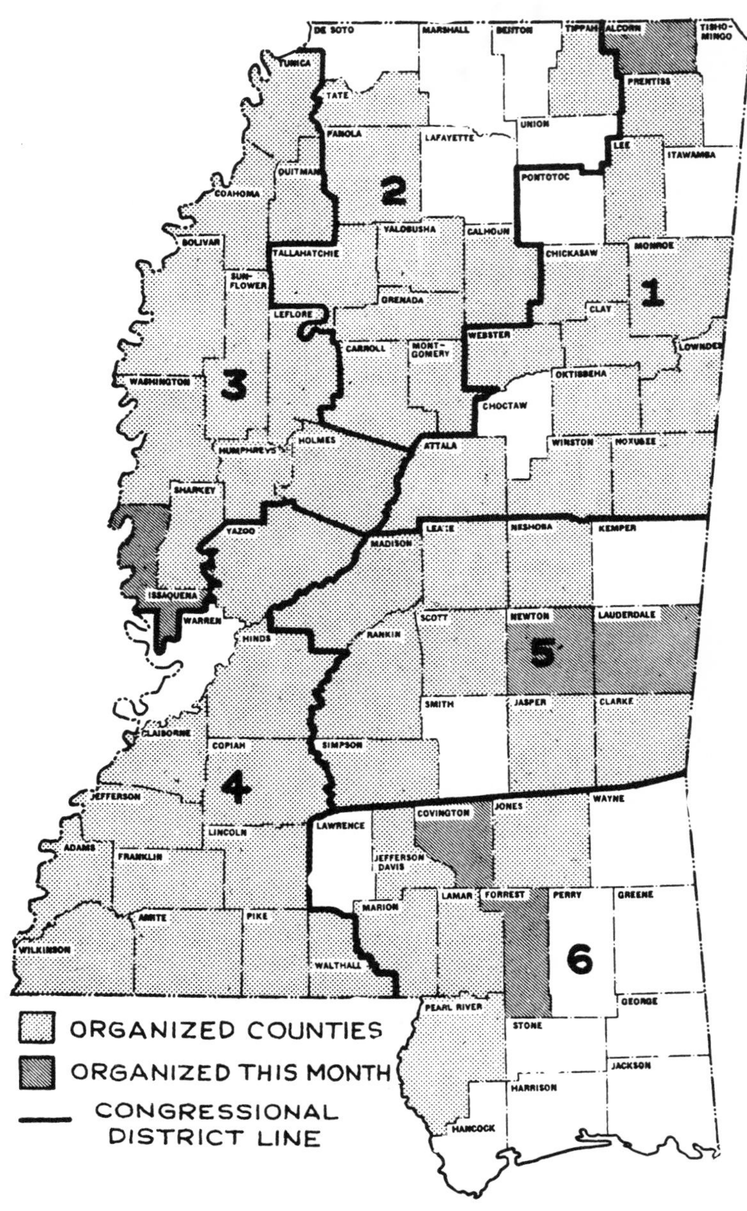

Map from *The Citizens' Council* showing counties organized in Mississippi by March, 1956.

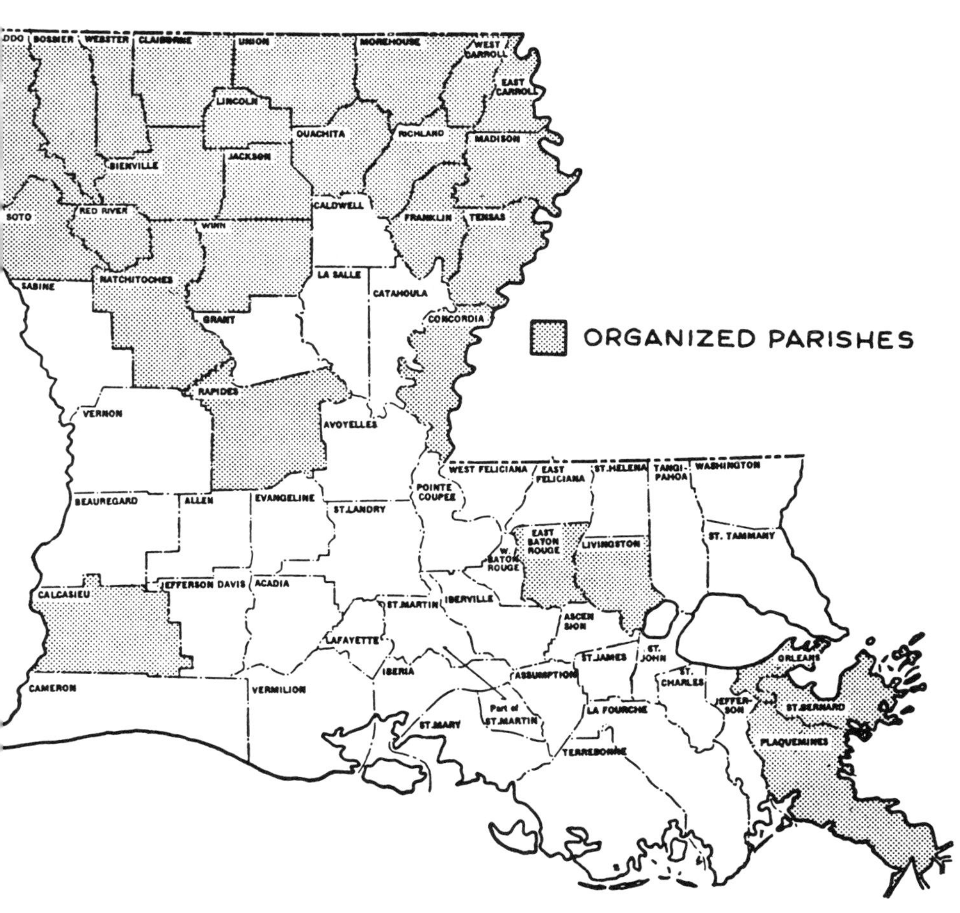

Map from *The Citizens' Council* showing counties organized in Louisiana by June, 1956.

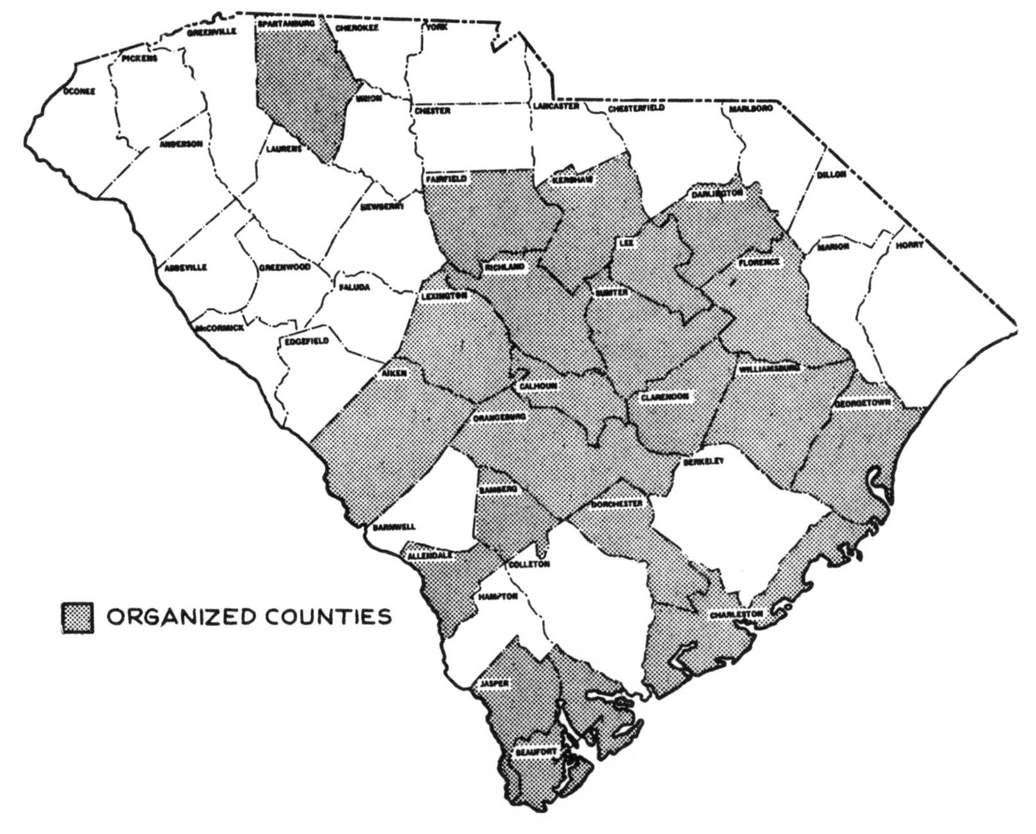

Map from *The Citizens' Council* showing counties organized in South Carolina by June, 1956.

supremacist."[72] In order to rescue the Illinois president's reputation from "such disgrace," the Citizens' Councils of America launched a national advertising campaign to acquaint the American people with the "real" Abraham Lincoln. A special Lincoln's birthday issue of *The Citizen* for February, 1964, was entirely devoted to quotations from his debates with Douglas, his first inaugural, and his speeches at Peoria (1854), Springfield (1857), and Chicago (1858)—all in an effort to equate the ideas of the Civil War statesman with those of massive resistance. Emerging from these carefully chosen excerpts was Lincoln, the impassioned critic of the high Court, who had warned that "if the policy of the government . . . is to be irrevocably fixed by the decisions of the Supreme Court . . . the people will have ceased to be their own rulers. . . ." An intractable champion of states' rights, the sixteenth president had denied that he possessed the constitutional authority to interfere with the institutions of the sovereign southern states. So fearful of miscegenation was he that he wished to carry racial disassociation to the point of deporting the Negro.[73]

Concomitant with the Lincoln issue of *The Citizen,* the CCA's information minister, Richard Morphew, announced a newspaper advertising scheme also designed "to save Lincoln's good name" by canonizing him as the patron saint of segregation. The objective was to blanket the North with a quarter-page publicity release, featuring "Lincoln's hopes for the Negro": "What I would most desire would be the separation of the white and black races." According to the organization's own calculations, the advertisement ran in more than six hundred "major" newspapers on February 10 and 11, and before the month had passed it had been printed in more than one thousand.[74]

Patently transparent though it was, the argument from history (like that from science and nature) did lend authority to the as-

[72] "The Big Lie about Lincoln," *The Citizen,* 8 (February, 1964), 1, 15.

[73] "Lincoln's Real Views on Race," ibid., 4–14. See also Richard D. Morphew, *The Citizens' Councils and the Negro Revolution: An Address to a Convocation at Beloit College, Beloit, Wisconsin* [*February 25, 1964*] (n.p., n.d.).

[74] Greensboro (N.C.) *Daily News,* September 1; Jackson *Daily News,* February 12, 25; Columbia (S.C.) *State,* March 2; San Francisco *Chronicle,* February 14; Los Angeles *Times,* February 13; New York *Times,* February 11, 1964.

sumptions of the segregationists. However, the movement resorted to levels of defense which lacked even that support. That oft-repeated affirmation that segregation's antonym, integration, would lead inexorably to miscegenation, that "horrifying byproduct" of racial coexistence, was perhaps the most compelling of these defenses. Council leaders tirelessly reiterated their Manichean conviction that segregation was the essence of all things good—"the freedom to choose one's associates, Americanism, state sovereignty, and the survival of the white race." Its alternative was an unqualified evil, representing only "darkness, regimentation, totalitarianism, communism, and destruction."[75] Integration always meant miscegenation, for by lowering the racial barriers in the public schools, the Supreme Court had opened the floodgates of "amalgamation."[76] Amalgamation, Council spokesmen declared, was precisely what the integrationists wanted. According to the "Manual for Southerners," the CCA's official handbook for the fifth and sixth grades: "The Race-Mixers even want Negroes and whites to date each other. They know that if the boys and girls share the school room, lunch room, dances, sports, rest rooms, and playgrounds, then the boys and girls will want to date each other."[77] "To integrate the races means to have them live with each other and marry each other. It is the Race-Mixers who want to integrate the races. Integration always leads the races to marry one another."[78] Certainly the Council had not created the segregationist's maxim that mixed schools meant mixed blood, but it seldom missed an opportunity to exploit the fears inspired by such a notion.

On its most dignified plane the case for segregation as the most effective means of preventing intermarriage took the form of a refurbishment of the cult of southern womanhood, that romantic adulation of femininity which Wilbur J. Cash has called "gyneola-

[75] *2nd Annual Report, August, 1956,* 2; Robert B. Patterson, *The Citizens' Council: A History* (Jackson: Citizens' Councils of America, [1963]), 5; Louis W. Hollis, *Integrity,* 5.

[76] For example, see a pamphlet by Herbert R. Sass, *Mixed Schools and Mixed Blood* (Greenwood: Association of Citizens' Councils, [1956]). This pamphlet was also published by the States' Rights Council of Georgia, Inc. The subtitle of Brady's *Black Monday: Segregation or Amalgamation, America Has Its Choice* also reflects the Councils penchant for the either-or dichotomy.

[77] "Manual for Southerners," *The Citizens' Council,* July, 1957, 3.

[78] "Manual for Southerners," *The Citizens' Council,* August, 1957, 3.

try." [79] Writing in *Black Monday,* Judge Brady expressed this chivalric mood in appropriately turgid prose: "the loveliest and purest of God's creatures, the nearest thing to an angelic being that treads this terrestrial ball is a well-bred, cultured white woman or her blue-eyed, golden-haired little girl." [80]

On a related but less lofty plane, Councilors sought to rout the enemies of separate-but-equal schools by drawing upon the white's darkest fears about integration. This approach focused on the popularly held conviction that the way to the bedroom was through the schoolhouse door.[81] Thus Council spokesmen like state Senator Walter C. Givhan of Alabama unhesitatingly exploited sexual anxieties by revealing that when the NAACP petitioned the courts for desegregation, it did so in order "to open the bedroom doors of our white women to Negro men." [82] Similarly, a pamphlet used by the movement in both Louisiana and Arkansas presented a cause-and-effect series of photographs under the caption: "Is this YOUR little girl's future?" The pictorial sequence began with a preschool-age girl in a party dress dancing with a Negro boy, and progressed to the denouement—Negro men passionately embracing provocatively attired white women.[83] Almost every issue of *The Citizens' Council* carried inflammatory headlines such as "White and Negro Marriage Is Goal," "Mixed Marriage Will Become Commonplace,"

[79] Wilbur J. Cash, *The Mind of the South* (New York: Vintage Books, 1941), 89.

[80] Brady, *Black Monday,* 45.

[81] See Calvin C. Hernton, *Sex and Racism in America* (Garden City: Doubleday, 1965).

[82] From an address at Linden, Alabama, in 1954, quoted in "How White Citizens' Councils Came to Alabama," *New South,* 10 (December, 1955), 11.

[83] Capital Citizens' Councils, *The Little Rock School Board's Plans for Your Child* (Little Rock: Capital Citizens' Council, n.d.); Greater New Orleans Citizens' Council, *Integration Today Means Racial and National Suicide Tomorrow* (New Orleans: Greater New Orleans Citizens' Council, n.d.). For other examples of the Council's exploitation of sex anxieties through pictures, see *The Arkansas Faith,* November, 1955; March, 1956; and the following broadsides: Tarrant Educational Citizens' Council, "Destroying the White Woman Destroys the White Race" (Birmingham: Tarrant Educational Citizens' Council, n.d.), and miscellaneous untitled broadsides, Southern Education Reporting Service, Miscellaneous Files. The latter, not bearing the Council's imprint, were enclosed in regular mailings by the Association of Citizens' Councils of Mississippi.

"Mixed Love for Negroes and Whites," "Sex Atrocity in Massachusetts: Blacks Rape White Girl Repeatedly," "Mixed Love in Kentucky," and "Sex Orgies in Iowa." Apologizing for printing such "sordid bit[s] of news," editor William J. Simmons explained that honest journalism required it; they are "becoming increasingly typical of stories filtering back from areas where racial integration is proceeding 'with all deliberate speed. . . .' "[84] Always there was the insinuation that at the root of the problem lay the Negro's own atavistic lusts. Or, as one Council spokesman explained it to the Commonwealth Club of California, "the Negro, in so far as sex is concerned is not immoral, he is simply nonmoral. He surely follows his natural instincts."[85]

Mounting sexual offenses were not the only effects of desegregation against which the white resistance group warned. Crime, disease, and violence, according to Council statisticians, also followed in the wake of racial mingling. In one statistical summary published by the Mississippi Association of Citizens' Councils entitled *Crime Report Reveals Menace of Integration*, the Negroid 10 percent of the population of the United States was credited with 63 percent of the arrests for murder, 62 percent for prostitution, and 40 percent for rape. The same single-sheet handout cited aggregate figures on the prison population in thirty-two states to "prove" that Negroes not only committed more crimes per capita than did whites, but that they ran afoul of the law far more frequently when segregation was not practiced.[86] Statistics such as these, Councilors believed,

[84] See *The Citizens' Council*, October, 1956, 3; November, 1956, 4; February, 1956, 1–2; August, 1957, 2; February, 1957, 3. Occasionally the Council focused on jazz music as a symbol of the sexual threats implicit in desegregation. In an early issue of *The Citizens' Council* it was pointed out that the word jazz "is a slang word which originally meant illicit sexual intercourse"; that jazz "originated in an atmosphere of illicit sex"; and that the "same [jazz] rhythms were known and used in Africa . . . for sexual orgies. . . ." (William Stephenson, "From Bawdy Houses to Parlor," *The Citizens' Council*, January, 1956, 4.)

[85] Tom P. Brady, *Segregation and the South: An Address to the Commonwealth Club of California, October 4, 1957*, 8.

[86] Association of Citizens' Councils of Mississippi, *Crime Report Reveals Menace of Integration* (Greenwood, n.d.). This one-page flier was offered for mass distribution by the Council's Greenwood office at a price of $1.00 for twenty copies.

demonstrated what perceptive southern white men—and intellectually honest scientists—had known all along: the Negro possessed genetically determined "criminal tendencies" which rendered him unfit for free association in white society.[87]

In addition to their greater proclivity for crimes of violence, Councilors believed that blacks were more prone to disease, especially social disease, than whites.[88] In this vein, the Capital Citizens' Council of Little Rock cautioned against the "diabolical venereal phase of integration." Releasing figures purporting to show that in Arkansas fifteen Negroes were syphiloid for every white who carried the disease, it warned that "uncontested" medical data demonstrated that little girls were "highly susceptible" to contracting the dreaded affliction from contact with drinking fountains, books, towels, and gym clothes.[89] Some Councilors believed that the very blood of the Negro was a carrier for disease and demanded that the American Red Cross label plasma and whole blood by race so that Caucasians would not contract sickle cell anemia and other diseases frequently found in "negroid blood." [90] With disease among Negroes, as with crime, Council statisticians demonstrated that the rates were much higher in such "integrated" states as Illinois, Massachusetts, New Jersey, and Ohio than in Alabama, Georgia, Louisiana, and Mississippi. "The moral restrictions inherent in segregation," hypothesized one anonymous Council pamphleteer,

[87] "Army Covering up Negro Crime Rate with Double Talk," *The Citizens' Council,* October, 1956, 2; George, *The Biology of the Race Problem,* 23; "Savages Stalk Corridors of Northern 'Blackboard Jungles,'" *The Citizens' Councils,* November, 1960, 4.

[88] Association of Citizens' Councils of Mississippi, *The St. Louis Story: Integrated Schools Hurting Both White, Colored Pupils* (Greenwood, n.d.). This single-sheet, legal-size flier contains tables on crime and disease based on statistics provided by the American States' Rights Association.

[89] Capital Citizens' Council, *The Little Rock School Board's Plans for Your Child,* 14.

[90] For example, see the anonymous pamphlet, *Sickle Cell Anemia* (n.p., n.d.), probably published by the Association of Citizens' Councils of Arkansas in its 1959 campaign on behalf of Arkansas House Bill 385, which would have required labeling of blood by race. See also Arkansas *Democrat,* February 16, 1959, for numerous Capital Citizens' Council-sponsored advertisements calling for labeled blood, and a letter to the editor by L. D. Poynter, president of the Association of Citizens' Councils of Arkansas, in the *Arkansas Gazette,* February 28, 1958, outlining the organization's case for blood labeling.

accounted for the relatively low incidence of disease, illegitimacy, and crime among the states of the Deep South.[91]

Segregation, then, was right. It was right not simply because of history, nor even because of science and religion. It was right because integration—the very quintessence of ignorance, evil, and unholiness—was so utterly wrong.

[91] Association of Citizens' Councils, *The St. Louis Story*.

CHAPTER X

Race and the Radical Right

ALTHOUGH not primarily a political movement, the Citizens' Council's ideology closely resembled the doctrines and beliefs of the States' Rights Democratic party of 1948. Like the Dixiecrat party, it was the child of dissent, sired by tradition-minded white men in reaction to advancing civil rights for Negroes. Like its predecessor, the Council's major objective was the preservation of the racial status quo. Like it again, the organization's appeal embraced not only racial anxieties but also such issues of general concern to southern whites as the increasing decline of the region's influence in national politics and the growing centralization of government. Desiring a shift in the balance of functions between state and federal governments and fearful of the trend toward big government, Councilors, perhaps not less than the Dixiecrats themselves, regarded their movement as the last bastion of constitutionalism. In their view, the growth of the general welfare state was not the logical extension of the American democratic experiment. It was a radical departure from the guidelines set down by the framers of the Constitution. To them, the great and noble nation founded as a "Republic of Sovereign States" had, through the erosion of the rights reserved exclusively for the several states by the Tenth Amendment, been reduced to a "totalitarian autocracy," a "Federal Government that is foreign to what the Framers had in mind." Indeed, so complete had been the encroachments of "creeping federalism" that by mid-century the once-sovereign states were mere colonies, "paying tribute" to Federal coffers.[1]

But the Council's economic and political conservatism, unlike its social conservatism, was not immediately apparent. From the outset, states' rights had been a major rallying cry of the movement; but its primary concern was the "right" of the southern states to isolate the Negro from white society, not lofty abstractions of Jeffersonian localism. Gradually, however, themes of broader appeal began to emerge. As early as July, 1955, nearly a year before Councilors from eleven states met in New Orleans to form the Citizens' Councils of America, William J. Simmons boasted that in the Council movement "much more is involved than the school segregation issue." Maintaining that his organization was not merely a white supremacist group, the Mississippian described the Council movement as the vanguard of an emerging "conservative revolt throughout the country." The problems that concerned the Council, he asserted, were not merely sectional problems, for "the trend toward the welfare state, the drift toward totalitarianism, the dangers of the United Nations" were transcendent issues confronting all of America.[2] In November, 1956, Simmons repeated his belief that the growth of the Council movement symbolized, "fundamentally, the first real stirrings of a conservative revolt in this country."[3] Increasingly thereafter, his public expressions affirmed his conviction that "integration is not the only battle in this wide-ranging social conflict." In his view the apparently ceaseless expansion of a centralized and bureaucratic government, the philosophy of the welfare state and the social gospel, the erosion of states' rights, confiscatory income taxes, and the increasingly collectivized pattern

1 See esp. Homo Americanus (pseudonym), "The New Federalist, Number One," and "The New Federalist, Number Two," *The Citizens' Council*, September, 1957, 1, 4, and November, 1957, 3–4, and Richard Morphew, *Ole Miss and the Constitution: An Address to the Associated Students of the California Institute of Technology, Pasadena, October 17, 1962* (n.p., n.d.).

2 Quoted in Jackson *Daily News*, July 23, 1955. See also Montgomery *Advertiser*, August 22, 1955. Simmons carried essentially the same message to audiences outside of the South. See *The Mid-West Hears the South's Story*.

3 Quoted in Betty E. Chmaj, "Paranoid Patriotism: The Radical Right and the South," *Atlantic Monthly*, 210 (November, 1962), 92.

of American life were all manifestations of "a total, all-out assault against American conservatism." [4]

The Council's growing identification with a broad conservative movement was also reflected in its publications. Initially, *The Citizens' Council,* official organ of the Association of Citizens' Councils of Mississippi, was devoted entirely to the race issue. But after the formation of the "national" organization and the adoption of the Mississippi tabloid as the voice of the entire movement, the newspaper offered a more diversified fare of interest to a wide range of right-wing readers. Increasingly, headlines read "U.N. Plans to Brain-Wash World Youth" and "Welfare State Crushes Constitutional Liberty," as well as "Survey Clearly Shows Racial Integration Has Lowered Standards of Public Education." [5] Once trained almost exclusively on the "mixiecrats" and the "National Association for the Agitation of Colored People," the range of the monthly's editorial cannons was extended to include "dupes," "do-gooders," and other "misguided pseudo-liberals" who subscribed to "federal oppression" and the "tyranny of big government." Similarly, *The Citizen,* successor to the original tabloid, differed but little from such organs of the far right as the *Dan Smoot Report* and H. L. Hunt's *Life Lines.* Thus, even before the first group was formed outside of the old Confederacy, the Council could claim that its "aims and objectives are nation-wide in scope and appeal," and its "program . . . designed to preserve ALL rights of EVERY state—not just those rights involving the South's segregation laws." [6]

In some respects, then, the movement's ideology matured as the organization grew. Racism remained the nucleus of its thought, but the Council's ideological circumference expanded to encompass the politico-economic attitudes characteristic of conservatism. This identification with the right wing was in some respects merely an exaggerated extension of ultraconservative Dixiecrat thought. But in a more profound sense, it represented a departure from the

[4] William J. Simmons, "Race in America: The Conservative Stand," *The Search for America,* ed. Huston Smith, 62. See also Simmons, *Civil Rights and the Oil Industry: An Address to the Desk and Derrick Club, Fort Worth, Texas, October 2, 1963* (n.p., n.d.).

[5] *The Citizens' Council,* July, 1956, 1, October, 1956, 1, 4, February, 1956, 1.

[6] Ibid., June, 1957, 4, September, 1957, 2.

legacy of 1948 and a growing intellectual alliance with what Seymour Martin Lipset has aptly called the "radical right." [7]

Although its claim of being a "nation-wide organization" can hardly be taken seriously, the national aspirations of the Councils' leadership cannot be doubted. As even the most myopic segregationist surely realized, such aspirations could never be achieved aboard the narrow vehicle of white supremacy. To attract the support of conservatives beyond Dixie's borders, the organization needed an issue of broader national concern than the social status of black Americans. In the decade of the 1950's, such an issue was anti-Communism. Certainly the Dixiecrats were no friends of the Kremlin, as Governor J. Strom Thurmond's campaign rhetoric readily illustrated. During the closing weeks of the frenzied presidential race of 1948, the States' Rights candidate from South Carolina not only attributed the Truman administration's entire civil rights program to the "demands of the parlor pinks and the subversives," but charged that the Fair Employment Practices Commission was "hatched in the brains of Communists." [8] But as Thurmond stumped the South in search of its 127 electoral votes, the Cold War was still in its infancy: the Communists had only the previous February seized the government of Czechoslovakia, Alger Hiss was still awaiting trial, China remained in the failing grasp of Chiang Kai-shek, and the Soviets had not yet detonated their first atomic bomb. These were but the opening salvos of a rapidly escalating international crisis that would soon make such faraway places as Panmunjom, Quemoy, Matsu, Budapest, and the Suez everyday words in apprehensive American households. The fears and frustrations engendered by this chain of events in the Cold War focused public attention on internal security as seldom before, and lent a disturbing aura of credibility to popular anxieties about Communist subversion. Linking race to these fears and frustrations, the Citizens' Council turned to anti-Communism with a virulence that could not have made sense in 1948, in those relatively innocent

[7] Lipset first used the term in "The Sources of the 'Radical Right,'" *The New American Right,* ed. Daniel Bell (New York: Criterion Books, 1955), 166–233.

[8] Quoted in Sarah McCulloh Lemmon, "The Ideology of the 'Dixiecrat' Movement," *Social Forces,* 30 (December, 1951), 166.

days before Senator Joseph R. McCarthy stepped into national prominence at Wheeling, West Virginia, to charge that Communist spies held strategic positions in the Department of State.

Fortunately for the nation's equilibrium, McCarthyism was not a long-lived phenomenon. Even as the Supreme Court overturned the *Plessy* doctrine in 1954, the senator who had brought the fear of domestic subversion to the level of national panic was falling precipitously from prominence. But, in pockets of extremism, the miasma of suspicion and malaise that he had encouraged lingered to haunt the sleep of frightened patriots. One of the largest of these reservoirs of McCarthyite hysteria, oddly enough, was to be found south of the Potomac.[9]

In many ways, the South was an unlikely environment for an anti-Communist crusade—if for no other reason than that the region had virtually no Communists. Despite its racial agitation, the South remained a section singularly untroubled by leftist influence. Indeed, this region which spawned so many organizations of the radical right proved almost impervious to the incursions of the radical left. With no apparent Communists in view, Dixie was inclined to look on indifferently while much of the rest of the nation indulged in the excesses of the McCarthy era. Yet while it had been (in the words of Nathan Glazer and Seymour Lipset) "the most anti-McCarthy section of the country" during the early 1950's, the South of the post-1954 period plunged headlong into superpatriotism.[10]

In part, at least, the explanation for this new vitality of anti-Communism in the post-*Brown* South may be traced to the swift

[9] For analyses of resurgent McCarthyism in the South since 1954, see Ralph E. Ellsworth and Sarah M. Harris, *The American Right Wing: A Report to the Fund for the Republic* (Washington: Public Affairs Press, 1962), passim; Chmaj, "Paranoid Patriotism," 91–97; Wilma Dykeman and James Stokely, "McCarthyism under the Magnolias," *The Progressive,* 23 (July, 1959), 6–9; Harry S. Ashmore's essay, "The New Know-Nothingism," in his *Epitaph for Dixie* (New York: W. W. Norton, 1957), 150–71; and Reese Cleghorn, *Radicalism, Southern Style: A Commentary on Regional Extremism of the Right* (Atlanta: Southern Regional Council, 1968).

[10] Nathan Glazer and Seymour Lipset, "The Polls on Communism and Conformity," *The New American Right,* 160; Dykeman and Stokely, "McCarthyism under the Magnolias," 6; Chmaj, "Paranoid Patriotism," 95.

rate of change which had so rapidly altered the face of the region. Already experiencing a difficult period of transition wrought by an economic revolution, a major war, and sweeping New Deal reforms, much of the South was ill prepared for the tremors loosed upon it by the quickening pace of civil rights. The economic dynamism that had transformed rural America into an industrialized and urbanized world power came late to the South—but it did come, and it came with astonishing rapidity. In its wake followed not only greater economic balance and diversity, but a threatening array of socio-economic changes which altered time-honored Dixie values and further diluted southern homogeneity.[11] Then came *Brown* v. *Board of Education*, with all of the domestic upheavals implicit in that decision, and many confused, resentful, and ultimately defiant Southerners began to look about for substantive explanations for the kaleidoscope of internal strains and divisive elements cracking the very substratum of traditional southern society. Vexed by labor unrest or troubled by rising Negro expectations, the conservative Southerner was not predisposed to view regional social change as an irresistible phase of democratic development. Unable and unwilling to objectify the sources of his anxieties, he learned to speak in vague terms of conspiracy. Just as an earlier generation of conservative Americans had seen a frightful red specter lurking behind labor unrest, the

[11] Studies which examine economic and social change in the South are numerous. See esp. Clark, *The Emerging South*, 104–23, passim; Dewey W. Grantham, Jr., *The Democratic South* (Athens: University of Georgia Press, 1963), 69–98; John C. McKinney and Edgar T. Thompson, eds., *The South in Continuity and Change* (Durham: Duke University Press, 1965); John M. Machlachlan and Joe S. Floyd, Jr., *This Changing South* (Gainesville: University of Florida Press, 1956), esp. Ch. 8, "This Changing South," 142–51; William H. Nicholls, "The South as a Developing Area," *Journal of Politics*, 26 (February, 1964), 22–40; Nicholls, *Southern Tradition and Regional Progress* (Chapel Hill: University of North Carolina Press, 1960); Allan P. Sindler, ed., *Change in the Contemporary South* (Durham: Duke University Press, 1963); C. Vann Woodward, "The Search for Southern Identity," *The South and the Sectional Image*, ed. Grantham, 173–86. More popularized accounts of the same subject include Harry Ashmore, *Epitaph for Dixie* (New York: W. W. Norton, 1957), 113–32; James McBride Dabbs, *The Southern Heritage* (New York: Alfred A. Knopf, 1958), 191–208; Ralph McGill, *The South and the Southerner*, 190–212, passim; and William T. Polk, *Southern Accent: From Uncle Remus to Oak Ridge* (New York: William Morrow Co., 1953), 231ff.

New Deal's "coddling" of the Negro, and such wartime innovations as the FEPC, the disquieted Southerner of the post-*Brown* period regarded the Negro revolution as a product of the "Communist conspiracy." [12] Thus, half a decade late, the region turned to militant anti-Communism.

The organized resistance movement took readily to Red-baiting. Almost from its inception, Council spokesmen equated the drive for Negro equality with a Marxist plot to destroy America by sapping its Caucasian energies through miscegenation. Such was the subject of a speech at the first statewide convention of the Citizens' Councils of Mississippi. Addressing this "great patriotic organization" and its "courageous, intelligent, and forthright" leadership in December, 1955, Senator James O. Eastland charged that in striking down separate-but-equal public education "the Court has responded to a radical, pro-Communist political movement in this country." Moreover, the *Brown* decision was "dictated by political pressure groups bent upon the destruction of the American system of government, and the mongrelization of the white race." [13]

These were themes to which the Mississippi senator would frequently return in future statements to the resistance movement. In a widely distributed Council pamphlet, for example, he mustered the full authority of his position as chairman of both the Senate Judiciary Committee and the Senate Internal Security Subcommittee to answer the question *Is the Supreme Court Pro-Communist?* with an emphatic affirmative. In the seventy-odd cases involving Communist or pro-Communist activities heard by the Court during the tenure of Chief Justice Earl Warren, Eastland charged, the nation's

[12] The appeal of the conspiracy theory of history to the radical right has been ably summarized by Victor C. Ferkiss, "Political and Intellectual Origins of American Radicalism, Right and Left," *The Annals of the American Academy of Political and Social Science,* 344 (November, 1962), 6–11. The theme of conspiracy in the era of McCarthy has been examined by several of the writers in the symposium assembled by Daniel Bell in 1955 and revised in 1963. See esp. Bell, "The Dispossessed—1962;" Talcott Parsons, "Social Strains in America—1955," Seymour M. Lipset, "Three Decades of the Radical Right: Coughlinites, McCarthyites, and Birchers—1962," *The Radical Right,* 1–38, 175–92, 313–69.

[13] James O. Eastland, *We've Reached Era of Judicial Tyranny: An Address before the State-Wide Convention of the Association of Citizens' Councils of Mississippi, Jackson, December 1, 1955,* 3–5.

highest tribunal "sustained the position advocated by the Communists" fully forty-six times.[14]

The corollary to the allegation that the Court had become a puppet of what another Council hero, Major General Edwin Walker, called the "control apparatus" of "international Communism,"[15] was the assumption that integration itself was a sinister phase of the Marxist plan to create a "raceless, classless, faceless" world.[16] Self-styled as "the only nation-wide organization dedicated to the preservation of the white race,"[17] the Council readily assumed the responsibility of exposing integration for what it was—a "Soviet scheme to mongrelize the races."[18] Second only to the question of race differences itself, Communist subversion became a principal tenet in the Council's defense of segregation.

Among the many professional Red-baiters attracted to the movement, few were more dedicated than Medford Evans, who had been, as he proudly declared, "a member of or a participant in a dozen different anti-Communist, pro-American, conservative organ-

14 Eastland, *Is the Supreme Court Pro-Communist?* (Richmond: Patrick Henry Group, n.d.).

15 Quoted in Bell, "The Dispossessed—1962," *New American Right*, 8.

16 *The Citizens' Council*, December, 1957, 1; April, 1959, 1.

17 This boast is on the Citizens' Councils of America letterhead.

18 *The Citizens' Council*, April, 1956, 1. Numerous examples showing the importance of anti-Communism to the Council movement are to be found in the publications of the state associations. See esp. the Association of Citizens' Councils of Georgia, *Bulletin*, October, 1964; July–August, 1965. This periodical's militantly anti-Communist line renders it almost indistinguishable from a Birch Society publication of the same name. Similar in tone are many issues of *The Defenders News and Views*, the official publication of the Virginia Defenders of State Sovereignty and Individual Liberties. The August–September, 1959, issue of this publication carried a revealing article entitled "Communism in Virginia," which pointed out that there were no "card-carrying Communists in Virginia" only because "the Communist Party no longer issues membership cards." But "the masterlist maintained only in Moscow" would reveal a surprising number of otherwise respectable Virginians, who "might themselves be surprised, for many of the camp-followers of communism are unconscious of the work they do, Ministers especially." Other articles in the same issue were entitled "Communism Has Invaded Every Aspect of Life in These United States" and "Why Are We Americans Fatheads about Reds?"

izations of one kind and another." [19] Quite obviously, his eight years in the cloak-and-dagger milieu of the AEC were reflected in his hypersensitivity to issues of national security and postwar international tensions. Like many Americans who had observed the deterioration of the wartime alliances, anxiously watched the euphoria of Yalta fade into the ominous reality of Potsdam, and seen their worst fears of Soviet duplicity realized in eastern Europe, the Council's chief anti-Communist specialist could only interpret the espionage cases of Alger Hiss and Julius and Ethel Rosenberg as documentary confirmation that insidious forces were boring from within the framework of the nation itself.[20] Although it can hardly be said that Evans brought intellectual vitality to the tired cliché of conspiracy, his advanced degree from a prestigious university and his wide reputation in conservative circles as a publicist of national circulation, as well as his long and intimate relationship with the occult world of atomic power, did lend a degree of dignity to the radical right.

In his opening salvo for *The Citizen*, "Forced Integration Is Communism in Action," Evans applied his devil theory of historical causation to the desegregation of public schools. Addressing himself to the question, "What is integration?" he examined the roots of contemporary racial unrest and concluded that "historically anlayzed [*sic*] and on the basis of the facts which we can see before us, it is a strategic campaign of the *world communist movement*. It is just that—nothing more and nothing less." [21]

[19] Medford Evans, "Forced Integration Is Communism in Action," *The Citizen*, 6 (September, 1962), 11.

[20] Evans believed that Mississippi was the primary target for Communist subversion in the United States. See his article, "Special Report: Why the Reds Say 'Mississippi Must Go!'" *The Citizen*, 9, (April, 1965), 4–15, an article also published in the April, 1965, issue of the Birch magazine, *American Opinion*. For examples of Evans's writing reflecting his obsession with national security and the Communist menace, see "Have They Really Got It? Fact and Myth about Soviet Atomic Strength," *Human Events*, 14 (June, 1957), 1–14; "The Atomic Disarmament Trap," *National Review*, 1 (November 26, 1955), 13–15; "An Open Letter to Dr. Oppenheimer," *National Review*, 2 (August 18, 1956), 18–19; *Civil Rights Myths and Communist Realities* (New Orleans: Conservative Society of America, 1965).

[21] Evans, "Forced Integration Is Communism in Action," *The Citizen*, 6 (September, 1962), 11.

Evans's suppositions about the genesis of desegregation were hardly novel. Indeed, in one of the earliest issues of *The Citizens' Council,* a banner headline warned of an "ANTI-WHITE PLOT HATCHED IN MOSCOW." "The Racial revolution seeking to wreck America's entire social system," the front-page story divulged, "is the offshoot of a diabolical plot first hatched in Soviet Russia by Communists nearly three decades ago." [22] Moreover, the nexus between the NAACP and the international Communist apparatus was the central motif of literally hundreds of Council speeches and publications.[23] As Georgia's militantly segregationist attorney general, Eugene Cook, told the Mississippi Citizens' Council on its first anniversary, the NAACP was in reality the "National Association for the Promotion of Communism." [24] The irony of such a charge against an increasingly cautious and conservative organization escaped most of the massive resisters.[25]

Publicly, at least, the Council indicted Communism for effecting the slow and agonizing death of Jim Crow. But there were those

22 *The Citizens' Council,* April, 1956, 1.

23 See, for example, the following Council-published pamphlets: *The Citizens' Council—What It Is* (Dallas: The Association of Citizens' Councils of Texas, n.d.); *The Undeniable Facts about the NAACP* (Montgomery: Citizens' Councils of Alabama, n.d.); Eugene Cook, *The Ugly Truth about the NAACP: An Address before the 55th Annual Convention of the Peace Officers Association of Georgia; The Story of the NAACP as Told by One of Its Founders* (Greenwood: Association of Citizens' Councils of Mississippi, n.d.). See also *The Citizens' Council,* May, 1957, which is devoted largely to the "[Communist] Front Records of Ten NAACP Leaders."

24 Quoted in *The Citizens' Council,* June, 1956, 1. Dykeman and Stokely in "McCarthyism under the Magnolias," 6–7, consider Cook's *The Ugly Truth about the NAACP* (which "was given saturation distribution throughout the South") a prime example of the region's post-*Brown* neo-McCarthyism.

25 Dykeman and Stokely, *Neither Black nor White,* 98. J. Edgar Hoover, whose statements on Negro crime and Communist subversion were frequently quoted by the Council, does not confirm this allegation against the NAACP. In his study of subversive activities in America, the FBI chief concluded that the NAACP's leadership has consistently thwarted Communist infiltration. (Hoover, *Masters of Deceit: The Story of Communism in America and How to Fight It* [New York: Henry Holt, 1958], 246–47.) At its forty-seventh annual convention, the NAACP reaffirmed its resolution of 1950, denying membership to "Communists and/or persons prominently identified with the Ku Klux Klan, White Citizens' Councils, or Communist front or Communist-line organizations. . . ." See NAACP, *Annual Report, 1956,* 66–67.

among the Council's leaders who entertained private doubts about the veracity of the conspiracy theory of racial problems. One such skeptic, oddly enough, was William J. Simmons himself. Under his editorial direction, *The Citizens' Council* and its more polished successor, *The Citizen,* burgeoned with sensational exposés of the Communist threat to southern institutions. In his columns and major addresses he frequently paid tribute to the conspiracy thesis through allusions to the "Communist-inspired and Communist-dominated" integration movement.[26] But in more candid moments he attributed the South's predicament to "a wave of equalitarian philosophy that started in the early part of the twentieth century, primarily with the progressive educationists such as John Dewey." This progressive equalitarianism, he believed, permeated the very fabric of American education and, through the influence of Franz Boas and his disciples, came to dominate American science. In his view, this spirit of equality "resulted directly in the Supreme Court school-integration decision." [27]

Simmons was not alone when he argued that the "equalitarian dogma," not Communism, was at the root of southern adversity. A sizable faction within the Council, including some of the most articulate professionals on the CCA staff, insisted that the movement must be anti-Negro first and foremost, and only incidentally anti-Communist. This was the spirit of an address by Richard Morphew, the Council's public relations director, at the annual leadership conference in 1965. In an obvious allusion to the Birch Society, Morphew warned that the Council must avoid overconcern with "side issues" such as anti-Communism, which had diverted many conservative organizations from the real issue—racial segregation.[28]

[26] See the following examples of Simmons's editorial writing: "Red Aims and Black Votes," *The Citizen,* 6 (February, 1962), 2, and "Survival Is the Issue," *The Citizen,* 9 (February, 1965), 2, 28.

[27] Quoted in Reese Cleghorn, "The Segs," *Esquire,* 61 (January, 1964), 135.

[28] Norman Kilpatrick, "Councils Divided over John Birch Society," undated manuscript, copy in Kilpatrick File, Southern Regional Council. Kilpatrick's role in the history of the Council movement is discussed in Ch. 10. According to Kilpatrick, "the official Council position is that race is the major domestic and foreign issue in the world today, and that while Communist influence can be seen in certain aspects of racial problems, and should be publicized,

Clearly Council leaders were not of a single mind on the relationship between Communism and the integration crisis. Their differences, however, were largely of degree rather than kind. They could all agree that race was the major domestic and international problem. In the final analysis, the question of whether the Communists caused the problem or merely complicated it did not diminish their determination to deny the Negro full equality before the law.

In terms of its rhetorical flag-waving, its overweening concern with Communist subversion, and its unabashed social Darwinism, the Council's ideology could scarcely be distinguished from the ideology of other American superpatriotic organizations. With only a little exaggeration, a CCA field director, Joseph Mitchell, could remark that "our philosophy is the same as that of the John Birch Society, but the Birch Society refuses to deal with the race issue." [29] It was scarcely remarkable, then, that Councilors and Birchers should cooperate in many areas. This was especially true in Florida, where, as one Council spokesman from the Sunshine State acknowledged, the patriots of the state's numerous Birch Society cells and the members of the Citizens' Council frequently combined their offensive against the imminent dangers of Communism.[30] Many of the Council's top leaders were Birchers, including not only Medford Evans, managing editor of its official journal, but William J. Simmons, its national administrator, and Louis W. Hollis, its national director.[31] Moreover, the personnel utilized by the CCA in its organizational activities outside the South were often Birchers. For example, the founder of the ineffectual New York Citizens' Council, Frank Purinton, was a Birchite who headed the Suffolk Freedom Fighters, an ultrapatriotic group which formally merged with the Birch Society in 1962.[32] Similarly, Kent H. Steffgen, the first CCA field director for California, had been a member of the Birch Society

---

race is a basic and inherent problem and must be put first in the thinking of all 'patriotic' Americans." See also the "White Book," 7.

29 Kilpatrick, "Councils Divided over John Birch Society."

30 Ibid.

31 The Birch Society is a secret society and membership is generally not made public, but Hollis has admitted to the press that both he and Simmons were Birchers. (Los Angeles *Times*, July 2, 1964.)

32 Report, Southern Office, Anti-Defamation League, June 1, 1965.

since its inception in 1958, as well as its paid coordinator for California, Missouri, Kansas, and Nebraska.

Yet for all of their apparent philosophical similarities, and for all of their frequently overlapping memberships, the Council and the Birch Society did have at least one fundamental difference—their attitudes on race. The Council's entire organization was structured around its anti-Negro attitudes. But the Birch Society, though many of its individual members may have been racists, managed to avoid the onus of Negrophobia as official policy. Indeed, a distinguishing characteristic of the far right of the Cold War period was its freedom from overt racism. Earlier twentieth-century manifestations of ultraconservatism in America, such as the Klan of the 1920's and the protofascist "shirt groups" of the 1930's, had been tainted by anti-Semitic and anti-Negro dicta. But beginning with the age of McCarthy, the racial theme began to disappear from right-wing ideology. If nothing else, the McCarthy era demonstrated that there need be no direct correlation between conservatism and racism.[33] Thus from his study of opinion polls Seymour Lipset concluded that rank-and-file McCarthy supporters were less likely to be anti-Semitic, and no more likely to be anti-Negro, than those who were critical of the Wisconsin senator.[34] Likewise, as we have seen, Robert Welch's organization officially declared its opposition to racial intolerance, whether anti-Jew or anti-Negro.[35] Even Tulsa's evangelistic parson, the Reverend Billy James Hargis, warned his fellow Communist-baiters that the Christian Crusade "cannot tolerate anti-Semitic statements, anti-Negro statements; we are not here to fight Jews . . . or Negroes. We are here to fight Communists."[36]

There were, of course, areas of difference other than race between radical-right groups and the segregation organization. To be sure,

[33] See Peter Viereck, "The Revolt against the Elite," *The New American Right,* 98–99; Ferkiss, "Political and Intellectual Origins of American Radicalism, Right and Left," 10; and Lipset, "Three Decades of the Radical Right: Coughlinites, McCarthyites, and Birchers—1962," 342–45.

[34] Lipset, "Three Decades of the Radical Right," 342–45.

[35] J. Allen Broyles, *The John Birch Society: Anatomy of a Protest* (Boston: Beacon Press, 1964), 127–29.

[36] Harold H. Martin, "Doomsday Merchant on the Far, Far Right," *The Saturday Evening Post,* 235 (September 28, 1962), 2.

there were elements within the Council which could agree fully with the Bircher maxim that the United States was a republic and not a democracy. Some, such as R. Carter Pittman, president of the statewide association in Georgia, would even equate democracy with Communism. For "a democracy," he believed, "is a government in which the will of the people is translated into action without regard to the constitution or laws." "Pure democracy is always the forerunner of communism. Communist dictators always dictate in the name of the people—the people's democracy." [37] But Pittman's distrust of the democratic process did not reflect the attitudes of rank-and-file Councilors—many of whom had probably never given the question serious consideration. Indeed, the segregationist movement took genuine pride in its "local grass roots organization"; its spokesmen frequently boasted that it was "the modern version of the old-time town meeting called to meet any crisis by expressing the will of the people." [38] Whatever disaffection Councilors may have occasionally exhibited toward democracy was motivated less by a mistrust of the majority will than by a fear of the full implications of color-blind equalitarianism.[39]

Similarly, there was a strain of anti-union sentiment among many Council leaders, and some, such as William N. Rainach, the leader of the movement in Louisiana and the first president of the Citizens' Councils of America, had been instrumental in the passage of state

[37] R. Carter Pittman, *The County Unit System Prevents City Political Machines from Controlling the State of Georgia: An Address to the Associated Industries of Georgia at Rome, Georgia, August, 1959* (Atlanta: States' Rights Councils of Georgia, Inc., n.d.). See also Pittman's *The Supreme Court, the Broken Constitution, and the Shattered Bill of Rights.*

[38] *2nd Annual Report: August, 1956,* 1; [Robert Patterson], *The Citizens' Council,* 1; Citizens' Councils of Alabama, *The Citizens' Council: The South's Only Answer,* 2. These pamphlets asserted that "history proves that the supreme power in government by the people always has been public sentiment."

[39] Pittman so feared the concept of equality that he dismissed the Declaration of Independence as a "Jeffersonian perversion" and "history's most effective piece of propaganda," "written to serve the temporary purposes of a sanguinary conflict." Pittman, "Liberty v. Equality: The Eternal Conflict," *American Bar Association Journal,* 46 (August, 1960), 873–80 (an article glowingly reviewed in *The Citizens' Council,* September, 1960, 3); and "The 'Blessing of Liberty' v. the 'Blight of Equality,'" *North Carolina Law Review,* 42 (Fall, 1963), 86–105.

"right-to-work" legislation.[40] But once again, rank-and-file Councilors—among whom were to be found a substantial number of union members in such industrial centers of the region as Birmingham[41]—opposed the extension of organized labor in the South largely for reasons other than an antipathy to trade unionism. The national labor organizations, particularly the Congress of Industrial Organizations, had been among the most consistent supporters of Negro equality. This pro–civil rights position, as well as the outspokenly hostile attitude of much of organized labor's leadership toward the Citizens' Council,[42] and not any widespread anti-union sentiment among Councilors themselves, accounted for the movement's opposition to the unionization of southern labor. However much this segregationist movement abhorred the equalitarian slogans of the national labor organizations, it did not officially endorse such conservative favorites as national right-to-work legislation or laws forbidding industry-wide collective bargaining.

[40] H. L. Mitchell, "On the Rise of the White Citizens' Council and Its Ties with Anti-Labor Forces in the South: A Preliminary Report" (unpublished paper, Southern Regional Council, January 30, 1956). See also Mitchell's "A Report on the Rise of the White Citizens' Councils in the South" (unpublished paper, Southern Education Reporting Service, November 21, 1955); and his "The White Citizens' Councils vs. Southern Trade Unions" (unpublished paper, Southern Regional Council, March 12, 1956). Mitchell was president of the National Agriculture Workers Union, an AFL-CIO affiliate.

[41] In 1956 Emmett Calhoun, chairman of the West End Citizens' Council in Birmingham and secretary of a local typographical union, estimated that 90 percent of the members of his Council's four hundred members were union people, and that 75 percent of the Council members in the Birmingham area belonged to a labor union. "Race Troubles Hurt Unions, Too: Drives to Organize the South Have Hit a Snag," *U.S. News and World Report,* 40 (April 6, 1956), 95–99. Similarly, a Columbia, South Carolina, official of the Textile Workers Union of America estimated in 1956 that 70 percent of the members of his local were members of the Citizens' Council. (Columbia *State,* May 19, 1956.)

[42] The AFL-CIO Executive Council, at its annual winter conference in Miami Beach, February 10, 1956, labeled the Citizens' Council a "new Ku Klux Klan without hoods [which] is ominous in its resemblance to . . . nazism and other totalitarian movements. . . ." (Quoted in Atlanta *Journal,* February 10, 1956.) Similarly, the Textile Workers Union of America, convening in Washington in 1956, resolved to "denounce the White Citizens' Councils and allied organizations as enemies of law and order and bitter foes of the labor movement. . . ." (Quoted in Columbia *State,* May 19, 1956.)

Much the same may be said for other conservative themes. At one time or another, upper-echelon Council spokesmen aligned themselves against a veritable cornucopia of liberal objectives, including minimum wage legislation, open housing laws, social security, medicare, graduated income taxes, repeal of the Walter-McCarran Immigration Act, public housing, and foreign aid. But these were sentiments of the conservative men who happened to lead the Citizens' Council. They were not attitudes upon which this essentially segregationist movement was founded, nor were they ever more than issues of tangential interest to the average Councilor.[43] "The Citizens' Councils . . . primary organizational purpose," declared the CCA's monthly newspaper in 1960, is "to restore the philosophies of States' Rights and racial integrity to their former pre-eminent position in our national, state and local governments throughout the United States. Other groups are organized to cope with fiscal matters, taxation, business and industry, and the other problems which confront our nation. We are the only national organization operating within our sphere."[44]

To a large degree, then, Council thought was essentially monistic. Racial difference was the ultimate reality before which all other issues paled in significance.

43 Perhaps the best example of the way in which issues of political and economic conservatism were subordinated to racial issues by the Citizens' Councils is to be found in the Association of Citizens' Councils of Mississippi, *The NAACP Legislative Scoreboard: The Civil Rights Crisis and the 84th Congress* (Greenwood, n.d.). In this fifteen-page pamphlet the voting records of the congressmen of the Eighty-fourth Congress were examined on issues which received the support of the NAACP: public housing, electoral college reform, extension of social security benefits, increase of minimum wage, and others. Because the NAACP had endorsed all of these issues, legislators who voted for any of them were considered to have "voted favorably to [the] NAACP." Not surprisingly, even Mississippi's own James O. Eastland, who voted for the extension of social security disability benefits and benefits for women, was found guilty of pro-NAACP voting behavior on two occasions.

44 Editorial, *The Citizens' Council,* September, 1960, 2.

PART IV

Action and Decline

CHAPTER XI

Black Challenge, White Response

IN the folklore of the Deep South there is no more cherished fiction than that of Negro contentment with segregation. According to this myth, southern black men recognized that the progress of their race could be attributed largely to the friendship and forbearance of southern whites; hence they wanted nothing more than to live out their days in peace and harmony under "our biracial system." Consequently, only the most cynical "racial agitators," heedless of the Negro's welfare, would seek to disrupt this mutually gratifying relationship.[1]

In one variation of this theme, a Council pamphleteer declared that 98 percent of both races preferred segregation. "Integration," the segregationist opined, "is urged by the NAACP, a few southern mulattoes, Northern Communist-front organizations and left-wing labor groups who would use the unsuspecting Negro as their tool." [2] To document this point, the organization's publications often carried statements by conservative Negro opponents of the NAACP,[3] and

[1] See, for example, Tom Ethridge, "Mississippi Notebook: Negro Progress Is Big Credit to White South," *The Citizens' Council*, February, 1956, 3.

[2] Brady, *Segregation and the South*, 4.

[3] See, for example, the following broadsides in the files of SERS: Association of Citizens' Councils, "Negro Archbishop Blasts NAACP Aims" (n.p., n.d.); and "Prominent Kingstree Negro Makes Frank Statement" (n.p., n.d.). See also *The Citizens' Council*, September, 1954, 4.

occasionally local Councils lowered the color barrier enough to permit black segregationists to address their meetings.[4] Moreover, local organizations in some states called upon "responsible negro leaders to cooperate with the Councils in the task of preserving racial harmony within the framework of segregation." In South Carolina, the state association encouraged its chapters to create race relations committees to elicit cooperation from the state's "right thinking" Negro leaders.[5] Claiming "the support of the thinking, conservative negro people," Mississippi Councilors even nurtured briefly a Parents-Teachers Youth Council as a kind of Negro counterpart to the Citizens' Council. The organization was designed to promote segregation by encouraging "race pride" among Negroes and exposing "agitators" in the black community.[6] But Negroes, understandably enough, demonstrated little enthusiasm for joint enterprises such as these. Ultimately even the Citizens' Councils of America acknowledged that one of the "most common errors in Southern thinking in the past few years has been . . . that negroes don't really want integration and will do nothing to aid its attainment." [7]

Indeed, many Negroes did desire desegregation, and, as the quickening tempo of black challenges to white supremacy indicated, not a few of them would do plenty to attain it. The first major attack on segregated schools in the post-*Brown* period came soon after the Court's implementation decree of May 31, 1955. Acting on instructions from the regional office, NAACP branches in seven southern states petitioned local boards of education to admit Negro pupils to all-white schools. Although more than eighty such petitions had been filed as classes convened in the fall, school officials in most instances neither replied nor publicly acknowledged the requests.[8]

4 Charleston *News and Courier*, May 11, 1957.

5 William J. Simmons, "A Statement of Policy: What Our Citizens' Councils Stand For," *The Citizens' Council*, February, 1956, 3; Martin, *The Deep South Says "Never"*, 64–66.

6 *Annual Report: August 1955*, 2; *The Citizens' Council*, February, 1956, 3; *Delta Democrat-Times*, July 24, 1955; *Southern School News*, August, 1955, 17.

7 "Three Southern Errors: Real Issues Now Unfold," *The Citizens' Council*, February, 1958, 4.

8 Petitions were filed in Alabama, Florida, Georgia, Mississippi, North

But in at least three states, whites answered with a vengeance. Spurred by local Citizens' Councils, militants in Alabama, Mississippi, and South Carolina met the black challenge with economic reprisal, social pressure, and in some cases violence.

Although repeatedly denying its role in white retaliation against Negroes, the Council, from its inception, advocated the use of intimidation as a means of quelling desegregation. At a July, 1954, meeting in Sunflower County, Mississippi, Arthur Clark, Jr., vice-president and one of the founders of the first Council, declared that the threat of desegregation could be effectively minimized by the removal of those who would "stir up discontent." "We propose to accomplish this," he indicated, "through the careful application of economic pressure upon men who cannot be controlled otherwise." [9] Duplicated and circulated to a carefully selected mailing list, and placed on a tape recording for use by early recruiting teams, Clark's "solution" found rapid acceptance in the nascent movement. Thus, in October, 1954, former state senator Fred Jones, an early Council stalwart and a member of the Mississippi association's first state executive committee, declared in a public statement that "we can accomplish our purposes largely with economic pressure in dealing with members of the Negro race who are not cooperating. . . ." [10]

Councilors in other states also took readily to the Mississippi plan. In neighboring Alabama, where the first Council was organized at Selma late in November, 1954, an early spokesman announced that the organization intended "to make it difficult, if not impossible, for any Negro who advocates desegregation to find and hold a job, get credit or renew a mortgage." [11] The following year when thirteen school desegregation petitions were filed in scattered districts across the state, Councilors urged angry whites in Bulloch,

---

Carolina, South Carolina, and Tennessee. See NAACP, *Annual Report: Progress and Reaction, 1955* (New York: NAACP, 1956), 21.

[9] Quoted in Anthony, "Pro-Segregation Groups," 5; and New York *Times*, November 21, 1954.

[10] Jackson *Clarion-Ledger*, October, 1954. See also Harold C. Fleming, "Resistance Movements and Racial Desegregation," *Annals of the American Academy of Political and Social Science*, 304 (March, 1964), 48; and *Annual Report: August, 1955*, 2.

[11] Quoted in "The Bite," *Time*, 64 (December 20, 1954), 54; *Southern School News*, January 6, 1955, 2.

Butler, and Dallas counties to employ economic reprisals. In Selma, where sixteen of twenty-nine signers of an August petition had lost their jobs by the first week in September, Council leaders expressed satisfaction with the "spontaneous" reaction of white employers. Although claiming neither "credit nor censure" for the firings, Dallas County Council president Alston Keith candidly observed: "I don't believe there would have been the unity of action that there was without the educational work of the Citizens' Council. They did just what we have been advocating right along."[12]

In South Carolina, where the first organization did not appear until August, 1955, Council leaders expressed a similar determination to bring economic pressure to bear on all persons identified with the NAACP. In Orangeburg whites were angered by the school petition; for, as the Orangeburg *Times and Democrat* expressed it, they were proud of having "pioneered in the equalization of schools and teacher's salaries, and . . . were sincerely convinced that they had dealt fairly and intelligently with racial problems."[13] Led by the mayor and W.T.C. Bates, an insurance agent who served as the head of the local Council, they retaliated with a campaign of systematic intimidation. Petitioners' names were printed in several issues of the *Times and Democrat*, and soon thereafter many were fired from their jobs and evicted from their rented homes. Several Negro merchants who had signed the appeal were unable to purchase merchandise from local wholesalers, and a service station operator was forced out of business by his gasoline distributor. New insurance policies were denied, credit terminated, and mortgages recalled. Confronted by pressures such as these, it was not remarkable that signers withdrew their names, declaring that they did not "fully understand" the meaning of the petition. By November, only twenty-six of the original fifty-seven signatures remained. Similar successes could be reported in other Palmetto State cities where

[12] Quoted in American Friends Service Committee, National Council of Churches of Christ in the United States of America, and Southern Regional Council, *Intimidation, Reprisal and Violence in the Southern Racial Crises* (n.p., n.d.), 10; and *Southern School News*, October, 1955, 8.

[13] Orangeburg *Times and Democrat*, as quoted in Edward Gamarekian, "The Ugly Battle of Orangeburg," *The Reporter*, 16 (January 24, 1957), 32.

Council boycotts were used, notably in Elloree and Summerton.[14]

Predictably, the boycott as an instrument of repression found most effective employment in a cotton center such as Yazoo City, Mississippi, the self-styled "Gateway to the Delta." The local Citizens' Council there was one of the state's oldest and largest, and as the Yazoo City *Herald* boasted, "from the very first this community's outstanding citizens have been members."[15] In a town of only 11,000 people the organization had grown from only 16 to nearly 1,500 by September, 1955. With such numbers, it was well prepared to meet the challenge of fifty-three signatures on a desegregation petition. In a full-page advertisement in the *Herald,* the Council published "an authentic list of the purported signers" of an NAACP petition. The list was also printed on large cardboard placards which were displayed in many of the community's stores, the bank, and even in cotton fields surrounding the city. As had happened elsewhere, economic sanctions followed and within a matter of weeks the petitioners' ranks were reduced to half a dozen. Again local Council leaders attributed the rash of reprisals to the "spontaneous reaction of public opinion."[16] Whatever the reason, a disapproving northern newspaper could observe with little exaggeration that, "with the awful spectre of Yazoo City before them, few Mississippi Negroes would sign a desegregation petition today."[17]

But the boycott, as the NAACP's southeastern regional office informed its branches, was "a two-edged sword."[18] In some areas of the Deep South, where white merchants depended heavily on the patronage of black consumers, Negroes could and occasionally did fight back with reprisals of their own. In Orangeburg, for example,

[14] Ibid., 32–34; William Gordon, "Boycotts Can Cut Two Ways," *New South,* 11 (April, 1956), 5–10; Quint, *Portrait in Black and White,* 51–52; Scheer, "The White Folks Fight Back," 9–12; Jacob Javits, *Discrimination—U.S.A.* (New York: Harcourt Brace, 1960), 201.

[15] Yazoo City *Herald,* August 8, 1957.

[16] American Friends Service Committee, *Intimidation,* 13; Jackson *Daily News,* December 11, 1955; David Halberstam, "A County Divided against Itself," *The Reporter,* 13 (December 15, 1955), 30–32.

[17] New York *Post,* as quoted in *Delta Democrat-Times,* January 31, 1957.

[18] NAACP, *Annual Report: The Year of the Great Decision, 1954* (New York: NAACP, 1955), 11–12.

a determined Negro population, comprising more than half of the town's total, demonstrated that economic pressure could indeed cut two ways. Orangeburg Negroes circulated their own list of twenty-three businesses known to be owned by councilors or their sympathizers. Joined by students at all-Negro South Carolina State College, the counterattack proved remarkably successful.

For months boycott and counterboycott continued, exacting a heavy toll on both sides. Although the Citizens' Council boasted that local whites had rallied with virtual unanimity to the side of the embattled merchants, this support proved insufficient. In the spring of 1956, Council President Bates announced his resignation for reasons of health and business. A spokesman for the local business community, however, acknowledged that Bates's dictatorial manner and his continuous pressure had caused resentment among many whites suffering from the Negro boycott. Moreover, as Republican county chairman, Bates himself may well have come to question the wisdom of reprisals—particularly when it might cost his party the support of Orangeburg's Negro Republican organization in the November election. At any rate, word quickly spread that petitioners could once again purchase goods and services from white businesses, and community boosters began to urge Negroes to shop at home instead of in nearby Columbia. Although the economic warfare gradually subsided, the basic issue remained unresolved. The number of petitioners was markedly reduced, but Negro parents continued to demand an end to segregation in the schools. No less resolutely, the white community continued to resist that demand.[19]

The Negro offensive in the "Battle of Orangeburg" was a particularly spectacular counterattack against white reprisals. More typically, Negroes resorted to defensive strategies. To assist the economically harassed, the NAACP sponsored a nationwide drive to obtain deposits for a special loan fund at the Tri-State Bank, a Negro-owned financial institution in Memphis. In its *Annual Report* for 1955 the civil rights organization stated that $300,000 had been made available in this way for secured loans to Negro victims of white boycotts. Smaller amounts were deposited for similar purposes

[19] Gamarekian, "The Ugly Battle of Orangeburg," 32–34; Gordon, "Boycotts Can Cut Two Ways," 7–8.

at a Negro-owned bank in Columbia, South Carolina. The NAACP also assisted in the resettlement and reemployment of some of the dispossessed, and charitable organizations in some cases distributed food and clothing to those in need.[20]

The Council's use of the boycott was widely deprecated both within and without the region. Repeatedly, the staunchly prosegregation Montgomery *Advertiser* condemned the Council's use of an "economic noose." "The night-riding and lash of the 1920's have become an abomination in the eyes of public opinion," the editor acidly observed, "so the bigots have resorted to a more decorous, tidy and less conspicuous method—economic thuggery." [21] In South Carolina, Lieutenant Governor Ernest F. Hollings cautiously expressed good will for the Council movement but suggested that "the organization of pressure is full of dangers." [22] Only a few weeks after the National Council of Churches of Christ in the U.S.A. registered its disapproval, the South Carolina Methodist Conference condemned "any action which seeks to strip a person of his means of livelihood." [23]

In the U.S. Congress, Representative Charles C. Diggs of Michigan demanded that the "credit squeeze" against members of his race be ended in the South and called for a "sweeping investigation" of the Citizens' Councils.[24] Even President Dwight David Eisenhower, in his State of the Union address of January 5, 1956, expressed concern that "in some localities allegations persist that Negro citizens are being . . . subjected to unwarranted economic pressure." [25]

Confronted by such criticism, the Citizens' Council hastily retreated from its original position of open advocacy for the boycott.

[20] NAACP, *Annual Report: Progress and Reaction,* 10; Oklahoma City *Black Dispatch,* January 22; Memphis *Commercial Appeal,* January 8; *Southern School News,* May 4, 1955; Gamarekian, "The Ugly Battle of Orangeburg," 32ff.

[21] Editorials, Montgomery *Advertiser,* November 30, 1954, September 13, December 13, 1955.

[22] Quoted in Charleston *News and Courier,* September 16, 1955. See also *The State,* September 16, 1955.

[23] *Christian Science Monitor,* June 30, 1955; *The State,* August 28, 1955; James McBride Dabbs, "Ironies of '55 Southern Style," *New South,* 10 (December, 1955), 2. See also Quint, *Profile in Black and White,* 50–51.

[24] Quoted in Norfolk *Journal and Guide,* April 9, 1955.

[25] *Congressional Record,* 84 Cong., 2 Sess., 1956, Part I, 143.

At an October, 1955, segregation rally in Charleston, William J. Simmons even denied that the organization had ever employed economic sanctions against Negroes. Its role, he asserted, had been limited to merely educating the public to the dangers in its midst. That same month, an article in the first issue of *The Citizens' Council* acknowledged that "individuals who belong to councils may have persuaded Negroes to remove their names from school integration petitions by various means short of violence"; but wherever reprisals were employed, they were adopted on "individual initiative and not as a group action." [26] Moreover, Robert Patterson, executive secretary of the Mississippi Association of Citizens' Councils, declared flatly: "We do not recommend economic pressure. That's false propaganda from the press. But of course we don't denounce 'freedom of choice' in business arrangements. If employers fire their help, that's their business." [27] Nevertheless, the charges persisted, and in 1957, Simmons, by then a chief spokesman for the movement in the South, reiterated the organization's case: "No, there never has been any economic pressure by the Councils as such. There never has been any organized attempt or recommendation to that effect by any Council. . . ." [28] Despite the frequency of the denials, the boycott, as one journal of liberal opinion expressed it, became "the trademark of the councils." [29] In the last analysis, Council professions of innocence in the face of seemingly incontrovertible evidence to the contrary were perhaps best explained by the Mississippi association when it noted in its *Annual Report* that "the Citizens' Councils think

26 Charleston *News and Courier,* October 5, 1955; Birmingham *News,* October 6, 1955; Thomas Waring, "Mississippi Councils Are Protecting Both Races," *The Citizens' Council,* October, 1956, 1.

27 Quoted in Wakefield, *Revolt in the South,* 45. Despite such denials, Patterson declared on numerous occasions in the 1960's that economic pressure was the most effective way to combat desegregation. See New Orleans *Times-Picayune,* March 7, 1960; Jackson (Tenn.) *Sun,* October 17, 1962; Jackson *Daily News,* February 26, 1963; and Robert Patterson, *The Road Ahead: An Address to Annual Leadership Conference of the Citizens' Councils of America, Montgomery, January 15, 1965* (Greenwood: Association of Citizens' Councils, n.d.).

28 Quoted in Carter, *The South Strikes Back,* 111.

29 Alfred Maund, "Grass Roots Racism: White Council at Work," *The Nation,* 181 (July 23, 1955), 70.

and plan as a group and then they are able to act as individuals. . . ."[30]

In many areas of the South a more immediate threat to white supremacy than school desegregation petitions was the Negro's access to the ballot box. In the course of a single decade—from the nullification of the all-white primary to the nullification of separate-but-equal schools—Negro registration in the eleven-state area had more than quadrupled. By 1956, there were at least 1,238,000 Negroes on the region's voting rolls.[31] Although that figure represented only 25 percent of the voting-age Negroes, as compared to 60 percent of the eligible whites, it nevertheless represented a substantial increase in the black man's political power and a growing threat to the white man's institutions. As the Council well understood, effective resistance to the *Brown* decision required the minimization of the Negro's role in state and local elections. In the campaign to limit, if not to eliminate altogether, Negro access to the polling places, the Council in Mississippi, as was its custom, stood in the vanguard.

Perhaps inevitably, Mississippi, the state with the highest percentage of Negroes in the nation, had the lowest percentage registered. Although Negroes comprised fully 41 percent of the state's voting age citizens in 1955, only 4 percent were officially eligible to vote. Alone among the southern states, the registration of black voters in Mississippi during 1953–55, the years immediately preceding and following the Court's desegregation ruling, leveled off and perhaps even declined.[32] Unquestionably, the paucity of black registrants in the Magnolia State reflected the unremitting hostility felt by an overwhelming majority of the state's white community toward even limited participation by Negroes in the political process. In 1954 that hostility was manifested in the form of a constitutional amendment tightening the state's registration law. Nevertheless,

[30] *Annual Report: August, 1955*, 2.

[31] In 1956, the Southern Regional Council, armed with a grant from the Fund for the Republic, deployed a small batallion of political consultants throughout the South to gather county-by-county data on Negro voting. For a summary of this data, see Price, *The Negro Voter in the South*.

[32] Ibid., 21.

extremist elements within the state, including the Citizens' Council which supported the amendment and even claimed credit for its passage, believed that the times required more stringent measures. Such measures were employed most notably in Belzoni, seat of Humphreys County, a Yazoo River town of some 4,000 inhabitants.

Before the appearance of the local Citizens' Council, 126 of Humphreys County's 16,000 Negroes were registered voters. Then, in the spring of 1955, Councilors began a systematic program of economic pressure. Negro registrants, like Negro petitioners, were fired, denied credit, and in other ways intimidated. Gradually, black registration declined to 95, or to what Medgar E. Evers, state secretary of the NAACP, called the "hard core." As Evers informed an Associated Press reporter in August, 1955, the Council then resorted to "other types of pressure." "They'd come and tell them 'You've lived in this community for a long time and if you want to stay here in peace, you'd better get your name off this list.'" These "personal visits," the Negro leader declared, reduced the voting rolls still further, to "about 35." [33]

One aspiring voter who would not be intimidated was Belzoni's NAACP president, Gus Courts, a sixty-six-year-old grocer who had never cast a ballot. Like the others, Courts was threatened, and in March he was evicted from his store. After he had opened for business in another location, he found it difficult to procure merchandise from wholesalers. Meanwhile, individually and in groups, Councilors—including the president of the Belzoni Guarantee Bank and Trust Company—"encouraged" him to withdraw his name. On several occasions he was even summoned before a three-member Council committee. As he later testified before a subcommittee hearing of the United States Senate: "They told me they were not going to let the Negroes in Humphrey County vote, and they told me they are not going to let the NAACP organization operate in Belzoni." [34] Undaunted, the Negro merchant persisted. During the summer primary he led a group of twenty-two Negro registrants to the polls, only to have their ballots invalidated by voting officials. The

[33] Quoted ibid., 42. See also Montgomery *Advertiser*, August 22, 1955.

[34] U.S. Senate Committee on the Judiciary, *Hearings before the Subcommittee on Constitutional Rights*, 85 Cong., 1957, 547.

following November, while working in his relocated grocery, he was critically wounded by a shotgun blast. Following his convalescence, Courts fled to Chicago, proclaiming himself an "American refugee from Mississippi terror." [35]

Perhaps because of his age or the relative security afforded by his self-employment, Courts proved more courageous than other members of Humphreys County's "hard core" registrants. At the time of the attempt upon his life, his name alone remained on the list of Negro registrants. Other less fearless voting aspirants had been dissuaded, either by Citizens' Council threats or the murder of the Reverend George Washington Lee, Belzoni's Negro minister. The first of his race to register in the county, Lee had often received anonymous warnings about his continued advocacy of Negro voting. One Saturday evening in May, 1955, after receiving a series of threatening notes and telephone calls, he was slain by two shotgun blasts while driving along Belzoni's Church Street. The sheriff, at first inclined to believe that the lead pellets found in the minister's mouth and face were dental fillings, ultimately concluded that he had been murdered by another Negro in an argument over a woman. No arrest was ever made.[36]

A second shotgun slaying of a Negro voting advocate in 1955 occurred in Brookhaven, the southern Mississippi hometown of Judge Tom P. Brady. There in the broad daylight of a mid-August afternoon, Lamar Smith, who had reportedly been urging the defeat of the incumbent in the Pike County supervisor's race, was murdered on the courthouse lawn. Although the county sheriff had actually witnessed the shooting, no arrest was made. Only two weeks later, the Magnolia State was the scene of yet another racial slaying; this time the victim was a fourteen-year-old Chicago youth. Kidnapped from his grandfather's home in Money, allegedly for having "wolf-whistled" at a white woman, Emmett Louis Till's body was found afloat in the Tallahatchie River on August 31. On this occasion two

[35] Ibid., 532. See also Charles J. Lapidary, "Belzoni, Mississippi," *The New Republic*, 134 (May 7, 1956), 12–13; Carter, *The South Strikes Back*, 114–15; and Rowan, *Go South to Sorrow*, 61–62.

[36] NAACP, *Annual Report: Progress and Reaction*, 23; Carter, *The South Strikes Back*, 115–16; Lapidary, "Belzoni, Mississippi," 12.

men were arrested for the kidnap-murder, but an all-white jury found neither guilty.[37]

Following the death of Till, Robert Patterson, in his capacity as state executive secretary, termed the murder "regrettable," but insisted that it was altogether unthinkable that the Citizens' Council could have been responsible. The NAACP, he suggested, should be held accountable for the recent rash of racial violence in Mississippi; for it had encouraged Negroes to challenge the state's racial customs.[38] But the Negro organization was not impressed by the logic of this argument. In a lengthy statement entitled *M Is for Mississippi and Murder,* the NAACP left few doubts as to its views on the question of Council guilt.[39] Moreover, the organization's New York headquarters filed a formal petition with the U.S. Department of Justice demanding that the government intercede to put an end to the "state of jungle fury" in Mississippi. The Council, the New York office charged, had created a violence-charged atmosphere which led to the deaths of the three Negroes.[40]

Although the NAACP's national headquarters was chary of directly implicating the white organization in any of the killings, state and local Negro leaders in Mississippi were not. In May, at a mass meeting called in Belzoni to protest the breakdown of local law enforcement, Dr. A. P. McCoy, state NAACP president, accused the Citizens' Council of being directly instrumental in the death of the Reverend Lee.[41] But the head of the Humphreys County Council, C. L. Puckett, denied that any member of his organization could have been the slayer, for "violence is against our constitution and by-laws." [42]

[37] NAACP, *Annual Report: Progress and Reaction,* 24–25; Carter, *The South Strikes Back,* 119ff.

[38] Memphis *Commercial Appeal,* September 8, 1955; Cook, *The Segregationists,* 55.

[39] NAACP, *M Is for Mississippi and Murder,* 2nd ed. (New York: NAACP, 1956.) See also a pamphlet by Alfred Baker Lewis, *Convict the Killers for a Change* (New York: NAACP, 1968), 3.

[40] Memphis *Commercial Appeal,* September 8, 1955.

[41] Cook, *The Segregationists,* 55. Gus Courts also linked the Council with Lee's death. *Hearings before the Subcommittee on Constitutional Rights,* 532, 545.

[42] Quoted in Carter, *The South Strikes Back,* 116.

Except in a general way, no attempt was made by the NAACP, or anyone else, to link the Council with the murders of Smith and Till. But Gus Courts, who survived to tell about his brush with death, accused the Humphreys County organization with complicity in the attempt against his life. Again the Council denied any involvement; and, after offering a $250 reward for information leading to the arrest and conviction of the guilty, it joined city officials and Belzoni's civic clubs in pious condemnation of racial violence.[43]

In combination with economic intimidation, violence in the Magnolia State—whatever the Council's role in it may have been—proved an effective deterrent to black voting. As an Associated Press survey in three scattered Delta counties demonstrated, the number of Negro registrants plummeted. Before the emergence of the Citizens' Councils, Montgomery, Sunflower, and Yazoo counties accounted for a total of 265 black registrants. By late August, 1955, however, the number had declined to 90. That same month, Senator Eastland proudly informed organized segregationists in Tate County that, "due largely to the Citizens' Councils," Mississippi's Negro voters had been reduced to no more than 10,000.[44] By election day in November, 1956, Hodding Carter III estimated that only 8,000 remained eligible to vote, and that in most rural counties of the black belt—the Council's stronghold—not even so much as a single black voter even tried to cast a ballot.[45]

Alabama's discriminatory voter qualification laws, like those in Mississippi, effectively barred all but a small percentage of Negro citizens from the voting booth. Through such legal deterrents as the poll tax and literacy test, the state had permitted only about 53,000 Negroes to register by 1956.[46] Although organized segregationists in

43 *Hearings before the Subcommittee on Constitutional Rights*, 545ff.; Martin, *The Deep South Says "Never"*, 35; Memphis *Commercial Appeal*, November 30, 1955. See also Luce, "The Mississippi White Citizens' Council," 90–96. Although he has no supporting evidence, Luce attempts to link the violence against Courts, Lee, Till, and Mack Parker to the Council.

44 Quoted in Memphis *Commercial Appeal*, August 14, 1955. See also Montgomery *Advertiser*, August 22, 1955; Price, *The Negro Voter*, 42.

45 Carter, *The South Strikes Back*, 124.

46 Price, *The Negro Voter*, 5, 11ff.; Donald Strong, *Registration of Voters in Alabama* (University, Ala.: Bureau of Administration, University of Alabama, 1956), 75.

this state experimented briefly with the economic boycott to discourage Negro voting, extralegal methods were less widely used in Alabama than in Mississippi. For its part, the Citizens' Council appeared content to leave the problem in the hands of the lawmakers—many of whom, including Senator Sam Engelhardt, executive secretary of the Citizens' Councils of Alabama, were Councilors themselves.

Despite his first-term tenure, Engelhardt possessed remarkable power within the legislature. A dignified and persuasive spokesman for segregation and a member of every major committee in the Senate, he was the principal architect of Alabama's legal defiance. Among the many proposals placed before the legislature by this resourceful Macon County segregationist, none were more remarkable than the several he designed to disfranchise black-belt Negroes. With a nonwhite population of more than 85 percent, Macon had the highest ratio of blacks to whites of any county in the United States. Of its more than 14,500 voting-age Negroes, only about 1,100 were registered in 1956. But insignificant though that percentage was, many whites recalled that there had been only 130 in 1948. And they feared that by 1960, Negro voters would actually be in the majority. To forestall that dreaded eventuality, the county's board of registrars employed every legal artifice at its disposal, and when all else failed its members resigned. Since 1948 this ploy had been used on at least three occasions, and during the seventeen months prior to June, 1957, there was in fact no board of registrars in Macon County. In that month, however, the U.S. House of Representatives approved and passed on to the Senate the bill that would become the first civil rights law since 1875. Endorsed by the upper house and signed into law by President Eisenhower in August, the Civil Rights Act of 1957 authorized, among other things, the federal government to bring suits in federal courts to prevent discrimination in the right to vote.

Even as the nation's lawmakers debated the merits of that significant measure, Engelhardt's bill to disfranchise Negroes in Tuskegee, seat of Macon County, passed both houses of the Alabama legislature without debate or even so much as a single dissenting vote. Local Act 140, as this gerrymander measure was officially known, transformed rectangle-shaped Tuskegee into a twenty-eight sided city to exclude Tuskegee Institute and all but 10 of its 420 Negro voters (but none of its white voters) from municipal elections. With only a little exaggeration an influential Negro newspaper, the Birmingham *World,* declared that the act in effect created a "White Citizens Council captive city"—"Tuskegee, WCC, Alabama."[47] When Governor James Folsom permitted the bill to become law without his signature on July 13, Negroes countered with a nearly unanimous protest. Supported by Negroes from surrounding Macon County, the city's black population boycotted Tuskegee's white merchants. They began to buy exclusively from the few local Negro stores, or from whites in towns twenty to fifty miles away. Although, at the request of the state attorney general's office, a circuit judge enjoined the all-Negro Tuskegee Civic Association from employing "force, threats, intimidation and coercion" to enforce the boycott, the buying strike proved a remarkable success. Protesting that it had never told people where to shop, the TCA remained in the background and the boycott of white merchants continued into the next year.[48]

Encouraged by the successful elimination of Tuskegee's Negro voters,[49] Engelhardt introduced a bill in July, 1957, to abolish Macon County itself by dividing it among neighboring counties. More-

[47] Birmingham *World,* June 12, 19, 26, July 3, 17, 1957. See also Lewis W. Jones, "Struggle for the Vote at Tuskegee," *Race Relations: Problems and Theory,* eds. Jitsuichi Masuoka and Preston Valien (Chapel Hill: University of North Carolina Press, 1961), 128–56; Lewis Jones and Stanley Smith, *Tuskegee, Alabama: Voting Rights and Economic Pressure* (New York: Anti-Defamation League, 1958); and Bernard Taper, *Gomillion versus Lightfoot: The Tuskegee Gerrymander Case* (New York: McGraw-Hill, 1962).

[48] Birmingham *World,* August 21, 1957; John G. Wofford, "The Ballot Box and the Grocery List," *The Reporter,* 17 (October 31, 1957), 23–26; Ed Cony, "Tuskegee," *Wall Street Journal,* November 5, 1957; Douglas Cater, "The Bitter Fruits of Southern Bitter Endism," *The Reporter,* 20 (January 23, 1959), 29–30; Jacquelyne Johnson Clarke, *These Rights They Seek: A Comparison of the Goals and Techniques of Local Civil Rights Organizations* (Washington: Public Affairs Press, 1962), 30–31. Engelhardt, who blamed the faculty at Tuskegee Institute for instigating the boycott, also considered the possibility of taking over this privately endowed institution as a state-supported and state-controlled Negro college. See Atlanta *Journal,* December 1, 1957.

[49] In *Gomillion* v. *Lightfoot* the Court found the Tuskegee gerrymander unconstitutional. See *Race Relations Law Reporter,* 5 (1960), 974ff.

over, he predicted that at least twelve and perhaps as many as fifteen additional counties would have to be similarly eliminated if the civil rights bill were enacted. As he believed, "in those counties where Negroes outnumber the whites there will be but two alternatives—face an almost certain integrated courthouse and legislature, or abolish the counties." Only by parceling out the territory possessed by black counties could Alabama hope to blunt the thrust of civil rights legislation.[50] Although it failed to pass, the bill's import could not have been lost upon aspiring Negro voters. With the state's white power structure willing to consider this kind of geographic butchery, surely the right of suffrage would be claimed by only the most stouthearted black citizen.

In Louisiana, Negroes were registered in far greater numbers than in either Alabama or Mississippi. Among the seven states with such statutory provisions, Louisiana had been the least stringent in the application of its literacy test. Indeed, with its voting population fully 18 percent Negro, Louisiana had the highest percentage of nonwhite registrants in the region.[51] Eager to remove the threat of 160,000 Negro voters, Pelican State Councilors began during the autumn of 1956 an ambitious and systematic purge of parish registration rolls. Leading the effort, and lending to it a quasi-official status, was state Senator William M. Rainach, chairman of the Joint Legislative Committee on Segregation and president of the Association of Citizens' Councils of Louisiana. On the issue of Negro disfranchisement, as on most white supremacy issues, Rainach was a tireless advocate. In his pamphlet, *Voter Qualification Laws in Louisiana,* and in numerous speeches across the state, the Claiborne Parish legislator expounded his belief that "the solution" to the region's race problem lay in the systematic expurgation of "illegally registered voters." "The thing that can stop the integration movement dead in its tracks and prevent a new reconstruction," he often asserted, "is a thoroughgoing clean-up of our registration rolls." Moreover, the state could be rid of the vast majority of its

[50] Interview with Sam Engelhardt; Montgomery *Advertiser,* July 26, 1957; *Southern School News,* October, 1957, 4. Engelhardt first considered the gerrymandering of county boundaries in 1951. See a cover story in *Alabama,* August 17, 1951.

[51] Price, *The Negro Voter,* 1, 5, 11ff.

black voters without resorting to extralegal methods, economic pressure, or even racial discrimination. As he informed parish registrars, state officials need not employ discriminatory practices against Negroes for "nature has already discriminated against them." Louisiana's voter qualification tests measured a citizen's intelligence, not his education—"and intelligence is something that is bred into people through long generations." [52]

Armed with Rainach's rationale and with state laws permitting duly registered voters to examine registration records and challenge the qualifications of other voters, Louisiana Councilors expended a considerable portion of their energies for nearly three years on "operation clean-up." Although official spokesmen often protested that the organization sought to achieve only "uniform enforcement" of voter qualification laws, the target was clearly and exclusively the Negro.[53] Systematically combing parish voter rolls in search of "illegal" registrants, Council committees, as one federal judge observed, "limited their examination almost exclusively to the registration records of Negro voters while making only token examination of records of white voters." [54] The most common reasons for disqualification were errors in spelling or grammar. One challenging affidavit signed by Councilors in Washington Parish even requested the removal of a Negro registrant because of an "error in spilling." [55] Others were challenged and duly disqualified for listing their ages in years instead of the exact number of years, months, and days, and some for miscalculating their ages by a few days. Still others were purged for filling in the blank for race with the letter "C"

[52] [William M. Rainach and William M. Shaw], *Voter Qualification Laws in Louisiana: A Manual of Procedures for Registrars of Voters, Police Jurors and Citizens' Councils* (Homer: Association of Citizens' Councils of Louisiana, Inc., n.d.); U.S. Commission on Civil Rights, *Report, 1959* (Washington: Government Printing Office, 1959), 101–5; U.S. Commission on Civil Rights, *Voting* (Washington: Government Printing Office, 1961), 39–72; New Orleans *Times-Picayune*, February 16, 1956.

[53] See, for example, letter, Association of Citizens' Councils of Louisiana, Inc., to "Dear Friend," n.d., reprinted in U.S. Commission on Civil Rights, *Hearings*, New Orleans, Louisiana, September 28, 1960, May 5–6, 1961 (Washington: Government Printing Office, 1961), 534.

[54] *U.S.* v. *McElveen*, 177 F. Supp. 355, as quoted in U.S. Commission on Civil Rights, *Voting*, 47.

[55] U.S. Commission on Civil Rights, *Report, 1959*, 101–5.

instead of the word "colored," and in some cases for using "Negro" instead of "black."[56]

In October, 1956, the Colfax *Chronicle* exposed the extent of the Council's commitment to uniform enforcement. In a scathing attack, the editor of this Grant Parish weekly newspaper revealed that the local Council had met with Senator Rainach, Representative John S. Garrett, and other officials of the state Council association at Dry Prong, and upon their urging voted unanimously to purge the parish of its 864 Negro voters. After sifting parish records for irregularities in registration forms, Councilors challenged more than 700 black voters. Applying the organization's own rigid standards, the *Chronicle*'s editor found among the first 100 white voters—none of whom had been challenged—only one who passed the test. Moreover, he reported that, if uniformly enforced, these same standards would have disqualified every member of the purge committee.[57]

Blatant discrimination such as this brought the Council's purgative activities to the attention of the Department of Justice. In October, 1956, Assistant Attorney General Warren Olney directed the attention of a Senate subcommittee to "mass disfranchisement" in several parishes, particularly in Ouachita, where a Council committee had removed more than 75 percent of some 4,000 registered Negroes. "One of the principal objects and purposes of the Ouachita Citizens' Council," Olney testified, "was and is to prevent and discourage persons of the Negro race from participating in elections in the parish."[58] Documentation for these charges came with an election-eve investigation by the Federal Bureau of Investigation in ten northern parishes which revealed that more than 8,500 Negroes had been challenged and purged through Council action. Within

[56] See letter, Assistant Attorney General Warren Olney III to Senator Paul Douglas, reprinted in *Congressional Record,* 85 Cong., 1 Sess., 1957, 13334–35. See also McCarrick, "Louisiana's Official Resistance to Desegregation," 59ff.; Lewis, *Portrait of a Decade,* 130–31.

[57] Colfax *Chronicle,* October 12, 1956, as reprinted in *Congressional Record,* 85 Cong., 1 Sess., 1957, 13335–36. See also New York *Times,* October 25, 1956.

[58] "Statement by Warren Olney III, October 10, 1956 [to Senate Subcommittee on Privileges and Elections]," reprinted in *Congressional Record,* 85 Cong., 1 Sess., 1957, 8607–8. See also NAACP, *Annual Report: New Threat to Civil Liberties, 1956* (New York: NAACP, 1957), 32.

another month that figure rose to a total of 11,000.[59] The investigation, Council leaders charged, was evidence of a "vast conspiracy" by federal officials to "nullify" the South's voice in the arena of national politics. Reconstruction-minded officials in the Eisenhower administration, Rainach contended, were using the FBI to "build a black Republican Party in the South" by intimidating the Citizens' Council. When a federal grand jury probe in December failed to discover any irregularities in the purge, he proclaimed that the Council had been vindicated and a Justice Department "plot to clamp a reign of terror on the South" foiled.[60]

The government's probe served only to embolden the purgers. Seeking not only to "purify" parish voting rolls but to curb all further Negro registration, the ACCL advised local officials to follow the letter of state law in handling Negro applicants—or face charges of malfeasance. One pamphlet, describing how "councils obtain their objectives," contained this suggestive passage: "It may come to the attention of a council that the registrar of voters in that parish is not complying with the law and is registering unqualified persons as voters. This jeopardizes the entire structure of parish government. The councils in the parish should be informed and should by proper resolution and delegations call the matter to the attention of the registrar. If no satisfaction is obtained from the registrar, the police jury and State board of registration can be contacted. With sufficient evidence, the registrar could then be disciplined or removed." [61] As a number of registrars could later testify, this was no idle threat. With such Council stalwarts as William M. Shaw, John S. Garrett, and William M. Rainach in virtual control of the Joint Legislative Committee to Maintain Segregation, the ACCL was in a position to speak authoritatively on such questions.

Serving from its inception as a kind of action arm for the Joint Committee, the Council's quasi-public role became increasingly obvious after the passage of the Civil Rights Act of 1957. While

59 State Advisory Committees to the U.S. Commission on Civil Rights, *The 50 States Report* (Washington: Government Printing Office, 1961), 219. See also *The Citizens' Council,* December, 1956, 4.

60 Quoted in New Orleans *Times-Picayune,* December 6, 1956. See also Columbia *State,* December 16, 1956.

61 *Citizens' Councils in Louisiana* (Homer: Association of Citizens' Councils of Louisiana, Inc., n.d.).

local Councilors busied themselves with parish registration records, their leaders conducted seminars on procedures for strict interpretation of the state's voter qualification laws. In a series of meetings sponsored jointly by the State Board of Registration and the Joint Legislative Committee in each of the state's eight congressional districts, Rainach, Garrett, and Shaw briefed parish registrars, district attorneys, sheriffs, and police jury presidents on ways and means of evading federal voting laws. During the course of each meeting, these public servants were informed that the Civil Rights Act was "clearly unconstitutional" because "voting is a privilege not a right." They were also given the Council's guide for local voting officials, *Voter Qualification Laws in Louisiana.* [62]

Occasionally the organization actually did bring charges against recalcitrant officials who persisted in registering Negro applicants. But such extreme measures were rarely necessary, for most officials found it inexpedient not to cooperate. As Mrs. Winnice J. P. Clement, registrar of Webster Parish, testified at a Civil Rights Commission hearing: "I was real strict in 1957, right after they did everything but shoot me." [63] Other harried registrars, unable to cope with the Council's pressure, resigned. And the registrar of Winn Parish, Mrs. Mary C. Flournoy, closed her office during most of August, 1959, rather than submit to the harassment of what she termed a "rabble-rousing mass" bent on challenging Negro voters for "minor" errors in their registration forms. "I'm for segregation right down the line," she acknowledged, "but I have a job to do, and I intend to be fair. . . ." Councilors insisted that she "follow the book" when it "suited their purpose," the registrar charged, but not when whites were involved. By her estimation, the Council's purge, if indiscriminately applied to every voter in the parish regardless of race, would have eliminated 93 percent of all registrants.[64]

Other more powerful official voices raised against "operation

62 U.S. Commission on Civil Rights, *Hearings, New Orleans,* 492, 534.

63 Ibid., 304. See also "Testimony of Quitman Crouch, Registrar of Voters, St. Helena Parish, Louisiana," ibid., 332–33, and New York *Times,* May 6, 1961.

64 Robert Wagner, "Vote Registrar Blasts Rainach: Winn Official Vacations in Face of Purge," New Orleans *Times-Picayune,* August 4, 1959, as reprinted in U.S. Commission on Civil Rights, *Hearings, New Orleans,* 519–20.

cleanup" included that of U.S. Senator Russell Long, who considered the purge both a personal embarrassment and a threat to segregation. Such activities, he believed, could only invite the intervention of the federal government on behalf of Louisiana's Negro citizens. More outspoken in his denunciation of the mass disfranchisement was Democratic National Committeeman Camille Gravel, one of the state's few political figures who openly endorsed the *Brown* decision.[65] Governor Earl Long also expressed his disapproval. But while he alone was in a position actually to minimize the effects of the Council's program, the governor chose to do nothing until 1959. Then, after Rainach carried the purge into Winn Parish, traditional seat of the Long machine, Long reacted by introducing to the legislature a pair of bills designed to undermine the effectiveness of the Council's endeavors. Although the governor personally appeared before both houses to win support, legislative segregationists, led by Garrett in the house and Rainach in the senate, were able to defeat both measures.[66]

Meanwhile, the Department of Justice had begun action of its own to protect the Negro's right to the ballot in Louisiana. On January 12, 1960, in the first action taken under the Civil Rights Act of 1957, a federal judge ordered the restoration of the names of 1,377 voters removed by Council initiative from the rolls of Washington Parish. During the next several years the government introduced numerous suits of similar nature, and by January, 1964, the Council's handiwork was undone. With the registration of fifteen Negroes in Tensas Parish—the first to register since Reconstruction—Negroes were qualified voters in every parish in the state.[67]

For all of its considerable success, the Negro voter purge, like the Council itself, was confined primarily to the parishes north of Alexandria. With the notable exception of the greater New Orleans

[65] McCarrick, "Louisiana's Official Resistance to Desegregation," 62–63; Shreveport *Times*, October 30, 1957.

[66] McCarrick, "Louisiana's Official Resistance to Desegregation," 45, 91–103.

[67] Ibid., pp. 62–63, 93–103; New York *Times*, January 12, March 1, June 8, 1960, August 22, December 29, 1961, January 8, 1964; New Orleans *Times-Picayune*, May 2, 1962; Baton Rouge *State Times*, November 28, 1961, January 31, February 22, 1962; Shreveport *Journal*, October 5, October 9, 10, 1962.

area, the Citizens' Council had little strength in French Catholic parishes, where the overwhelming preponderance of the state's Negro registrants were concentrated. Ironically, then, in those parishes where the organization was sufficiently powerful to curb Negro voting, there were in fact comparatively few Negro voters to curb. Thus, to a remarkable degree, Louisiana mirrored the dilemma of the Council movement throughout the South. It prospered only amid the very racial, economic, and social conditions which tended to minimize Negro political activity. As voting studies of the mid-1950's indicate, Negroes were least likely to register in the predominantly rural, large plantation counties of the Deep South where they comprised a large proportion of the total population. Such counties generally proved most responsive to the appeal of organized racism. Conversely, in states such as Arkansas, Florida, North Carolina, and Texas, where comparatively advantageous conditions permitted the registration of significant numbers of Negroes, segregation groups had neither the numerical strength nor the political influence to pose a serious threat to the black voter.[68]

But whatever their locality, organized white supremacists viewed with alarm the quickening tempo of federal activity on behalf of Negroes after 1957. Confronted by growing Negro militancy and an increasingly determined national government, even the most ardent advocates of resistance recognized that boycotts, purges, and even social separation could never be more than short-range "solutions" to the problem of black men in a white society. "Segregation," as William J. Simmons liked to say, "is at best a temporary palliative. The real solution is to establish a Negro state. Nothing less than physical separation of the races will solve the problem." [69] To be sure, following the passage of a second Civil Rights Act in May, 1960, and the adoption of strong civil rights planks by the platform

[68] See Price, *The Negro Voter*, 42; and three articles by Donald R. Matthews and James W. Prothro: "Negro Voter Registration in the South," *Change in the Contemporary South*, 142–43, "Social and Economic Factors and Negro Voter Registration in the South," *American Political Science Review*, 57 (March, 1963), 24–44, and "Political Factors and Negro Voter Registration in the South," *American Political Science Review*, 57 (June, 1963), 355–67.

[69] Quoted in Cook, *The Segregationists*, 73. See also Cleghorn, "The Segs," 136.

committees of both major parties during the following summer, segregation appeared to be more temporary than ever. With the gravity he characteristically reserved for his most dire predictions, Simmons informed Councilors in August that if either party enacted 60 percent of its civil rights proposals, "indescribable chaos" would ensue.

In order to avert this eventuality, the Council offered a seven-point platform of its own. In addition to such standard white supremacist planks as "the recognition of racial differences as fact," "strict enforcement of state voter qualification laws," and "separate public schools and other facilities," the platform called for the creation of a federal commission charged with the task of finding ways and means of geographically separating the races. The segregation group did not indicate whether this separation would be compulsory. But it did suggest that, until actual geographic separation could be accomplished, a workable substitute would be "the movement of Negroes and white people who desire to live among their own kind to communities populated exclusively by members of their race."[70] Yet satisfactory though such South African–style "Bantustans" may have been, Council leaders generally preferred the colonization of Negroes in their "homeland." Toward that end, the Citizens' Councils of America convened in New Orleans in May, 1962, to adopt a resolution urging Congress to proceed with hearings on, and to expedite the enactment of Senator Russell B. Long's Senate Bill 759, which provided for the "voluntary repatriation in Africa of those Negroes who wish to leave this country."[71]

Clearly, the vision of a pure white America was tantalizing to the Negrophobe. But few were sufficiently deluded to believe that it could ever be realized—even through the revival of well-worn nineteenth-century racist schemes. But by encouraging the long-range demographic trend of Negro outmigration, many proponents of organized resistance believed that the problem of black men in concentrated numbers could at least be ameliorated. In order to reduce the "proximal factor in racial discord," the CCA endorsed Senator Richard B. Russell's voluntary "Negro relocation plan" to

[70] "A Citizens' Council Platform," *The Citizens' Council*, August, 1960, 2.

[71] "Resolutions Adopted at Meeting of Citizens' Councils of America, May 19, 1963," *The Citizen*, 6 (May, 1962), 4.

facilitate a "more equal distribution" of Negroes throughout the United States. In terms of national average, a "surplus of Negro population" existed in the District of Columbia, Delaware, Maryland, and the eleven former Confederate states. In the remaining thirty-seven states, on the other hand, "a deficit Negro population" existed. Thus, by resettling Georgia's 1960 "surplus" of 708,569 Negroes in Vermont, New York, and Pennsylvania, which shared a combined "deficit" of 720,832 Negroes, the South would not only be "send[ing] the problem to the folks who are sure they have the answer" but would virtually eliminate "an unbearable economic and political liability." According to a Council brochure, such a program would constitute a genuinely "Christian and humanitarian" means of reducing racial strife and improving inter-sectional understanding.[72]

The continuing northward migration of Negroes had other advantages as well. As the Citizens' Councils of America asserted in an official statement during August, 1961, "one million more Negroes in New York City or Chicago will provide the South with an argument far more powerful than mere words." The following May the regional organization urged its state and local affiliates "to expedite volunteer migration of any dissatisfied Negroes from the South."[73] In effect, the resolution was an endorsement of "Freedom Rides North," an inverted version of the "freedom rides" sponsored by the Congress of Racial Equality during the spring of 1961 to test the Interstate Commerce Commission's 1955 ruling against segregation in trains, buses, and terminals involved in interstate commerce. Adopted as an official project of the Greater New Orleans Citizens' Council, the "reverse freedom rides" were conceived by George Singelmann, an administrative assistant of Leander H. Perez and charter member of the Crescent City Council. Under his direction, New Orleans Councilors in April, 1962,

72 "U.S. Negroes Are Moving North!" *The Citizen*, 6 (May, 1962), 4–12; "Migration Is the Answer," *The Citizens' Council*, November, 1956, 4; "Relocation of Negroes Urged," *The Citizens' Council*, January, 1959, 1, 4; *Migration, the Only Reasonable Answer* (Greenwood: Association of Citizens' Councils, n.d.); Association of Citizens' Councils of Mississippi, *Keep the Dark Tide Moving North: Redistribution of Negroes* (Greenwood, [1967]).

73 New Orleans *Times-Picayune*, August 27, 1961, May 20, 1962; Augusta *Courier*, June 4, 1962.

began sending indigent Negro families by bus to northern cities that had shown leadership in racial desegregation. Although welfare cases were given top priority, the criminal element was also favored. Notices were posted on bulletin boards at the Orleans Parish Prison and the state penitentiary at Angola so that Negro convicts whose terms were expiring might take advantage of free transportation out of the state.[74]

Following the New Orleans Council's lead, the Capital Citizens' Council of Little Rock also began sending Negroes north. Among the first to go were two husbandless mothers on welfare with families totaling twenty children. Each family was provided with one-way bus tickets to Hyannisport, Massachusetts, and sixty dollars for expenses. The organization's motives were not merely "beneficent and humanitarian," as CCC spokesman Amis Guthridge explained. "We want to see if northern politicians really love the Negro or whether they love his vote." [75]

Soon after the endorsement of "Freedom Rides North" by the Citizens' Councils of America, Councilors in other states began dispatching unemployed Negroes from a number of southern cities, including Macon, Georgia, Montgomery, Alabama, and Shreveport, Louisiana. During the summer months of 1962, perhaps as many as 250 "reverse riders" left the South, although Council spokesmen had hoped to send more than 1,000. Favorite targets were New York City, Washington, D.C., and especially Hyannisport, where President John F. Kennedy maintained a summer home. Despite Massachusetts Governor John A. Volpe's condemnation of this "traffic in human misery," and the inability of Cape Cod authorities to provide either adequate housing or employment, Councilors shipped some ninety-six impoverished people to that resort town by mid-October, 1962. When it became apparent that the daily provisioning of this jobless throng was taxing local welfare resources, the Louisiana Citizens' Council named the chief executive's youngest brother, senatorial candidate Edward M. Kennedy, honorary chair-

[74] Letter from George Singelmann to "Dear Friend," April 4, 1962, Southern Office, A-DL; Baton Rouge *State Times* and New Orleans *Times-Picayune,* March 31, 1962; Washington *Post,* April 14, 23, 1962; *Newsweek,* May 7, 1962, 30–33.

[75] Quoted in *Arkansas Gazette,* May 4, 11, 21, June 15, 1962.

man of a proposed "Southern Care Package Committee." For distribution by this committee, Pelican State Councilors promised, but did not provide, chitterlings, hog jowls, opossums, grits, and sweet potatoes. In similar mock philanthropy, the Little Rock Council shipped to former residents of Arkansas in Massachusetts a goat named Samson in a red, white, and blue crate for a Fourth of July barbecue.[76]

Such callous disregard for human dignity brought condemnation from major newspapers across the South, including such staunch defenders of segregation as the Birmingham *News,* the Columbia *State,* the Montgomery *Advertiser,* and the Richmond *Times-Dispatch.*[77] To be sure, many whites agreed with Senator Allen J. Ellender of Louisiana when he offered his support for the project, declaring, "I want Negroes from the South to learn they are better taken care of in the South." [78] But many others did not. In Little Rock alone, the reverse rides drew the censure of the city's board of directors, its mayor, the chamber of commerce, the Greater Little Rock Ministerial Alliance, the Little Rock Conference of the Methodist Church, the Presbyterian Synod of Arkansas, and the Downtown Lion's Club.[79]

If Council spokesmen were dismayed by such criticism, they gave few indications. "Nothing has so caught the imagination of the

[76] By the week before Christmas, only one family, an Arkansas mother with eleven children, remained in Cape Cod, where only summer employment was available. (Charleston [W. Va.] *Gazette,* December 22; Providence *Evening Bulletin,* June 11; *Arkansas Gazette,* June 13, 15; Washington *Post,* June 2, 1962.)

[77] For examples, see editorials in the following issues: Birmingham *News,* April 23; Columbia *State,* April 26; Montgomery *Advertiser,* June 30; Richmond *Times-Dispatch,* April 25, 1962.

[78] Senator Russell Long also lent his support, as did a number of state lawmakers. Louisiana even considered passing legislation to underwrite the project with state funds. See *Urban League of Greater New Orleans Warns People Not to Fall for Crackpot "Freedom Ride" Bait* (New Orleans: Urban League, 1962); and Richmond *Times-Dispatch,* April 29, 1962.

[79] The *Arkansas Gazette,* June 2, 1962, ran an "Honor Roll" of those organizations which had censured the project. See also *Christian Science Monitor,* June 5; Louisville *Courier-Journal,* June 20, 1962; "Southern Business Denounces Reverse Freedom Rides," *The Christian Century,* 79 (June 6, 1962), 706.

nation," chortled Willie Rainach, the first president of the Citizens' Councils of America. "For the first time, we are on the offensive. We have exposed the hypocrisy of the people of the North." [80] So pleased was the CCA with the effort that in September, 1962, some forty delegates from eight states met to plan a second series of reverse rides. George Singelmann was named regional coordinator to oversee the transportation of Negroes to the hometowns of northern liberal politicians in time for Christmas. But the successful experience of the summer was not to be repeated. By mid-December only the Greater New Orleans Council was preparing to send new riders. Selecting Senator Hubert H. Humphrey as its target, the group planned to send a delegation of Negro welfare cases to Minneapolis for Christmas dinner. "Most people eat turkey for Christmas," Singelmann cracked, "but we'd like to fix it [so] that the great humanitarian . . . will eat crow instead—and Jim Crow at that." Although the scheme was canceled when the Minnesota senator indicated that he would remain in Washington for the holidays, Singelmann was confident that the Council had made its point: "We knew he was a hypocrite. We just wanted to prove it." [81]

Little more was heard of the reverse freedom rides.[82] In view of the shrinking revenues of the organized resistance movement, it had been an expensive enterprise. Certainly it proved ineffective as a means of reducing the South's "surplus" Negro population. During the decade preceding 1960, Bureau of Census data indicate that nearly 1,500,000 nonwhites migrated from the South.[83] At that rate more Negroes left in a single day than Councilors had been able to export during an entire summer. But cost accounting criteria

[80] Quoted in Shreveport *Journal,* July 10, 1962.

[81] Montgomery *Advertiser,* September 23; Shreveport *Journal,* December 4, 24; Jackson *Daily News,* December 13, 1962; "Integration: Crow for Christmas," *Newsweek,* 60 (December 17, 1962), 22.

[82] Probably the last reverse ride occurred in February, 1963, when the Louisiana Citizens' Council sent a Negro family of ten to Trenton, New Jersey, the home of Assistant U.S. Attorney General Nicholas de B. Katzenbach's aged mother. The family was given seventy-five dollars and a dozen cans of sardines. Their luggage was marked "Remember Mississippi." (Jackson *Daily News,* February 9, 1963.)

[83] New York *Times,* April 29, 1962.

seem hardly adequate for the task of evaluating "Freedom Rides North." As perhaps no other phase of the resistance movement had, the project indicated the moral bankruptcy of the racial extremist. In the eyes of the white supremacist, the Negro—despite his rising status throughout the nation—remained a human commodity from an inferior race whose numbers, like so many bales of cotton, were measurable in the economic terminology of surplus and deficiency. Quite clearly, though many decades had passed since the last Virginia slave trader shuttled the last black coffle overland to the markets of New Orleans and Natchez, the legacy of human bondage still lay heavily upon the land.

CHAPTER XII

Racial Orthodoxy and the White Community: The Case of Mississippi

IN many quarters of the embattled South, the right of free expression was one of the earliest casualties in the war to defend segregation. Traditionally, societies under siege have found it inexpedient to permit open debate and internal division, and the experience of the post-*Brown* South proved no exception. Not unlike proslavery zealots of the 1850's, the prosegregationists of a century later were inclined to brook no latter-day abolitionism among fellow Southerners. Indeed, the perils which many whites believed implicit in the Court's school desegregation decision required nothing less than the closing of southern ranks and the suppression of intraregional dissent. In this repressive atmosphere the moderate was vilified and he who was found "soft" on integration was adjudged treasonous.

In the chorus of racial conformity the voices were numerous, but none was so loud and none was more insistent than that of the Citizens' Council. Believing, as William J. Simmons expressed it, that "an all-out war is being waged against the white race,"[1] the

1 Simmons, "Organization: The Key to Victory," *The Citizen*, 6 (February, 1962), 7–8. These words also comprise the first sentence of the "White Book," 7.

Council was quick to equate nonconformity with disloyalty. Through the columns of its monthly newspaper, this self-appointed guardian of the status quo warned that "the scalawag Southerner" who urged compliance with the law of the land was "an enemy of his own people," worthy of the "distaste, contempt, and ostracism that any proud people will feel for a traitor." Repeatedly it called upon "patriotic" and "dedicated Southerners" to form an "impregnable front" against those "enemies who would destroy our way of life and put an end to the traditions so precious to our people." [2]

Councilors in every southern state strove to forge an "impregnable front," but nowhere with greater success than in Mississippi. Without effective opposition for nearly a decade, the organization was instrumental in creating what James W. Silver has chosen to call "a hyperorthodox social order." According to this former University of Mississippi professor, "the totalitarian society of Mississippi imposes on all its people an obedience to an official orthodoxy almost identical with the pro-slavery philosophy. . . ." [3] In "Mississippi: The Closed Society," a presidential address to the Southern Historical Association at Asheville, North Carolina, on November 7, 1963, and in an identically titled book-length exposition of the same theme, Silver identified the Citizens' Council as the self-appointed but virtually unchallenged administrator of the "official orthodoxy." [4] In so doing he gave academic expression to a condition which many of the nation's journalists had been describing for more than half a decade.

One of the earliest such descriptions appeared in the New York *Daily News* during November, 1955. Written by veteran reporter James Desmond, this series of five articles affirmed that "the specter

[2] *The Citizens' Council,* May, 1956, 2; November, 1959, 1.

[3] James W. Silver, "Mississippi: The Closed Society," *The Journal of Southern History,* 30 (February, 1964), 5.

[4] Ibid., 35–43, and passim. In a paradoxical refutation of Silver's "closed society" indictment, then U.S. Representative John Bell Williams expressed the view of many Mississippi segregationists when he declared "it's time we call his [Silver's] bluff and get rid of him." The state must "fumigate its college staffs," he believed, and replace those eliminated with "professors who will teach Americanism and not foreign ideologies." Quoted in editorial, *Delta Democrat-Times,* November 12, 1963.

of thought control that the White Citizens Councils brought to Mississippi has become a monstrous cloud blotting out nearly all dissent."[5] Only a few months later, *The Christian Century* observed that "the citizens' councils have in fact become the government of Mississippi. At every level from the village mayor to the United States Senate, these councils have taken over the role once played by the Nazi party in Germany and now played by the Communist party in Russia."[6] In January, 1957, the New York *Post* ran a fortnight-long series by Stan Opotowsky revealing "The Inside Story of the White Citizens' Councils." Again it was asserted that Mississippi, as well as much of the South, was "held captive today by a brigade of bigots whose total domination of the populace can be matched only by the Communist Party within Russia."[7]

Liberal southern journalists, no less than their northern colleagues, took note of the coercive influence of the movement in the Magnolia State. "The Citizens' Council as of January, 1958, stands virtually unquestioned in its dominance of the white community in Mississippi," wrote Hodding Carter III, son of the Pulitzer prize-winning editor of the Greenville *Delta Democrat-Times*.[8] Again in 1961 he reported that "to a degree which is hard to convey to someone who does not live in Mississippi, the Citizens' Council has managed to divert the antipathy of most white Mississippians for integration into a mold which includes the total rejection of any deviation from the status quo."[9] In September, 1963, Ralph McGill, nationally syndicated columnist and distinguished publisher of the Atlanta *Constitution*, charged that "Mississippi is ruled by a network of white Citizens' Councils. Their political control and their coercive power in economic affairs is so vast as to be difficult to comprehend."[10]

[5] James Desmond, New York *Daily News*, November 22–26, 1955.

[6] "Tornado Weather in Dixie," *The Christian Century*, 73 (February 29, 1956), 263–65.

[7] Stan Opotowsky, "Dixie Dynamite: The Inside Story of the White Citizens' Councils," New York *Post*, January 7, 1957. This series ran from January 7 through January 20, 1957.

[8] Carter, *The South Strikes Back*, 196.

[9] Hodding Carter III, "Citadel of the Citizens' Council," *New York Times Magazine*, November 12, 1961.

[10] Quoted in Patterson, *The Citizens' Council: A History*, 1.

Characteristically, the Council's reaction to such imputations was ambivalent. On the one hand, it delighted in the attention it received from so large a segment of the press. As Executive Secretary Robert Patterson put it, coming from a "left-wing publisher" such as McGill, the most abusive attack "must be considered a tribute to the effectiveness of the organization." On another occasion William J. Simmons observed: "We are proud that the Citizens' Council movement has been singled out [for attack]. . . . It means that our movement is effective; that it is doing its job well; and that it has the Reds and their liberal-left associates worried." But Councilors also regarded this "vicious campaign of hate, smear and distortion" as but one phase of an attack on the South and its racial customs. The real target of the mounting torrent of journalistic invective, the organization's spokesmen averred, was not the Council at all but the "southern way of life." By vilifying its most ardent and effective champion, the critics of segregation could hope to destroy the institution itself.[11]

In order to impede the interregional flow of equalitarianism, the Council, not unlike proslavery fire-eaters of the previous century, sought to erect a *cordon sanitaire* around the South. In an age of mass communications, such a task was infinitely more difficult than that which confronted the antebellum opponents of social change. For modern media, through their ability to cut across such traditional barriers to effective communication as region, race, and religion, have tended to promote national consensus and homogeneity in a most profound way. In order to neutralize this external barrage and to insulate the South from ideas they believed to be subversive, Council leaders charged that the nation's "controlled" communications industry had conspired to erect "a barrier to free communication," a "paper curtain," around the South. The objective, they declared, was to prevent the white Southerner from receiving "a fair hearing in the market-place of national public opinion." Through skillful manipulation of the news, the South-hating propagandists who dominated the media defamed the region and its inhabitants by portraying them in "the sorriest light possible." [12]

11 Ibid.; "Consider the Source," *The Citizens' Council*, April–May, 1961, 2.
12 Patterson, *The Road Ahead*, 3; "Let's Tear That Paper Curtain," *The*

The measure of the Mississippi Council's resolution to close the frontiers of the state—and whenever possible the region—to undesirable external influences was perhaps best illustrated by the organizations it blacklisted. In November, 1959, *The Citizens' Council* carried an "official list" of seventy-four public and private associations and agencies identified as favoring " 'civil rights' and anti-South force legislation." The offenders on the list, which grew to nearly one hundred by the following August, ranged alphabetically from the Amalgamated Meat Cutters and Butchers Workmen of North America to the Young Women's Christian Association. Listed among "The Enemy" were such likely candidates as the American Friends Service Committee, the Anti-Defamation League, the NAACP, and the Southern Regional Council. But there were also the Benevolent and Protective Order of Elks and twenty-seven religious organizations, including the Methodist and Episcopal churches. Even the U.S. government was to be found among the foes of the South. Ten governmental agencies were listed, among them the "Department of the Air Force," the Department of Justice, the Department of the Treasury, and the Interstate Commerce Commission.[13] Perhaps because it was such an obvious choice, the Supreme Court did not appear in the Council's inventory of antagonists.

Another means by which the Council sought to curtail the flow of intellectual contraband was through a program of indoctrination for the region's youth. Believing that "for too long Southern children have been 'progressively educated' to scorn their origins and the reasons for our bi-racial society," [14] the Mississippi Associa-

---

Citizens' Council, June, 1956, 1; "Key Words as Weapons," *The Citizens' Council,* March, 1957, 2; Workman, *The Case for the South,* 62.

[13] "Here Is the Enemy!" *The Citizens' Council,* November, 1959, 4; "Another Enemy," January, 1960, 4; "Here Is the Enemy!—Part II," August, 1960, 4. The Montgomery *Advertiser,* December 6, 1959, noted that of the seventy-four "enemies" on the original list, only two had been identified by Congress as Communist-front organizations.

[14] "A Manual for Southerners," *The Citizens' Council,* February, 1957, 1. Simmons believed that "there are many adults who might benefit from a review of these fundamental truths." In the third installment (April, 1957) he added that it "served also to present to Americans everywhere the basic causes for our position." The editor refused to identify the authors, saying

tion published a handbook for elementary school children. Serialized in *The Citizens' Council,* the manual was written in two parts. The first, designed for use in grades three and four, was subdivided into such topics as "GOD PUT EACH RACE BY ITSELF," "WHITE MEN BUILT AMERICA," "WHITE PEOPLE LIKE TO BE FREE," and "MIXING RACES MAKES AMERICA WEAK." The manual's second part, written for fifth- and sixth-graders, contained similar insights into what Simmons referred to as "fundamental truths." Among these truths were the duplicity of social liberals and the subversive intent of the integration movement. One section entitled "YOU CAN'T BELIEVE RACE-MIXERS" reminded southern children that the integrationists owned most newspapers and radio and television stations. Another warned that "RACE-MIXERS HELP COMMUNISTS." A third disclosed that "The Race-Mixers are like the Communists. . . . These people are trying to change our way of life. They know we will be unhappy if we change. Then our country will not be strong." [15]

The Citizens' Council was quick to report the success of the manual. Following the appearance of the first installment, Simmons noted that public reaction had been both "keen and widespread," indicating great interest in a long-neglected field of education. Largely on the strength of the handbook, he declared, school teachers were requesting bundles of the monthly newspaper for use as classroom current events assignments. Unquestionably, the manual was well received in some quarters.[16] Yet the demand for it could not have been great. A projected edition for junior and senior high schoolers never materialized, and an independent printing of the several installments, although promised, did not appear.

It was also necessary, Mississippi Councilors recognized, to shield the state's school children from the inculcation of false notions of equalitarianism. To protect the plastic minds of the young, the organization maintained not only a surveillance over

---

only: "they are two public school teachers in Mississippi. They don't want to be identified for fear of reprisals."

15 "A Manual for Southerners," *The Citizens' Council,* August, 1957, 3. The "Manual" for grades five and six appeared serially in the following issues of *The Citizens' Council:* March, 1957, 1–4; April, 1957, 2; June, 1957, 3; July, 1957, 3; August, 1957, 3–4.

16 "Something You Can Do," ibid., March, 1957, 2, April, 1957, 4.

school textbooks but sought to sterilize other aspects of schoolroom life, including library books, reference tools, and educational films. This phase of the program was conducted by Mrs. Sara McCorkle, a past president of the Mississippi American Legion Auxiliary who became director of the Council's youth activities division in January, 1958. By July, 1959, this vigorous lady Councilor, according to the organization's own reckoning, had spoken to students in nearly every high school in the state, advised local Councils on their youth programs, and conferred with numerous PTA groups across the state on the most effective ways of educating children to "the dangers of integration." [17] Working closely with the American Legion, the Daughters of the American Revolution, and the United Daughters of the Confederacy, she also scrutinized instructional materials used in public schools for possible "brain washing" devices. Among her earliest discoveries was "Playtime Farm," an educational toy with plastic figures used in some elementary schools. As she revealed to the Florence, Mississippi, Citizens' Council, the family group in this set had a dark-skinned father and a white mother. Quite obviously, it was a subtle effort to promote intermarriage.[18]

The Council also found the educational film "High Wall" objectionable. Donated by the Anti-Defamation League—"one of the most aggressive and highly financed pressure groups for integration in this country"—the film had been used in Mississippi's public schools for six years. But in 1959, Council censors discovered that it taught "children to pity their prejudiced parents who did not enjoy the enriching experience of intermingling with persons of different racial, ethnic, and cultural backgrounds." Although the state audio-visual director observed that "this meaning has never been read into it" and state Superintendent of Education J. M. Tubb found "nothing objectionable about it," the film was withdrawn from use.[19]

In the *World Book Encyclopedia,* Council inquisitors found yet

[17] *Southern School News,* February, 1958, 5; "Councils Put Accent on Youth," *The Citizens' Council,* July, 1957, 1.

[18] Jackson *Daily News,* January 3, 1958.

[19] Ibid., October 10, 12; New York *Times,* October 18, 1959; Silver, *Mississippi: The Closed Society,* 64–65.

another example of educational materials used as "propaganda tools to fool otherwise alert American lovers of liberty. . . ." In a front-page exposé in *The Citizens' Council,* the organization revealed that the popular reference work was unfit for southern homes and schools because it was hostile not only to the South but to the American spirit of free enterprise. Moreover, its publisher, Marshall Field, was the "grandfather of a negro sired boy, backer of a far-left New York daily, author of a book outright plugging for the destruction of the American way of life, and one of the most outspoken advocates of the NAACP and integration." In volume *N,* an essay written by a "professional agitator" "glorifying the Negro" contained such "shocking" assertions as: "The term Negro is used loosely to mean a member of the Negroid group, but no sharp line can be drawn between the so-called 'races'. . . . Negroid physical traits are also found among other racial groups." [20]

In addition to its censorial activities, Mrs. McCorkle's youth activities division sponsored an annual statewide high school essay contest to promote patriotism, states' rights, and racial integrity. Contestants could choose one of four topics: "Why I Believe in Social Separation of the Races of Mankind"; "Subversion in Racial Unrest"; "Why the Preservation of States' Rights Is Important to Every American"; and "Why Separate Schools Should Be Maintained for the White and Negro Races." For the best boy and girl essayist in the state the awards were $500 college scholarships, provided by the Council's Educational Fund. Lesser amounts were awarded to second, third, and fourth place winners, and local Councils on occasion gave prizes of $50 to the winners of high school contests.[21]

When the winning essays for the first competition were an-

[20] "Especially for Children: Grandpa's World Book Exposed," *The Citizens' Council,* January, 1958, 1, 4. In a "World Book Sequel" (April, 1958, 2), Simmons noted that, following the Council's exposé, Field Enterprises, Inc., agreed to submit the article in question to "a panel of critics to be reviewed from the standpoint of Southerners and from the standpoint of the free enterprise system to insure the articles are not slanted or biased either way." *World Book* also requested a reference article from the CCA on the Citizens' Council for inclusion in its second printing of 1958.

[21] Jackson *Daily News,* April 24, 1958; *The Citizens' Council,* September, 1958, 4.

nounced in July, 1959, it seemed apparent that the essayists had broad familiarity with the Council's list of recommended "research and reference" materials, including works by Judge Tom P. Brady, Theodore G. Bilbo, James J. Kilpatrick, Stuart O. Landry, and Herman Talmadge.[22] In her first-place entry, a pretty coed from Hattiesburg High School wrote that white southerners would never bow to the will of the federal judges, "however exalted their seats or black their robes and hearts." "Rather, we intend to obey the laws of God and the . . . Constitution. As long as we live, so long shall we be segregated." In a similarly recalcitrant mood, her male counterpart, a senior from Morton, endeavored to explain "why we fight and will continue to fight until we have succeeded in maintaining segregation, our way of life, or until the Communists, with the aid of our own Supreme Court, have caused us to crumble from within and to fall like Rome of old."[23] With sufficient reason, *The Citizens' Council* considered these annual contests to be the most successful function of the youth activities division. In July, 1960, it reported that more than 8,000 students from 163 secondary schools participated and that English teachers in some high schools listed the contest as required work in English classes, giving credit for term papers submitted as entries.[24]

In arrogating the right to oversee the education of Mississippi's

[22] The Council's suggested reading list included the following: Theodore G. Bilbo, *Take Your Choice: Separation or Mongrelization* (Poplarville, Miss.: Dream House Publishing Company, 1947); Brady, *Black Monday;* Claude Bowers, *The Tragic Era* (Cambridge: Literary Guild of America, 1929); Ernest Sevier Cox, *White America* (Richmond: n.p., 1923); James Jackson Kilpatrick, *The Sovereign States* (Chicago: Henry Regnery Co., 1957); Stuart O. Landry, *The Cult of Equality* (New Orleans: Pelican, 1945); Herman Talmadge, *You and Segregation.* See *Fourth Annual Report,* July, 1958, 4; *Delta Democrat-Times,* October, 1958.

[23] *The Citizens' Council,* July, 1959, 1.

[24] Ibid., July, 1960, 1, 3; *Winning Essays in the 1960 Contest* (Greenwood: Association of Citizens' Councils, [1960]). Mrs. McCorkle resigned her position in 1961 and thereafter the Council's youth activities division became inactive. During the fall of that year, she was instrumental in the organization of the Patriotic American Youth (PAY), an anti-Communist organization for Mississippi high school and college students. Under her direction, PAY offered scholarships for the best essay on "What America Means to Me." See Jackson *Daily News,* November 7, 1961; Patriotic American Youth, *Statewide College Scholarships Essay Contest* (n.p., n.d.).

youth, the Council did not limit itself to the elementary and secondary levels. Of particular concern was the screening of out-of-state lecturers at state university campuses. During the spring of 1956 the Reverend Alvin Kershaw, an Episcopal minister from Oxford, Ohio, was scheduled to appear as a Religious Emphasis Week speaker at the University of Mississippi. But upon learning of his donation of some $32,000 in television quiz show winnings to the NAACP, the Council objected and pressured the university administration to cancel his appearance. Over the protest of the school newspaper and a significant number of the students, the harassed administration capitulated and Kershaw's invitation was withdrawn. Thereafter, the board of trustees required that all future speakers must be screened and approved.[25] Expressing the view of the extreme segregationists, the Jackson *Daily News* commented editorially that "the Citizens' Council of Mississippi . . . asked that the invitation be withdrawn because it sincerely believed that any man who gives aid or comfort to the NAACP is an open enemy of the Southern way of life. . . . There is no escape from the logic of that reasoning."[26]

That same logic also extended to private institutions of higher learning. When the student religious council at Millsaps, a small Methodist-affiliated liberal arts college in Jackson, organized a forum on race relations in the spring of 1958, the institution's administration came under attack. The capital city's Citizens' Council demanded that racial liberals be prohibited from addressing students. Ellis W. Wright, president of the Jackson organization and a prominent funeral director, advised college administrators in an open letter to be mindful that "the Citizens' Councils and patriotic public officials are engaged in a life and death struggle for our very existence against an enemy with whom there is no compromise." Insisting that it was "intolerable" for Millsaps to be anything but totally committed to segregation, Wright informed Dr. H. E. Finger, president of the college, that a showdown was imminent: "Either you and your faculty are for segregation, or

25 Jackson *Daily News*, November 12, 1955; Muse, *Ten Years of Prelude*, 170; Silver, *Mississippi: The Closed Society*, 108–9.

26 Editorial, Jackson *Daily News*, November 15, 1955.

you are for integration."[27] Although one antisegregation address in the forum's series was canceled—because it "had been singled out for special notice"—President Finger was not intimidated. In his reply, he advised Wright that as president of a private institution, he was answerable only to the trustees. Striking a sensitive nerve, he reminded the states' rights advocate that "in an age when we are alarmed by the increasing controls of government, we should be strengthening those institutions which preserve and support freedom of speech. " When differences of opinion are no longer tolerated, he concluded, there can exist only "dreaded thought-control."[28] The logic of Finger's argument was wasted on the Council, which accused him of evasion. The Millsaps president, *The Citizens' Council* charged, had obscured the issue with a "thick smoke screen of 'academic freedom.' "

Having failed to force the administration to bow, the segregationists turned to the board of trustees, demanding a statement of its views on racial separation. Brushing aside all "irrelevant remarks" about academic liberty and free speech, the Jackson Citizens' Council's open letter to the trustees warned that an equivocal response could be interpreted only as a profession of integrationist sentiment. In its reply the board rejected this either-or proposition: "segregation always has been, and is now, the policy of Millsaps College." Affirming its devotion to free inquiry, the trustees declared that "the purpose of a college is not to tell people what to think but to teach them how to think." After commending Finger for his fidelity to the institution's traditional principle of intellectual freedom, the statement concluded with an expression of confidence in both faculty and administrators. Simmons reprinted the board's reply in full, noting that "it is certain that many Mississippians remain acutely conscious of the climate of opinion on the Millsaps campus."[29] The last word was truly the Council's. Soon after the board issued its statement, John Satterfield, a lawyer

[27] Ibid., March 17, 1958.

[28] Quoted in Hodding Carter, "Ellis Wright and Bill of Rights," *New South* (May, 1958), 8–9.

[29] For both the board's statement and Simmons's reply, see *The Citizens' Council*, March, 1958, 4. See also Jackson *State Times*, March 14, 1958.

with a statewide reputation and an active supporter of the Citizens' Council, delivered a prosegregation address on the Millsaps campus.[30] On that note, the issue was closed.

The open disregard demonstrated by the organization for academic freedom at the Methodist college became unqualified contempt whenever a state university was involved. "For too long," *The Citizens' Council* proclaimed in 1961, "Southern states have kept on their payrolls college professors and others who have worked single-mindedly to break down Southern traditions. It is time for drastic action. . . ."[31] College faculties and administrations, Simmons often said, should never be immunized from local pressures: "I think they ought to be responsive to the views of their community." In similar tones the state association's executive secretary, Robert Patterson, acknowledged that while a college professor "has a right to say what he thinks, he also has a responsibility to accept the results of what he says."[32] Clearly one of the results which Patterson had in mind was involuntary unemployment for any teacher who questioned the sanctity of segregation.

During the desegregation crisis at the University of Mississippi in the fall of 1962, the Council urged faculty moderates either to accept segregation or resign. Improvising on a favorite refrain, *The Citizen* declared: "This is no question of 'academic freedom.' It is rather, a simple matter of morality." Because "every faculty member at every state-supported school in Mississippi signs a loyalty oath every month—by the simple act of endorsing his paycheck"—personal honesty required the resignation of all "pro-integration" professors.[33] Once James H. Meredith was uneasily attending classes at the university, Councilors harassed faculty and administrators who befriended him. Local members inundated them with "honorary nigger" postal messages; and the state association circu-

30 For a detailed account of the entire incident and its aftermath, see Carter, *The South Strikes Back,* 180–84.

31 The statement was made in conjunction with a demand that some three hundred faculty members from the University of Georgia be fired for having signed a "pro-integration petition." "We Say Fire Them!" *The Citizens' Council,* January, 1961, 2.

32 Quoted in Cleghorn, "The Segs," 135; Silver, *Mississippi: The Closed Society,* 61.

33 "Simple Matter of Morality," *The Citizen,* 7 (November, 1962), 2.

lated postcards addressed to the state board of trustees and Chancellor J. D. Williams bearing the printed message: "As a taxpayer supporting state schools and as a loyal Mississippian promoting Americanism, I respectfully demand that Dean [of the Law School Robert J.] Farley, [Professor of History James W.] Jim Silver, [Vice-Chancellor]Alton Bryant, and [Professor of Political Science Russell H.] Barrett and all other integrationists be removed immediately from the pay roll of Ole Miss." [34] Another message from Greenwood warned an elderly English professor that "the Citizens' Councils are busy taking names too, and when this thing is over, some Southern renegades are going to lose their jobs." Executive Secretary Patterson also distributed lists containing the names and telephone numbers of faculty members who signed a cautiously worded AAUP resolution of October 3, "deploring the tragic events" and declaring "that the attempt of men in prominent positions to place all the blame for the riot on the United States marshals is not only unfair and reprehensible but is almost completely false." There followed, as one signer recalled, a "long siege of harassing telephone calls to faculty at inconvenient hours." [35]

More reprehensible still was the Council's role in the publication of the *Rebel Underground,* a crude and anonymous weekly which appeared throughout the fall and winter of 1962. Whether urging the execution of that "Marxist Monster," President John F. Kennedy, or lampooning university personnel and agents of the federal government as "comsymps," "professionals of the party," and "betrayers," this literary venture represented perhaps the most scurrilous aspect of the Council's entire effort to block desegregation at the Oxford campus.[36] Aspiring as it did to middle-class respectability, the organization did not identify the publication as

[34] Postcard, Eugene Cox Materials, Mitchell Memorial Library. See also *Southern School News,* December, 1962, 16.

[35] Russell Barrett, *Integration at Ole Miss* (Chicago: Quadrangle Books, 1965), 179–81, 205; Silver, *Mississippi: The Closed Society,* 129; and Louis Joughin, "The University of Mississippi Situation: A Review of the Association's Interest and Action," *AAUP Bulletin,* 48 (Winter, 1962), 317–20.

[36] *Rebel Underground,* Vol. 3, No. 2, distributed January 6, 1963. Scattered copies of this publication are to be found at Mitchell Memorial Library and SERS.

one of its own. But soon after the appearance of the first edition, David Webb, editor of the weekly Meadville *Franklin County Advocate,* revealed that it was typed on the machine used by Robert Patterson in the production of his frequent newsletters. Moreover, the country editor noted, the texts of one of Patterson's letters and the first issue of the *Rebel Underground* bore striking similarities. On October 24, the executive secretary had written to "Dear Friend": "We hereby serve notice on the racial perverts and ruthless politicians who would destroy the South: 'We have only begun to fight.'" The first issue of the *Underground* concluded similarly: "We serve notice to the forces of integration that 'we have only begun to fight.'" [37]

Shabby though these vituperations surely were, they represented much less a threat to the university's welfare than did other aspects of the Council's campaign to restore the institution's "racial integrity." In an obvious reference to the white supremacist organization, Vice-Chancellor Bryant charged that "adult agitators," "essentially moral and physical cowards," were manipulating extremist student sentiment in order to create further disorders on the campus and thereby close the university.[38] The vice-chancellor's remarks, made during an address to the Jackson Junior League in early November, followed by only several days the appearance of *Operation Ole Miss,* an eight-page pamphlet proposing the closure of any state institution which the federal government "seizes by force." Published by the Jackson Council and written by a "prominent attorney" under the pseudonym "James Cincere," the pamphlet suggested that any institutions so closed by authority of a public referendum could then be reopened as a private school.[39] Such a strat-

[37] Meadville *Franklin County Advocate,* November 1, 1962. See also Robert Patterson, "What Does Oxford Prove?" *The Citizen,* 7 (October, 1962), 2. Additional evidence of the Council's role in the production of these broadsides has been assembled by Terry Alford, "The Underground Press in Mississippi Since the Ole Miss Crisis of 1962" (unpublished paper, copy in possession of author), 1–10. Alford identified at least five issues of the *Rebel Underground* as the Council's handiwork.

[38] Jackson *Daily News* and New Orleans *Times-Picayune,* November 9, 1962.

[39] James Cincere [pseud.], *Operation Ole Miss* (Jackson: Jackson Citizens' Council, [1962]). See also McComb *Enterprise Journal,* November 5, 1962; *Southern School News,* December, 1962, 16.

agem was impossible to fulfill, as the Council's "prominent lawyer" should have known. In 1961, a federal court in New Orleans ruled that selective closure of state schools violated the Fourteenth Amendment's equal protection clause, and that public-supported private schools constituted in fact public education. Morever, the proposal was not well received. Almost immediately after its appearance, the Ole Miss Alumni Association announced its intentions to oppose any attempt to close the university.[40] Thereafter the Council lost interest, and the idea was forgotten.

Accreditation, however, was yet another matter. The untoward conduct of the administration of Governor Ross Barnett and the disruptive course pursued by the board of trustees during the desegregation crisis at Oxford moved the Southern Association of Colleges and Schools to place Mississippi's eight public institutions of higher learning on "extraordinary status" and "under continued and careful observation." At a meeting of its executive council late in September, the SACS issued a stern warning against "any encroachment by pressure groups, investigating committees or other agencies upon the freedom of faculties and administrations or the students to learn or teach."[41] The Council's reaction to this threat came in several forms. In its November issues *The Citizen* carried a guest editorial by James J. Kilpatrick, editor of the Richmond *News Leader*, calling for the "unfrocking" of "these self-ordained high priests of education." By enacting state laws prohibiting state-supported institutions from recognizing or affiliating with the Southern Association, the editorial suggested, taxpayers could escape the tyranny of a "gang of gowned educators bearing holy orders from Columbia Teachers College." A similar expression of the organization's views came from Circuit Judge M. M. McGowan, a leading Council activist in the state judiciary. In an article in the Jackson *Daily News*, this spokesman called for the abolition of the "arrogant" accrediting association, for it demanded that Mississippi take up the "hammer and sickle" in the defense of "the veritable hordes of socialist-minded professors."[42]

[40] Memphis *Commercial Appeal*, November 11, 1962.

[41] Quoted in Sarratt, *Ordeal of Desegregation*, 147–48.

[42] James J. Kilpatrick, "A Time for Unfrocking," *The Citizen*, 7 (November, 1962), 17–18; Washington *Post*, December 23, 1962; Barrett, *Integration at*

The attack on accreditation and the proposal to close the university were indicative of the extreme measures to which the organized segregationists would resort in order to preserve the racial status quo. Another more ominous measure of that extremism was the increasingly belligerent attack on the region's white moderates or, as *The Citizens' Council* called them, the "pseudo-Southerners," the "planted voices in the South."[43] Almost instinctively, Mississippi Councilors recognized that a few southern moderates provided a greater threat to the resistance movement than all the "outside agitators" and northern "mixicrats" combined. The experience of the upper South, they believed, had shown that whenever schools or lunch counters had been successfully desegregated it had been an "inside job." It had been true in Hoxie, Arkansas, and Clinton, Tennessee, and it had been true in Little Rock, where "fifth column treachery" brought "peaceful surrender to the totalitarian pressure groups." It had also been true in Virginia, where Governor J. Lindsay Almond's "massive betrayal" and "massive capitulation" brought an end to massive resistance in February, 1959. Similarly, in Nashville (where "profit-hungry merchants ignominiously capitulated to Negro 'sit-down' agitators" in 1960) and in Memphis (where a "small group of self-serving moderates" and "collaborators" engineered a "shameful surrender" to desegregate some all-white schools in 1961) the "duplicity" of the "die-easys" had been made abundantly clear.[44]

It was with some uneasiness, then, that soon after the desegregation of Ole Miss *The Citizen* acknowledged "the appearance of a few 'moderates' advising peaceful surrender" in Mississippi. As the editor reminded his readers, "a 'moderate' is for segregation but he's chicken! " The same issue carried a brief article about a Biblical "moderate," Pontius Pilate, and "unyielding" and "impossibly inflexible" Jesus Christ, who "was, in effect, creating a riot in Jeru-

---

Ole Miss, 201–2. For an expression of other views by this circuit judge on behalf of the Citizens' Council, see his article, " 'Integration Amendment' Was Never Legally Adopted!" *The Citizen,* 7 (November, 1962), 9–15.

43 *The Citizens' Council,* October, 1957, 1, 3.

44 *The Educational Fund of the Citizens' Council; The Citizens' Council,* October, 1957, 1; February, 1959, 1, 4; May, 1960, 1; July–August, 1961; "We Have a Plan!" *The Citizen,* 6 (October, 1961), 2.

salem." To preserve order and permit "business . . . to go forward as usual," Pilate, "like any moderate man," chose to mollify a "crowd crying for blood."[45] If, as this remarkable analogy clearly suggested, the Council was like Christ, "unyielding" and "inflexible," there could be no question but that the Pilates of Mississippi were those business and civic leaders who counseled that the state must accept at least token desegregation in order to prevent further bloodshed.

The ways and means whereby moderate voices in the white community could be suppressed were among the organization's first concerns. During the early developmental stages of the movement, it became apparent that the so-called Information and Education Committees had functions other than those described in the organization's public relations brochures. One of four standing committees possessed by each local Council, this committee, in some instances at least, was vested with the responsibility for assembling dossiers on community "agitators." As an Indianola planter who doubled as an organizer told a prospective group of Councilors in England, Arkansas, the committee "gathers information on people who are giving trouble—agitators and groups—and, in general, educates the people of the community."[46] While there is much that is not yet known about this aspect of the Council's operations, it seems certain that some groups did collect information on racial dissidents, both black and white. During 1955, for example, the Jackson Citizens' Council apparently made extensive use of mimeographed "confidential communiques" to identify "troublemakers" in the city. Thus "Confidential Communique Number 14" alerted the membership to the integrationist activities of Arrington High, a Negro newspaper publisher. No course of action was suggested, but High was soon forced to withdraw his money from a local bank and his home was subjected to acts of vandalism.[47]

[45] "Won't They Ever Learn?" and "A Moderate," *The Citizen*, 7 (January, 1963), 2, 4.

[46] *Southern School News*, April 7, 1955, 3. Even in the semi-secret "White Book," the "primary responsibility" of the Information and Education Committees was listed only as "presenting the Citizens' Council story to the public and to the members." ("White Book," 38–39.)

[47] Wakefield, "Respectable Racism: Dixie's Citizens' Councils," 339–40; Dan Wakefield, *Revolt in the South* (New York: Grove Press, 1960), 46.

As the largest and most ably led Council in the state, the Jackson organization also pioneered in the collection of dossiers and permanent files on the "expected conduct" of white citizens in the event of a racial crisis. In what U.S. Representative Frank Smith of Greenville, Mississippi, called "a skilled plan to search out anyone who deviated in the slightest and to bludgeon into silence those who had any differing ideas," [48] Jackson Councilors proposed to interview every white family in the metropolitan area in their so-called "Freedom of Choice" survey of 1958. Letters sent to whites preceding this block-by-block canvass explained that the "NAACP and other groups" were plotting not only against the white schools but also against the white residential areas as well, and were encouraging "mass voting by Negroes as a bloc." The canvass would "determine how our citizens in Jackson would react to a positive program under responsible leadership to meet these threats." Although councilors reported that fully 98 percent of the white community promised to give the organization full cooperation, it seems unlikely that this opinion survey was ever completed. As Congressman Smith observed, "even the Council found it impossible to inspire enough volunteers for such an ambitious program." [49] Nevertheless, its impact on public opinion was unmistakable. With considerable candor, one Mississippian wrote the editor of the Jackson *State Times:* "If a group of serious-minded individuals armed with pencils and a known philosophy of 'you're either with us or against us,' comes around to your door, demands to know your personal views and applies the pressure, only a Mongoloid idiot would fail to give the right answer." Similar surveys were also conducted in Greenwood and McComb; but the house-to-house canvass of the South urged by CCA President Roy V. Harris was never attempted.[50]

The very presence of a strong and active Council in any given community was usually sufficient to silence dissent. But occasionally

[48] Smith, *Congressman from Mississippi,* 272.

[49] Ibid.; *The Citizens' Council,* April, 1958, 1; *Delta Democratic-Times,* April 25, June 3; Washington *Post,* June 4; Memphis *Commercial Appeal,* June 5, 1958.

[50] Silver, *Mississippi: The Closed Society,* 41; *Southern School News,* August, 1956, 5.

more tangible methods were employed against racial deviants—real or imagined. One of the most remarkable examples of these methods came to light when Billy Clyde Barton, a University of Mississippi student, implicated the Citizens' Council, the governor, and the State Sovereignty Commission in a conspiracy to prevent his election as editor of the student newspaper. During the Spring of 1961 this journalism major from Pontotoc, Mississippi, revealed that as managing editor of *The Mississippian* he had been advised to "write a conservative editorial, [because] you're on the Citizens' Council's 'Black List.'" From a fellow student, John Ellis, he learned that the blacklist was used to deny employment to liberal graduates. Barton also charged that, in order to insure his defeat and pick its own candidate for editor-in-chief, the Council had promised to commit "any amount of money necessary," and circulated a confidential report on his alleged integrationist activities.[51] The origin of that report dated from a letter written on August 17, 1960, by William J. Simmons to Albert Jones, director of the Sovereignty Commission. In this communication, the Council chieftain related information he had received from Georgia States' Rights Council official William A. Lufburrow on Barton, a "very dangerous" summer employee of the Atlanta *Journal*. According to this information, the Ole Miss student participated in several Atlanta lunch counter sit-ins and was being groomed by Ralph McGill for future service in the "left-wing apparatus." In Simmons's view, this intelligence—all of which he said had been confirmed by the Georgia Bureau of Investigation—"indicates the painstaking efforts of the pro-integration people to plant sympathizers in key positions in our college campuses, where they can exert a maximum influence on student opinion."[52]

There the matter rested until December when the student editor of *The Mississippian* wrote to Governor Barnett requesting information on Barton, whom he believed to be a member of the NAACP.

[51] "Mississippi: 'Very Dangerous' Cub," *Newsweek*, 57 (March 28, 1961), 26; Carter, "Citadel of the Citizens' Council;" *Southern School News*, April, 1961, 15. See also the transcript of a complaint to U.S. Court of the Western Division of Northern District of Mississippi, *Barton* v. *Association of Citizens' Councils of Mississippi, et al.*, in Cox Materials, Mitchell Memorial Library.

[52] Simmons's letter is quoted in full by Cook, *The Segregationists*, 85–86. See also *Delta Democrat-Times*, March 13, 15, 1961.

Barnett turned the request over to the Sovereignty Commission, and the Commission in turn forwarded Simmons's report to the Ole Miss campus—taking only the precaution of inking out the Council's letterhead and the signature. Ultimately it fell into the hands of Barton, who vehemently denied the accusations. Subsequent polygraph tests confirmed that he told the truth when he declared that he had attended a sit-in only as a news reporter; that he did not know McGill, who, he pointed out, edited the Atlanta *Constitution* and not the *Journal;* and that he had no relationship with the NAACP.

With Barton threatening to sue all those concerned for defamation of character, even Governor Barnett, although insisting that he personally had not been involved, acknowledged that the editorial candidate was probably not dangerous. Moreover, the Jackson *Daily News,* intractable champion of segregation and perhaps the most intemperate daily newspaper in the South, admitted that the "Sovereignty Commission and Citizens' Council have pulled a boo-boo." "As to the young Mr. Barton's claim that he has been slandered," the *Daily News* noted further, "it is hoped his hide is tough enough to take it in a measure of degree that Barnett and personnel of the Sovereignty Commission and Citizens' Council are doing." Upon this philosophical note, the newspaper wished Barton success in his "intriguing campaign" for the editorship of *The Mississippian,* and advised Mississippians to forget this "dime novel" episode and "go fishing."[53] Ironically for Billy Barton, who lost the spring election by a wide margin, one of his professors informed a news magazine reporter that had the Council not intervened, Barton would have been regarded as the conservative candidate in a race against a campus liberal.[54]

There were those who did not "go fishing" after the Barton case. Indeed, the affair unleased a torrent of criticism upon the Council, the likes of which it had never before confronted. Paced by Hodding Carter's *Delta Democrat-Times,* a significant portion of the state's press attacked what the Greenville journalist called its "police state maneuverings."[55] Carter was, of course, a natural

[53] Editorial, Jackson *Daily News,* March 17, 1961.

[54] "Mississippi: 'Very Dangerous' Cub," 26.

[55] Editorial, *Delta Democrat-Times,* March 19, 1961.

leader for such an attack. His frequent thrusts against the organization, which he had likened on one occasion to "a pack of baboons yelling, grinning and making faces," won him a vote of censure in 1955 from "89 angry jackasses" in the Mississippi House of Representatives. Yet, though censured and condemned, Carter was beyond the reach of what he contemptuously called "the lash of organized intolerance."[56] As perhaps the state's most progressive and urbane city, Greenville, despite its location in the conservative Delta region, was never a stronghold of the Citizens' Council. But even had it been, Carter's immense national reputation would probably have afforded him considerable immunity from its pressures.

No less courageous an anti-Council crusader was Hazel Brannon Smith, editor and publisher of the Lexington *Advertiser,* the Durant *News,* and several other Delta newspapers. Although she lampooned the Council's "spy actviities" and its "cheap game of character-assassination," Mrs. Smith, like virtually all Mississippi moderates (Hodding Carter among them), was a segregationist and often said so. But her refusal to embrace the negative programs of massive resistance and her unrelenting campaign against racial excesses marked her as a traitor to her race and an enemy of the region in the eyes of white militants. So it was with considerable pride that she boasted in 1963 that "the editor of this newspaper has opposed the racist Citizens' Council from the very beginning—not because we oppose racial segregation and constitutional government they now claim to foster—but because in 1954 we recognized it as a serious threat to the personal freedom, peace and security of every living Mississippian—and its potential as a real Gestapo to take over the state." With only a little exaggeration, she could add: "that we have survived at all is a miracle that we attribute only to God."[57]

She was, to be sure, no stranger to trouble. Years of editorial warfare against bootlegging, gambling, and slot machine racketeer-

[56] See Jackson *Daily News,* January 18, 1960; Hodding Carter, "A Wave of Terror Threatens the South," *Look,* 19 (March 22, 1955), 32–34; "The South and I," *Look,* 19 (June 28, 1955), 74; and editorial, *Delta Democrat-Times,* October 22, 1955.

[57] Editorial, Lexington *Advertiser,* as reprinted in *Delta Democrat-Times,* March 23, 1961; editorial, Lexington *Advertiser,* June 20, 1963.

ing in Holmes County won her a reputation as a fighting journalist —and enemies as well. In 1943, she was found guilty of contempt of court when she interviewed a witness, the widow of a black man who had been whipped to death by vigilantes. In 1954, she was found guilty of libel against the sheriff of Holmes County for her coverage of his shooting of a Negro.[58] Then, in 1957, after her repeated attacks on Council excesses, her enemies, led by persons prominent in the Holmes County Citizens' Council, formed the *Holmes County Herald* to drive her out of business. The state legislature joined the effort in 1962 when it passed a bill to permit any town in the county—and only in that county—to publish its official proceedings in newspapers outside of the municipality. Throughout it all, indeed until December, 1969, the organized segregationists endeavored to enforce an advertising boycott of her papers.[59] But try as it did the Council failed to break Hazel Smith. Defiantly she told the organization and its advocates: "this is not a lone woman editor you are fighting, it is not just a newspaper . . . it is an institution interwoven into your life and the life of the community and county." For 121 years the *Advertiser* had recorded the triumphs and tribulations of Holmes Countians, and, she promised, "it will still be around to carry your obituary." True to her word—even in the face of several unexplained attempts to destroy her operations by dynamite and fire—this moderate voice of protest persevered. But for all of her courage, it must be recorded that Mrs. Smith, like Hodding Carter, spoke from a position of relative security. Despite the power of the Council in Holmes County, her diversified operation rendered her less vulnerable than those who produced but a single weekly paper.[60]

One such editor was P. D. East. His Petal *Paper* was in the truest sense a one-man operation. Not only was he its editor and publisher,

58 Although a county court awarded the sheriff $10,000, the state supreme court reversed the ruling, affirming Mrs. Smith's right to print facts.

59 Interview with Hazel Brannon Smith, September 23, 1970; "Mississippi: Determined Lady," *Columbia Journalism Review*, 2 (Fall, 1963), 37–38; *Delta Democrat-Times*, January 5, 1962; Silver, *Mississippi: The Closed Society*, 38–39; Smith, *Congressman from Mississippi*, 267–69.

60 Quoted in Carter, *South Strikes Back*, 156. The New York *Times*, March 30, 1961, quoted Hazel Smith to this effect: "We've managed to stay in business because we publish not one but four papers and work like dogs."

but he wrote the copy, sold the advertising, and often even personally mailed the weekly edition. Unlike either Carter or Smith, he was an inveterate iconoclast and, as he remarked, "having been corrupted by the Constitution," an outspoken critic of segregation. An eccentric and volatile man, East vented his rage against the oppressive atmosphere of conformity through a powerful sense of ridicule and an often outlandish sense of humor. When the Citizens' Council organized Forrest County in south-central Mississippi, the seat of his tiny operation, he greeted it with his now-famous "Jack Ass Ad." Headlined "Yes, YOU too, can be SUPERIOR," the full-page "advertisement" invited readers to "Join the Glorious Citizens Clan" and enjoy such new freedom as the "freedom to wonder who is pocketing the five dollars you pay to join," and the "FREEDOM TO BE SUPERIOR WITHOUT BRAIN, CHARACTER, OR PRINCIPLE!"[61] A few months later, in November, 1956, he devoted another full page to the Citizens' Council, which he now called the "Bigger and Better Bigots Bureau." After proposing to "present below our views on the good that has been, and is being done, by the citizens councils of Mississippi since they went into business," he ran an empty page.[62]

East's position was not calculated to win support among segregationists. Nor did it. By 1959 his local circulation had fallen from a high of 2,300 to none at all. Somewhat proudly he announced in the January, 1959, issue of *Harper's*: "My newspaper has the lowest local per capita circulation of any in the world." His local advertising was likewise nonexistent, and he managed to survive—but only temporarily—through the grace of out-of-state subscribers and advertisers. How great a role the Council played in this economic squeeze East himself did not know, although he was inclined to credit it heavily.[63] Yet, because he made no effort to conceal his

[61] Petal *Paper*, March 14, 1956. In his book, *The Magnolia Jungle: The Life, Times and Education of a Southern Editor* (New York: Simon and Schuster, 1960), 179, East noted that the "advertisement" had "gone into all fifty states, Canada, Japan, England, Ireland, Australia, France, Italy, and Germany (West Germany, that is)." It was also reprinted in several major magazines. See Albert Vorspan, "The Iconoclast of Petal, Mississippi," *The Reporter*, 16 (March 21, 1957), 33–35; and East, "How to Be a Man of Distinction," *Harper's*, 217 (January, 1959), 12–18.

[62] Petal *Paper*, November 22, 1956.

[63] After losing 50 percent of his standing advertisements in a single month,

views, an organized boycott was hardly necessary. Almost axiomatically, a community in which the Citizens' Council prospered would prove to be a community singularly unresponsive to East's brand of journalism.

The Petal *Paper*, the *Delta Democrat-Times*, and the Lexington *Advertiser*, each in its own way, were exceptional. Indeed, as one student of southern journalism has written, they were "islands of unorthodoxy in a monolithic sea."[64] Certainly their unrelenting hostility toward organized segregation did not represent the views expressed by an overwhelming majority of the state's press. In varying degrees most Mississippi newspapers reflected the attitude of the archconservative Hederman press, whose morning Jackson *Clarion-Ledger* and evening *Daily News* vied with one another in offering praise for the Citizens' Council.[65] Reciprocating in kind, the Council honored the Jackson newspapers in November, 1955, for their "fair stories about the Councils." On another occasion, the *Daily News* editor, Major Frederick Sullens, was presented a plaque by William J. Simmons in recognition of his courageous defense of "our Southern way of life."[66]

Some editors of course held contrary views—but they expressed them cautiously. Typical of the circumspection of a large segment of the state's moderate press was a series of editorials written by

---

East learned that Councilors had been suggesting to local merchants that advertising in the Petal *Paper* could be an economic liability. Telephone interview with P. D. East, January 24, 1971. See also East, *Magnolia Jungle*, 210–11; and "How to Be a Man of Distinction," 12.

[64] Hugh Davis Graham, *Crisis in Print: Desegregation and the Press in Tennessee* (Nashville: Vanderbilt University Press, 1967), 316.

[65] Silver has noted that "the extremist Jackson *Clarion-Ledger* and the *Daily News* dominate Mississippi thought. . . . To read the Hederman press day after day is to understand what the people of the state believe and are prepared to defend." See *Mississippi: The Closed Society*, 30.

[66] Birmingham *News*, November 25; Jackson *Daily News*, October 28, 1955. The relationship between the Council and the Hederman press was indeed a warm one. The *Daily News* and the *Citizens' Council* occasionally exchanged editorials. *Daily News* cartoonist Bob Howie also served as cartoonist for the *Citizens' Council*—although he did not sign his work for the latter. For examples of editorials defending the Council from its detractors, see *Daily News*, December 18, 1955, June 13, 1956. See also editorial, "Join the Citizens Councils," *Clarion-Ledger*, September 27, 1957.

J. Oliver Emmerich, editor of the Jackson *State Times,* Hederman's short-lived competitor. Proposing "A Positive Program for the South," the editor noted that "some publicity, perhaps unfair, has placed the Citizens' Council in the awkard position of appearing to favor the negative, emotional, frenzied approach to the problem [of desegregation]." The *State Times,* Emmerich was careful to add, did not subscribe to this accusation, and in the "spirit of genuine cordiality," it offered the "sincere suggestion" that the Council make every effort to channel its energies into a "constructive and amicable program" for solving the racial dilemma.[67]

In the aftermath of the Barton case, Emmerich was considerably bolder. Decrying "secret-police procedure," even when "done in the name of patriotism," he declared that "witch-hunting . . . is just as wicked in Mississippi as in Russia." [68] Similarly, other moderate papers, notably the Batesville *Panolian,* the Pascagoula *Chronicle,* the Rollingfork *Deer Creek Pilot,* and the Tupelo *Daily Journal,* leveled their editorial cannons at what Paul Pittman of the Tylertown *Times* chose to call "an insidious fifth column [which] is at work in our state, undermining individual rights, perverting individual freedom and creating a hateful state of suspicion and fear among our people." [69]

A growing restiveness in some quarters of the press was only the most obvious manifestation of Hodding Carter's belief that "Mis-

[67] Editorial, Jackson *State Times,* March 30, 1958. It seems likely that Emmerich's early caution can be attributed to the fate of his predecessor, Norman Bradley, the first editor of the *State Times.* According to Mississippi journalist Raymond Milner, Bradley had been fired after his repeated calls for racial moderation and for criticizing the Citizens' Council. As Milner reported, the *State Times,* fighting for circulation and advertising against Hederman, could not afford the luxury of antagonizing the Citizens' Council. (*Delta Democrat-Times,* March 11, 1956.) The *State Times* began its operation on February 28, 1955, and suspended it January 16, 1962. Its equipment was then sold to Hederman's Mississippi Publishers Corporation. (New York *Times,* January 17, 1962.)

[68] Editorial, Jackson *State Times,* March 16, 1961.

[69] See editorials from Tylertown *Times* and Rollingfork *Deer Creek Pilot,* reprinted in *Delta Democrat-Times,* March 16, 20, 1961; Batesville *Panolian,* January 26, 1961; and Ira B. Harkey, Jr., *Smell of Burning Crosses* (Jacksonville, Ill.: Harris-Wolfe, 1967), passim. See also New York *Times,* March 30, 1961, on the general reaction of Mississippi's press to the Barton case.

sissippians are getting a little tired of Mr. Simmons" and those racial extremists "who believe that any means are acceptable so long as they can preserve the status quo." [70] The formation of the Mississippi Council on Human Relations during the early 1960's was less conspicuous but perhaps not less important. In vain a few moderates had endeavored to form such a group in 1957, but extremist opposition and an attempted assassination made it impossible to find suitable officers. In the fall of 1961, however, a human relations organization was formed at Tougaloo Southern Christian College, a Negro coeducational institution near Jackson. Almost immediately Council spokesmen declared that it "could serve only to create undermining from within our peacefully segregated social structure," and expressed every confidence that "the members of the Jackson Citizens' Council will know how to deal with this threat to our community." [71] Confronted with such opposition, the group functioned rather furtively at first. Yet it survived, and by 1965 James W. Silver cited it as evidence that a "revolution" had begun in the Magnolia State. "The Mississippi Council on Human Relations," he wrote in a third and enlarged edition of his *Mississippi: The Closed Society,* "is not only a healthy reality, with a paid executive director and a paid assistant, but it has several branches meeting regularly in several parts of the state." [72]

The Mississippi Advisory Committee to the Federal Commission on Civil Rights had a similar history. In October, 1958, as the Commission was endeavoring to find prominent Mississippians willing to serve on the advisory group, Simmons sounded the tocsin in a front-page editorial entitled, "The Carpetbaggers Are Coming." In the chief Councilor's view, "no decent or responsible citizen in the South will be so stupid as to allow himself to be used for the betrayal of his own people, or so callous as to be insensible to the ostracism that will inevitably follow." [73] For more than a year this threat of social blacklisting was sufficient to dampen whatever

[70] Editorial, *Delta Democrat-Times,* May 18, 1961.

[71] Interview with Kenneth Dean, executive director, Mississippi Council on Human Relations, June 26, 1970; Jackson *Daily News* and *Clarion-Ledger,* May 5, 1962.

[72] Silver, *Mississippi: The Closed Society,* 358.

[73] *The Citizens' Council,* October, 1958, 1. See also, Jackson *Daily News,* October 26, and Jackson *State Times,* December 9, 1958.

enthusiasm the state's moderates may have felt for such a committee. And when the search for advisers was renewed in November, 1959, Simmons again called upon whites to "DEFY the Federal Civil Rights Commission in its efforts to employ Mississippians as collaborators, to spy and report on their fellow citizens." Again he warned "disloyal or unthinking Mississippians"—the "Quislings in our midst"—to be mindful that cooperation with the federal agency would bring certain banishment.[74] Nevertheless, in December, 1959, a state advisory group was formed, and soon thereafter it began a series of hearings on the administration of justice in Mississippi. When its report was released in January, 1963, it confirmed what many concerned Mississippians had long suspected —that "justice under law is not guaranteed for the Negro in Mississippi in the way that it is for the white man"; and that "much of the basic meaning of being an American citizen is denied to nearly half the state." "Terror hangs over the Negro in Mississippi," the report averred, "and is an expectancy for those who refuse to accept their color as a badge of inferiority. . . ."[75]

Individually, the formation of the state advisory committee on civil rights, the appearance of a human relations council, the outcry over the Barton case, and the faint appeals for moderation in the wake of rioting at Ole Miss could have meant little. But collectively these occurrences represented the disenchantment felt by an ever-widening audience of white Mississippians toward the bitter-end segregationists who would sacrifice all to bar even so much as a single black child from the state's all-white school system. Thoughtful whites were becoming increasingly aware of the federal presence

[74] "The Carpetbaggers Are Coming—Again!" *The Citizens' Council*, November, 1959, 1–2. See also *Southern School News*, December, 1959, 5; February, 1960, 7.

[75] Employing the understatement, the advisory group reported: "The Committee's work was difficult from the first. In addition to official obstacles put in their path by the State Government . . . the Committee members were . . . subjected to personal abuse from private sources. . . . [One] member was threatened by a sheriff, who was also the president of the local White Citizens' Council, and was hit in the face by his neighbor. . . ." Others were ostracized and one's home was bombed. (Mississippi Advisory Committee to the U.S. Commission on Civil Rights, *Administration of Justice in Mississippi* [Washington: Government Printing Office, 1963], 23, 32–33.)

in Mississippi—a presence made possible not merely by judicial fiat, but by a succession of civil rights statutes enacted by the Congress and signed into law by the nation's President. Squarely confronted by the three branches of a determined United States government, continued defiance became a practical impossibility. Not insignificantly, then, the May, 1964, issue of *The Citizen* failed to celebrate the tenth anniversary of Mississippi's successful evasion of the Court's writ. The entire issue, like that of the previous month, was devoted to a section-by-section analysis of "the vicious 'Civil Rights bill'" then pending before the House.[76]

Thus even before the Civil Rights Act of 1964 could be enacted, the Citizen's Councils of America announced that it had already begun "a nationwide campaign" for its repeal. Meanwhile, it advised Mississippians not to "surrender our American liberties in blind compliance," and to continue resistance by "all lawful means." The Association of Citizens' Councils of Mississippi expressed confidence that much, if not all, of the act was unconstitutional. Because the measure carried no criminal penalties and persons discriminated against had no recourse save that of injunction, the organization advised owners of public accommodations and other businessmen to continue their practice of segregation, secure in the knowledge that "persons involved in litigation resulting from resistance to the 'Civil Rights Act' should have the backing of the community and should have financial assistance from a White Citizens' Legal Fund." For its part, the Jackson Citizens' Council took a characteristically hard line, warning that "businessmen cannot play both sides of the street; they must ultimately choose whether to serve white or Negro customers." White businesses found to be in compliance with the "force bill," it warned, would be subject to massive white boycotts.[77]

That such threats no longer served to keep the white community in line became immediately apparent. Within twenty-four hours after President Lyndon Baines Johnson affixed his signature to the act, several Jackson hotels and a leading downtown motel quietly

[76] See undated Citizens' Councils of America press release, file of Wilson Minor; and *The Citizen*, 8 (April, 1964) 5–20; (May, 1964), 4–15.

[77] "Official Citizens' Council Statements on the 'Civil Rights Act,'" ibid., 8 (July–August, 1964), 6–9; *Aspect*, July, 1964.

began to desegregate their services. That same day the executive council of the capital city's chamber of commerce released a declaration favoring compliance. Although the Council quickly condemned this "secret rump session [called] to pass a Washington sponsored integration resolution," it was clear that some public officials and business leaders in the very citadel of segregation had already abandoned massive resistance.[78]

Additional opposition to the Council's policy of no compromise appeared in the form of the Mississippians for Public Education, an organization of "parents, taxpayers and citizens" dedicated to the preservation of the state's school system—segregated or otherwise. Formed in the early summer of 1964, soon after the issuance of federal court orders requiring desegregation the following September in four Mississippi cities, this statewide group urged support for school authorities and other public officials in their efforts to effect a peaceful transition. Like similar citizens' organizations in other states, the MPE gingerly avoided the issue of segregation and based its campaign exclusively on that of open schools. Composed primarily of mothers and led by a Jackson housewife, Mrs. Gordon Henderson, it effectively countered the Council's charge that it was fronting for the "NAACP and other Communist-led forces of integration." [79] Due in no small measure to the endeavors of this public-spirited organization, desegregation proceeded on schedule in September, without incident and without school closure.

Following the admission of black children to formerly all-white classrooms in Biloxi, Carthage, Clarksdale, and Jackson, the MPE was joined by other voices of moderation and accommodation. In October, Jackson's mayor, Allen Thompson, once regarded as a Council stalwart, publicly attacked William J. Simmons, Louis Hollis,

[78] *The Citizen,* 8 (July–August, 1964), 9; *Wall Street Journal,* July 6, and New York *Times,* July 4, 1964.

[79] Knoxville *News-Sentinel,* September 3; Memphis *Commercial Appeal,* October 3; Memphis *Press-Scimitar,* October 21, 1964. For representative examples of the Council propaganda materials used against the MPE, see Lauderdale County Citizens' Council advertisement, Meridian *Star,* August 3, 1964; and a two-page mimeograph throwaway, Association of Citizens' Councils of Mississippi, "Facts about School Integration," July 21, 1964, personal collection of Terry Alford, State College, Mississippi.

and other top CCA leaders for their persistent efforts to disrupt the city's program for orderly desegregation under court decree.[80] In December, George Keith, the president of the Mississippi Press Association, and Erle Johnston, chairman of the State Sovereignty Commission, sniped at the organized extremists in separate speeches to the Public Relations Association of Mississippi and the Mississippi Sheriff's Association, respectively. Echoing a theme from Governor Paul B. Johnson's inaugural address of January, 1964, both urged whites to work together to overcome the state's reputation for racial lawlessness. As Johnston informed the sheriff's assemblage, "we cannot win our tomorrows by longing futilely for yesterday." Mississippi, he added, was in a "period of transition whether you like it or not." [81] A similar view was expressed soon thereafter by the Mississippi Economic Council, the state's chamber of commerce. Following the adoption of resolutions by both the Association of Citizens' Councils of Mississippi and the Citizens' Councils of America urging local school boards to forfeit federal monies rather than sign desegregation pledges as required under Title VI of the new civil rights legislation, the businessmen's group issued a statement of principle: "Mississippi is not an island unto itself, but an integral and responsible part of the United States. We recognize the Civil Rights Act of 1964 . . . cannot be ignored and should not be unlawfully defied. Resistance to the law should be through . . . the ballot boxes and the courts. We should adjust ourselves to the impact of the legislation, regardless of personal feeling and convictions, and limit our resistance to the stated methods." [82]

But the most telling testimony of the Council's failing grip on the white community in Mississippi came not from the state's business and political leadership, but from within the very ranks of the organization itself. From its earliest development, no Mississippian had been more closely identified with white southern resistance

[80] Jackson *Daily News,* October 2; New York *Times,* October 6, 1964.

[81] Quoted in Memphis *Commercial Appeal,* December 13, 1964. See also New Orleans *Times-Picayune,* December 13, 1964.

[82] Quoted in Silver, *Mississippi: The Closed Society,* 281. See also Meridian *Star,* January 20; Jackson *Daily News,* April 7, 8, 1965; and "A Timely Warning," *The Citizen,* 9 (January, 1965), 2–15.

than Judge Tom P. Brady. His *Black Monday* had inspired the first Council, and his appointment to the state supreme court in 1963 was generally regarded as evidence of the organization's enormous influence with the administration of Governor Ross Barnett. Even after taking his seat on the bench, the Brookhaven lawyer continued to serve on the Council's state executive committee. But as a member of Mississippi's court of last resort, Brady came to recognize what few if any of his fellow Council leaders had—that the tides of justice were flowing ever more strongly against the cause of white supremacy. However personally repugnant the colorblind spirit of the Constitution may have been, he could have no doubt that its letter was explicitly equalitarian. Prior to his appointment as an associate justice, he could indict the "High Priests of Washington" for committing "legal legerdemain" in their *Brown* decision. He could defiantly proclaim that "a law is never paramount to mores"; that "the Supreme Court can play King Canute to its heart's content—but laws like bullets cannot kill a sacred custom." He could even predict that, whenever a law runs counter to local customs, "invariably strife, bloodshed and revolution follow in the wake of its attempted enforcement." [83] But once elevated to the state's highest seat of judgment, his views on the efficacy of the law were to change markedly. Thus in an opinion of 1965 he admonished that "irrespective of how erroneous it may appear, or how odious it is, a decision of the United States Supreme Court is still the ultimate in judicial determination and is binding on the tribunals and citizens of the respective states in comparable cases. As a self-governing agency, it is imperative that this state operate under law and law alone." [84] Again the following year, he wrote the majority opinion in a state supreme court reversal of the grand larceny conviction of a Montgomery County Negro on the ground that blacks were systematically excluded from jury duty. Among the precedents he cited, Brady included not only previous rulings of the U.S. Supreme Court but the Civil Rights Act of 1964. Not unmindful of the irony, the Councilor-jurist would later recall that this unpopular opinion was followed by a spate of

[83] Brady, *Black Monday*, 44–45.

[84] *Bolton* v. *City of Greenville*, 253, *Miss. Reports*, 656 (1965). See also "The Education of Tom Brady," *Time*, 86 (October 22, 1965), 94–95.

harassing midnight telephone calls branding him a "nigger lover." [85]

Although he adamantly denied it, Justice Brady had become a moderate. To an extraordinary degree, his dilemma was that of white supremacists generally. For, although Mississippi's segregationists were for the most part no more ready to embrace the black citizen as their equal than they had been a decade before, a growing number of them recognized by the mid-1960's that last-ditch defiance was utterly futile. If the "closed society" had not already toppled, it was surely rent with irreparable fissures. Even many of its erstwhile guardians were breaking ranks to accept tokenism.

[85] *Hopkins* v. *State,* 254, *Miss. Reports,* 484–87 (1966); interview with Judge Brady.

CHAPTER XIII

The Lily-White Schoolhouse

IT was surely one of the most interesting anomalies of the post-*Brown* period that, in a region not notable for the excellence of its public schools, education should become the focus for a monumental expenditure of legislative energy. Whether striving to restrict desegregation in the upper South or to avoid it altogether in the Deep South, the state legislatures of the former Confederacy lavished attention on the public schools as never before. During the course of the first decade of the new era, no fewer than 450 acts and resolutions designed either to prevent, delay, or limit the attendance of Negroes in white schools were adopted in the eleven-state area. Far and away the leader in this legislative fusillade, Louisiana alone accounted for ninety-two such measures during its one regular and five extraordinary sessions of 1960–61.[1] Although the mood varied from one state to the next, legislators throughout the region wrote their allegiance to the lily-white schoolhouse into law. And in every state but one, the extent of that allegiance could be measured by the statutes permitting or requiring the closure of public schools as a "last resort." Schools were actually closed in Little Rock, several areas of Virginia, and briefly in Alabama; yet the abandonment of formal education was an expediency to which all but the most extreme segregationists were loath to turn. Clearly preferable were laws which would keep classrooms open as well as segregated.

1 "Ten Years in Review," *Southern School News,* May, 1964, 1B, 5B.

The heart of resistance legislation throughout the South was the pupil placement law. Although varying from state to state, this device usually established elaborate criteria "other than race" as the basis for assigning students to particular schools. Patently transparent though they were, pupil assignment laws were effective deterrents to widespread desegregation in the peripheral South, and until late in the first decade after the Court's decree, they served as seemingly insurmountable barriers in the Deep South. In every southern state compulsory attendance laws were either amended or repealed, and so-called "freedom of choice" provisions were enacted in each to prevent children of one race from being "forced" to attend schools with those of another. Excepting only North Carolina and Texas, resolutions of interposition were universally adopted on the specious theory that by interposing its "sovereignty" between its citizens and the federal government a state could nullify the effects of a federal edict within its own boundaries. Other legislative mainstays included measures permitting or requiring the withholding of funds from desegregated schools, laws permitting the sale of public school property for use by private institutions, and enactments authorizing or encouraging the creation of private schools. In six states teacher tenure laws were altered so that "pro-integration" teachers might be more easily dismissed. State laws also authorized local boards in Alabama, Florida, Louisiana, Tennessee, and Texas to segregate children by sex so that white girls need not attend classes with Negro boys. In some states it became a misdemeanor to teach a desegregated class, and in Mississippi it was declared unlawful to attend a desegregated school. Georgia made it a crime for a teacher of one race to offer instruction to pupils of another; Louisiana denied promotion or graduation to students who attended biracial classes; Arkansas permitted segregated classes within desegregated schools.[2]

[2] The most complete source on school segregation laws is *Southern School News*. Among the several brief analyses of the patterns of resistance legislation are James T. Leeson, "The First Ten Years," *Phi Delta Kappan*, 45 (May, 1964), 362–70; "The Crumbling Legal Barriers to School Desegregation," *Southern Education Reports*, 2 (October, 1966), 10–12; James W. Vander Zanden, "Seven Years of Southern Resistance, *Midwest Quarterly*, 2

To protect this jerry-built legal edifice from the erosive effects of litigation, the region also launched a massive counterattack against the NAACP. Every state but North Carolina adopted laws designed either to curb or hinder the activities of the organization. Most frequently these measures assumed the form of barratry or champerty statutes, but laws requiring the filing of lists of members, making it a misdemeanor to employ a member, and requiring the dismissal of public employees who were members were also adopted. In several states the NAACP was subjected to "investigations" by legislative committees and state sovereignty commissions, usually intending to link it to the "Communist conspiracy." [3]

But even the anti-NAACP laws were scant protection, for whenever carried to the court of last resort they too were found invalid. Political weapons, however adroitly wielded, could only delay the implementation of the Court's writ. As the perimeter of segregation contracted following the exhaustion of public resources for resistance, private groups were pressed into service. Early monuments to the disruptive effects of these extralegal instrumentalities were the disturbances at Clinton and Hoxie. But it was not until the crisis at Little Rock that their incendiary potential became fully apparent.

If mere long-range planning were a valid index to peaceful desegregation, Little Rock's submission to the dictates of the *Brown* decision would have been accomplished without incident. While its program of preparedness was neither as well conceived nor as effectively executed as those in the border cities of Louisville and St. Louis, the Little Rock school board began preparing for desegregation immediately after the Court's ruling. On May 18, 1954, the board instructed Superintendent of Schools Virgil T. Blossom to formulate a plan for compliance. Unenthusiastic though he was, Blossom set to work, and within a year he presented a functional

---

(July, 1961), 273–84. See also, Ch. 2, "The Legislators," in Sarratt, *Ordeal of Desegregation*, 28–46.

[3] Walter F. Murphy, "The South Counterattacks: The Anti-NAACP Laws," *Western Political Quarterly*, 12 (June, 1959), 371–90. See also Stanley Rowland, "Legal War on the NAACP," *The Nation*, 184 (February 9, 1957), 115–16.

blueprint for tokenism at the high school level beginning in September, 1957.[4] Although failing to utilize fully the flourishing moderate community within this upper-South capital city, Blossom undertook a constructive program of public education. In a series of some two hundred addresses, he lectured service clubs, businessmen's organizations, and church groups, emphasizing that while desegregation was neither his nor the school board's desire, there was no practical alternative. Perhaps because, as one NAACP spokesman believed, "Superintendent Blossom was more interested in appeasing the segregationists by advocating that only a limited number of Negroes be admitted than in complying with the Supreme Court's decision,"[5] significant opposition to the Little Rock Phase Program did not materialize until the summer of 1957. The vanguard of that opposition was, of course, occupied by the Capital Citizens' Council.

Although it was the largest organization of its type in Arkansas, the CCC was but a pale reflection of its Deep South counterparts. Unquestionably the vast majority of the city's whites considered themselves segregationists, but only a relative few were willing to join the organized resistance movement. At peak strength, the CCC could boast of only some five hundred dues-paying members, and fewer than three hundred of these actually resided in the capital city. Its public rallies never attracted large crowds, nor did it enjoy the support of what might be called the city's "substantial" middle class; and, unlike those of many another southern city, the organization's officers were not drawn from the city's traditional civic leadership. A measure of the Council's standing in the community was provided by the school board election of March, 1957. In that month, voters rejected a pair of Council-endorsed candidates—one of whom was the organization's president—in favor of two others pledged to uphold the school board's desegregation plan.[6] But how-

[4] For the best account, see Numan V. Bartley, "Looking Back at Little Rock," *Arkansas Historical Quarterly*, 25 (Summer, 1966), 101–16.

[5] Daisy Bates, *The Long Shadow of Little Rock* (New York: McKay, 1962), 51–52. For a similar view, see Colbert S. Cartwright, "Lesson from Little Rock," *The Christian Century*, 74 (October 9, 1957), 1193–94.

[6] Virgil T. Blossom, *It Has Happened Here* (New York: Harper, 1959), 32.

ever much they lacked in terms of numbers and status, the members of the Citizen's Council possessed the advantage of an established organization and leadership. As one student of Little Rock politics has written, they comprised "the most vocal and potent group within the community."[7] Events would prove that their disruptive capacity could be enormous.

For all practical purposes, the opening salvo in the campaign to prevent desegregation at Central High came when CCC President Robert E. Brown, the recently defeated candidate for the school board, addressed an open letter to Governor Orval Faubus in the late spring of 1957. Reminding Faubus that Governor Allan Shivers had successfully flouted a federal court order and prevented desegregation in Mansfield, Texas, Brown observed that "in order to preserve domestic tranquility" he could block the school board's program. "As the sovereign head of the state," the city's chief Councilor added, "you are immune to federal court orders."[8] As Superintendent Blossom would later recall, this letter became the basis for "hundreds of thousands of circulars and many full-page advertisements."[9] But the governor was apparently unmoved. As late as mid-July he indicated that he would have nothing to do with defiance. "Everyone knows no state law supersedes a federal law," he told a press conference. "If anyone expects me to try to use them to supersede federal laws they are wrong."[10]

Quite obviously, the use of state laws for such purposes was precisely what some segregationists had in mind. Throughout the summer the Council's efforts to sabotage the desegregation plan continued. Whether creating disorders at open meetings of the school board, organizing letter-writing campaigns to urge the governor to invoke "police powers," or urging defiance through numerous newspaper advertisements, the organization managed to keep the sensitive issue before the public's eye. Typically, it sought to exploit the white community's darkest fears about racial co-

[7] Henry M. Alexander, *The Little Rock Recall Election*, Eagleton Institute Case Studies in Practical Politics (New Brunswick: Rutgers University Press, 1960), 4.

[8] Quoted in *Southern School News*, June, 1957, 9.

[9] Virgil T. Blossom, *It Has Happened Here*, 34.

[10] Quoted ibid., 36.

mingling. "If you integrate Little Rock Central High in September," one CCC-sponsored newspaper advertisement inquired of the school board, ". . . would the negro boys be permitted to solicit the white girls for dances?" In integrated drama classes, "when the script calls for . . . tender love scenes, will those parts be assigned to negro boys and white girls?"[11] Other Council advertisements "exposing" the "plot" between Blossom and the NAACP, urged parents to "disrupt [the] vile schemes" of a "small clique of white and Negro revolutionaries."[12] Repeatedly segregation leaders linked "the Blossom race-mixing plan" with black militants, and at one Council rally a speaker said that it may have been drafted by the "hidden hand which is the invisible world government."[13]

Persistent rumors of impending violence, fed by the ominous predictions of the extremists, served only to cloud the issue still further. Amis Guthridge, the furniture dealer and lawyer who served as the Council's most articulate spokesman in Little Rock, gravely warned that desegregation at Central High School could only be followed by "hell on the border."[14] The Reverend J. A. Lovell, a Dallas radio minister imported by the CCC for a midsummer public meeting, warned that "there are people left yet in the South who love God and their nation enough to shed blood if necessary to stop this work of Satan." Quickly affirming its nonviolent principles, the Council denied that Lovell's statement meant that the organization would condone physical resistance; Guthridge even publicly advised members that expulsion would follow any act of violence. Nevertheless, the organization's resolute commitment to segregation at any price contributed to widespread uneasiness within the city as the first day of school approached.[15]

The acme of the summer-long crusade came late in August with the appearance at a Council fund-raising dinner of Georgia's Governor Marvin Griffin and its former speaker of the house, Roy

11 *Southern School News*, August, 1957, 7. For Blossom's answers, see *It Has Happened Here*, 41–43. See also Wilson Record and Jane Cassels Record, *Little Rock, U.S.A.: Materials and Analysis* (San Francisco: Chandler, 1960), 32.

12 Quoted in Birmingham *News*, July 19, 1957.

13 Quoted in *Arkansas Gazette*, July 17, 1957.

14 *Southern School News*, July, 1957, 10.

15 Ibid., August, 1957, 7.

V. Harris. Prior to the engagement, Governor Faubus, fearful lest their visit spark disorder, telephoned Griffin in Atlanta to express his apprehension. Although the Georgia governor replied that "I was gonna give 'em hell on the Constitution and Roy was gonna give 'em hell on the civil rights thing," he offered his assurances that there would be no inflammatory statements. Thus satisfied, Faubus invited the pair to be his guests at the governor's mansion during their stay in Little Rock.

To be sure, these roving ambassadors of resistance did not incite to riot. But their defiant speeches left little doubt that when and if the court ordered Georgia to desegregate there would be no peaceful submission. Amid tumultuous applause, the vow was made that as a last-ditch measure the Griffin administration would summon "every white man in Georgia" to defend "our cherished institutions." [16]

These intimations were clear not only to Little Rock's militant segregationists but to Faubus as well. Soon after his guests departed, the governor reported that "people are coming to me and saying if Georgia doesn't have integration why does Arkansas have it?" [17] Certainly the appearance of Harris and Griffin had a galvanic effect. Until their arrival, Superintendent Blossom believed "we had a chance of getting people to accept the gradual integration plan." But afterward, popular opposition solidified.[18] In his testimony before an August 29 hearing at Pulaski County chancery court where segregationists sought an injunction against Little Rock school desegregation and again in a nationwide broadcast early in September, Faubus expressed agreement. Sentiment in the city had undergone a profound change, he said, and Griffin had "triggered" it.[19] Griffin himself was inclined to view his role as

[16] Ibid., September, 1957, 6–7; Brooks Hays, *A Southern Moderate Speaks* (Chapel Hill: University of North Carolina Press, 1959), 131–32; Fletcher Knebel, "The Real Little Rock Story," *Look*, 21 (November 12, 1957), 32–33; George B. Leonard, Jr., "Georgia: Rallying Point of Defiance," *Look*, 21 (November 12, 1957), 32–34; *Arkansas Gazette*, August 22, 23, 1957.

[17] Quoted in *Southern School News*, September, 1957, 6–7.

[18] In his testimony before a federal court, Blossom declared that Griffin's appearance in Little Rock "had more to do with strengthening opposition than anything that happened." Quoted in Atlanta *Journal*, June 5, 1958.

[19] *Southern School News*, September, 1957, 6–7.

catalytic. Soon after Faubus called out the state militia, ostensibly to prevent "tumult, riot and breach of the peace" [20]—but also to bar the admission of nine Negro students to Central High—the Georgian conceded: "I think my visit did make a little contribution to the unity of the people." [21]

Less certain was the degree to which the archsegregationists influenced Faubus's own decision to follow the destructive route of defiance. Almost until the very moment of his September 2 proclamation activating the National Guard, Faubus had been vilified by white militants. Indeed, there was little in the record of this upcountry politician to suggest that he would become the hero of the resistance movement. Raised in Negro-sparse Madison County, he recognized early the advantages accruing from a discreet cultivation of the state's growing number of black voters. Following his first-term election in 1954, he became the first Arkansas governor to appoint Negroes to the state Democratic central committee. During the Democratic gubernatorial primary campaign of 1956, he courted and won a majority of the state's Negro voters to gain a second nomination over the opposition of segregationist candidate James Johnson, a former state senator and the head of the statewide Council organization. When racist ire was raised over desegregation at Hoxie, he ignored all pleas for intervention to preserve all-white schools in that troubled village; even during the very peak of the crisis at Little Rock, he recalled with pride that peaceful desegregation of the state colleges had occurred during his tenure.[22] Precisely because his generally constructive, although not enthusiastic, attitude of compliance invited favorable comparison with other moderate upper South governors, notably Frank G. Clement of Tennessee and Luther H. Hodges of North Carolina, he became the target of the extremists. From its first issue in November, 1955, the *Arkansas Faith*, monthly organ of the state's early Council movement, lampooned "Governor Oval

[20] See Faubus's proclamation to the National Guard, September 2, 1957, as printed in *Race Relations Law Reporter*, 2 (October, 1957), 937.

[21] Quoted in Corrine Silverman, *The Little Rock Story* (University: University of Alabama Press, 1959).

[22] Colbert S. Cartwright, "The Improbable Demagogue of Little Rock, Arkansas," *The Reporter*, 17 (October 17, 1957), 23–25; Bartley, "Looking Back at Little Rock," 110–11; Silverman, *The Little Rock Story*, 10.

'Fabalouse'" (also "Awful Faubus"), whose anxieties to "appease" the integrationists had made him "unable to remember whether he received his college training at the communist Commonwealth College or at a mule barn." [23] Even as late as the fund-raising banquet at the Hotel Marion, Griffin and Harris felt obliged to apologize for accepting the governor's hospitality. As Harris reassuringly explained, "having us at the mansion's the worst thing could happen to Faubus. It'll ruin him with the integrationists and the liberals." [24]

But however moderate his previous record, Faubus chose to bend with the current of racial extremism. Perhaps to his own consternation, he was swept along into the very vortex of massive resistance. Having deployed the National Guard to block the execution of a federal mandate, the governor flirted with armed rebellion for seventeen days. Only after a series of complicated maneuvers involving the President, the Department of Justice, and a federal judge—and the issuance of a federal injunction against further obstruction—did he withdraw the guard on September 20.[25] On the twenty-third, when Negroes at last gained admission, an unruly mob gathered outside the school. Just three and one-half hours after their appearance, apprehensive school and city administrators, fearful lest there be bloodshed, ordered the removal of the black students by a side exit.[26] That same day President Eisenhower issued an emergency proclamation urging the angry crowd of whites to disperse. When the jeering throng appeared for a second day, the President federalized the Arkansas National Guard and ordered in a thousand-troop battle group from the 101st Airborne Division.[27] For nearly a month, while a sullen calm

[23] *Arkansas Faith*, November, 1955, March, 1956. See also Rowan, *Go South to Sorrow*, 156–57, and *Arkansas Gazette*, October 4, 1957.

[24] Knebel, "The Real Little Rock Story," 32–33; Hays, *A Southern Moderate Speaks*, 131–32.

[25] Little Rock Congressman Brooks Hays, a participant in these manueverings, has written "The Inside Story of Little Rock," *U.S. News and World Report*, 46 (March 23, 1959), 118–35.

[26] Blossom, *It Has Happened Here*, 103–9.

[27] Major General Edwin A. Walker, commander of the Arkansas Military District, directed the federal military operation at Little Rock. Although he carried out his assignment with efficiency and even lectured white students on proper deportment before the Negro pupils arrived at Central High, Walker, who became a Council hero, would later declare that he had fought

settled over the city, the nine Negro children attended school with a troop escort. On November 27 the last regular Army forces were withdrawn, leaving a shrinking detachment of federalized Guardsmen until the commencement of the summer recess on May 29, 1958.

Although the Capital Citizens' Council heralded the day the troops left Little Rock as "Liberation Day," [28] there is little reason to believe that the occasion was a particularly joyous one for the organization. Since desegregation had been achieved, its preoccupation had been the creation and maintenance of an atmosphere so unrelentingly hostile that a permanent federal garrison would be required to keep the peace. During a return engagement in mid-January, 1958, Roy Harris, this time in the company of Robert Patterson and Federation for Constitutional Government President John U. Barr, expressed well the mood of Little Rock's Councilors. "Little Rock has Ike over a barrel," he informed more than one thousand segregationists assembled in the city's largest hotel ballroom. "If the people of Little Rock stand pat and he is forced to keep troops here from now on he soon will be the laughing stock of the nation and the world." In similar language, Patterson encouraged militants to persist in their defiance: "Little Rock has proved that forced integration is impractical if not impossible." [29]

To insure that integration would remain impractical at best, the organized segregationists met the arrival of Negroes at the all-white school with a vow of eternal resistance. Having urged whites to "peacefully assemble," [30] the Capital Citizens' Council may be at least partially credited for the appearance of the milling throngs of people that appeared so often around the high school during the month of September. An additional manifestation of its approval

---

on the "wrong side" in 1957. On the tenth anniversary of the *Brown* decision, he returned to the capital city as a guest of the CCC to deliver an address on "The Road from Little Rock: The Unprecedented Exposé of an American Soldier's Battle with the World Police State." School officials refused to let him speak from the steps of Central High. (Memphis *Commercial Appeal,* May 18, 1964.)

[28] *Arkansas Gazette,* May 27, 1958.

[29] Quoted in *Southern School News,* February, 1958, 12. See also *Arkansas Gazette,* January 15, 16; editorial, January 18, 1958.

[30] Columbia (S.C.) *State,* September 3, 1957.

of mob action came when it formed the "Freedom Fund for Little Rock" and toured the Deep South for contributions to defray the legal expenses of the seventy-five persons arrested during the disorders.[31] In its persistent harassment of school officials, the organization endeavored unsuccessfully to bring charges of malfeasance and nonfeasance against Blossom and members of the school board. Failing here, it supported a recall election law in hopes of effecting their removal by other means.[32]

Through it all, Councilors continued their inflammatory efforts to equate communism and the NAACP with school desegregation. During December, 1957, they circulated a broadside charging that the state president of the NAACP, "'Mrs.' Daisy Bates, Little Rock's 'Lady' of the Year," was the "unofficial 'principal' in charge of lecturing white students at Central High who 'cross' any of her 'brave' nine negro students." The circular, which carried police photographs of Mrs. Bates and a transcript of her "record" (failure to register the NAACP, "gaming," and "contempt of court"), indicated that "iron-clad censorship" and "prison-like fear" prevented white pupils from telling even their parents of the horrors of student life inside an integrated school.[33] With similar disregard for credibility, state Council leader James Johnson advised members of the Mothers' League of Central High School that an "active Communist cell in your own community" was "pulling the strings" throughout the summer and fall of 1957. Given sufficient time, the former state senator promised the prosegregation organization that he could even produce the "card numbers" of Little Rock's "Communist organizers."[34]

[31] Birmingham *News*, Charlotte (N.C.) *News* and Charleston *News and Courier*, November 20; Columbia *State*, November 22, 1957; *Southern School News*, November, 1957, 11.

[32] See CCC editorial, Monroe (La.) *Morning World*, January 22, 1958; *Southern School News*, February, 1958, 12; Blossom, *It Has Happened Here*, 150.

[33] Broadside, "Mrs. Daisy Bates," Miscellaneous Files, SERS. The NAACP state president informed the press that her 1946 contempt charge was dismissed on appeal, and that the 1952 gaming charge stemmed from a police raid on a private home where Mrs. Bates, her husband, and another couple were playing "penny ante" poker. (Memphis *Commercial Appeal*, December 18, 1957.)

[34] Quoted in *Arkansas Gazette*, March 21, 1958.

Tactics such as these contributed substantially to a general crystallization of white attitudes against continued compliance. Evidence that extremists had gained support in the wake of the military and legal proceedings which ended with federal troops in position at Central High School came on November 5, 1957, in a citywide government election. Although decisively defeated in a school board election the previous spring, the militant element made a surprisingly strong showing in the election of the first seven-member city manager board. Only one of the candidates endorsed by the Capital Citizens' Council was elected, but the voting was extremely close. The narrow margin of victory for the six moderate candidates came in wards where Negro voting was heaviest and in Pulaski Heights, the "silk stocking" section of the city.[35]

Undoubtedly encouraged by this mood of mounting intransigence, Faubus responded to a Supreme Court reversal of a lower court decision granting Little Rock a two and one-half year "tactical delay" without further desegregation by closing the city's high schools for the 1958–59 academic year.[36] Hailing Faubus's action as a major blow for "racial integrity and states' rights," Little Rock's segregationists began planning immediately for the reopening of the high schools on a private basis. Although the governor endorsed the plan and declared it not only "sound and workable" but beyond the reach of the "so-called 'law of the land,'" a federal court intervened to prevent the transfer of public school facilities and the diversion of public revenue.[37] Nevertheless, the newly formed Little Rock Private School Corporation opened tuition-free T. J. Raney High School late in October in a two story, thirty-two-room former orphanage. Not officially a Capital Citizens' Council project, the Private School Corporation was in everything but name a Council enterprise. Among its six incorporators were to be found such stalwarts of the organization as Guthridge and Pruden. Its treasurer was Dr. Malcolm G. Taylor, an osteopath who became

[35] *Southern School News*, December, 1957, 2–3.

[36] *Race Relations Law Reporter*, 3 (August, 1958), 630–41, 644–48; *Southern School News*, October, 1958, 5, 7.

[37] *Southern School News*, October, 1958, 5–7.

the president of the CCC in January, 1959.[38] Moreover, the Private School Corporation was a chief beneficiary of Citizens' Council philanthropy. The October issue of *The Citizens' Council*, monthly organ of the Council movement, carried a front-page appeal for "CONTRIBUTIONS TO LITTLE ROCK." To stimulate generous giving, Little Rock Councilors—occasionally in the company of Faubus himself—made solicitation tours to several southern cities.[39]

The returns were impressive. In its November issue, *The Citizens' Council* reported that "the Little Rock Private School Corporation is receiving financial support from citizens in every Southern state and many parts of the North." Paced by the Morehouse Parish, Louisiana, Citizens' Council, which collected $11,000 in a "Four Blocks for Little Rock campaign to ring the courthouse with silver dollars, American segregationists and their sympathizers from as far away as South Africa contributed generously to Arkansas' lily-white private school. Before the drive was a month old, the corporation's president could boast the collection of $175,000 of the estimated $600,000 necessary to operate the segregation academy for a year.[40]

Meanwhile, the embattled school board remained the focus of the controversy. During the months following the school closing, the Mothers' League joined the Council in a campaign for the recall of the five moderate board members. When the sixth and favored member, Dr. Dale Alford,[41] defeated Representative Brooks Hays in a write-in campaign for the fifth district congressional seat, the moderates resigned in recognition of "the utter hopelessness, helplessness and frustration of our present condition." When the new board was elected in early December, 1958,

38 Ibid., November, 1958, 8–9.

39 *The Citizens' Council*, October, 1958, 1; New Orleans *Times-Picayune*, November 10, 1958.

40 *The Citizens' Council*, November, 1958, 1; December, 1958, 2; *Southern School News*, November, 1958, 5; December, 1958, 12; Montgomery *Advertiser*, October 3, 1958; Muse, *Ten Years of Prelude*, 155.

41 For Alford's views on race, see a book much vaunted in Council circles: Dale Alford and L'Moore Alford, *The Case of the Sleeping People (Finally Awakened in Little Rock School Frustrations)* (Little Rock: Pioneer Press, 1959).

three of its members carried the endorsement of the Citizens' Council, and three represented a so-called "businessmen's ticket" which Councilors branded as "integrationist."[42] With the board thus equally divided, Faubus's supporters in the state legislature introduced a bill to permit the governor to appoint three additional members. Opposed by Little Rock PTA groups and the Women's Emergency Committee to Open Public Schools, a thousand-member moderate counterpart to the Mothers' League, the board-packing measure failed to pass.[43]

Defeated but unruffled, Faubus and the Council-endorsed board members joined the city's organized segregationists in demanding the removal of the principal of Central High, his two vice-principals, and the principal of all-Negro Horace Mann High School. The issue came to a head after months of rumors about a mass purge of school personnel in a meeting of the school board early in May. Following a fruitless morning of deadlock over the renewal of teacher contracts, the moderates withdrew. In their absence the pro-Faubus trio voted to replace Superintendent Terrell E. Powell with T. H. Alford, father of Dale Alford, and to discharge forty-four teachers and administrators for "integrationist" activity.[44]

The outcry was instantaneous. No sooner had the purge been announced than the Little Rock Classroom Teacher Association declared the action illegal. The following day PTA groups held mass protest rallies in at least five schools. In a statement of censure, the Little Rock PTA Council urged citizens to "carefully consider all legal measures allowed by Arkansas law to achieve recall of officials who use their positions to jeopardize our public school system." Within a week seventeen of the city's twenty-five PTA's

42 *Southern School News*, December, 1958, 12–13; January, 1959, 14.

43 House Bill 546, as the board-packing measure was known, was introduced on February 26 at the request of Faubus and Edward I. McKinley, Jr., one of the Council-endorsed school board members. According to its legislative sponsor, the bill was "a little on the dictatorship side, but we have no choice. The people voted the man [Faubus] back to do whatever he can to preserve their way of life." Quoted in *Southern School News*, March, 1959, 2.

44 *Arkansas Gazette*, May 6, 1959: *Southern School News*, June, 1959, 2–3.

endorsed the central council's demand for a recall, and the committee to Stop This Outrageous Purge (STOP) was organized by 179 prominent business and civic leaders to promote the effort.

Fighting back, the segregationists organized a committee and a recall campaign of their own. The Citizens' Council and the States' Rights Council united with the Mothers' League in the formation of CROSS, the Committee to Retain Our Segregated Schools. With opposing petitions filed and the election set for May 25, both camps campaigned vigorously. Limiting itself to the issue of the purge—to the specific exclusion of a stand on desegregation—STOP waged a dignified battle. CROSS, on the other hand, indiscriminately identified all those who protested the firings as "integrationists," "left-wingers," "fellow travelers," and "Communists."[45] Echoing CROSS, Council spokesmen labeled such open-school advocates as the Little Rock Chamber of Commerce and the PTA as "communist frontiers" and pawns in a "race-mixing conspiracy." U.S. Representatives Dale Alford and John Bell Williams also assisted by speaking at CROSS rallies, as did Faubus, who made two appearances on local television in support of the purge and recall of the moderates.[46]

On May 25, the voting was heavy and the margin narrow, but STOP emerged the victor. With the purgers themselves purged by the voters and the moderates exonerated, the always neutral *Southern School News* could report that "for the first time since September, 1957, there was widespread opposition to Faubus at

[45] CROSS also invited Dr. Wesley A. Swift to address a rally. Given advance billing as "State Director, Anti-Communist League of California and pastor of a well-known Los Angeles Church," the Reverend Swift arrived in Little Rock but did not appear at the segregationists' rally. When the *Arkansas Gazette* revealed that he had been a former Klansman and bodyguard for Gerald L. K. Smith, CROSS canceled his scheduled address and used local talent. See editorial, "The Contrast between CROSS and STOP," *Arkansas Gazette,* May 19, 1959; and Alexander, *Little Rock Recall Election,* 28.

[46] The most balanced and comprehensive analysis of this entire episode is Alexander's *The Little Rock Recall Election.* See also "STOP and CROSS: School Board Election," *Time,* 73 (June 8, 1959), 20–21; Jerry Neil, "The Education of Governor Faubus," *Nation,* 188 (June 6, 1959), 507–9; "How They Beat Faubus in Little Rock," *New Republic,* 140 (June 8, 1959), 7–8; and Silverman, *The Little Rock Story,* 30–31.

Little Rock on a school matter." In less measured tones, a jubilant *Arkansas Gazette* proclaimed: "The air is clearer today, and the future brighter." [47]

Unquestionably, the future of public education was brighter in the months after the recall election. In June a federal court struck down Arkansas's school closure statutes and ordered the school board to proceed with its original desegregation plan. For its part, a reconstituted school expunged the action taken during the rump session of May 5 and prepared for the reopening of the city's four high schools.

With public institutions slated for reopening, the already hard-pressed private schools began to fold. Baptist High School, able to register only twenty-two students by mid-July, scuttled its plans for reopening as a permanent Christian academy. About the same time, Trinity (Episcopal) Interim Academy advised its pupils to enroll in the public schools and closed its doors. By the end of the month, only T. J. Raney High School, the largest of the private institutions, was preparing to open its classrooms in the fall. Despite a projected enrollment of more than 1,200 students and plans for a twenty-eight-room addition to its physical plant, even Raney was floundering. Ineligible for state aid and unable to repeat its spectacular fund-raising of the previous year, the heretofore free school announced early in the summer that it would charge a monthly tuition of fifteen dollars. Then in August, to the surprise of friend and foe alike, the corporation declared its insolvency and terminated its operations.[48]

No less suddenly, the school board, perhaps maneuvering to foil any plans the governor may have had for a special legislative session, announced on August 4 that city high schools would reopen on August 12, nearly a month early. The Citizens' Council met the move with a long statement condemning the "cowardly yellow quiters [*sic*]." Dr. Taylor, its president, taking note of the sharply

47 *Southern School News,* June, 1959, 2; editorial, *Arkansas Gazette,* May 27, 1959. The significance of the purge and the recall election has been ably treated by a Little Rock minister, Colbert S. Cartwright, "Hope Comes to Little Rock," *The Progressive,* 23 (August, 1959), 7–9.

48 *Southern School News,* July, 1959, 8; August, 1959, 6; September, 1959, 1–2.

rising incidence of poliomyelitis during the past year, charged that "our schools are in the hands of reckless daredevils who are willing to open schools in the height of a polio epidemic in order to force integration." Failing to arouse public indignation here, Councilors accused downtown merchants of integrationist sentiment and called for a "buyer strike" to commence the day before school opened. They failed again. According to the Federal Reserve Bank, Little Rock department stores enjoyed a sales increase of 1 percent that week.

Having exhausted every other means of resistance, the organized segregationists took to the streets. On the morning school reopened the Council participated in a mass segregation rally on the state capitol grounds. Although some one thousand people attended, only about two hundred heeded the call of Robert J. Norwood, president of the States' Rights Council, to march on Central High fifteen blocks away. Chanting "two, four, six, eight, we don't want to integrate," the demonstrators were intercepted and dispersed by police. When twenty-one were arrested, Guthridge and Pruden called a press conference to condemn the "Hungarian Gestapo tactics" used by police officers.[49] On yet another occasion, a CCC spokesman charged that the mayor and city manager board had "ordered the police to bash in the faces of defenseless women and children while they were peaceably assembled in a public street. . . ."[50] The Council's attorney represented those arraigned in municipal court.

With some disorder, then, but without major mishap, Central High School was once again desegregated. All remained peaceful until Labor Day, the second anniversary of the appearance of the National Guard at the school. Then the calm of the sultry summer night was shattered by a series of dynamite explosions—one damaging the school board office, another the front of a building in which the mayor maintained an office, and a third a city-owned automobile parked in the driveway of the chief of the fire department (who had helped disperse the mob on August 12 with high-pressure hoses). A fourth and unsuccessful bombing attempt was

[49] Ibid., September, 1959, 1–3.

[50] Malcom G. Taylor to Mayor Werner C. Knoop, Little Rock, February 25, 1960, Miscellaneous Files, SERS.

made on the office of a member of the city manager board. The culprits were readily apprehended, and during the course of the trial in November, testimony revealed that the dynamitings had been planned at a Ku Klux Klan meeting. But it was E. A. Lauderdale, Jr., a member of the CCC's board of directors, the owner of a Little Rock lumber company, and a twice-defeated candidate for the city manager board—and not a Klan leader—who was indicted for masterminding the plot. Convicted and sentenced to three years in prison, Lauderdale did not begin serving his term until February, 1961. Scarcely six months later, Faubus pardoned him.[51]

Midway between Lauderdale's conviction and his imprisonment, the Council in Arkansas was linked yet another time with violence and the hooded legion. During July, 1960, Emmett E. Miller—who had served the cause of racial integrity in various capacities, most notably as founder and president of the Crittenden County Citizens' Council, local campaign manager for Justice Jim Johnson, and, more recently, Klan recruiter—was charged with planting thirty sticks of dynamite in a classroom at all-black Philander Smith College in Little Rock. Perhaps coincidentally, several hours after the attempt was made at the Negro campus, a warehouse owned by the Little Rock school district was partially destroyed by an unknown bomber.[52]

Although available evidence does not suggest CCC complicity in these violent acts, the resort to dynamite by those associated with the Council served further to discredit the organization. With its vein of potential lawlessness thus laid bare and its pretensions to

[51] *Arkansas Gazette,* September 10, 11, 1959, September 15, 1961; *Southern School News,* October, 1959, 2; December, 1959, 3–4; March, 1961, 15. Fulfilling a promise made during Lauderdale's trial, Guthridge opposed the prosecuting attorney, J. Frank Holt, in his bid for the attorney generalship. Guthridge charged that Holt was a tool of "the integrationists" who had rigged a jury to put Lauderdale in prison. Guthridge was defeated. (*Southern School News,* June, 1960, 6; August, 1960, 5.)

[52] *Southern School News,* August, 1960, 5; September, 1960, 10. Miller later became identified with the militantly anti-Semitic and anti-Negro National States' Rights Party. He was listed in the party's publication, *The Thunderbolt,* May, 1962, as an officer of both the Little Rock and the West Memphis, Arkansas, units.

respectability stripped away, the Council rapidly ceased being a significant factor in the city's political life. Symbolic of its declining influence in Little Rock and across the state was the overwhelming defeat in November, 1960, of a proposed constitutional amendment providing for the closure of schools by local option in order to prevent desegregation. Despite the Council's declaration that a negative vote was a vote for racial amalgamation, and Governor Faubus's last minute endorsement, the measure failed to carry even a single county and was defeated by a margin of three to one.[53] Having once tasted the bitter fruit of defiance, Arkansas clearly wanted no more of it.

In time even Governor Faubus alienated himself from the Council. Unerringly playing his role as barometer for popular sentiment in the state, he demonstrated his consummate political virtuosity by moving full circle by 1962. Opposed by Representative Alford for an unprecedented fifth two-year term during the summer of that year, the erstwhile hero of the massive resistance movement ignored the race issue, condemned extremists on either side, and unabashedly posed for the voters as an apostle of moderation. Although the CCC did not openly endorse Alford, its most articulate spokesmen waged a radio campaign against Faubus, charging that he had joined the "ranks of the gutless." But Arkansas voted for Faubus, as it would again two years later.[54]

During the thick of the furor at Central High in October, 1957, Amis Guthridge observed with characteristic overstatement that "Little Rock is the last battle. If we win in Little Rock, integration is dead. If we lose in Little Rock, the Republic of the United States is gone forever."[55] These grave predictions to the contrary, the republic did in fact survive the defeat of extremism there. And, as time and events would prove, the stand of the archsegregationists in that city was not even the last redoubt for massive resistance.

By 1960 the *Brown* ruling had secured a somewhat tenuous beachhead in most of the cities of the upper South, but it had yet

[53] *Southern School News,* November, 1960, 13; December, 1960, 11.

[54] *Arkansas Gazette,* July 11, 12, 31, 1962; *Southern School News,* August, 1962, 6; January, 1963, 11.

[55] Quoted in *Southern School News,* November, 1957, 11.

to penetrate the heart of Dixie. In November of that year, when Deep South resistance barriers were breached for the first time in New Orleans, it was Little Rock all over again. Although under school desegregation orders since 1956, the Crescent City's white community was unprepared for compliance when classes convened in the fall of 1960. As only experience could demonstrate, local predictions of easy accommodation to desegregation proved unrealistic. It was true that Louisiana politics since the days of Huey P. Long had been more often preoccupied with issues of economic welfare than race. It was true again that Pelican State Negroes, particularly those in urban centers and predominantly French Catholic areas, participated more freely in politics than did Negroes in other Deep South states. But it was also true that the state legislature was dominated by representatives of rural communities whose values, traditions, and fears were not substantially different from those of their counterparts in Mississippi or Alabama. Moreover, during the four years preceding the school crisis in New Orleans, the effective political power traditionally wielded by the governor in Louisiana had passed from the hands of an inept and unassertive Earl K. Long to a coterie of extreme segregationists within the legislature. Even the resignation from the senate of Willie Rainach, the most powerful member of this group, and the election of a new governor in 1960 failed to restore either gubernatorial hegemony or racial moderation to state politics. As an avalanche of legislative defiance would reveal during the one regular and five special sessions of 1960–61, the racial extremists were more securely in control than ever.[56]

Notwithstanding the defiant mood of lawmakers in Baton Rouge, it was not altogether inconceivable that adjustment to desegregation in New Orleans could have been accomplished without major discord. This cosmopolitan, enlightened, multiracial city was notable for the apparent harmony of its Negro-white relations. Under the leadership of de Lesseps S. Morrison, its liberal Roman Catholic

[56] See Morton Inger, *Politics and Reality in an American City: The New Orleans School Crises of 1960* (New York: Center for Urban Education, 1969), 21–22; Pinney and Friedman, *Political Leadership and the School Desegregation Crisis in Louisiana*, 3ff.; McCarrick, "Louisiana's Official Resistance," 132–74.

mayor, it had tranquilly obeyed federal orders to end discrimination in city buses and parks, and in 1958 Louisiana State University in New Orleans desegregated its professional schools. While by no means progressive, the city's two major newspapers, the jointly owned *Times-Picayune* and *States-Item*, were at least moderate by Deep South standards. But as the school crisis of 1960 unfolded, the voices of stability were strangely silent; the mayor vacillated; and not until the eleventh hour did the press timidly express editorial support for the public schools.[57] Lacking constructive counsel from the traditional power structure, the city became easy prey for extremists, and, as the Louisiana Advisory Committee on Civil Rights observed, "The White Citizens Council . . . by default became the dominant political force in the community." [58]

The Council movement was indeed a potent force in New Orleans throughout the turmoil-packed months of 1960–61—despite the enduring schism of 1958 which had divided its membership. Its most prominent spokesman, Leander Perez, whose political influence extended well beyond the oil-rich parishes of Plaquemines and St. Bernard, figured prominently behind the scenes in the frenetic legal action waged by lawmakers in the state capital.[59] The president of the statewide Council organization (with which both the South Louisiana Council and the Greater New Orleans Council were affiliated) was Representative John S. Garrett, who served as Rainach's successor as chairman of the powerful Joint Committee on Segregation and vigilant guardian of the movement's best interests in the legislature. On the Orleans Parish school board, Councilors had a friend and a fellow member in Emile A. Wagner, Jr., the banker-lawyer who managed Rainach's gubernatorial campaign in 1959. An unyielding segregationist, Wagner alone among

[57] Editorials, New Orleans *Times-Picayune* and New Orleans *States-Item*, August 26, November 11, 1960. The Louisiana State Advisory Committee to the U.S. Commission on Civil Rights has severely criticized the reluctant, belated, and very minimal role of leadership assumed by the Times-Picayune Publishing Company. See *New Orleans School Crisis*, 34–35.

[58] Louisiana State Advisory Committee, *New Orleans School Crisis*, 39–40. See also Claude Sitton, "Citizens' Council Fuels Louisiana Resistance," New York *Times*, November 27, 1960.

[59] See Pinney and Friedman, *Political Leadership and the School Desegregation Crisis in Louisiana*, 7.

the five members of the board preferred no schools at all to desegregated schools.[60] To dignify their mass meetings, Councilors could and did call upon the state's most influential segregationists, including Governor Jimmie H. Davis, Attorney General Jack P. F. Gremillion, Secretary of State Wade O. Martin, Jr., State Sovereignty Commission Chairman Frank H. Voelker, Jr., and State Superintendent of Education Shelby M. Jackson.[61]

But as important as the support of these political luminaries may have been to the realization of the Council's objectives, more important still was the large body of white New Orleanians who, although not directly affiliated with the organized resistance movement, would support its demands to the point of sacrificing public education. Partial revelation of the extent of that body came in a school board poll of May, 1960, when parents of public school children were asked to indicate whether they preferred the schools closed rather than integrated. Much to the consternation of the moderate members of the board, more than 80 percent of the nearly fifteen thousand white respondents indicated a preference for closure.[62]

As they endeavored to tap this reservoir of segregationist sentiment, New Orleans Councilors used many of the same techniques found effective in Little Rock. The moderates on the school board were portrayed to the public as the villains in the school crisis, and petitions demanding their removal were circulated periodically.[63] Civic organizations formed to support public schools were identified as "pro-integrationist," no matter how carefully they avoided the

60 An assessment of Wagner's considerable influence in New Orleans during the several public and parochial school desegregation crises between 1956 and 1962 may be found in Cook's essay, "Sin and Sociology in New Orleans," in *The Segregationists*, 229–46. See also Workman, *The Case for the South*, 101, and *Southern School News*, November, 1959, 13.

61 Louisiana State Advisory Committee, *New Orleans School Crisis*, 38–39.

62 When Negro and white votes were combined, the results of the parents' poll revealed a slim majority favoring open schools: whites for closure, 12,229, against closure, 2,707; Negroes for closure, 679, against closure, 11,407. Ibid., 6–7. See Appendix I, Inger, *Politics and Reality*, 101.

63 New Orleans *Times-Picayune*, July 20, 1960, January 31, 1961. See also petitions printed and circulated by the Greater New Orleans Council against the school board moderates, files of Southern Office, A-DL.

issue. Thus a newspaper advertisement paid for by the South Louisiana Council charged that "Save Our Schools" (SOS), the most successful of these, was in collusion with "several national organizations who have publicly espoused total integration in the South." The Greater New Orleans Council labeled it "pro-Communist" and demanded that state and federal authorities investigate its financial base.[64]

As always, the most effective device for keeping racial sentiment high proved to be the mass meeting. On the evening of November 15, 1960, the day following the admission of four Negro girls to first-grade classes in formerly all-white Frantz and McDonough No. 19 schools, more than five thousand people crowded into the Municipal Auditorium to hear Council orators call for a march on the school board building and city hall. Only through "scorched earth" tactics and acts of "civil disobedience," declared former Senator Rainach, could "the runaway courts" be checked. In characteristic fashion, Leander Perez related the court-ordered desegregation of the previous day to a satanic conspiracy by Communists and "Zionist Jews" to destroy the nation. "Don't wait for your daughters to be raped by these Congolese," he urged. "Don't wait until the burr-heads are forced into your schools. Do something about it now." [65] In the view of some eye witnesses, it was "a gathering straight out of Nazi Germany." [66]

The following morning perhaps as many as two thousand people, mostly truant teenagers, set out to "do something about it." Met by police at City Hall, the chanting, snake-dancing youths converged in the school administration building on Carondelet. Waving Confederate flags and crudely lettered protest placards, the crowd was confronted by mounted police and high-pressure hoses. Once dispersed, they roamed the narrow streets of the French Quarter. Angry crowds also assembled around the desegregated schools

[64] New Orleans *Times-Picayune,* August 17, 1960; Louisiana State Advisory Committee, *New Orleans School Crisis,* 6.

[65] New Orleans *Times-Picayune,* November 16, 1960; *Southern School News,* December, 1960, 1, 8–10; George Sherman, "The Nightmare Comes to New Orleans," *The Reporter,* 23 (December 8, 1960), 24–26.

[66] Louisiana State Advisory Committee, *New Orleans School Crisis,* 14.

where Council leaders had urged "a few peaceful demonstrations." Throughout the week, sporadic disturbances continued, and on Friday school recessed for a week-long Thanksgiving vacation.[67]

As school reconvened, the Council shifted from mob appeal to boycott. By encouraging the angry crowds that gathered about the schools daily and stationing "observers" at all entrances, Councilors discouraged all but the most determined white parents from bringing their children. Pre-desegregation enrollment reached 1,038, but by the end of the month daily attendance at the two schools had stabilized at six.[68] Hoping to empty the schools altogether, the organization, through Emile Wagner, sought a court order to force parish School Superintendent Dr. James Redmond to release the names of attending students. Failing here, it circulated lists containing descriptions of automobiles and phone numbers of the volunteers who transported white children to Frantz school. With hostility toward nonboycotters mounting daily, the safe passage of pupils became a question of major concern. Following a series of threatening incidents, including a two-mile chase and an attempt to ram one of the vehicles, federal marshals escorted white as well as Negro children to classes.[69]

Despite the successful boycott of the schools, the unflagging support of the governor, and the willingness of an apparently indefatigable legislature to execute virtually every conceivable tactic of evasion and delay, the extremists waged a losing battle. Federal District Judge J. Skelly Wright was unwavering in his resolve to uphold the *Brown* decision. Supported by the Fifth Circuit Court of Appeals, he set aside state laws, overruled state administration orders, and at one point enjoined 170 state officials—including

[67] New Orleans *Times-Picayune,* November 17, 1960; *Southern School News,* December, 1960, 8–10; "D-Day in New Orleans," *Time,* 76 (November 28, 1960), 19; "Louisiana Nightmare," *Newsweek,* 56 (November 28, 1960), 19–20.

[68] See Council advertisement, New Orleans *Times-Picayune,* November 14, 1960. See also New Orleans *Times-Picayune,* November 29, and New York *Times,* November 17, 1960.

[69] New Orleans *Times-Picayune,* November 30, December 3, 1960; Louisiana State Advisory Committee, *New Orleans School Crisis,* 16–17.

Governor Davis and every member of the legislature—from interfering with the operation of the two elementary schools.[70]

Moreover, with the city's business in sharp decline[71] and its carefree reputation badly tarnished, the long-quiescent moderate community began to stir. Throughout the spring and summer months preceding desegregation, SOS and a companion organization, the Committee for Public Education (CPE), had fought to create broad community interest in an open schools movement. But not until the school board election of November 8 did their lonely effort begin to succeed. Running against a field of three segregationists, the moderate incumbent, Matthew Sutherland, won the endorsement of ninety-eight business, professional, and religious leaders and enough votes (55.6 percent) to be reelected.[72] Then in early December forty-six prominent Protestant, Catholic, and Jewish clergymen joined in a public plea for orderly compliance and an end to "this period of unrest."[73] A few days later the Junior Chamber of Commerce issued a statement criticizing the state's official posture of massive resistance. Continued defiance, the young businessmen's group declared, could only jeopardize public education.[74] On December 14, a group of 105 business and professional leaders issued an "appeal to reason" in a six-column advertisement in the *Times-Picayune*. Urging public support for the school board, the group called for an end to "threats, defamation and resistance."[75] During the same month, more than three hundred

[70] Pinney and Friedman, *Political Leadership and the School Desegregation Crisis in Louisiana*, 8–9, 13.

[71] See James Harwood, "New Orleans Caught in Economic Squeeze in Integration Fight," *Wall Street Journal*, November 18, 1960, and Claude Sitton, "New Orleans Rift Takes Trade and All," New York *Times*, November 28, 1960.

[72] See advertisement by Business and Professional Men's Committee for Sutherland, New Orleans *Times-Picayune*, November 7, 1960; Pinney and Friedman, *Political Leadership and the School Desegregation Crisis in New Orleans*, 11; Louisiana State Advisory Committee, *New Orleans School Crisis*, 11–13, 40–41.

[73] New York *Times*, December 4, 1960.

[74] Ibid., December 9, 1960.

[75] New Orleans *Times-Picayune*, December 14, 1960. See also New York *Times*, December 14, 1960, and Harnett Kane, "Dilemma of the Crooner-Governor," *New York Times Magazine*, January 1, 1961, 33.

Tulane University faculty members signed a public statement endorsing the position of the businessmen, while nearly two hundred New Orleans public school teachers issued a similar statement of their own.[76]

Hoping to abate this rising spirit of moderation, Councilors called forth the specter of perfidy and treason. Charging that self-serving "integrationists" sought to sacrifice the welfare of white children to satisfy the demands of federal jurists, they sponsored a second public meeting. But despite predictions of a record crowd and the well-advertised appearance of a galaxy of state and local political dignitaries, attendance at the mid-December rally was considerably below that of the previous November (estimates ranged from 1,000 to 2,500). Following the usual round of speeches in praise of all-white schools and the intractable posture of the Citizens' Council, a troupe of small children in plain and blackface gave "a little demonstration of what integration means." While the young actors lavished biracial kisses and caresses upon each other, Dr. Emmett L. Irwin, chairman of the GNOCC, inquired of the audience, "Is this what you want for your children?"[77]

These histrionics served only to underscore the growing impotence of the extremists. As had been true in Little Rock, the appeal of the radical racists began to weaken almost as soon as the community's civic and business leadership asserted itself. Nevertheless, the boycott remained in force; for the remainder of the academic year white students at Frantz rarely exceeded a dozen, and at McDonough there were none at all.[78] But it is not implausible to say that the empty desks resulted as much from the socio-economic composition of the ninth ward (in which the two schools were located) as from Council pressure. Of all the predominantly white wards in the city, the ninth, as the state Committee on Civil Rights reported, was among the least prepared for social

76 Louisiana State Advisory Committee, *New Orleans School Crisis*, 18–19.

77 New Orleans *Times-Picayune*, December 16, 1960; State Advisory Committees, *The 50 States Report*, 195; *Southern School News*, January, 1961, 11.

78 A brief effort to break the total boycott at McDonough ended when a drug clerk, citing economic and social intimidation as the reason, withdrew his nine-year-old son from school and moved his family out of town. See *Southern School News*, March, 1961, 8.

change. "Inhabited by extremely poor and racially prejudiced whites," many of whom lived in ramshackle housing developments, the neighborhood, the Committee observed, "was ripe for dissidence." [79]

The following year, when four additional schools admitted eight more Negroes on September 6, 1961, all was peaceful. The governor and the legislature were silent. Even Emile Wagner advised a Council gathering to adjust to an accomplished fact and refrain from further demonstrations. The federal government, he acknowledged, would prevent any effort to close the schools. The only practical recourse now remaining was private education. And so, after a brief and futile attempt to reimpose the boycott, Councilors discontinued their effort altogether.[80]

Encouraged by the ease of desegregation in the public schools, the Roman Catholic hierarchy made preparations for similar action in the 164 parochial schools of the archdiocese of New Orleans. In March, 1962, Archbishop Joseph Francis Rummel, with full support from the priests under his jurisdiction, announced that desegregation would begin the following September. Immediately, an old battle between southern Louisiana's liberal Catholic leadership and the Catholic laymen who led the organized resistance movement was rejoined.[81] The feud dated from February, 1956, when the archbishop, denouncing segregation as "morally wrong and sinful," called for the gradual desegregation of the elementary schools in the archdiocese. Led by Jackson Ricau, a Greater New Orleans Council official, and Emile Wagner, segregationists responded by forming the Association of Catholic Laymen, an organization limited to "persons of the Caucasian race who profess

[79] Louisiana State Advisory Committee, *New Orleans School Crisis*, 14, 25. A similar view is expressed by Inger, *Politics and Reality*, 37–39.

[80] *Southern School News*, October, 1961, 3. See also a South Louisiana Council advertisement in New Orleans *Times-Picayune*, September 16, and New Orleans *States-Item*, September 15, 1961.

[81] The prevalence of anticlericalism among southern Louisiana Catholics, expressed whenever the hierarchy attempts to buck popular political or racial attitudes, has been recognized by William C. Havard. Leander Perez, Havard observes, has been particularly successful in the exploitation of this sentiment. (*Louisiana Election of 1960*, 71.)

the faith of the Holy Catholic Church." But under threat of excommunication, the association's board of directors announced its dissolution on May 1.[82]

Taking a more direct tack than that employed by the lay Catholic group, the Citizens' Council sponsored a parade down Canal Street and a massive open-air protest meeting at Pelican Stadium on May 17, the second anniversary of "Black Monday." While a responsive crowd estimated at six thousand booed at every mention of his name, a string of orators denounced the "pro-integrationist" archbishop. Afterward, in the early morning hours, an eight-foot cross was set ablaze before Rummel's residence. The Council was held responsible for the fiery display by the Commission on Human Rights of the Catholic Committee of the South, a liberal lay organization which denounced the segregation rally as "anti-American, anti-Southern, anti-Catholic and irreligious." Calling this an "untrue and libelous accusation," a Council statement reported that the "Black Monday" gathering had been the occasion for the intonation of the Lord's Prayer and the singing of both "Dixie" and the "Star Spangled Banner." As for the burning cross: "The Citizens' Council does not do this kind of thing."[83]

Throughout the spring and summer the organization attacked an ever-widening circle of Catholic leaders, and in August it identified the archbishop himself as an accomplice, although perhaps unwitting, of world Communism. In a proclamation issued "in the name of God's justice and with Christian charity for all," it labeled Rummel's grade-a-year desegregation plan as "surreptitious infiltration" designed to "condition the minds of Catholic parents in truly Communist fashion."[84] Under this blistering attack, the

[82] See Ricau's account of this episode in his pamphlet, *The Tragic Truth about the Catholic Race-Mixing Program in New Orleans,* 3ff. See also an advertisement purchased by the Association of Catholic Laymen in New Orleans *Times-Picayune,* March 28, 1956; and Cook, *The Segregationists,* 236–37.

[83] *Southern School News,* July, 1956, 8–9; New Orleans *Times-Picayune,* May 17, 25, and Montgomery *Advertiser,* May 25, 1956.

[84] Quoted in New Orleans *Times-Picayune,* August 30, 1956. See also Jackson *Daily News,* June 15, 1956, and an anonymous handbill distributed by the Greater New Orleans Citizens' Council in the files of SERS. This document invited Catholics into "Archbishop Rummel's Black Melting Pot"

octogenarian archbishop retreated. Just six months after his initial statement, he issued a second pastoral letter acknowledging that "we are not now prepared to introduce integration generally." Instead, he said, desegregation would commence in September, 1957. But that school opening, and a succession of others, passed without further action.[85]

When the archbishop again ordered the desegregation of church schools during the spring of 1962, he did so with greater determination. In letters of "paternal admonition" to the city's more vociferous Catholic segregationists, he warned that attempts to provoke opposition to the new directive would be met with severe action. Heedless of the prelate's warning, Jackson Ricau, executive director of the South Louisiana Citizens' Council, Mrs. B. J. Galloit, the Bible-quoting president of Save Our Nation, Inc., and Leander Perez continued their segregationist activity. On April 16, they were excommunicated.[86]

Unrepentant, the trio continued to lead defiance against what Perez called "a Communist brainwashed" church hierarchy. In the April issue of *The Citizen*, Ricau told "The Revealing Story of My Excommunication," and pledged "to continue the fight until the evil, Communist-inspired forces of integration are resoundingly and finally defeated."[87] For his part, Perez declared it "better excommunicated than integrated" and challenged archdiocesan officials to enforce their desegregation edict in his home parish. Styling himself still "a Catholic but not an Archbishop's Catholic," the aging segregationist organized the Parents and Friends of Catholic Children in order to encourage whites to withdraw their children from church schools.[88]

When school opened in the fall, Perez proved as good as his

---

and charged that "Catholic Churchgoers Face Jungle Law/Murder-and-Rape/or Excommunication." For examples of subsequent attacks on liberal Catholicism, see the monthly bulletin of the South Louisiana Citizens' Council, *The Citizens' Report*, January, 1961.

85 Quoted in Lewis, *Portrait of a Decade*, 156.

86 *Southern School News*, April, 1962, 6; May, 1962, 2–3; Baton Rouge *State Times*, March 29, 1962; and Washington *Post*, April 7, 1962.

87 Jackson Ricau, *The Citizen*, 6 (April, 1962), 4–8.

88 Baton Rouge *State Times*, April 26, 1962; Shreveport *Journal*, June 28, 1962.

word. In the village of Buras, near the center of Plaquemines Parish, the admission of five Negroes brought a total boycott by the more than three hundred white students of Our Lady of Good Harbor School. When the Negroes withdrew, their efforts at integration frustrated, the school was closed. Just prior to its scheduled reopening the following year, it was partially destroyed by arson. Although later repaired, it remained closed for want of approval by the parish building inspector.[89]

But where the patriarch of Plaquemines could succeed within the narrow confines of his own political preserve, the Citizens' Council could not within the larger arena of New Orleans. Despite the determined endeavors of the archsegregationists, there were only minor disorders in the suburb of Westwego, when, for the first time in sixty-seven years, New Orleans' formerly all-white Catholic schools lowered their racial barriers to admit some 150 black students on September 4, 1962.[90]

The emergence of biracial parochial schools in New Orleans was an anticlimax. As key figures on both sides of the issue well understood, once token compliance had been accomplished in the public schools, it could only be a matter of time before Catholic education fell into line. Indeed, this initial breakthrough in a Deep South state fully mobilized for resistance was an achievement of enormous symbolic significance, not just for New Orleans but for the entire region as well. As the Southern Regional Council observed in the fall of 1960, desegregation in the "Queen City of the South," even though court-ordered and grudging, heralded "the beginning of a new phase in the struggle to win in reality what was granted in law by the Supreme Court decision of 1954." [91]

89 Sarratt, *Ordeal of Desegregation,* 281. Perez's persistent domination of schools in Plaquemines Parish was demonstrated once again in September, 1966, when the public schools there were desegregated under court order. After twenty-eight Negroes entered Woodlawn High School, all of the white pupils and the staff (except the principal) moved over to a newly opened private school established in a hastily converted mansion owned by Perez's daughter. The Negroes were then withdrawn and Woodlawn was closed. With lesser degrees of success other desegregated schools in the parish were also boycotted. See James T. Leeson, "Violence, Intimidation and Protest," *Southern Education Report,* 2 (December, 1966), 30.

90 New York *Times,* September 5, 1962.

91 Quoted in Wilma Dykeman and James Stokely, "Integration: Third

During the course of the next four years, massive resistance collapsed in the four remaining states of the Deep South. There was, of course, no wholesale swing to total compliance—nor would there be in the foreseeable future. Yet as Mississippi, the last of the hard-core states, yielded to federal demands to begin desegregation in several cities during September, 1964, the formidable process of reconciling the region's social patterns with the nation's fundamental law had at least begun.

There was no hint of reconciliation, however, in the mood of the organized resistance movement. Unable to adjust to what its official tabloid chose to call even "a token few perfumed, beribboned, bedecked, hand-picked, cotton-pickin', educated, elucidated, fumigated, super-de-looper, de-luxe pickaninnies, who speak better English than any Southern white you ever saw quoted in Time or Life," the Citizens' Council persistently advocated the closure of public schools and the creation of private ones as the ultimate weapon in the defense of segregation.[92] In May, 1959, with racial barriers crumbling in each of the peripheral states, William J. Simmons warned that "no one [need] labor for one minute under the mistaken notion that Deep South states would hesitate to go out of the public school business. . . ." Should school closure "become necessary," the chief Councilor reported, "a satisfactory system of white private schools would be quickly devised." [93]

---

and Critical Phase," *New York Times Magazine,* November 27, 1960, 24–25.

92 See *Annual Report: August, 1955,* 1; "How to Keep Schools Open," *The Citizens' Council,* May, 1959, 2.

93 "How to Keep Schools Open," *The Citizens' Council,* May, 1959, 2. Initially, at least, Simmons and other Council spokesmen believed that state school systems could be operated precisely as before, except under private auspices. Public schools under desegregation orders, they contended, could be converted into "private" institutions, operated in the same manner with the same financial support and the same physical plant as the public schools. But even before Deep South segregationists could turn in earnest to the problems of abandoning the public schools, federal courts in Arkansas (1958) and Louisiana (1961) ruled against the public-private school idea. For its part, the Supreme Court—although specifically avoiding the question of whether a state could abandon its system of public education altogether—sustained lower-court rulings against publicly operated "private" education and the selective closure of individual schools within a state to avoid desegregation. Once public-private school systems became a practical impossibility,

Unquestionably, Simmons spoke the mind of the vast majority of the organization's rank and file. Councilors in every state preferred no schools at all to token integration. As one North Carolina leader phrased it, "we consider it more important to preserve the white race" than to educate it.[94] Likewise, a spokesman for the Tennessee Federation for Constitutional Government urged state legislators to abolish public schools as a last resort: "I don't agree that they are essential. Let the people educate their own children." [95] Although the private school movement did not begin in earnest until after the passage of the Civil Rights Act of 1964, state and local resistance groups in the upper South, at least as early as 1958, endeavored to provide an alternative to biracial public education. As we have seen, Capital Citizens' Councilors were largely instrumental in the formation of the Little Rock Private School Corporation. In the Old Dominion, the Defenders of State Sovereignty and Individual Liberties played a similarly primary role in the organization of the Virginia Education Fund, a private corporation formed to promote all-white private institutions.[96]

By 1959 even some Deep South Councils were assessing possibilities for private education in their states. Soon after his appointment in March of that year, Executive Secretary Farley Smith of the Association of Citizens' Councils of South Carolina launched a statewide survey to determine what facilities might be available for future use. At segregation gatherings across the state, he emphasized

---

organized resistance leaders pinned their hopes to tuition-grant or grant-in-aid private schools. Although every southern state except Florida, Tennessee, and Texas had statutes permitting the payment of public funds for private, nonsectarian school tuition, only Virginia and Louisiana actually paid substantial sums for this purpose. By the autumn of 1967, federal courts on a state-by-state basis had barred tuition grant payments for segregated private schools in every state but Alabama, Mississippi, and Virginia—and in each of these, grants were under legal attack. See James T. Leeson, "Private Schools Continue to Increase in the South," *Southern Education Report,* 2 (November, 1966), 22–25; and Leeson, "Private Schools for Whites Face Some Hurdles," *Southern Education Report,* 3 (November, 1967), 13–17.

94 Quoted in Charlotte *News,* July 9, 1959.

95 Quoted in Memphis *Commercial Appeal,* February 26, 1956. See also Nashville *Tennessean,* February 26, 1956.

96 *Defenders News and Views,* September–October, 1958; Muse, *Virginia's Massive Resistance,* 55–56.

that Palmetto State Councilors would never compromise with "partial or token integration." Should it "become necessary," Smith indicated, the association was preparing to "carry out peacefully with as much order as possible the transition from public to private schools."[97] About the same time, the Councils of Montgomery County, Alabama, began to formulate plans for a similar transition. "If and when the ultimate integration comes," a local spokesman informed the press, "we won't be caught flat-footed."[98] During the fall of 1960, Louisiana Councilors assisted in the formation of the New Orleans Educational Foundation, which operated the Ninth Ward Private School in a converted machine shop. Earlier that same year Greater New Orleans Council leaders were also behind the formation of the White Educational Association, an organization devoted to assisting white parents in the establishment of so-called private school cooperatives as an alternative to integrated public schools.[99]

The professional leadership of the Citizens' Councils of America watched the nascent private school movement with growing interest. But not until desegregation became imminent in Mississippi did it actually become involved. Late in August, soon after the passage of the 1964 Civil Rights Act and the issuance of federal desegregation orders to school boards in Biloxi, Carthage, Clarksdale, and Jackson, preliminary plans for the formation of Council School No. 1 were divulged. Explaining the CCA's position on private education in the September issue of *The Citizen,* William Simmons averred that heretofore desegregation, that "potentially lethal virus," had only "slightly infected" the region's "excellent public school systems." But the newly enacted and "misnamed" civil rights legislation, permitting the Department of Justice to initiate school desegregation suits, carries the "death sentence" for all public schools. No longer responsive to the will of the community and no longer con-

[97] Quoted in Charleston *News and Courier,* March 19, 1959. See also Charleston *News and Courier,* January 7, 1959; *Southern School News,* December, 1958, 16; April, 1959, 13.

[98] Quoted in *Southern School News,* April, 1959, 3. See also Birmingham *News,* October 2, 1958.

[99] Louisiana State Advisory Committee, *New Orleans School Crisis,* 8, 10; New Orleans *Times-Picayune,* July 14, August 17, 20, 1960, January 31, 1961; *Wall Street Journal,* April 6, 1962.

trolled by the people, public schools were in fact "government schools." In Simmons's view, "concerned parents who do not wish to surrender their children" had no recourse but to turn to private academies. Hoping to hasten this transition, the editor devoted the entire September issue to a manual on "How to Start a Private School."[100]

Written by the Council's "educational consultant," Dr. Medford Evans, the manual was an optimistic sixteen-page catechism on the ease with which a determined and enterprising citizenry could abandon "government schools" and fabricate educational institutions better equipped to "teach the importance of racial integrity." In Evans's view, such "minimum" essentials as a school building and "a concerned and determined school board" presented the only real problems. Once these were obtained, the rest would be easy. Even the acquisition of efficient administrators and competent instructors presented no difficulties. Retired educators were in plentiful supply, as were "otherwise well-educated" people who lacked only "certain paper 'qualifications.'" Even the cost of private education, Evans assured, need not be burdensome; for, when combined with tuition grants available in many southern states, "the equivalent of cigarette money for the average young couple" would be more than sufficient to meet the necessary fees. Moreover, because the all-white academies would be a bulwark for southern values against "alien encroachment," a sense of community spirit would doubtless lead many childless citizens to contribute generously. Similarly easy in solution were many other problems, including accreditation ("it need not be despised, but it should not be revered"), transportation ("if you have a good school the parents will find a way to get their children to you"), school lunches ("there was a time . . . when school children took their lunch in a paper bag . . . or went home") and curriculum ("the main job is teaching the 'three R's'"). Some states, such as Mississippi, even provided free textbooks. Although conceding that such "handouts" may be "an instrument of

100 "Government School," *The Citizen*, 8 (September, 1964), 2; Jackson *Daily News*, August 24, 1964. See also T. Robert Ingram, "Government or Public Schools," *The Citizen*, 12 (April, 1968), 10–21, and Medford Evans, "The Road Ahead in Private Education," *The Citizen*, 13, February, 1969, 16–25.

cultural retardation and socialistic regimentation," the Council's manual advised against "ideological puritanism" in this regard.[101]

In November, 1964, the Council School Foundation opened Council School No. 1, its "pilot or demonstration operation." Despite considerable fanfare and early predictions of an enrollment in excess of one hundred, the project began inauspiciously. Following a delay in procuring and renovating a two-story frame dwelling in a once-fashionable section in northern Jackson, classes were temporarily convened, nearly a month after those of the public schools, in the home of Foundation president Dr. Charles Neill, a prominent Jackson neurosurgeon. Handicapped by a basic tuition of $375 per pupil (only $185 of which was defrayed by the state grant), the new academy had only twenty-two pupils scattered among its six grades. Funds for a small library were raised by a benefit bridge party at the elegant antebellum-style home of Governor and Mrs. Ross Barnett.[102]

In September, 1965, the school reopened with a full twelve-grade program and 110 students. During the following year, pupil enrollment reached 260 in the Council School Foundation's fully accredited, three-school system: CS No. 1, grades one through seven; CS No. 2, grades one through eight; and CS No. 3, grades eight through twelve. With the future looking brighter and a $300,000 building campaign under way to accommodate increasing enrollment, Simmons confidently advised the four members of the

[101] "How to Start a Private School," *The Citizen,* 8 (September, 1964), 4–19. The issue also contained a sample charter. Subsequent issues frequently carried articles of a similar nature. See for example, W. J. Simmons, "The Citizens' Councils and Private Education," *The Citizen,* 10 (February, 1966), 8–11; Dr. Charles L. Neill, "How to Start a Private School," *The Citizen,* 10 (May, 1966), 7–15; Richard Morphew, "A Parent Compares Private and Public Schools," *The Citizen,* 10 (May, 1966), 16–21; John T. Synon, "Private Schools and the Citizens' Councils," *The Citizen,* 12 (October, 1967), 4–5, 20.

[102] Interviews with Medford Evans and William J. Simmons, May 26, 1967; Medford Evans, "Council School No. 1: As New as Childhood, and as Old as Truth," *The Citizen,* 9 (July–August, 1965), 4–15; Memphis *Commercial-Appeal,* October 3; Jackson *Daily News,* October 11, 12, 1964; Silver, *Mississippi: The Closed Society,* 314–15. See also a pamphlet, *Why Should I Join the Councils School Corporation* ([Jackson: Jackson Citizens' Council], n.d.).

first graduating class—one of whom was a National Merit Scholar—that "you are, in truth, the leading edge of the wave of the future." [103]

Simmons's commencement oratory to the contrary, there was no wholesale shift away from public schools in the immediate aftermath of desegregation. Yet private schools did enjoy increasing prosperity—particularly after an impatient Supreme Court unanimously ruled on October 22, 1969 (*Alexander* v. *Holmes County Board of Education*) that "all deliberate speed," its own standard for fourteen years, be replaced by desegregation "at once." By the spring of 1970, an estimated 300,000 children were enrolled in some 300 to 400 southern academies. In Mississippi alone, at least 100 private all-white schools were in operation by that date; in Jackson, despite the court-ordered termination of state tuition grants, the Council School Foundation could boast of an enrollment of 3,100 students in its three-school system.[104] Although the CCA has claimed much of the credit for this "burgeoning independent school movement," most of the region's segregation academies were in no way Council connected. To be sure, a few were official projects of local organizations; still others, despite their nominally independent status, owed both their origin and survival to Council efforts.[105]

[103] Jackson *Clarion-Ledger,* July 19, September 16, 1966, Leeson, "Private Schools Continue to Increase," 24; "Council School No. 1," *The Citizen,* 9 (September, 1965), 4; "Jackson's Council High School Holds First Graduation Exercises," *The Citizen,* 10 (June, 1966), 16–17; Jackson Citizens' Council (Monthly Bulletin), *Aspect,* 5 (April, 1967).

[104] On the growth of private academies following the *Alexander* decision, see James Jackson Kilpatrick, "Back to Segregation, by Order of the Courts," *National Review* (June 16, 1970), 611–26; and Wilson F. Minor, "Mississippi Schools in Crisis," *New South* (Winter, 1970), 31–36. For a history of the Council schools, see *Welcome to Council School: A Handbook of Information and School Policy* (Jackson: Council School Foundation, 1970).

[105] Typical of the latter category was the Southwest Mississippi Christian Academy in Pike County. Although Charles Neill and William Simmons were instrumental in its formation in July, 1965, and local Council officials dominated its board of directors, the Academy's spokesmen informed Justice Department investigators that the school had no connection with the Citizens' Council. See Summit (Mississippi) *Sun,* July 15, 22, 1965, and Jackson *Clarion-Ledger,* June 4, 1966. See also [Association of Citizens' Councils], *School Tomorrow* (Greenwood: Greenwood-Leflore Educational Foundation, n.d.).

But if Council contributions to the private school movement were somewhat less consequential than its leaders have claimed, they were nevertheless considerable. As the nation's largest organization dedicated exclusively to segregation, it was in a position to provide leadership for whites who could not or would not accept biracial schools. From the outset, it had pledged to "assist all persons who wish to operate private, nonsectarian, segregated schools." Toward that end, Council headquarters in Jackson served as "a clearing house of information," maintaining a register of private schools and available instructors and administrators, as well as potential physical facilities.[106]

Indeed, so thoroughly preoccupied did the organization become with the private school movement that by January, 1966, Executive Director Louis W. Hollis could inform the CCA's Eleventh Annual Leadership Conference that the "promotion of segregated private education is [now] the major project of the Citizens' Councils." [107] Indeed, in its haste to embrace "free enterprise schools," the organization's ultraconservative leadership all but abandoned "socialized education" to the race mixers.[108] The Eleventh Annual Meeting—"the most significant education event of the Mid-Century" [109]—was itself wordy corroboration of this fact. Featuring a spate of "authoritative and respected speakers" and a panel discussion by some fifty private school students, the two-day conclave in Chattanooga was structured around the theme "How Can We Educate Our Children?" According to *The Citizen,* the 303 delegates (111 of whom were from Mississippi) from nineteen states agreed by "common consent" that the 1966 Citizens' Councils of American Leadership Conference was "the finest and most rewarding" ever held.[110] To

106 Evans, "How to Start a Private School," *The Citizen,* 8 (September, 1964), 19.

107 Louis W. Hollis, "Never!" *The Citizen,* 10 (March, 1966), 30.

108 Interview with William K. Scarborough, Mississippi segregation leader, May 24, 1970; John J. Synon, "Why Not Try Free Enterprise Schools?" *The Citizen,* October, 1965, 18–19.

109 *Over Dues: A Dialogue by and for Concerned Citizens* (Jackson: Citizens' Council of America, n.d.).

110 "A Big Success," *The Citizen,* 10 (January, 1966), 2, 23. See also Chattanooga *News-Free Press* and Chattanooga *Times,* January 8, 1966; Citizens' Councils of America, *Annual Leadership Conference: How Can We Educate Our Children* (n.p., n.d.).

Simmons, who was now professing that the "destiny" of the organization lay in the field of private education, the "overwhelming success" of the Chattanooga conference was living testimony to the constancy of the Council movement in its efforts "to win victory in this war for the survival of our race." "Never, since the earliest days of the movement, have Citizens' Council members lost sight of the first war aim of all—the education of their children." [111]

But if the "war aim" remained unchanged, the campaign itself was markedly altered. In the course of a single decade the organization originally founded to do battle for segregated public schools had fallen back to become the fortress of private education. Perhaps it cannot be said that the war for "racial integrity" was lost, but without question the forces of bitter-end segregation were no longer in command of the field.

111 William J. Simmons, "The Citizens' Councils and Private Education," *The Citizen*, 1 (February, 1966), 9, 13. Speeches delivered at the Chattanooga conference were reprinted in five successive issues of *The Citizen:* February, 1966–June, 1966.

CHAPTER XIV

The Politics of Racial Integrity

LIKE many interest groups actively endeavoring to influence governmental processes at the local, state, and federal levels, the Citizens' Council frequently asserted that it was both nonpartisan and nonpolitical. Introducing the still inchoate organization to the Mississippi legislature in September, 1954, state Representative Wilma Sledge assured lawmakers that "it is not the intent or purpose of the Citizens' Councils to be used as a political machine."[1] More pointedly William Simmons declared: "The Citizens' Council is definitely a nonpartisan organization and is not engaged in politics. There's no reason to be in politics in Mississippi for the Citizens' Council because there is no disagreement among candidates. . . . The Citizens' Council is simply not a political organization."[2]

The Council was in fact not a political organization in the sense of political party. But in the race-centered political atmosphere of the post-*Brown* South, it was unquestionably a political action group of formidable power in some states. Perhaps the most candid description of the movement's political character is to be found in the constitution of the Citizens' Council of Alabama—"a civic,

[1] Quoted in *Southern School News*, October 1, 1954, 9.

[2] Quoted in Carter, *The South Strikes Back*, 49. In a May 26, 1967, interview with the author, Simmons reiterated the substance of this quotation, noting that in the state Democratic primary of 1967, each of the five gubernatorial candidates was a Council member.

political, nonpartisan, non-secret body" pledged to the defense of white supremacy by "adequate political action." Article II, Section 5 of this charter proclaimed that the organization would not only endorse "worthy" candidates but that it would "expose and publish names of political traitors . . . who advocate principles destructive to white civilization." [3]

Even spokesmen for the Citizens' Councils of America occasionally acknowledged that a major objective of the movement was to capture and control political power. Conceding that "the most frequent charge leveled at the Citizens' Councils of Mississippi . . . has been that they have captured the so-called power structure in our state," CCA executive director Louis Hollis outlined the national organization's policy for state and local officers at an Annual Leadership Conference in the following terms: "We *all* work to capture the power structure of our local community, or county, through a strong locally autonomous Citizens' Council. And then go to work to make our influence felt at the state level. When we have enough states in this category, it will be no problem to drive the rascals from our national government." [4] Similarly, the "White Book" remonstrated that the principal "objective is to see that racial integrity is an open issue in every political campaign." The official guide for Council activities adjured, moreover, that "each local and state group should work to create a climate of opinion so strong that it would be unthinkable for any candidate for public office to be less than ardent in supporting segregation to the utmost."

In the Deep South, where virtually every office-seeker in any given election was an avowed white supremacist, Councilors only rarely endorsed individual candidates. As the "White Book" observed, it would be the "height of folly for the organization to split over personalities in such cases." But wherever racial moderates sought public station, the official handbook declared that "no stone should be left unturned in an all-out campaign to defeat the traitors to our race." [5]

In many states the Council served as a self-appointed clearing

[3] "Constitution of the Citizens' Council of Alabama," unpublished document in the files of the Southern Office, A-DL.

[4] Hollis, *Integrity*, 1–2. See also Hollis, *John H. Wisdom*, 16.

[5] "White Book," 40, 50.

house for political aspirants. Among their standing committees most Councils had a Political and Education Committee to evaluate the segregation credentials of office-seekers.

In Alabama, Louisiana, Mississippi, North Carolina, South Carolina, and Tennessee this screening process was facilitated by the use of questionnaires designed to elicit the attitudes of candidates toward the organized resistance movement and white supremacy generally. Typical of these was a seven-point query mailed by the Association of Citizens' Councils of South Carolina to all aspirants for the U.S. Senate and House of Representatives as well as for all statewide offices in the 1956 state Democratic primary. Candidates were instructed to answer: "YES or NO" to such questions as: "Do you give your whole-hearted support to the actions to maintain segregation that have already been taken by the State of South Carolina?" "Do you, here and now, promise not to seek the Negro vote, directly or indirectly?" "Are you a member of a Citizens' Council?" "If not, will you join a Citizens' Council?" [6]

Although even that "unofficial organ of the Councils," the Charleston *News and Courier,* conceded that the questionnaire "seems to imply pressure on candidates to join the Councils if they want the support of their substantially large membership," [7] the response was overwhelming. Nearly every candidate replied—including the state's entire congressional delegation—but five incumbent U.S. representatives refused to renounce the votes of "good Negroes." In a joint letter they reminded the organization's officials that "there are in South Carolina many patriotic colored citizens who are working at the local level with our white citizens to solve this complex problem. They are helping to promote unity among our people at a time when it is most needed." In a separate letter to ACCSC Executive Secretary S. Emory Rogers, Representative L. Mendel Rivers, the only Councilor among the candidates, explained further that many Negroes were segregationists too: "If we make it impossible for Negroes like those who rode with Hampton to help us in

[6] W. D. Workman, Jr., untitled, unpublished field report, SERS, May 27, 1956. See also *Southern School News,* June, 1956, 14; and Charleston *News and Courier,* May 6, 1956.

[7] Editorial, "We Support the Citizens' Council," Charleston *News and Courier,* May 18, 1956. See also Quint, *Profile in Black and White,* 50.

our way of life, I think it is wrong." In his reply, former Governor J. Strom Thurmond, a frequent speaker at Council rallies, indicated that, as a U.S. senator, he thought it inadvisable to join—"but I am in thorough accord with the Council and have encouraged their work all I could." Likewise, Senator Olin D. Johnston indicated his inability to become a member, but reminded the group that he had often appeared at its mass meetings. He pledged his continued support, "so long as the Councils remain in the hands of responsible and law-abiding citizens such as you." [8] Although some of these replies were more carefully qualified than many Councilors may have wished, the state association judged the entire slate to be "sound" on the issue of race.

When upper-South groups employed the same tactic, the results were invariably less satisfactory. In Tennessee, for example, the Federation for Constitutional Government mailed questionnaires to some 308 candidates for the state legislature in June, 1956. Warning that "mere lip-service" to states' rights and segregation was insufficient, Federation President Donald Davidson advised office-seekers to stick to "the main issues" and avoid such "empty cheats" as vows of defense for TVA and pork-barrel promises of higher teachers' salaries and better roads and hospitals. Despite these admonitions, more than two-thirds of the recipients disregarded the questionnaire altogether. Of the one hundred who did reply, more than one-fifth expressed reservations about Federation tactics and programs.[9]

The fate of the Federation's questionnaire was representative of the plight of the organized resistance movement in states where the political tenor was one of relative moderation. To be sure, Tennessee had pockets of unyielding white supremacist sentiment, particularly in the counties surrounding Chattanooga and Memphis, but its leadership at the highest level was generally moderate. Excepting only Prentice Cooper, an aging Crump politician who served three terms as governor during the 1940's, no politician of

[8] W. D. Workman, Jr., unpublished field report, SERS, May 27, 1956; *Southern School News*, June, 1956, 14; Charleston *News and Courier*, May 6, 1956. See also "Olin D. Johnston Backs Citizens' Councils," *The Citizens' Council*, October, 1955, 1.

[9] Nashville *Banner*, June 5, July 24, 1956; Graham, *Crisis in Print*, 92.

statewide standing became identified with organized resistance. While latter-day fire-eaters like Senators James O. Eastland of Mississippi and J. Strom Thurmond of South Carolina intimately allied themselves with the segregation movement, Tennessee's senators, Albert Gore and Estes Kefauver, remained steadfastly aloof. Similarly unfriendly Frank G. Clement, who had aroused racist ire in 1955 by vetoing a pair of segregation bills, adroitly outmaneuvered extremists in the state legislature when he won the enactment of a "mild" school bill package in January, 1957. Indicating that more severe measures would be vetoed, the youthful governor preempted the field of segregation legislation with five ambiguously worded and relatively innocuous laws. In so doing, he spared the state from such statutory excesses as school closing laws and resolutions of interposition.[10]

To the Federation for Constitutional Government, which had drafted its own list of legislative proposals in November, 1956, Clement's program was just one more artful pirouette by an administration that had "failed its citizens at every crucial point." In his annual statement to the membership in 1957, Davidson could only report that state lawmakers had not heeded the Federation's *Message to the Members of the General Assembly of the State of Tennessee, Containing Proposals for Legislative Action to Preserve the State Education System and to Safeguard and Maintain the Sovereign Rights of the State of Tennessee and Its People.* Instead of enacting the stringent measures necessary for the creation of "a secure bulwark against the encroachment of a socialistic and tyrannical federal government,"—including "a strong resolution of interposition"—the legislature had flaccidly succumbed to the governor's machinations.[11]

The frustrations of the politically impotent Tennessee Federation for Constitutional Government were widely shared by its counterparts elsewhere in the upper South. Excepting only defiant Virginia, the peripheral resistance movement fared best in Arkansas, but even there the Citizens' Council's impress on public policy was seldom

[10] For an account of this episode, see Graham, *Crisis in Print,* 120.

[11] Donald Davidson, *Report of the State Chairman, Tennessee Federation for Constitutional Government* (Nashville, 1957); Nashville *Tennessean,* June 16, 1957; *Southern School News,* July, 1957, 2.

very consequential. Until Governor Orval Faubus's defection from moderation in 1957, its most influential patron was its founder, James D. Johnson, whose political credentials were dubious at best. Defeated in successive bids for the state attorney generalship (1955) and the governorship (1956), the former state senator was without a public forum until his election to a seat on the state supreme court in 1958. Even the election to Congress of one of its more ardent well-wishers, Dale Alford, and the development of a warm (if somewhat ephemeral) relationship with Governor Faubus failed to open the corridors of power to the Council in Arkansas.

In Florida, North Carolina, Tennessee, and Texas, the forces of organized resistance exercised even less influence over state policy. In each of these states the preponderance of white public sentiment was unequivocally opposed to desegregation; and in each there existed sizeable blocs of legislators who were deeply committed to the defense of the status quo. Yet Councils or Council-like groups were of such marginal respectability that their active support was not always considered an asset in these states.[12] Thus in Texas, when oilman Robert Cargill, chairman of the Longview Citizens' Council, organized a successful state referendum on three segregation proposals in 1956, he did so under the banner of the Texas Referendum Committee—and not the Associated Citizens' Councils of Texas, which had been largely instrumental in securing the 150,000 signatures necessary to place the measures on the ballot.[13] Lacking mass memberships or even statewide followings and unable to attract influential community support, resistance groups outside the Deep South never directly participated in the decision-making processes of state government. With only one major exception, theirs was a rearguard action waged on the fringes of the political arena.

[12] See, for example, editorial, Dallas *Morning News,* June 28, 1957.

[13] So pleased was Simmons with the Council's little-advertised role in the referendum that he ran a special edition of *The Citizens' Council* in August, 1956, under the title "TEXAS VOTES FOR SEGREGATION." Excepting only the headline story and an article by Dr. B. E. Masters, chairman of the Associated Citizens' Councils of Texas, the special edition was identical to the edition published earlier that month. See also *Southern School News,* April, 1956, 3; June, 1956, 4, and O. Douglas Weeks, *Texas One-Party Politics in 1956* (Austin: University of Texas Press, 1957), 37.

Larger and far more powerful than any other organization of its kind in the peripheral South, the Virginia Defenders of State Sovereignty and Individual Liberties played a major role in the drama of defiance in the Old Dominion. Indeed, until 1959, when Virginia's policy of massive resistance collapsed, the Defenders' legislative program, "A Plan for Virginia," served to a remarkable extent as the legal basis for the state's continued operation of segregated schools.[14] To a large degree the organization's successes were the result of its strength in the politically powerful fourth district. Like many black-belt areas, the fourth district, or Southside as it was known locally, had a disproportionately strong influence on the course of state policy. This phenomenon, when coupled with the Defenders' generally dignified deportment—a factor which made it easier for many of the state's most important politicians to become involved in its affairs—gave the group an enviable voice in state politics. While it is true that the group was never overtly identified with Senator Byrd, it was also true, as one student of Virginia's recent past has observed, that "the Defenders came to carry the expression of the [Byrd] organization's sentiment on racial affairs."[15]

Paying tribute to the Defenders' contributions to the state's continued efforts to evade desegregated schools, Governor J. Lindsay Almond, Jr., observed at the organization's annual convention in the winter of 1958: "Virginia has led in this fight, and the Defenders have led Virginia." On the same occasion, state Attorney General Albertis S. Harrison, Jr., added: "We are indebted to this organization, because in the past four years it has led Virginia in the fight for our dual government and Constitution with integrity, dignity, and honor."[16] But Virginia's fight to maintain segregation was nearly over. Confronted by both state and federal court orders, the Almond

[14] *A Plan for Virginia, Presented to the People of the Commonwealth by the Defenders of State Sovereignty and Individual Liberties* (Richmond, 1955). See also Richmond *Times-Dispatch,* June 9, 1955. For a comparative analysis of the Defenders' legislative proposals and the segregation legislation adopted by the Virginia General Assembly, see *Defenders News and Views,* November, 1956.

[15] Smith, *They Closed Their Schools,* 97. See also Gates, *The Making of Massive Resistance,* 48–50, 97, 150–66.

[16] Quoted in *Defenders News and Views,* February–March, 1958.

administration retreated from massive resistance as an official state policy five years after the rendering of the *Brown* decision. Almost immediately the Defenders' position of influence began a precipitous decline.

Angered by the governor's "betrayal" and insistent that "Massive Resistance Did Not Fail—It Was Never Tried," the Defenders made a determined effort in the spring and summer of 1959 to lead white Virginia to the polls to "change the complexion of the Assembly" by purging the moderates. But instead of a reaffirmation of faith in massive resistance, the voters in the July Democratic primary delivered a decisive rebuff to the Defenders. When the new assembly convened in January, 1960, the issue of school segregation—for the first time in more than five years—was not a major legislative concern.[17]

Not unlike the Virginia Defenders, the Citizens' Council of South Carolina numbered among its staunchest supporters some of the state's most influential political leaders. Indeed, upon its formation the Association of Citizens' Councils of South Carolina received the unanimous commendation of both houses of the state legislature. In a joint resolution adopted during February, 1956, the General Assembly expressed its appreciation to "those who have engaged in the formation of such Citizens' Councils in the State of South Carolina," and extended "its approval and encouragement of all others who desire to form such councils." Additional evidence of the organization's political stature was to be found in the endorsement it received from many of the state's most powerful spokesmen. At an early statewide Council rally in Columbia, for example, such notables as U.S. Senators J. Strom Thurmond and Olin T. Johnston, U.S. Representatives L. Mendel Rivers and John J. Riley, former Governor James F. Byrnes, and state Representative Burnet R. Maybank, Jr., graced the speakers' platform.[18]

Attestations to the effectiveness of the Council's role in molding public policy in South Carolina were numerous. But perhaps the

17 Defenders' mimeographed broadside, in files of SERS; Richmond *News Leader*, February 26, May 5, 1959; *Southern School News*, June, 1959, 7; Muse, *Virginia's Massive Resistance*, 164–65.

18 South Carolina State *Journal*, February 9, 1956, 248–49; *Southern School News*, March, 1956, 9; Quint, *Profile in Black and White*, 50.

most compelling came from the lips of state Senator L. Marion Gressette of Calhoun County, one of the General Assembly's most influential leaders. Speaking before a group of one hundred Council leaders during the summer of 1959, Gressette, the chairman of the legislature's powerful Special Segregation Committee, affirmed that "it is good to know that you are organized and that your influence and support can be depended upon to crystallize the right sentiment and attitude on the part of our people." A strong Citizens' Council, he observed, was like a strong army—"we may never need it but it is good to know that it is around." [19]

Even though ready to offer public testimonials of good will, leading Palmetto State politicians were decidedly unready to follow the Council's leadership into an open break with the national Democratic party. Nevertheless, during the campaign of 1956, Micah Jenkins, chairman of the statewide Council association, endeavored to forge a third party from dissident Democrats. Following an unsuccessful effort to win the endorsement of a slate of independent electors by the state convention, Jenkins and other stalwarts of the state Council movement, including S. Emory Rogers and Farley Smith, formed the South Carolinians for Independent Electors. Initially uncommitted, the Independents' electoral slate was ultimately pledged to Senator Harry F. Byrd of Virginia and Representative John Bell Williams of Mississippi for president and vice-president respectively. Although the Byrd-Williams ticket generated considerable enthusiasm in low-country counties where Council strength was greatest, it proved singularly incapable of attracting prominent Democratic leaders to its standard. In November, the vast majority of the state's Democratic voters heeded Governor George Bell Timmerman's appeal for political loyalty and voted for the party's national nominees.[20]

In Alabama and Louisiana, the Council also figured prominently in state political life. To be sure, Council leaders in both states

[19] Quoted in editorial, Charleston *News and Courier,* June 25, 1959. See also *Southern School News,* July, 1959, 10.

[20] James F. Byrnes was the only prominent Democrat in the state to lend his name to the Independents. In March, 1958, the faction made an unsuccessful attempt to capture the state Democratic chairmanship. See Charleston *News and Courier,* June 17, October 22, 1956; and Quint, *Profile in Black and White,* 128–44.

doubled as the foremost spokesmen for white supremacy within the legislature. The principal architect of Louisiana's official resistance was Senator Willie Rainach, president of the Association of Citizens' Councils of Louisiana. As head of the Joint Legislative Committee on Segregation, he steered through both houses—often without even a dissenting vote—a prodigious body of segregation measures. Not a lawyer himself, this Claiborne Parish segregationist relied heavily on the legal skills of fellow Council chieftain Leander Perez, who wrote most of the so-called "watch-dog" committee's bills during Rainach's chairmanship.[21] When Rainach resigned from the Senate and retired as head of the Council to run unsuccessfully in the gubernatorial race of 1960, state Representative John S. Garrett became his successor both as chairman of the Joint Legislative Committee and president of the ACCL.

In Alabama the chairman of the legislative study committee in charge of drafting segregation laws was Senator Albert Boutwell, a Birmingham lawyer and Council stalwart. Other spokesmen for segregation in the state's upper house were Samuel Martin Engelhardt, executive secretary of the Citizens' Council of Alabama, and Walter C. Givhan, one of the state's earliest Councilors and ultimately the chairman of the state Council organization. In the lower house, Charles W. McKay, Jr., youthful chairman of the Sylacauga Citizens' Council and author of the state's nullification resolution, was the organization's most notable representative. But despite its numerous champions in public office, the Alabama Citizens' Council encountered difficulty in attracting support from the highest level of the state's power structure. In order to attract crowds at organization rallies, Councilors frequently imported such regionally celebrated segregationists as Mississippi's Senator James O. Eastland and Georgia's former Governor Herman Talmadge. As a speaker at one Council gathering in Montgomery lamented during the autumn of 1955, governors in many southern states were in the vanguard of the organized resistance movement, but "we haven't a single U.S. Senator who has opened his mouth, nor have we a single Congressman who has said a word." Similarly, in June, 1956, at a Selma rally featuring Representative John Bell Williams of

[21] See Anthony, "Pro-Segregation Groups," 62–63; *Southern School News*, December, 1957, 8; McCarrick, "Louisiana's Official Resistance," 16, 86–87.

Mississippi, Senator Givhan called upon Alabama's congressional delegation to "join us in this fight so we won't have to go to Mississippi, Georgia or South Carolina to get speakers for such programs as this." [22]

Following Givhan's complaint, the Montgomery *Advertiser*—which had itself expressed "a cool and reserved attitude towards the White Citizens' Council"—polled members of Alabama's congressional delegation regarding their availability for Council speaking engagements. All eleven expressed their willingness, and two, Representatives Frank Boykin of the first district and George Grant of the second, acknowledged their membership in the organization. The *Advertisers'* poll, however, could not have been a great comfort to Council organizers. For, although Alabama talent was more readily available for segregation rally oratory thereafter, the responses to the newspaper's inquiry were generally unenthusiastic. Senators Lister Hill and John Sparkman seemed to speak for a majority of the delegation when they replied that it was their policy never to refuse to speak to any responsible group of constituents—whether it be the Eastern Star, the plumbers' local, or the Citizens' Council.[23]

Similarly without enthusiasm for the organized resistance movement was James T. Folsom, successor to Governor Gordon Persons in January, 1955. Even less willing than his moderate predecessor to identify his administration with extreme segregationists, "Big Jim" became an outspoken critic of the Council. As a candidate for national Democratic committeeman in 1956, the governor refused to return a Council political questionnaire.[24] Protesting that the organization was led by "Nullicrats," "the same faces, rank and serial number and issues that led the Dixiecrats in 1948," he flatly refused "to swear allegiance to . . . any group that's trying to tear up the Democratic party in Alabama." Although facetiously protesting that he supported "the White Citizens' Council, Black Citizens' Council, Yellow Citizens' Council, Red Citizens' Council and any

[22] Quoted in Birmingham *News,* October 4, 1955; and *Southern School News,* June, 1956, 10–11.

[23] Montgomery *Advertiser,* February 19, July 8, 1956.

[24] The questionnaire was reprinted in full in *Newsweek,* 46 (April 2, 1956), 26.

other color you might mention," Folsom, who represented the northern and urban sections of the state, was a frequent vetoer of segregation measures favored by the black-belt organization. With the probable exceptions of his reputation as a "friend" of the Negro, his attempt to gain legislative approval for a biracial commission to ease racial tensions, and his hospitable reception of Representative Adam Clayton Powell in the governor's mansion, Folsom's greatest transgression in Council eyes was his dismissal of an Alabama resolution nullifying the *Brown* decision as "just a bunch of hogwash." With similar indelicacy, he likened the legislature which adopted it to "a hound dog baying at the moon." [25]

For his racial moderation, Folsom paid the bitter price of defeat at the hands of a Councilor. As a gubernatorial candidate in 1954, he had carried sixty-two of the state's sixty-seven counties. But in his bid for the post of Democratic committeeman in 1956, he lost in all but five counties to Representative Charles McKay. While it did not formally endorse McKay, the Council waged an unstinting campaign for the governor's defeat. With some justification, then, Executive Secretary Engelhardt claimed that his organization could be credited with 75 percent of the anti-Folsom vote.[26]

Decidedly less successful were the efforts of Engelhardt and his fellow Councilors to influence the state's role in national politics during the campaign of 1956. In Alabama, state delegates to the national convention were chosen by direct election rather than a state party convention. With full Council backing, Laurie Battle, a militant Birmingham segregationist and former state representative, led the ticket in the statewide race for delegate-at-large, polling nearly 26,000 more votes than Senator John Sparkman, the runner-up. But Sparkman, who (like Folsom) had ignored the Council's

[25] Quoted in *Southern School News*, February, 1956, 6–7, April, 1956, 5; Birmingham *News*, April 15, 1956; and Montgomery *Advertiser*, March 8, 1959. As a first-term governor in 1948, Folsom had opposed the States' Rights Democratic Party's successful effort to capture the machinery of the Democratic party in Alabama. That year he was defeated in his bid for a seat on the state delegation to the national convention.

[26] Interview with Sam Engelhardt; "The White South Today: A Political State of Mind," *Newsweek*, 47 (May 21, 1956), 38, 43; *Southern School News*, June, 1956, 10; Birmingham *News*, May 2, 1956.

questionnaire, was named to lead the state delegation to Chicago in August. Failing to win the delegation chairmanship for its favorite, the Council then sought to win state convention support for a caucus of the South immediately prior to the national convention. But a majority of the state delegation, like Chairman Sparkman himself, apparently believed that the South could fight its political battles most effectively through the machinery of the Democratic party. Perhaps fearing that an eleven-state conference to map a regional strategy could lead to a repetition of the Dixiecrat performance of 1948, the Alabama convention did not initiate the call; indeed, there was no regional caucus of delegates. Although Council leaders did manage to qualify a slate of unpledged electors for the November ballot, its appeal, like similar slates in Mississippi and South Carolina, was limited. The state's eight electoral votes were cast for the liberal Democrat from Illinois, Adlai E. Stevenson.[27]

Upon the inauguration of Governor John M. Patterson, the Council's relationship with the state's chief executive improved markedly. Patterson, whose racial views won the support of a wide variety of segregationists—including that of national Grand Wizard Robert M. Shelton of the Knights of the Ku Klux Klan—believed that "we need to have more organized groups such as the Citizens' Councils."[28] In a show of accord with the organized resistance movement, he met with state Council leaders soon after assuming office to discuss his segregation program. Similarly congenial was his successor, Circuit Judge George C. Wallace of Barbour County, whose first official appearance as governor outside of the state was before the Mississippi legislature and the Jackson Citizens' Council. Although some Council leaders bitterly resented his "racial liberalism" of the early 1950's, Wallace became a favorite and frequent Council orator. Both during and after his term in the statehouse (1962–66), the "Little Judge" often invited citizens from across the region "to join

[27] Birmingham *News*, April 22, May 20, July 1, 25, October 31, November 4, 1956.

[28] Quoted in *Southern School News*, November, 1958, 12. On Patterson's connection with the Klan, see Birmingham *News*, May 16, 17, 21, and Montgomery *Advertiser*, May 15, 17, 18, 22, 1958.

with me in becoming an active member of your local Citizens' Council."[29] At a time when the movement was in severe decline throughout the South, the alliance of the Citizens' Council of Alabama with this immensely popular state official was an invaluable asset for the segregation group.

Momentarily, at least, it seemed likely that Governor Jimmie H. Davis might play a comparable role in the Pelican State. Enjoying the favor of neither Governor Robert Kennon nor his successor, Earl K. Long,[30] the Association of Citizens' Councils of Louisiana enthusiastically followed defeated candidate Willie Rainach's lead in mustering segregation support for the popular songwriter and former governor in the runoff primary of 1960. Although the enigmatic Davis has been generally recognized as a man who "almost never demonstrated definite convictions about anything,"[31] he was a determined segregationist and, it appeared, a willing friend of the organized resistance movement. During the New Orleans school desegregation crisis his defiant posturing won, in the words of a Citizens' Councils of America resolution, the "admiration and respect of all freedom loving Americans." Praised by Council leaders for his "courageous conduct" and "priceless contribution to the cause of constitutional liberty and state sovereignty" during the six legislative sessions of 1960–61, Davis was accorded a status in the hierarchy of southern resistance heroes only slightly lower than that enjoyed by Ross Barnett and George Wallace.[32]

But if Louisiana Councilors expected Davis to revitalize their rapidly disintegrating movement, they were to be sorely disappointed. Plagued by factionalism and declining membership and

[29] Interview with Sam Engelhardt; Birmingham *News,* November 28; Memphis *Commercial Appeal,* November 25, 1962; *Aspect,* June, 1964; *The Citizen,* 9 (December, 1964), 16.

[30] In the Louisiana gubernatorial election of 1956, the ACCL campaigned actively against Earl Long, and it opposed virtually every position he took as governor. For his part, Long was often critical of the Council, which he believed to be comprised of "extremists" and "hot heads." See *Delta Democrat-Times,* January 20, 1956; *Southern School News,* June, 1956, 3.

[31] Harnett Kane, "Dilemma of the Crooner-Governor," *New York Times Magazine,* January 1, 1961, 30–33.

[32] A complete text of the resolution appears in *The Citizens' Council,* March, 1961, 1. See also New Orleans *Times-Picayune,* February 26, 1961.

wanting in effective leadership, the organization was perhaps beyond salvation. And, for his part, the easygoing governor lacked the inclination to champion a dying cause. Indeed, his less-than-resolute commitment to the Council's welfare became apparent during his first year in office. In return for Rainach's support in the second primary, Davis agreed to establish a powerful and autonomous State Sovereignty Commission with the Claiborne Parish Councilor as its chairman. Such a commission was in fact created by the legislature in 1960, but it was neither autonomous nor powerful. As Davis must surely have anticipated, Rainach refused the chairmanship once it was known that the commission's operation would be under the control of the governor's office. Despite the South Louisiana Citizens' Council's bitter reminder that it had been Rainach's endorsement "that made you governor of the state of Louisiana for the second time," Davis considered his obligation fulfilled. He then appointed one of his own intimates, Frank H. Voelker, Jr., to fill the post.[33] Thus deprived of a forum, Willie Rainach drifted back into the obscurity whence he had emerged less than a decade before. With Rainach eliminated as an important political figure and desegregation an accomplished fact in New Orleans, the governor's early interest in organized extremism rapidly waned.

Although influential in Alabama, Louisiana, South Carolina, and Virginia, organized resistance achieved its greatest power in "unyielding Mississippi." In this, the Council's mother state, the organization men of southern defiance manipulated popular opinion, forged political alliances, and so thoroughly blurred distinctions between public and private authority that they virtually dominated many areas of public policy. From the first stages of its development, the Council's Mississippi leadership recognized that effective resistance to desegregation began with the capture and control of the local power structure. Despite his boast that "it's a grass-roots movement—it's an organization of the people," Robert Patterson was careful to recruit the business and civic elite of Indianola to serve as cofounders of the original Council in Sunflower County. These community leaders—including the mayor, the city attorney, a banker, a dentist, a pharmacist, and some of the more substantial

[33] New Orleans *Times-Picayune,* June 2, 1960; McCarrick, "Louisiana's Official Resistance," 104–6.

merchants—strove in turn to enlist men of comparable substance in surrounding counties. Only after securing the support of the power structure in the rural communities and county seats of the Delta did the Council come out into the open actively to seek mass support.[34]

Almost at once, indications of the fledgling organization's potential political muscle became apparent. In October, 1954, immediately after its formation, the Association of Citizens' Councils of Mississippi pledged full support to a proposed voter qualification amendment to the state constitution. Although a similar measure aimed at reducing Negro suffrage had failed to pass in 1952, the amendment was adopted in the November election by a vote of 75,488 to 15,718. In his first *Annual Report,* Patterson heralded the victory as "the first major accomplishment and the first project undertaken by our Councils on a state level. . . ." The extent to which Council support proved decisive, however, was uncertain; for a broad spectrum of influential spokesmen, including Senators James O. Eastland and John Stennis, the Hederman Press, and four leading candidates for the forthcoming gubernatorial race, endorsed the measure. Nevertheless, the voting was heaviest and most favorable in counties well organized by the Council, and in Sunflower County not even 1 of the 114 registered Negro voters went to the polls.[35]

Still another 1954 constitutional amendment to which the Council laid claim was one authorizing the state legislature by a two-thirds vote to abolish the public schools should desegregation become imminent. Although the voting was unusually light, the measure received a two-to-one endorsement in the December election. As before, the twenty-six counties known to be Citizens' Council strongholds gave the measure an overwhelming endorsement. In the segregation organization's home county, only 64 out of more than 1,900 votes cast were opposed to ratification.[36] Once again the de-

[34] Patterson noted in his first *Annual Report: August, 1955,* 1, that early in the Council's development "the concept of assembling non-political community leaders into a unified body to provide the best thinking on the local level, dealing with local problems, became deeply rooted."

[35] Ibid.; Patterson, *The Citizens' Councils: A History,* 3; Anthony, "Pro-Segregation Groups," 6; Carter, *The South Strikes Back,* 41–42.

[36] *Annual Report: August, 1955,* 1; *Southern School News,* December 1,

gree to which the election was influenced by Council support was in question. As one student of Mississippi politics has noted, election figures suggest that the density of a county's Negro population was the most important variable in the referendum.[37]

Whether or not its support was decisive, the Citizens' Council distinguished itself by becoming openly identified with the passage of these two segregation amendments. Even its most outspoken critics—and there were few critics in Mississippi who were outspoken—acknowledged that in a very short time it had emerged as a highly potent force in state politics. As *Delta Democrat-Times* editor Hodding Carter expressed it, "in the first six months of the Councils' existence they have won each fight they've entered, or objective they've sought, without physical violence. . . . Not a single office seeker in a state which will hold state-wide elections this summer has publicly criticized the Councils, even though some have privately wrung their hands over their actions." [38]

Carter could, indeed, speak with authority on the Council's power within the state. Following the publication of an article in a national magazine in which he analyzed the white resistance group's potential for violence, Mississippi's House of Representatives censured him by a vote of 89 to 19 for having "lied, slandered . . . and betrayed the South." Among those who opposed the resolution of censure was Representative Joel Blass of Stone County, the leader of the futile fight to defeat the public school abolition bill. In his remarks in defense of Carter on the house floor, Blass indicated that he, too, had been "smeared" by the segregation group as an instrument of the NAACP; he, too, had "felt the lash of the Citizens' Councils." [39]

Further evidence of the organization's growing power within the

---

1954, 8; January 6, 1955, 10; Atlanta *Journal and Constitution,* December 26, 1954.

[37] Carter, *The South Strikes Back,* 45–47.

[38] Hodding Carter, "A Wave of Terror Threatens the South," *Look,* 19 (March 22, 1955), 33.

[39] Ibid., 32–36; editorial, "Liar by Legislation," *Delta Democrat-Times,* April 3, 1955; Hodding Carter, "The South and I," *Look,* 19 (June 28, 1955), 74–80.

state came during the Democratic gubernatorial primary in the summer of 1955. In their first and only joint appearance of the campaign the five aspirants appeared before a Madison County Citizens' Council rally to affirm the orthodoxy of their racial views. Each offered assurance that if elected governor, segregation would be preserved, and each—except Attorney General James P. Coleman—was effusive in his praise for organized resistance. Apparently unaware of the attorney general's oversight, Patterson expressed his satisfaction with the entire slate. No public endorsement was given, but Coleman, as the "least immoderate candidate,"[40] was clearly not the Council's favorite. He nevertheless won enough votes to enter the runoff primary against Paul Johnson, a seasoned gubernatorial candidate whose most apparent political asset was a truly remarkable command of the idiom of white supremacy. With tensions already running high in the wake of an NAACP school desegregation petition campaign, this son of a former governor made an active bid for the votes of the state's sixty thousand Councilors. But despite Johnson's hard line on race, despite his endeavors, in the attorney general's words, "to wrap the cloak of the councils around him,"[41] Coleman emerged as the victor in the August 23 election. Immediately after the election, the Democratic nominee (in Mississippi, as in much of the South, the Democratic nomination was tantamount to election) issued a "solemn pledge" that during his term of office Mississippi's children would continue to attend only segregated schools.[42]

Although never as outspokenly hostile as Alabama's Governor Folsom, Coleman's relationship with the organized resistance movement was never more than cool. While he steadfastly refused to become a member, he was always careful to note, as he did on a "Meet the Press" telecast in 1957, that he did not "disapprove of the objectives of the association." "My official duty," he declared "[is] to represent everybody, those who belong to the organization and

40 Douglas Cater, "Beyond Tokenism," *The Reporter,* 29 (October 10, 1963), 23–27. See also *Southern School News,* July 6, 1955, 4.

41 Quoted in Memphis *Commercial Appeal,* August 18, 1955.

42 Carter's book, *The South Strikes Back,* 49–105, provides the fullest published account available of Coleman's election and subsequent administration. Coleman's protracted conflict with the Council has been sensitively portrayed by Wilson Minor in "The Citizens' Councils."

those who do not." On another occasion he was quoted as saying that "I am not a member of the Citizens' Council and never have been. I believe that a governor of the state should act purely on what he believes to be right as governor and not because of any organization." At one point he even predicted the ultimate demise of organized resistance. Expressing his belief that, through responsible legal action, Mississippi might permanently forestall the threat of desegregation, he declared: "When the urgency [of the racial crisis] passes, I feel that the Citizens' Council will pass along with it."[43]

With views like these, it was not remarkable that Coleman and the Council were at perpetual loggerheads. An unremitting opponent of extremist legislation, he resisted pressure to outlaw the NAACP, vetoed a measure intended to cripple FBI civil rights investigations, and issued frequent statements condemning those who sought to sensationalize race crises. Although he did sign a declaration of interposition passed by the state legislature in March, 1956, he was unimpressed by the logic of nullification. To William J. Simmons and his legions, nullification may have been "the lodestone of the Citizens' Councils" and a "philosophy of government rooted in the very nature of our Union of forty-eight separate political communities,"[44] but to James P. Coleman it was sheer "legal poppycock." Furthermore, he reminded the advocates of this dubious stratagem that even if its constitutionality were more certain, there was always that one simple reality—"Mississippi can't whip the whole United States." He clashed with the Council once again when his administration supported the donation of state land for an integrated Veterans Administration Hospital in Jackson. State and local Councils protested vigorously in editorials and resolutions that integration would cause "deep psychological reactions in physically helpless war veterans," and these groups

[43] Quoted in *Southern School News,* July, 1957, 1–5; Martin, *The Deep South Says "Never"*, 134; Memphis *Commercial Appeal,* October 8, 1956.

[44] Editorial, "Interposition—Basic Principle of States Rights," *The Citizens' Council,* January, 1956, 1. In the same issue, see also M. M. McGowan, "Interposition or Nullification," 1–2; "Interposition—A Plan for Action Now!" December, 1955, 1, 4; and the text of an interposition resolution adopted by the executive committee of the Association of Citizens' Councils of Mississippi, February, 1956, 1.

went as far as petitioning Congress to require that the operation of VA hospitals conform to local "customs, traditions, and laws." But Coleman stood his ground, and when Council supporters introduced a bill in the state legislature to prevent the land transferral to the VA, forces sympathetic to the governor quietly buried it in committee.[45]

Perhaps an even more important victory for Governor Coleman in his undeclared war with the organized extremists involved the selection of state delegates to the Democratic national convention. During his own campaign for election, he had warned Councilors of the peril of meddling in partisan issues. Should Council leaders "become mixed up in politics," he advised, they would only "hurt and perhaps destroy the effectiveness" of their organization.[46] But during May, 1956, the statewide association projected itself into the very maelstrom of an intraparty battle. In a resolution sent to each of the county Democratic organizations, the Council demanded that the Mississippi delegation be bound to support only those candidates for national office who were deemed sympathetic to the state's resolution of interposition. Additionally, the resolution called for a recessed state convention, to be reconvened immediately after the nomination of the national ticket in Chicago, and the selection of electors "unequivocally" dedicated to the principle of state sovereignty. Already on record as favoring an uninstructed delegation, Coleman accepted this challenge to his control of the state convention. With full support from the state Democratic executive committee chairman, he met the Council head-on in a month of intense fighting at the precinct, county, and district levels. When the state convention met on July 16, Coleman had the support of an overwhelming majority of the 280 delegates. In the third district, which encompassed virtually the whole of the Delta, Council supporters did manage to block the selection of Representative Frank E. Smith, a racial moderate and an articulate

45 *Southern School News,* January, 1956, 6; February, 1956, 16; Minor, "The Citizens' Council"; "Official Resolution," *The Citizens' Council,* June, 1957, 1; "By Formal Resolution Veterans and Councils Blast VA Integration," *The Citizens' Council,* July, 1957, 1, 4; "Monuments to Integration," *The Citizens' Council,* January, 1958, 4; Jackson *Daily News,* May 22; *Delta Democrat-Times,* May 30, 1957.

46 Quoted in Memphis *Commercial Appeal,* August 18, 1955.

critic of organized resistance. But even here Coleman had the final word. The state convention made Smith a delegate-at-large to the national convention.[47]

Following the Chicago convention, some individual Councilors, unable to accept either the national Democratic party ticket or its platform, joined in a feeble effort to win popular support for a slate of electors "pledged to principle rather than party." Instrumental in the formation of this movement, the Mississippians for States' Rights, were such prominent Council personalities as William J. Simmons, Ross R. Barnett, and Circuit Judge M. M. McGowan. The Citizens' Council itself, however, did not officially endorse the slate, and it was ignored by the state's entire congressional delegation, all but one of whom supported Adlai E. Stevenson and Estes Kefauver. In November, the state voted solidly Democratic.[48]

Like virtually every other successful Mississippi politician, Coleman could resort with ease to the argot of race-baiting whenever the occasion demanded it. Against even a regional backdrop, many of his pronouncements on race were extreme. But though "soft" on segregation only by Deep South standards, Coleman was often vilified for his racial moderation. In Judge Tom P. Brady's derisive phrase, he was "Fair-minded Jim." Repeatedly and with apparent indignation, Coleman protested that he was not a "moderate" but rather a "practical segregationist."[49] Nevertheless, at that troubled juncture in the state's history, he was probably about as moderate as a governor of Mississippi with further political

[47] Association of Citizens' Councils of Mississippi, "Resolution," undated, SERS files; *Southern School News,* July, 1956, 12; *Delta Democrat-Times,* June 3; Jackson *Daily News,* May 30, 1956; Carter, *The South Strikes Back,* 68–69; Bartley, *The Rise of Massive Resistance,* 158–59; Smith, *Congressman from Mississippi,* 265.

[48] See Jackson *Daily News,* May 30; Memphis *Commercial Appeal* and *Delta Democrat-Times,* May 31, 1956; and Carter, *The South Strikes Back,* 69. Simmons's dissatisfaction with the national tickets and platforms of both major parties was reflected in his editorial, "Our Next Move," *The Citizens' Council,* September, 1956, 2. In October the Citizens' Councils of America adopted a kind of platform of its own. See "Blueprint for Victory Is Mapped at National Rally," *The Citizens' Council,* November, 1956, 1.

[49] Quoted in Walter Lord, *The Past That Would Not Die* (New York: Harper and Row, 1965), 79; *Southern School News,* July, 1959, 11.

aspirations could afford to be. At any rate, time would prove (despite his defeat in the gubernatorial primary of 1963 by Paul B. Johnson) that he was not only a shrewder politician but a far shrewder segregationist than his successor.

The inauguration of Ross Barnett in January, 1960, heralded a new day for the Citizens' Council in Mississippi. Held at arm's length not only by Coleman but also by his predecessor, Governor Hugh L. White, the organization, for all its strength in the state legislature and its more than eighty thousand members, had until that winter day been conspicuously without influence with the state's chief executive. Under the new governor, however, it would enjoy not only official blessings but generous state subsidies.

An early convert to organized resistance, Barnett was active in the Jackson Citizens' Council almost from its inception. In 1957 he journeyed to Knoxville to assist the Tennessee Federation for Constitutional Government in the defense of the fifteen eastern Tennessee "patriots" who had been charged, along with Frederick John Kasper, with unlawful interference with desegregation at Clinton High School. In 1958 he took an active part in the Jackson Council's "Freedom of Choice" canvass. And during his gubernatorial campaign in 1959, he often spoke before Council gatherings. Amid a field of four committed segregationists, his attack on racial moderation was by far the most strident. Thus, at a meeting of the Wilkinson County Citizens' Council, he could praise the movement because it "did not pursue in any manner the avenue of moderation"; nor did it "sit around and do nothing with sweet thoughts and apathy."[50] In a similarly complimentary mood at a benefit dinner for the Citizens' Council "Forum" in September, 1959—his first postelection address—he informed an appreciative audience of some one thousand persons: "I am proud that I have been a Citizens' Council member since the Council's early days. I hope that every white Mississippian will join with me in becoming a member of this fine organization. The Citizens' Councils are fighting your fight—they deserve your support."[51]

[50] Quoted in Jackson *Daily News*, November 18, 1958. See also *Southern School News*, July, 1959, 11.

[51] Barnett spoke on the topic, "The Voice of the South." See William J. Simmons to "Dear Member," August 31, 1959, Special Collections, Mitchell

It was not remarkable, then, that for his inaugural invocation the sixty-two-year-old governor-elect chose Dr. Willie M. Caskey, head of the department of political science and economics at Mississippi College. A devout Baptist layman and unofficial chaplain-at-large for the resistance movement, Caskey had often called down providential blessings on Council rallies.[52] Nor should readers of the Jackson *Daily News* have been startled by a postinauguration news article of January 27, 1960, headlined: "COUNCIL ACTIVITIES KEEP BARNETT BUSY." Apparently unencumbered by the myriad tasks which customarily preoccupy new governors, Barnett found time during his first days in office to confer with the professional staff from the CCA headquarters, meet delegations of local Council leaders from Little Rock and Jackson, and even address an Association of Citizens' Councils of South Carolina fund-raising banquet in Columbia. As an appreciative *Daily News* reporter suggested, "Governor Ross Barnett should have proclaimed this week as 'Citizens' Council Week' in Mississippi."[53]

To many observers both within and without Mississippi, every week was "Citizens' Council Week in Mississippi" during most of Barnett's tenure. Indeed, unlike his predecessor, who dealt with racial problems wholly from within the framework of state government, Barnett characteristically worked through the Citizens' Council whenever issues of race were concerned. Even before taking the oath of office, he anticipated a close working relationship between his administration and the resistance organization.

Memorial Library; *The Citizens' Council*, August 1959, 1; September, 1959, 1; Jackson *Daily News*, September 12, 1959; *Southern School News*, October, 1959, 3; Memphis *Commercial Appeal*, October 4, 1959.

[52] For 11½ minutes, Dr. Caskey prayed that the Eternal would assist the new governor in keeping Mississippi segregated during his term of office. (Columbia [S.C.] *State*, January 21, and *Delta Democrat-Times*, December 18, 1960.) Caskey's views on states' rights and race are presented in his booklet, *The South's Just Cause* (Clinton, Miss.: by the author, n.d.). See also *The Citizens' Council*, December, 1960, 1.

[53] Jackson *Daily News*, January 27; Columbia *State*, January 21, 1960; *Southern School News*, March, 1960, 7; *The Citizens' Council*, February, 1960, 1, 3; "Address by Governor Ross R. Barnett of Mississippi to Statewide Citizens' Council Banquet, Columbia, South Carolina, January 29, 1960," Southern Regional Council files.

Immediately following his landslide victory in the runoff primary, he spoke expansively about his plans for "total mobilization" in this "life-or-death fight" before a Council gathering in Jackson: "There are certain fields where private agencies—such as the Citizens' Councils—can be most effective. There are other activities that the people should undertake through our state government."[54] Although not spelling out specifically those areas of public concern that might best be solved through the medium of organized resistance, he clearly envisioned a kind of semi-official status for the Council.

After Barnett's inauguration, the organization did in fact exercise what one of the state's more prominent historians called "a position of power and prestige seldom if ever achieved before by any extralegal group in the history of Mississippi." Echoing this view, Hodding Carter III declared in 1962 that with the election of Barnett, its "unabashed front man," the Council gained a "stranglehold" on state politics.[55] Perhaps the best measure of the organization's influence was the role of leadership it assumed in the unpledged elector campaign of 1960. During the campaign of 1956, Councilors or members of Council-like organizations in at least nine states were actively involved in some form of third-party effort. In Alabama, Mississippi, and South Carolina, Council leaders identified themselves with slates of "free" or "independent" electors. And in Arkansas, Louisiana, Georgia, Tennessee, Texas, and Virginia, spokesmen associated with the Council movement were instrumental in forming States' Rights parties. With but few exceptions, statewide Council associations maintained an official neutrality throughout the campaign, and the newly organized Citizens' Councils of America, although obviously sympathetic, did not openly encourage a third-party campaign in the South.[56] The

54 Quoted in Jackson *Daily News*, September 12, 1959. Barnett expressed this sentiment to Council groups elsewhere in the South as well. See, for example, a reprint of his address at a New Orleans Council meeting, *Strength through Unity*, 6.

55 Silver, *Mississippi: The Closed Society*, 11n; Hodding Carter III, "Mississippi: Deluded and Still Defiant," *The Nation*, 195 (October 13, 1962), 214.

56 On the "Dixiecrat revival" of 1956, see Bartley, *The Rise of Massive*

election of 1960, however, was quite another story. With Barnett in the vanguard, the Mississippi professionals who led the CCA plunged into an ambitious crusade to mold the South's 128 electoral votes into a solid bloc committed only to the principles of "states' rights and racial integrity." Employing the same strategy of electoral juggling used by the Texas "Regulars" in 1944 and the Dixiecrats in 1948, the organization hoped to deadlock the electoral college by denying either major candidate the necessary 269 votes. The election would then be forced into the House of Representatives, where the region would be in "a good trading position." By adroitly manipulating the balance of power, southern congressmen could perhaps even name a segregationist as the thirty-fifth president of the United States.[57]

Preliminary planning for Dixie's unpledged elector campaign occurred at a Citizens' Councils of America meeting in Montgomery during February, 1959. But the effort did not begin in earnest until after Barnett's victory in the runoff primary. Addressing Jackson Councilors in his first postelection appearance, the future governor called for "active consultation among our political leaders" in order "to unite the South behind a bold and determined program that will breathe new vitality into the words 'Solid South.'" Warning that "our enemies will use the age-old strategy of divide and conquer," he declared that "the South must go to the Democratic National Convention united—and the South must remain united, either IN the Convention or OUT!"[58]

Resistance, 150–69; *Southern School News,* September–December, 1956, passim.

[57] See M. M. McGowan, "Electoral College System Explained: How Do Unpledged Electors Function," *The Citizens' Council,* September, 1960, 3. Similar explanations are offered by John J. Synon, conservative columnist and staff member of Americans for Constitutional Action, in "President from Dixie?—The South Holds the Cards for a Spectacular Upset," *Human Events,* 17 (April 28, 1960), 1–4; and Hall E. Timanus, a conservative Texas lawyer, in "Presidential Elections: A Study of the Appointment and Function of Presidential Electors," *U.S. News and World Report* (July 11, 1960), 100–2. Synon's article was reprinted, in part, in *The Citizens' Council,* June, 1960, 1, 4.

[58] "Will the South Beat the Democrats?" *U.S. News and World Report,* 46 (April 6, 1959), 56–58; *The Citizens' Council,* September, 1959, 1; Birmingham *News,* February 1; Jackson *Daily News,* September 5, 1959.

To be certain there were few Councilors who believed that the national party would nominate a white supremacist ticket. At a two-day "southern unity" conclave in Montgomery in September, the second such meeting of the Citizens' Councils of America during 1959, state and local leaders were urged to begin grass-roots campaigns to place unpledged electors on the ballot of their respective states. Although Barnett escorted a Mississippi delegation comprised largely of Council members to the Democratic National Convention in Los Angeles, the organization's strategy was to concentrate on the selection of uncommitted electors rather than party delegates. As Robert Patterson observed, "we are not too much concerned about the convention, because they aren't going to nominate any man acceptable to the South. But we can make ourselves heard if enough Southern states will get together and elect free and unpledged presidential electors."[59]

But try as they did, Barnett and the Citizens' Council were not able to generate great enthusiasm in much of the region for a Dixiecrat-style rebellion. Indeed, the dream of southern political unity proved more illusory in 1960 than in 1948; for even had voters in the peripheral states of Florida, North Carolina, Tennessee, Texas, and Virginia desired to vote for independent electors, they could not have done so. Only in the five Deep South states and Arkansas did state laws permit such electoral slates on the ballot.[60] And in these six states there were few Democratic politicians of consequence who were willing to break openly with the national party. In Arkansas, for example, the chairman of the Senate Foreign Relations Committee, J. William Fulbright, the chairman of the Senate Government Operations Committee, John L. McClellan, and the chairman of the House Ways and Means Committee, Wilbur Mills, shared a vested interest in party loyalty. They were willing enough to offer the necessary lip service to states' rights and segregation on the campaign trail, but they could

[59] *The Citizens' Council,* September, 1959, 3; Montgomery *Advertiser* and Birmingham *News,* September 20, 1959; *Southern School News,* October, 1959, 8.

[60] Legislators in Georgia (1958) and Arkansas (1959) adopted laws permitting state parties to "free" electors from any responsibility to the nominees of national parties.

hardly be expected to lead a bolt against the source of their own immense congressional power. Similarly, both Richard B. Russell of Georgia, chairman of the Senate Armed Services Committee, and Olin D. Johnston of South Carolina, chairman of the Senate Post Office and Civil Service Committee, had offered their public blessings to the organized resistance movement; but they were no more ready than such relative moderates as Louisiana's Allen J. Ellender, chairman of the Senate Agriculture and Forestry Committee, and Alabama's Lister Hill, chairman of the Senate Labor Committee, to become identified with what was in fact a third-party effort. Even Senator James O. Eastland, Mississippi's bellicose "traveling salesman for the Citizens' Councils," responded to the realities of party politics with a grudging endorsement of the national ticket. "If I would bolt the Democratic party," he explained, "I would be removed as chairman of the Judiciary Committee." [61]

Southern governors provided another source of support for party regularity. Initially, several chief executives expressed deep dissatisfaction with both the Kennedy-Johnson ticket and the party platform, but only Governor Jimmie Davis of Louisiana was prepared to join Ross Barnett in open defection. And even with Davis's assistance, the states' rights or unpledged faction within the Louisiana party's central committee failed to capture the Democratic emblem on the ballot.[62] With varying degrees of enthusiasm, the recalcitrant governors who remained fell into line. After some coy flirtation with "southern unity," Arkansas's Orval Faubus, who was himself the unwilling presidential nominee of the National States' Rights Party, shied away from the independent movement.[63] Early in the campaign, Governor Ernest F. Hollings of

[61] Quoted in *Southern School News,* November, 1960, 14. See also Charles J. Lapidary, "Ol' Massa Jim Eastland," *The Nation,* 184 (February 9, 1957), 121.

[62] See Robert J. Steamer, "Southern Disaffection with the National Democratic Party," *Change in the Contemporary South,* 164–65; Abraham Holtzman, *The Loyalty Pledge: Controversy in the Democratic Party,* Eagleton Institute Case Studies in Practical Politics (New Brunswick: Rutgers University Press, n.d.), 30.

[63] *Southern School News,* May, 1960; Arkansas *Gazette,* September 29, 1960. After Faubus specifically denied his candidacy, the NSRP was withdrawn from the ballot in Florida. But in Alabama, Arkansas, Tennessee, and

South Carolina expressed public reservations about the ticket and even recommended that the state Democratic convention place two slates on the ballot, a pledged and an unpledged one. But in August, when the state convention reconvened, he reversed himself to plea for loyalty and won the endorsement of a slate pledged to Kennedy and Johnson. Another holdout, Governor Ernest Vandiver of Georgia, suddenly switched from tacit support for, to outright opposition to, unpledged electors following a late-August conference in Washington with the party's national nominees. Although a statewide referendum in September seemed to indicate a popular preference in Georgia for "free" electors, he personally headed a slate pledged to support the Democratic ticket.[64]

In Alabama, states' rights advocates did manage to place six unpledged electors on the party's eleven-man slate—but they did so over the opposition of Governor John Patterson and the state Democratic executive committee chairman, Samuel M. Engelhardt. Labeled "Quislings" and "Judases" by the militant segregationists they "betrayed," this unlikely pair of loyalists—the governor who as a candidate befriended the Grand Wizard of the Knights of the Ku Klux Klan and the former executive secretary of the Citizens' Council—symbolized the futility of the entire independent movement. Armed with only the single issue of race and lacking effective party organization and even a candidate, the unpledged elector campaign was hardly a match for the national party. By effectively wielding the formidable threats of a loss of patronage, the denial of presidential cooperation on desired legislation, and perhaps even forfeiture of committee assignments, Kennedy and Johnson were able to undermine the appeal of the free elector scheme. As one politician after another jumped on the Democratic bandwagon, Barnett and the Council professionals could only ineffectually rail against those "cowards" and "traitors" willing to surrender to the "South-haters." In a fist-swinging, election eve address to the Capital Citizens' Council of Little Rock, the gover-

---

Delaware the party's ticket of Faubus and retired Admiral John G. Crommelin was presented to the voters. In Arkansas it polled 7 percent, in Tennessee 1 percent, and in Alabama and Delaware less than 1 percent. "National States' Rights Party," *Group Research Reports*, Sec. 1-ORG (April 8, 1964), 4, 6.

[64] Holtzman, *The Loyalty Pledge Controversy*, 30.

nor, perhaps speaking from one of the many texts prepared for him by Simmons, conceded that his "southern unity" crusade had fallen short of the mark: "This fall we are treated to a spectacle which would be amusing were it not so alarming—the spectacle of Southern leaders who were elected on platforms promising total and unremitting efforts to preserve the Southern way of life, now speaking in behalf of candidates and platforms pledged to destroy the South and all that we stand for." [65]

In November, only fourteen Democratic electoral votes, eight in Mississippi and six in Alabama, were withheld from the national ticket. In Louisiana, the only other state which gave a substantial vote to a slate of unpledged electors, the independents ran third, well behind the electors pledged to John F. Kennedy and to Richard M. Nixon. Despite the poor showing of the unpledged electors, Councilors were heartened by Kennedy's narrow margin of only thirty-four votes. In its postelection edition, *The Citizens' Council* ran a banner headline proclaiming that the "PRESIDENTIAL RACE ISN'T OVER YET." Optimistically, its lead article announced that "the people of the south still have their best opportunity in over a century to put a Southerner in the White House!" In a front-page editorial, "How You Can Help Elect a Southern President," Simmons called upon "patriots" in the six states carried by the national ticket to persuade Democratic electors to withhold their ballots from Kennedy. "Call them. Write them. Form committees to visit them," he instructed. "Be sure they are aware that it is within their power to bring the forced integration campaign to a halt virtually overnight." The effort came to naught, however, and on December 19, after a prolonged meeting with top officials from the Citizens' Councils of America, the free electors from Alabama and Mississippi cast their fourteen futile ballots for Senator Harry F. Byrd of Virginia.[66]

[65] Ibid., 27–28, 31; Allan P. Sindler, "The South in Political Transition," in McKinney and Thompson, eds., *The South in Continuity and Change*, 312–13; *Southern School News*, January, 1959, 6; April, 1959, 3; November, 1960, 13; Montgomery *Advertiser*, March 21, 1959; *Arkansas Gazette*, September 29, 1960.

[66] *The Citizens' Council*, November, 1960, 1; Charleston *News and Courier*, December 13; *Delta Democrat-Times*, December 18, 1960; Minor, "The Citizens' Council."

The close alliance between the governor and the organized resistance movement apparent throughout the presidential campaign became the pattern for the Barnett era. Councilors were appointed to numerous governmental posts, including key positions on the state Sovereignty Commission and a seat on the state Supreme Court.[67] But more important, the professional staff of the Citizens' Councils of America, conveniently situated in a modern office building adjacent to the governor's mansion, comprised a kind of cabinet extraordinary for racial affairs. They advised the chief executive on segregation matters, wrote many of his speeches, and traveled in his official entourage.[68] Particularly high in the governor's esteem was the suave and articulate national administrator, William Simmons. Although Barnett would later emphatically deny that the chief Councilor offered anything but "occasional suggestions," Simmons was—to use James W. Silver's only slightly exaggerated phrase—the administration's "prime minister of racial integrity." [69] Whether accompanying the governor on his travels across the region, sitting in as an "observer" at closed meetings of the Sovereignty Commission, or acting as the governor's chief strategist during the Ole Miss crisis, Simmons was the embodiment of Council influence in administration circles. Although no one close to Barnett dared criticize the Council head, the governor's own friends were known to complain privately that Simmons had him "surrounded." Thus, with little fear of contradiction, one of the state's most astute political observers could report that the administrator had Barnett "in his hip pocket." [70]

67 In 1961, four members of the Sovereignty Commission were on the board of directors of the Association of Citizens' Councils of Mississippi. Three others, including the governor, were Council members. Associate Justice Thomas Pickens Brady, a member of the statewide executive committee, was appointed to the state bench in 1963. (New York *Times,* March 31, 1961. See also Smith, *Congressman from Mississippi,* 274.)

68 Jackson *Clarion-Ledger,* April 28, 1963; Samuel Dubois Cook, "Political Movements and Organizations," in Leiserson, ed., *The American South in the 1960's,* 138–39; Silver, *Mississippi: The Closed Society,* 41–44; Carter, "Citadel of the Citizens' Council," 22ff.

69 Interview with Ross Barnett, June 23, 1970; Silver, *Mississippi: The Closed Society,* 44.

70 For two particularly able accounts of Simmons's relationship with Barnett, see William B. Street, "Simmons Plays Much Discussed Role in

An effective advocate of segregation at any cost and a skillful behind-the-scenes manipulator, Simmons enjoyed power and influence such as is rarely accorded an individual of nonofficial status. Suggestive of his peculiar position of authority was a letter written early in the summer of 1962 by a state legislator (who wished to remain anonymous) to Erle Johnston, public relations director of the Sovereignty Commission, editor of the weekly *Scott County Times*, and an outspoken critic of the chief Councilor. "It's hard for us sometimes to consider a bill on its merits, if there is any way Bill Simmons can attach an integration tag," the lawmaker wrote.

> For instance, a resolution was introduced in the House to urge a boycott of Memphis stores because some of them have desegregated. I knew it was ridiculous and would merely amuse North Mississippians who habitually shop in Memphis. The resolution came in the same week that four Negroes were fined in court for boycotting Clarksdale stores. Yet the hot eyes of Bill Simmons were watching. If we had voted against the resolution he would have branded us. So there we were, approving a resolution urging a boycott while a Mississippi court was convicting Negroes for doing what we lawmakers were advocating. It just didn't make sense.[71]

A similar letter came to the same editor from yet another legislator, who rued that during the previous May he had voted against his conscience on a house bill to permit county and municipal governments to donate public funds to the Citizens' Council. Believing the bill both unwise and unconstitutional, he nevertheless cast an affirmative ballot. "If I had voted against the Councils," he explained, "Bill Simmons would brand me as an integrationist." [72]

Although passed by a substantial majority in the house, the bill to permit local governments to subsidize the "educational" activities of segregation organizations operating within their jurisdictions

Mississippi Politics," Memphis *Commercial Appeal*, January 13, 1963; Minor, "The Citizens' Council."

[71] Quoted in editorial, *Scott County Times*, June 6, 1962.

[72] Ibid.

was defeated in the senate judiciary committee.[73] Drafted by Yazoo City's John Satterfield, the president of the American Bar Association and a long-time supporter of the Council movement, the measure was almost identical to one introduced in 1958 by Senator Hayden Campbell, an active member of the Jackson Citizens' Council. Campbell's bill won wide support, particularly among Delta lawmakers, and in separate versions passed both the House and Senate. But it was opposed by a number of the state's newspapers—although not by the Jackson *Daily News* and *Clarion-Ledger*—and Governor Coleman termed it a "raw grab for political power." Under threat of veto, it died in a joint House-Senate committee.[74]

Although denied public subsidy by statute, the Council was nevertheless the beneficiary of state largess. Since the spring of 1960, the State Sovereignty Commission had been generously subsidizing the Council's radio and television series, the Citizens' Council "Forum." A pet project of James P. Coleman, the commission was established by the state legislature in 1956 "to protect the sovereignty of . . . Mississippi and her sister states from encroachments thereon by the Federal government." Created as a propaganda and investigative arm of the legislature, the anti-integration agency was designed to carry the "Mississippi story" to points outside the region and to keep tabs on "racial agitators"—reportedly through a "network of Negro informers blanketing Mississippi." But, though it had a division of investigation headed by a former sheriff and one-time chief of the state highway patrol, the commission apparently made little use of secret agents and spy tactics

73 *Journal of the House of the State of Mississippi*, Regular Session, January 2–June 2, 1962, 1028; *Journal of the Senate of the State of Mississippi*, Regular Session, January 2–June 2, 1962, 1006; Jackson *Daily News*, May 22; *Delta Democrat-Times*, May 27, 1962. An earlier attempt to provide tax funds for Council purposes occurred in 1956. Introduced by three Holmes County representatives, two of whom were leaders of their local Citizens' Councils, the measure would have permitted county boards of supervisors to make unrestricted donations of public funds to the prosegregation group.

74 *Journal of the Senate of the State of Mississippi*, Regular Session, January 7–May 10, 1958, 419; *Journal of the House of the State of Mississippi*, Regular Session, January 7–May 10, 1958, 679–85; Tupelo *Daily Journal*, March 31; *Delta Democrat-Times*, March 25; Jackson *Daily News*, March

under the Coleman administration. Preferring "friendly persuasion" to police state methods, Coleman channeled the agency's energies into "public relations" activity.[75]

Upon the inauguration of his successor, however, this policy was reversed. Almost immediately, secret investigators began spying and compiling dossiers on the activities of such dangerous "conspirators" as Hazel Brannon Smith and Billy Barton,[76] and the once-active propaganda bureau virtually abdicated the field in favor of the Council's "Forum." In May, 1960, only months after Ross Barnett assumed office, the commission over which he presided made the first of its periodic contributions of public funds to the private organization. In announcing the grant, commission director Albert Jones commended the "Forum's" "record of solid accomplishment." Its effort to counter the national media's "anti-South propaganda," he affirmed, "merits the active financial support of all patriotic Mississippians. . . ." [77] After an initial payment of $20,000, monthly contributions were fixed at $5,500. Scaled down first to $4,500 in 1962 and then to $2,000 somewhat later that same year, the donations totaled $193,500 by 1964, when they were terminated altogether.[78]

24; Jackson *State Times,* March 23; Memphis *Commercial Appeal,* April 18; New Orleans *Times-Picayune,* April 10, 1958.

[75] Silver, *Mississippi: The Closed Society,* 8n; Carter, *The South Strikes Back,* 64; *Southern School News,* June, 1956, 5. Typical of the Sovereignty Commission's activities during this period was its sponsorship during October, 1956, of a tour of the state by twenty-eight New England newspaper editors so that they might see "the Mississippi side of the integration question." See William Rotch, "Cotton, Cordiality and Conflict," *New South,* 12 (February, 1957), 9–11; Rotch, "Cotton, Cordiality and Conflict," *New South,* 12 (March, 1957), 6–9; and "South Increases Propaganda," *New South,* 14 (May, 1959), 3–6.

[76] Russell Barrett, himself a subject of investigative concern for the Commission, noted that its secret inquiries were "clumsy efforts to track down enemies of segregation, including the Negro [Clyde Kennard] who attempted to enter the University of Southern Mississippi; newspaper editors . . . college professors, and other such dangerous adversaries." (*Integation at Ole Miss,* 28–29.)

[77] Quoted in *Southern School News,* August, 1960, 3–4. See also Jackson *Daily News,* July 10, 1960.

[78] Fully $169,000 of that sum came during the Barnett administration. (In-

There were, of course, whites in Mississippi who were not altogether certain that patriotic duty demanded a public subsidy for the Citizens' Council. Speaking for the state's "silent minority," its white moderates, Oliver Emmerich, editor of the McComb *Enterprise-Journal* and Jackson *State Times,* sharply criticized this "grave error in judgment." Protesting that the Council, through its "ever-growing unofficial role" in state government, had already become "deeply enmeshed" in the Barnett administration, the editor asserted that even "many of the Citizens' Council members are aware of the danger of it becoming . . . a dominating force [in] . . . the affairs of our state." [79] More telling still was an argument used by the Ackerman *Plaindealer.* With the circumspection characteristically used by those who attacked the organization, the editor of this country weekly noted that "we do not oppose the Citizens' Council per se," but if the state could legally grant it aid, so too could it aid the NAACP and the AFL-CIO.[80]

These views were echoed by a few other papers, most notably the *Delta Democrat-Times* and the Lexington *Advertiser.* But a substantial majority of the state's daily press either maintained a timid silence or joined the Jackson *Daily News* in lauding the donations. As the West Point *Daily Times Leader* expressed it, "the State Sovereignty Commission HAS channeled a portion of its appropriations to the Mississippi Citizens Council. And wisely so! Those who think the state officers of the Citizens Council are a bunch of wild-eyed red necks with lynch ropes behind their backs are dead wrong. . . . They are cool-headed, soft-spoken, intelligent Mississippians, who realize that their state has a story to tell to the nation." Embroidering on this view, the Meridian *Star* urged its subscribers to rally around "your local Citizens Council." "In times such as ours, there is a definite need for such an organization." [81]

---

terview with Erle Johnston, Jr., director of the State Sovereignty Commission, 1963–68, June 25, 1970. See also Jackson *Daily News,* January 23, 1965.)

[79] Editorials, Jackson *State Times,* July 17, 1960; McComb *Enterprise-Journal,* May, 10, 1961.

[80] Editorial, Ackerman *Plaindealer,* July 2, 1960.

[81] Editorial, West Point *Daily Times Leader,* as reprinted in Jackson *Daily News,* January 12; editorial, Meridian *Star,* January 10, 1961.

Despite the support given the tax fund subsidies by most of the state's major dailies, the policy fell under increasing attack. In January, 1961, a liberal Jackson attorney, joined by two labor officials and a Negro grocer, initiated action in federal court to end the donations.[82] During the following April, state Attorney General Joe T. Patterson, ex officio member of the State Sovereignty Commission and long-time Council member, opposed the grant, as did state Representative Karl Wiesenburg, a moderate Pascagoulan and persistent critic of the excesses of the Barnett administration.[83] In December, 1961, three hundred students from twenty-nine high schools and ten colleges participating in the Mississippi Youth Council, an annual young people's forum sponsored by the Mississippi Speech Association, voted overwhelmingly against public assistance for the resistance organization. The North Mississippi Conference of the Methodist Church during the following spring protested against state support for an "extremist organization." [84]

In May, 1962, this festering dissidence came to a head when Erle Johnston, editor and publisher of the *Scott County Times* and public relations director of the Sovereignty Commission, launched a sustained public attack on the Citizens' Council. For his opening salvo, this self-styled "disillusioned charter member" of the Forest Citizens' Council chose a commencement address at Grenada High School, his alma mater. Mentioning neither the Council nor the NAACP by name, the former president of the Mississippi Press Association condemned "militant hotheads in

[82] Almost immediately, two of the plaintiffs, an officer of a local International Brotherhood of Electrical Workers and the local director of the Communications Workers of America, withdrew from the case under pressure from union rank and file. A third, attorney William L. Higgs, subsequently became involved in the case to admit James Meredith to the University of Mississippi and was disbarred from further practice in the state. Early in 1963 he left the state, saying that he feared for his life. The case itself was never prosecuted. See *Southern School News*, February, 1961, 4; Silver, *Mississippi: The Closed Society*, 79–80, 96–98.

[83] Moss Point *Advertiser*, April 21, 1961. Joe Patterson resigned from the CC after the organization opposed his reelection in 1963. See Memphis *Commercial Appeal*, April 4, 1965.

[84] Jackson *State Times*, December 4, 1961; editorial, *Scott County Times*, June 6, 1962.

both races"—a "five-letter organization financed by outsiders" and "a group which believes in threat and intimidation"—for systematically closing the avenues to racial reconciliation in the state. Calling himself "a practical segregationist who believes in recognition, cooperation and consideration of the colored race," the editor urged Grenada's class of 1962 to work together to bring a new day for race relations in Mississippi. "We can be practical," he advised, "without being radical. We can be realistic without being ridiculous." [85]

The Council's reaction was both immediate and predictable. Although not mentioning the incident in *The Citizen,* William J. Simmons used an interview with a United Press International correspondent to castigate the Barnett appointee to the Sovereignty Commission for his unseemly moderation. "Johnston sounds like he is ready to surrender," the national administrator asserted. "His approach is the sure way to integration." J. Paul Faulkner, Simmons's confidant and former president of the Jackson Council, added: "I think he [Johnston] has already surrendered." [86]

Replying in kind in the June 6 edition of his weekly newspaper, Johnston charged that "Mississippians can hardly make a move or say a word without approval of the Rajah of Race, Williams [*sic*] J. Simmons, who is Mr. Citizens' Council." Simmons and his professional staff, the editor continued, used "smoke screens of 'moderation' and 'integrationist' " to becloud every issue confronting the state. They had generated "fear and hysteria," turned "neighbor against neighbor," and encouraged "strife, confusion and violence." "Regardless of the original intentions of the Citizens Councils," he concluded, "it has degenerated into a handful of leaders who depend for their very existence on the friction, tension and emotionalism they can create. Its chief objective in Mississippi now appears to be making white people hate other white people." [87]

Even as the Johnston-Simmons feud unfolded, the state was girding itself to resist the court-ordered desegregation of the Uni-

[85] Interview with Erle Johnston. For the text of that address, see *Scott County Times,* May 30, 1962.

[86] Quoted in *Southern School News,* July, 1962, 2. Medgar Evers, speaking for the NAACP, was also extremely critical of Johnston's address.

[87] Editorial, *Scott County Times,* June 6, 1962.

versity of Mississippi. Given the temper of the times and the tenor of the Barnett regime, it appeared to many that the editor-public relations director had sacrificed his career in state government on the altar of moderation. Amid a spate of rumors, the *Clarion-Ledger*—"one of the trumpets of the Simmons policy," as Oliver Emmerich called it—reported that Johnston's resignation was forthcoming. The *Delta Democrat-Times,* in a rare moment of accord with the Hederman Press, agreed that "Erle Johnston's days are apparently numbered." "The Citizens Council's hatchet was out for Johnston," Hodding Carter observed, "and in this administration that's all that is needed to end someone's public career." As Johnston himself recalled, it was not so much a question whether he would be fired, but whether he would also be "hanged, drawn and quartered, or burned at the stake." [88]

But to the surprise of nearly everyone, the governor resisted Council pressure for Johnston's head. Not unmindful that it was his long-time friend from Scott County who had directed the publicity for his successful gubernatorial bid of 1959, Barnett postponed the Commission's June meeting so that tempers might cool. Then in July, after a heated two-hour session, Barnett (as the Commission's ex officio chairman) emerged to read a statement affirming that the state's anti-desegregation agency would take no stand in the Johnston-Simmons feud. Both men, the official resolution declared, were "dedicated segregationists. Both, in their respective fields, have made valuable contributions to the success of our cause. Mississippi needs . . . both men." Behind the neutral rhetoric, there was implicit in the July resolution a vote of confidence in Erle Johnston. In words reminiscent of those used in his Grenada commencement address, the Commission approved a "policy of cooperation with Negroes in an effort to maintain segregation in Mississippi as being in the best interest and welfare of both races." Those familiar with the scrappy country editor's skill as a political infighter were not surprised to learn later that—without the knowledge of the governor and all but one of the commissioners—the author of the "watch dog" agency's resolution was Johnston himself.[89]

[88] Editorials, McComb *Enterprise-Journal,* July 31; *Delta Democrat-Times,* July 23, 26; Jackson *State Times,* June 14, 1962; interview with Erle Johnston.

[89] The fullest and most useful account of this episode is Johnston's own

A more emphatic triumph for Johnston came in March, 1963, when he was named to succeed commission director Albert Jones. Although made over the strong objection of the organized segregationists, the appointment met the full approval of the governor. Recalling his feud with Simmons, Johnston could boast some years later that he was "the first state official ever to attack publicly the Citizens' Council leadership and not only survive politically, but to be promoted politically." Despite bitter extremist opposition, Johnston soon began to dismantle much of the "watch dog" committee's spy apparatus and place into "dormancy" its dossiers.[90] Consistently his policy was one of promoting conciliation and accommodation between the races. It must be noted, however, that throughout Johnston's tenure (1963–68), the Sovereignty Commission kept under surveillance "subversive outsiders" active in the civil rights movement in Mississippi.[91]

Before Mississippi could become aware that the Council had sustained its first major setback of the Barnett era, the state was plunged into the debacle at Oxford following the admission of James Howard Meredith to the University of Mississippi. The degree to which the organization influenced the chain of events culminating in a night of rioting at the Ole Miss campus remains conjectural. Doubtless the Reverend Murphey C. Wilds, pastor of the First Presbyterian Church of Oxford, exaggerated when he charged that "the governor's actions [throughout the crisis] were not so much his own as those of the council." [92] But it can be said without overstatement that no group did more to create the

---

untitled, unpublished, undated manuscript, in the file of Wilson Minor. See also *South*, 27 (August 6, 1962), 11; Memphis *Commercial Appeal*, October 28, 1962; *Southern School News*, November, 1962, 19.

90 Johnston, untitled manuscript; Birmingham *News*, March 25; *Delta Democrat-Times*, March 27, 1963; Silver, *Mississippi: The Closed Society*, 270–71.

91 In November, 1967, the Commission prepared for key state officials a 10,000-word secret report on its "intelligence operation." In an interview with the author, Johnston acknowledged that this confidential document was leaked to the press. For excerpts, see New York *Times*, July 29, 1968.

92 Quoted in Memphis *Commercial Appeal* and Jackson *Daily News*, December 5, 1962.

miasma of defiance and bigotry in which the violence of September 30–October 1, 1962, thrived. But even had it not been actively and directly involved in Mississippi's challenge to federal authority, the Citizens' Council, as the foremost advocate of resistance at any cost, would have to be held more than a little accountable for the turmoil. In fact, the Council's high command, despite its recent reversal in the Sovereignty Commission, remained privy to the maneuverings of the Barnett administration. Before delivering his televised executive proclamation of September 13, directing all state officials "to interpose the State Sovereignty and themselves between the people of the state and any body-politic seeking to usurp such power," the governor had sought the advice of the state's most outspoken champion of interposition, William J. Simmons. It was Simmons once again who stayed in the governor's suite at the Alumni House and served as Barnett's personal representative in Oxford during the week prior to Meredith's admission. Moreover, while the CCA's national administrator huddled in official strategy conferences on the campus and even addressed state law enforcement officers there on proper conduct, his chief aides, notably Executive Director Louis Hollis and Public Relations Director Richard Morphew, conferred regularly with Barnett in Jackson.[93]

Characteristically, the organization worked to create a resistance mentality through extralegal as well as legal channels. The barrage of incendiary statements and literature dispensed by state and local Councilors accounted in no small way for the high degree of student agitation apparent in a mob willing to assault—with bottles, bricks, fragments of concrete, and Molotov cocktails—battle-ready federal marshals. Whether encouraging students to defy university authority or, as the London *Economist* charged, "directing the hundreds of hoodlums to the university grounds on the night of the riot,"[94] the Council strove to foment sufficient

[93] "Mississippi Still Says 'Never'!" *The Citizen,* 6 (September, 1962), 6–10; New York *Times,* October 5, 1962; New Orleans *Times-Picayune,* January 13, 1963; Barrett, *Integration at Ole Miss,* 127–28.

[94] London *Economist,* January 12, 1963, 111. There is evidence which

bedlam to prevent desegregation. Although the group officially denounced violence, it appears that among its followers there were some who contemplated armed insurrection against the U.S. government. For example, an out-of-state Council spokesman, Willie Rainach, arrived on the university grounds at one point prior to the rioting promising to "organize a voluntary march to Oxford to join in the defense of Governor Barnett and the State of Mississippi." "Indications are that more than ten thousand Louisianans would join this march upon the proper call," the former Pelican State senator informed newsmen at an informal press conference. "They would come as volunteers, provided they would be given enlisted status in the Mississippi National Guard and assured a proper command." [95]

Also calling for a show of arms was retired Major General Edwin A. Walker, idol of the resistance movement and one-time commander of the 24th Infantry Division in West Germany. Walker believed, as he informed a Jackson Council rally only the previous December, that "the resolute determination with which the State of Mississippi has defended its sovereignty is related to the fact that few states have as high a percentage of men and women who know how to use firearms!" To insure effective mobilization and experienced direction of that "resolute determination," the man billed by the Citizens' Councils of America as "the general they couldn't muzzle" offered his assurances over a Shreveport radio station on September 26 that a federal "invasion" would bring him to Mississippi. Urging patriots everywhere to follow his lead, he called for "10,000 strong, from every state in the union" to "rally to the cause of freedom." [96] Fortunately, irregular armies such as

---

suggests that Simmons spent more than six hundred dollars in telephone calls to points across the South, urging militant segregationists to come to the campus "for a showdown with the federal government." See New Orleans *Times-Picayune,* January 13, 1963; and Lord, *The Past That Would Not Die,* 176–77.

[95] Quoted in Michael Dorman, *We Shall Overcome* (New York: Delacorte Press, 1964), 38.

[96] For a full text of Walker's address to the Jackson Council, see "There Is No Substitute for Victory!" *The Citizen,* 6 (January, 1962), 8–25. The Council also reproduced the general's address on a fifty-minute, high-fidelity phonograph record and a thirty-minute film. Both were entitled "The

these never materialized. Fearing that "thousands would be killed," Barnett did not encourage his enraged supporters from across the South to descend upon Oxford.[97] Nevertheless, General Walker did appear and, according to some accounts, actually led a charge against federal forces.

In the state capital, Council leaders were similarly at work fanning the flames of extremism across an already overwrought white populace. On Sunday afternoon, September 30, a short while before twenty-four federal marshals secretly escorted James Meredith to Baxter Hall on the Ole Miss campus, the Jackson Citizens' Council was inciting mob action against imagined federal intruders. Playing tape recordings of the state's official song, "Go Mississippi," and the governor's campaign theme, "Roll with Ross," the group assembled a throng of whites on the street between the headquarters of the CCA and the executive mansion. When approximately two thousand had gathered, immediate past President John R. Wright leaned from a window in the Council's third-floor suite with an electronic megaphone to read defiant statements from General Walker and Judge Brady. He warned that according to "reliable sources" federal forces were then en route to "seize" the governor. The angry, rebel flag–waving multitude complied when he directed them to form a human wall, five-deep around the mansion.[98]

Barnett, who in fact was already under heavy guard by the state highway patrol, did not need this kind of protection. To be sure, he had spent part of that day and several previous days effecting a detente with federal officials. Unknown even to many of his most intimate advisers—including Council professionals—he had agreed, in a series of secret telephone conversations with President John F. Kennedy and Attorney General Robert F. Kennedy, to a face-saving charade which called for his capitulation before a show of

General They Couldn't Muzzle." See also George B. Leonard, T. George Harris, and Christopher S. Wren, "How a Secret Deal Prevented a Massacre at Ole Miss," *Look*, 29 (December 31, 1962), 20; "Rebellion in Mississippi," *New Republic*, 197 (October 8, 1962), 3–4; Barrett, *Integration at Ole Miss*, 119.

[97] Interview with Barnett, June 23, 1970.

[98] Jackson *Daily News*, October 1, 1962; *Southern School News*, October, 1962, 12.

federal force.[99] As planned, he appeared on television at 7:30 p.m. to announce: "We are physically overpowered" and "surrounded on all sides by the armed forces and oppressive power of the United States of America." "My heart still says 'Never'," the governor intoned, "but my calm judgment abhors the bloodshed that would follow [further resistance]." Meredith was already on the campus.[100]

From this point forward, the Council's fortunes in Mississippi began to slip. Although it was not immediately apparent, the state's moderate voices achieved, in the aftermath of the Ole Miss crisis, a degree of saliency unknown for nearly a decade. Forces already at work undermining Council influence in state government were accelerated following the night of terror which brought death to two, injury to 375, and incalculable notoriety to Mississippi.[101] Almost at once, word circulated that Council professionals were being treated with perceptible coolness by the administration. By late October, the *Delta Democrat-Times* could even optimistically foresee a day when Council activities in the state would soon "dwindle down to the scope of a yapping dog—as they have in Arkansas, Louisiana, Tennessee and Georgia." Enheartened by rumors that Barnett was "infuriated" by Simmons's activities in connection with the Ole Miss crisis, editor Hodding Carter noted

99 Leonard, Harris, and Wren, "How a Secret Deal Prevented a Massacre at Ole Miss," 18–24, 29–36.

100 Barnett's "surrender" statement is quoted in full in Barrett, *Integration at Ole Miss,* 146. The Council's stunned reaction to this statement has been recorded in Leonard, Harris, and Wren, "How a Secret Deal Prevented a Massacre at Ole Miss," 19; and Lord, *The Past That Would Not Die,* 228.

101 The Citizens' Council had quite another view of the impact of the Ole Miss crisis on the organized resistance movement, and of the sequence of events in the rioting itself. See esp. letter from Robert Patterson to "Dear Friend," October 24, 1962, Mitchell Memorial Library; "Victory at Oxford," *The Citizen,* 6 (September, 1962), 2, 4; Richard D. Morphew, *Ole Miss and the Constitution, an Address to Associated Students of the California Institute of Technology, Pasadena, October 17, 1962* (n.p., n.d.). *Oxford: A Warning for Americans* (Jackson: Mississippi State Junior Chamber of Commerce, 1962) also reflects a point of view to which the Council subscribed. These accounts of the rioting should be compared with "Mississippi: The Sound and the Fury," *Newsweek,* 60 (October 15, 1962), 23–29; and "Though the Heavens Fall," *Time,* 30 (October 12, 1962), 19–22.

that the chief Councilor "had to cool his heels while waiting to see the governor recently. For a man who prior to September 30 seemed to be the governor in fact if not in title, this was a unique experience." [102]

There was additional evidence as well, for on October 18 the Sovereignty Commission announced that monthly payments to the Council "Forum" would thereafter be reduced from $4,500 to $2,000. Within six months, Erle Johnston, an opponent of the state subsidy, was appointed commission director; in July, 1963, the Council's tax fund subsidies were temporarily suspended.[103] In November, the subsidy was resumed, but the Council's days as a beneficiary of public revenues were clearly numbered. In December, 1964—amid charges that the "Forum's" audience had been vastly exaggerated, that its programs were, indeed, seen regularly in only a handful of stations in Mississippi and surrounding states [104]—payments were again suspended pending receipt by the state Budget Commission of a detailed accounting of all expenditures. The Council protested that during the six months prior to the last suspension it had provided 6,668 radio tapes and 520 television programs to local media in forty-six states, but it either could not or would not identify participating stations. No further payments were made by the Mississippi State Sovereignty Commission. In early 1965, however, its sister agency in Alabama contributed $1,500.[105]

[102] Editorial, *Delta Democrat-Times,* October 25, 1962. See also Memphis *Commercial Appeal,* December 7, 1962, January 13, 1963.

[103] Jackson *Clarion-Ledger,* October 19, 1962; *Southern School News,* November, 1962, 19; October, 1963, 2; November, 1963, 7; Jackson *Daily News,* October 19, 1963.

[104] In 1961, Hal DeCell, editor of the *Deer Creek Pilot* and former publicity director of the Sovereignty Commission, offered $100 to anyone able to produce a list of radio and television stations using the "Forum" outside the South. Having no takers, he concluded that the Council's national coverage was a "farce." Similarly, Robert Pittman, a Jackson *Daily News* reporter, surveyed the television stations claimed to be carrying the series. He learned that not more than eight stations, all of them southern, carried "Forum" programs regularly. See *Delta Democrat-Times,* December 29, 1961; and Minor, "The Citizens' Councils."

[105] In a letter to Erle Johnston, William Simmons refused to provide a list of "Forum" stations lest "pressure and harassment" be used against them. Unimpressed by Simmons's logic, Johnston later recalled his belief that the

The Council's alienation from the state government of Mississippi, a process begun during the Barnett administration, was completed following the inauguration of Governor Paul B. Johnson in January, 1964. A long-time supporter of organized resistance and a bellicose white supremacist who campaigned as the candidate who had "personally blocked" Meredith's initial effort to enter Ole Miss, Johnson so ardently wooed the segregationist vote that the daily press in Jackson could write approvingly of his "apparent romance" with the Citizens' Council. Widely recognized as the "Council candidate,"[106] he decisively defeated former Governor James P. Coleman in the runoff primary. As Democratic nominee he was a featured speaker at the CCA's annual leadership conference in Jackson during October. Addressing himself to that favorite Council theme, "Organization Is the Key to Victory," Johnson informed resistance spokesmen from sixteen states that the region's governors could hope to preserve segregation only if "people in every county or parish . . . band[ed] themselves together into strong local Citizens' Councils." According to *The Citizen,* which carried excerpts from the address in an inauguration eve edition, the message clearly charted "Mississippi's course for the next four years."[107]

But the promise of Paul Johnson's leadership conference address was never fulfilled. The next quadrennium would prove disastrous for the Council. Johnson's enthusiasm for organized extremism

---

"Forum's" range was "extremely limited" outside of the state. (Simmons to Johnston, March 15, 1965, copy in Cox Materials, Mitchell Memorial Library; interview with Erle Johnston, June 25, 1970. See also letter, Joe T. Patterson, attorney general, to Erle Johnston, March 26, 1965, copy in the file of Wilson Minor; financial report of the Citizens' Council Forum, Inc., to Mississippi Commission of Budget and Accounting, copy in Cox Materials; letters, Eli Howell, executive secretary, Alabama State Sovereignty Commission, to William J. Simmons, February 18, March 23, 1965, copies in Cox Materials.)

[106] Jackson *Daily News,* April 8; Jackson *Clarion-Ledger,* April 28; *Delta Democrat-Times,* August 2, 1963; Cook, "Political Movements and Organizations," in Avery Leiserson, ed., *The American South in the 1960's* (New York: Praeger, 1964), 139. For an example of Johnson's pre-gubernatorial views on the Citizens' Council, see *The Citizens' Council,* June, 1961, 1, 4.

[107] *The Citizen,* 8 (December, 1963), 8–11.

did not even survive the inauguration ceremonies. Indeed, no sooner did state Supreme Court Justice Tom P. Brady administer the oath of office than the new governor pledged that "hate, prejudice or ignorance" would not be forces motivating his administration. Warning that "we are Americans as well as Mississippians," that "[we are] a part of this world, whether we like it or not," he obliquely dismissed the negative programs of the Citizens' Council as a "rear-guard defense of yesterday." Mississippi, he declared, must now begin "an all-out assault for our share of tomorrow."[108]

Perhaps it may not be said that during his term of office Paul Johnson was an unswerving apostle of progress. But he must be ranked among that growing number of the state's business, civic, and political leaders who recoiled from violence and recognized the futility of bitter-end resistance. For all of his strident electioneering, this belated convert to moderation recognized the erosive effects of extremism on the welfare of the state and on its image within the nation. Although capable of damning the *Brown* decision and the Civil Rights Act of 1964 in the most colorful language, he knew, as he told an audience of Jackson businessmen, that "we are our own architects of the doghouse in which we find ourselves."[109] Under his capable and constructive leadership, the state moved toward a grudging accommodation with the law of the land.

Johnson did not openly break with the Council, but he managed to disassociate himself from it. During and immediately following his campaign, he often spoke at its gatherings. But after his inauguration he became unavailable. When the Jackson Citizens' Council staged its "White Monday in Mississippi" rally on the eleventh anniversary of the Supreme Court decision, he was conveniently out of the state. Although Governor George C. Wallace was the principal speaker and gubernatorial courtesy seemed to require the Mississippi governor's presence, Johnson found it necessary to be in Washington for last-minute instructions to the Mississippi Marketing Council then en route to Europe on a trade

[108] Quoted in Memphis *Commercial Appeal*, January 22, 1964.

[109] Quoted in Meridian *Star*, January 30; New Orleans *Times-Picayune*, March 7, 1965.

mission. In his stead, former Governor Barnett was called upon to introduce the visiting dignitary to an enthusiastic crowd of perhaps 6,500 whites waving Confederate flags and "Wallace for President" signs. Newspaper accounts reported that cries of "Where's Paul" were heard and that placards bore such messages as "We're through with LBJ and PBJ."[110] Similarly, when the CCA's annual leadership conference for 1965 convened in Montgomery, Johnson was conspicuously absent. Once again it was Ross Barnett who represented Mississippi "officialdom," who posed beneath a Confederate flag for photographs with Governor Wallace, and who lectured to the gathering on a "Strategy for Survival."[111]

Johnson's determination to disengage himself from the organization with which he had so long been identified was also apparent during the presidential election of 1964. Almost alone among the Democratic governors of the South, he broke with his party to endorse openly the Republican candidate, Senator Barry Goldwater of Arizona. But unlike Barnett four years before, he did not link his defection with the efforts of the Citizens' Council. Yet, with or without the governor's leadership, the organization remained determined to elect a president sympathetic to the objectives of the resistance movement. Apparently undaunted by the debacle of 1960, there were indications as late as the fall of 1963 that Councilors in several states were determined to wage another unpledged elector campaign.[112] But by the spring of 1964, as Governor Wallace entered presidential primaries in Wisconsin, Indiana, and Maryland and the Republican nomination of Senator Barry Goldwater loomed ever more certain, all serious consideration of such a venture was abandoned. When Wallace withdrew his third-party candidacy in mid-July in deference to the conservative Republican standard-bearer, the movement's professional

110 Simmons devoted the entire June, 1965, issue of *The Citizen* to the "highlights" of the "White Monday" rally. See also Jackson *Daily News*, May 18; *Delta Democrat-Times*, May 19; McComb *Enterprise-Journal*, as quoted in *Delta Democrat-Times*, May 24, 1965.

111 See the entire issue of *The Citizen*, 9 (March, 1965) for details of the conference, including Barnett's address.

112 Jackson *Daily News*, July 17, October 27; Lexington *Advertiser*, June 20, 1963.

leadership began mustering states' rights support for the Arizona senator, who had voted against the Civil Rights Act of 1964. Although the Citizens' Councils of America remained officially neutral, its major spokesmen did express their support for the GOP candidate; and Roy V. Harris, then serving his sixth consecutive one-year term as president of the CCA, organized a "Democrats for Goldwater" group in his home state of Georgia.[113] There was, however, no concerted Citizens' Council campaign for Goldwater on state and local levels in the South. To be sure, with membership at an all-time low and many state and local organizations either inactive or on the verge of collapse, it can hardly be said that there was even a regional Council movement by 1964.

Nevertheless, the organization men in Jackson's Plaza Building—doubtlessly encouraged by the decision of Senator J. Strom Thurmond to change his partisan affiliation in order to campaign for Goldwater[114]—predicted that the Republican party would ride the crest of a white southern backlash vote to victory. Late in the campaign, Simmons even released a Citizens' Councils of America "survey" purporting to show that on election day it would be Goldwater by a "landslide of major proportions." While virtually all professional polls—including those commissioned by the Republican national committee—indicated Johnson to be a heavy favorite, the Council's opinion sample revealed that the Arizonian's electoral total could be as high as 405 votes.[115]

[113] See Association of Citizens' Councils of Georgia, *Bulletin*, October, 1964; Ross Barnett, "Why the South Will Win This Fight!" *The Citizen*, 8 (July–August, 1964), 14; Roy V. Harris, "What Does the Election Prove?" *The Citizen*, 9 (November, 1964), 6–7; Atlanta *Constitution*, July 18; Houston *Chronicle*, July 22; New York *Times*, September 15; Washington *Post*, August 11, 1964.

[114] In the entire southern congressional delegation, the only other bolters were Representatives Albert Watson of South Carolina and John Bell Williams of Mississippi. Among the region's governors, only Wallace of Alabama and Johnson of Mississippi crossed party lines to support openly the GOP ticket. See Stanley Kelley, Jr., "The Presidential Campaign," *The National Election of 1964*, ed. Milton C. Cummings, Jr. (Washington: Brookings Institution, 1966), 68.

[115] Ibid., 43–45, 70; Stephen C. Shadegg, *What Happened to Goldwater? The Inside Story of the 1964 Republican Campaign* (New York: Holt, Rine-

Whether the Council's survey reflected faulty sampling techniques or, as seems more likely, an advanced case of wishful thinking, it did not reflect the verdict at the polls. For although the Republican ticket did win considerable support in the traditionally Democratic South, it sustained one of the worst defeats in American history. Carrying only his home state and the five states of the Deep South, the man considered by many dedicated segregationists to be the "candidate of the southern white man" polled 47 percent of Dixie's total vote; but nationally, he was buried by a Democratic popular majority of 61 percent.

Without so much as a sideways glance at its preelection forecast, the organization expressed delight that "more than 26½ million white Americans had backlashed their way to the polls—despite the G.O.P.'s seeming efforts to drive them away." Far from a mandate for the Johnson administration's "pro-Negro" policies, the election of 1964, as *The Citizen* interpreted it, demonstrated conclusively the folly of a timid stand on racial integrity. Although sound on most questions of domestic and international concern, the conservative wing of the Republican party, like the John Birch Society, refused to recognize the "realities" of race. By studiously avoiding the segregation issue, the nation's most salient issue, it failed to win the support of "uncounted millions" who believed that "America is still a white man's country." But, despite his misdirected focus, Goldwater's "eminently respectable showing" reflected a vast "power base" of discontent with the "Liberal Establishment." "Judicious cultivation" of that discontent during the next four years, the monthly journal asserted, could result in the election of a segregationist in 1968.[116]

Clearly, *The Citizen*'s election post mortem analysis indicated

---

hart and Winston, 1965), 241; Memphis *Commercial Appeal,* November 8, 1964; Silver, *Mississippi: The Closed Society,* 324.

116 "The Backlashers," *The Citizen,* 9 (November, 1964), 2, 23. In the same issue, see also Harris, "What Does the Election Prove?" 4–7; and Edward Hunter, "Don't Be Downhearted—Here's Why," 13–21. Perhaps the Pollyanna-ish tone of the Council's postelection analysis was best explained by Hunter, chairman of the ultrarightest Anti-Communist Liaison: "Anyone on our side who spreads despondency is doing the work of the enemy. . . . They must be shut up for the sake of our survival in freedom!"

that the Council was unready to say after Frederick Douglass that "the Republican party is the island; all else is the sea." Indeed, the GOP's "obsessive concentration on extraneous trivia" to the exclusion of race only reinforced a belief widely held in segregation circles that the political home of the white supremacist was not to be found within the two-party system. Unable to find fulfillment even within the conservative wing of the Republican party, the organized resistance movement turned once again to the politics of desperation. The campaign of 1968 found the organization devoting all of its energies to the election of American Independent Party candidate George C. Wallace. One of the few politicians of national prominence still willing to identify openly with the movement, Wallace remained the personification of Council aspirations. Although he skillfully substituted such code words as "law and order" for his more customary brand of strident Negrophobia, the Deep South segregationist's message was unmistakable. As Roy V. Harris, state chairman for Wallace in Georgia, predicted early in the campaign, "When you get right down to it, there's really only going to be one issue, and you spell it n-i-g-g-e-r." [117]

Protesting as always that the organization was nonpolitical and nonpartisan, Council professionals, nevertheless, made every effort to link their movement to the rising political star of its long-time ally. Although Wallace ran with the support of a wide range of extremist groups, including Kent Courtney's Congress of Conservatives, the Minute Men's Patriotic Party, and Robert Shelton's United Klans of America, *The Citizen* boasted that, among all nationwide conservative groups, it alone possessed an "infrastructure" adequate to elect the Alabama firebrand.[118]

Almost from the moment of the Goldwater debacle, the Council began boosting Wallace; in February, 1967, even before he announced his formal candidacy, it kicked off its own "Stand up for America" campaign to promote the "new force" in American politics. Across Dixie and beyond, Councilors figured prominently in

[117] Quoted in Lewis Chester, Godfrey Hodgson, Bruce Page, *An American Melodrama: The Presidential Campaign of 1968* (New York: Viking Press, 1969), 280.

[118] *The Citizen*, February, 1967, 15. On Wallace's right-wing support, see Cleghorn, *Radicalism*, 10–12.

the third-party effort. Top Council leaders serving as chairmen or co-chairmen of the Wallace movement in their respective states included William J. Simmons, Leander Perez, and William K. Shearer, as well as Roy Harris. And the organization's rank and file was numbered solidly in the hard core of Wallace support.[119] Without much exaggeration, one Council spokesman could declare that "every member of the Citizens' Council is for George Wallace." [120]

Not taken seriously at first by many critics, Wallace nevertheless proved to be the most formidable third-party contender since 1912. But for all of his broad financial support and impressive strength at the polls (36 percent of the southern vote and 13.5 of the national total), he, too, was a disappointment to the segregationists. While he engendered considerable enthusiasm among lower-middle-class and blue-collar voters in the North, he failed to win a large vote in any industrial state. Mistrusted by respectable conservatives both within and without the region, unable to stem the rising tide of New South Republicanism in peripheral states, the Alabamian failed even to match Goldwater's southern vote of 1964. Nevertheless, the Council's organization men could review the election statistics with some optimism. With little fear of contradiction they pointed to the events of 1968 as evidence that a heightened sense of "racial awareness" was abroad in the land north of the Potomac—a development which could only augur well for organized resistance. Perhaps, as one sympathetic observer declared, they could even view the nearly 10 million Wallace voters in fifty states as a "potential membership." [121]

Thus, even before the placards of 1968 were pulled down, Council leadership launched a "Wallace in '72" movement. Through the creation of a permanent, national American Independent Party, they could cling to the hope of electing a segregationist president. If, in the process, the resistance movement should be revitalized, that too would be a welcome development.

[119] Interview with William J. Simmons, June 26, 1970; *The Citizen* (April, 1967); New Orleans *Times-Picayune*, February 18; and Chicago *Defender*, February 25–March 3, 1967.

[120] *The Citizen*, April, 1967, 8. See also the issue for January, 1969, 8.

[121] John J. Synon, "My Friends of the Citizens' Council," ibid., January 1969, 4.

PART V

Epilogue

CHAPTER XV

Southern White Resistance and the Second Reconstruction

From the tenuous vantage point of 1956, C. Vann Woodward designated the revolutionary era in race relations ushered in by the Supreme Court's school desegregation decision of 1954 as the "New Reconstruction." Although careful not to strain the analogy, he suggested that the Second Reconstruction, perhaps not less than the first, was an "all-out effort by the majority to impose its will upon a recalcitrant and unwilling minority region." Federal efforts to effect sweeping social change within the South during the post-*Brown* period, like those of the post–Civil War period, were jeopardized by widespread white determination to resist. Although cautiously confident that the Second Reconstruction would succeed where the first had not, the liberal historian of the South conceded that "the optimism of 1954 has given way to the prevailing pessimism of 1956," and that "many minds are hounded by the prospect that the New Reconstruction is doomed in the end to repeat the frustration and failure of the Old Reconstruction." [1]

[1] C. Vann Woodward, "The 'New Reconstruction' in the South," *Commentary,* 21 (June, 1956), 501–8. Woodward provided a more fully developed statement of this theme in "From the First Reconstruction to the Second," *Harper's,* 230 (April, 1965), 127–33; and Ch. 5, "The Declining Years of Jim Crow," in *The Strange Career of Jim Crow,* 2nd rev. ed. (New York: Oxford University Press, 1966), 143–51.

Not remarkably, organized resistance leaders found this analogy immensely appealing. Particularly comforting was Woodward's appraisal of the Citizens' Council's own role in the growing "contagion of defiance." Noting that white resistance had coalesced around the Mississippi Plan of 1890 to disfranchise the Negro, he reported that a third Mississippi Plan, the Citizens' Council, had emerged in 1954 to place the Magnolia State once again in the vanguard of the unsubmissive South. Already disposed to view their organization as the last bastion against a vicious federal tyranny, the Council's professional spokesmen applauded Woodward's "surprising candor" and then adopted his historical parallel as their own. In the columns of the organization's monthly newspaper, its pamphlets, and its public statements, they asserted that the "stark terror" of "black Reconstruction" was once again abroad in Dixie.[2] Thus, in an address to the Jefferson Society of the University of Virginia in March, 1963, William J. Simmons charged that "Reconstruction II," "backed by forces even more powerful and insidious" than "Reconstruction I," had endeavored for nearly a decade to destroy the very foundations of southern civilization. From the "violent parallel of military occupation" in Little Rock and Oxford to the "star chamber prosecution" of state officials by federal judges, a "radical coalition" of northern fanatics, self-seeking carpetbaggers, faithless scalawags, and ignorant blacks was "following the familiar pattern of the First Reconstruction." In the Civil Rights Commission, the CCA administrator even discovered a "modern Freedmen's Bureau," luring the "massive Negro bloc vote" with "the bait of surplus commodity handouts and cash welfare payments instead of forty acres and a mule." [3]

Unquestionably, a white supremacist organization could find a kind of perverse satisfaction in indulging its fantasies in lurid

[2] See, for example, editorials, "Issue Has Been Force," and "New Reconstruction Compared with Old," *The Citizens' Council*, December, 1956, 2–4; William J. Simmons, *A Comparison of Attitudes during Reconstruction I and II: Address to Jefferson Davis Camp No. 635 Sons of Confederate Veterans, Jackson, Mississippi, April 5, 1962* (n.p., n.d.); Hollis, *John H. Wisdom, the Man Who Saved Rome.*

[3] William J. Simmons, *Civil Rights and the Second Reconstruction: An Address to the Jefferson Society, University of Virginia, Charlottesville, March 22, 1963.*

comparisons between the post-*Brown* and the postbellum periods. No less certainly, its recruiters recognized that the traditional portrait of Reconstruction—etched as it was in darkly tragic hues of unrelieved brutality, scandal, and licentiousness—could be exploited to inflame white southern sentiment. But it was as a portent of the future, rather than as a distorted image of the past, that Councilors found Woodward's analogy most serviceable. Pointedly, Simmons reminded the movement's rank and file that "the white South won a total victory in Reconstruction I by showing its determination to fight and by organizing from one end of the region to the other." So, too, he asserted, could a determined white South, united under the standard of the Citizens' Council, emerge triumphant over Reconstruction II. Mid-twentieth-century "radicals" and "scalawags" to the contrary, then, desegregation was not inevitable; it had been evaded once, and it could be evaded again.[4]

There were, of course, aspects of the earlier battle for southern redemption—and particularly the original Mississippi Plan—with which the Citizens' Council sought no identification. Foremost among those were the paramilitarism and violence used by the defeated Confederates with such telling effect to intimidate the freedman and frustrate the designs of his white advocates. Although organized terrorism during Reconstruction was most frequently attributed to the Ku Klux Klan, there were numerous secret, quasi-military societies variously identified as the Sons of Midnight, Native Sons of the South, Knights of the Black Cross, Society of the White Rose, and Red Spirited Brandy Wine Tigers. Whether drilling as irregular militia in areas of heavy Negro population during broad daylight or engaging in hooded adventures under cover of darkness, these organizations sought systematically to intimidate all those unsympathetic to white supremacy and the defeat of congressional Reconstruction.

The similarities between these organizations and the segregation groups of the post-*Brown* years were obvious, particularly to critics. To most northern observers, and to many southern moderates and liberals as well, the Council was simply a middle-class variant of the Ku Klux Klan. It was a "new, sinister Ku Klux

[4] Simmons, *Comparison of Attitudes during Reconstruction I and II.*

Klan," a "current version of the Ku Klux Klan," a "scrubbed-up cousin of the Klan," a "white-collar Klan," an "uptown Klan," a "button-down Klan," and a "country club Klan."[5] Typical of the views of much of the nation's opinion-forming media was the reaction of the editor of the Milwaukee *Journal,* who identified the organization as the "hateful specter of the old Ku Klux Klan riding again, without robes or nooses or whips, but practicing the same sadism and terrorism with more subtle weapons for the same purpose."[6]

In reality, the Council demonstrated a marked preference for the subtler forms of intimidation. Disdaining exotic rituals, secret oaths, and paraphernalia of disguise, just as it eschewed the rope, fagot, and whip, it forswore lawlessness and pledged itself to strictly legal means of defiance. Whatever may have been the theoretical relationship between the explosive atmosphere it so often created and the actual outbreak of violence, there is no tangible evidence which suggests that it engaged in, or even overtly encouraged, criminal acts. From time to time individual Council members were implicated in acts of vigilantism, including homicide and bombing, but the organization itself was never directly linked with these things.[7]

With some pride, then, a brief, official history of the movement could note from the perspective of 1964 that the "channeling of popular resistance to integration into lawful, coherent and proper

[5] See, for example, editorial in *Arkansas Gazette,* February 10, 1960; Jack Anderson and Drew Pearson, "Washington Merry-Go-Round," Atlanta *Journal,* September 16; *The Christian Century,* February 22, 1956; McGill, "The South Has Many Faces," 92; and Newby, *Challenge to the Court,* 6.

[6] Quoted in J. J. Seldin, "The Dixie Boycott: Is Your Brand 'Pure White'?" *Nation,* 182 (April, 1956), 360.

[7] Perhaps the most celebrated such case was that of Byron de la Beckwith, accused murderer of NAACP leader Medgar Evers. A fertilizer salesman and prominent member of the Greenwood, Mississippi, Citizens' Council, Beckwith enjoyed the full support of the statewide organization during his trial. Key Council leaders, including Ellett Lawrence, state finance chairman, and R. F. Parish, state treasurer, organized a White Citizens' Legal Fund to underwrite the expenses of the Greenwood Councilor's trial. The episode ended in two mistrials. (Memphis *Commercial Appeal,* July 9; Greenwood *Commonwealth,* June 24, 1963; Jackson *Daily News,* February 4, 1964; several untitled and undated broadsides distributed by the White Citizens' Legal Fund, SERS.)

modes" was perhaps the "outstanding accomplishment of the Citizens' Council."[8] By that date, however, there were few other durable contributions to which the organization could point. The counterrevolution it once claimed to lead managed only to slow the processes of change, not to still them. Despite a dogged white southern determination to resist, despite even an elaborate regional network of legal devices designed to circumvent the Court's school desegregation decision, the federal government remained unshaken in its resolve to guarantee equality for black Americans. In the face of seemingly irresistible pressures for compliance, the vast majority of the region's whites were making at least token adjustments to the nation's changing pattern of race relations. Undesirable though even limited segregation may have been, all but the most intractable clearly evinced a preference for the new order to the chaos that last-ditch defiance would surely bring. To be sure, there was no wholesale compliance. Nor had the American dilemma, as posed by Gunnar Myrdal some two decades before, been resolved. Yet few could doubt that the Second Reconstruction promised to be an enduring phenomenon, and fewer still would deny that it had already wrought a modest revolution within a reluctant South.

A principal casualty of this "revolution" was, of course, the resistance movement itself. The advance of desegregation, agonizingly slow though it was, critically eroded the Council's popular appeal. In the years immediately following the 1954 ruling, whites from every station of southern life—fearful lest any disruption of the color-caste system be followed by social upheaval—pledged themselves to defend the status quo. Confident in the oft-tendered assurance that regional social customs would remain undisturbed if they, even as had their forebears, but organized to resist the federal intrusion, they rallied by the thousands to the banner of "states' rights and racial integrity." They were soon to discover, however, that the Citizens' Council was frail protection against the leveling force of the Second Reconstruction. For it could no more halt the march of social change in an increasingly democratic and equalitarian society than it could restore the intellectual tenability of the old dogmas of white supremacy. Perhaps inevitably, then,

[8] Patterson, *The Citizens' Council: A History*, 4–5.

once it became apparent that some degree of desegregation was unavoidable, that the nation's much-vaunted commitment to racial justice could not again be deferred indefinitely, widespread popular ardor for organized defiance cooled.

Having promised much more than it could deliver, the movement began to decline soon after the confrontation of state and federal governments in Little Rock. Thereafter, as total defiance gave way to token compliance in state after state, it grew increasingly ineffective. By 1961, it had all but disappeared in the peripheral states, and in the Deep South, where its power and prestige had always been greatest, the movement was demoralized and in disarray. An ambitious regional remobilization drive, begun in that year by the Citizens' Councils of America, resulted in the reorganization of many local and most state Councils. But it did not restore the movement to its original vitality. The CCA did manage, however, to assume greater control over state and local affairs. This accomplished, it began a drive in 1964 to create a nationwide Council network by carrying the movement into northern and western states. Although the organization softened its position on race in favor of issues more appealing to nonsouthern conservatives, this attempt proved largely unsuccessful.

For all of its long-range failures, the Council figured prominently in the history of both region and nation during the formative years of the second great age of civil rights. Despite its minority status even in the states of the Deep South, it was an effective defender of white supremacy. That it did not stem the gradual retreat of institutionalized segregation should not obscure the role it played in minimizing the impact of the larger implications of the *Brown* ruling on the land south of the Potomac. In the Deep South, the Council exercised formidable, sometimes even decisive, influence over state and local politics, enforced a rigid conformity to racial orthodoxy among whites, and employed a systematic program of fear and reprisal to minimize black challenges to segregation. In the upper South, however, the organized resistance movement was vibrant only in Virginia. Although occasionally authoritative on the local level, statewide Councils or Council-like groups in Arkansas, Florida, North Carolina, Tennessee, and Texas possessed neither public influence nor popular esteem.

Although scarcely resembling the grass-roots protest of the early post-*Brown* years, the Citizens' Council survives to the present day. The vitality of its appeal long since sapped, its legion of followers thoroughly dissipated, its negative programs almost universally discredited, the organization obstinately perseveres as a poignant, perhaps even pitiable, symbol of that distressingly large minority of Americans who are unable or unwilling to pay more than lip service to the nation's equalitarian ideals. To be sure, the bitter-enders who march in its shrunken ranks betray no sign of a softening of attitude. They cling desperately to the faith that the indomitable will of the southern white man will ultimately triumph over federal law to bring redemption once again to the troubled South. Grasping at straws, they place great store in the mounting national impatience with racial unrest. Unquestionably, they are encouraged by recent developments along the nation's uneasy racial front—by the widespread protest against lawless black militants; by the astonishing political appeal of backlash candidate George C. Wallace; by the apparent influence in conservative Republican circles of such unreconstructed neo-Confederates as J. Strom Thurmond; by the implications, both real and fancied, of President Richard M. Nixon's much-discussed and much-denied "southern strategy"; by the nationwide outcry against busing to achieve racial balance in the schools; by the waning of white northern zeal for equalitarianism in the face of federal recognition of de facto as well as de jure segregation; and, most of all, by the federal judiciary's belated discovery of race discrimination on the northern side of the Mason-Dixon line.

In the somber light of such developments, one finds small comfort in the knowledge that the horizons of citizenship have broadened appreciably for black Americans since 1954. For the gulf between the customary national cant about human equality and the grave realities of racial injustice in this democracy remains disturbingly wide. Surely this is the burden of white America, and this, too, its tragedy.

Bibliographical Note

The following essay does not represent an effort to list all sources used in the preparation of this study. Materials not herein discussed are to be found either in the footnotes or the author's unpublished manuscript located in the Joint Universities Library, Nashville, Tennessee.

MANUSCRIPT COLLECTIONS

Manuscript sources available to students of the organized resistance movement, like those of the Ku Klux Klan, are in short supply. The Citizens' Councils of America made available a formidable body of printed matter; but with the major exception of its "White Book of Citizens' Council Organization" (unpublished volume, rev. ed., Jackson, Mississippi, 1965), a semi-secret manual for Council leaders, it politely refused all requests for material of a more intimate nature. Similarly, private archives of state Council associations either did not exist or were closed to researchers. Quite unlike many Klan leaders, however, Councilors often proved willing not only to answer letters of inquiry but to submit to personal interviews. On two occasions William J. Simmons, the organization's most authoritative spokesman, reminisced at length for the author's benefit. Other Council leaders and their allies who either permitted interviews or wrote long and informative letters were Ross Barnett, Judge Tom P. Brady, Lola Lee Bruington, Samuel M. Engelhardt, Medford Evans, Louis W. Hollis, Willie M. Rainach, William K. Scarborough, J. Barrye Wall, and William D. Workman. The recollections of other firsthand observers, including Erle Johnston, Hazel Brannon Smith, Kenneth Dean, Wilson Minor, and Claude Ramsey, also proved valuable. A particularly useful source of information was Mrs. Meredith Crown, who in telephone conversations and extensive correspondence revealed much about the movement's organizational endeavors on the West Coast.

Although future students of organized resistance can hope to exploit the records of governmental agencies, particularly those of the Department of Justice, such vital material was unavailable at this early date. Fortunately, other manuscript collections were open. The Eugene Cox Materials and the Segregation File, both in the Mitchell Memorial Library, Mississippi State University, have letters and other unpublished documents of major importance to the history of Council growth and activity in Mississippi. Special Collections at the same library contain a complete file of transcripts from Citizens' Council "Forum" television and radio series. The Citizens' Council Files of the Anti-Defamation League's Southern Office in Atlanta also contain a wealth of primary source material. In addition to Council letters and unpublished by-laws and constitutions from many states, the A-DL has preserved memoranda from its field agents (undercover and otherwise) whose firsthand reports of Council activities are extremely useful. Also very helpful were the Miscellaneous Files of the now-defunct Southern Education Reporting Service in Nashville, Tennessee. SERS endeavored to collect not only all printed material pertaining to the Council but many manuscript sources as well. This major collection has been microfilmed and is available through *Facts on Film* (164 rolls, 1958–1967). A similar, though less extensive collection is the Resistance Group Files of the Southern Regional Council in Atlanta. Although this file contains an abundance of primary sources, it is most noteworthy for the materials gathered by Norman Kilpatrick, a Maryland civil rights activist who infiltrated the movement. Small private collections owned by Terry Alford, State College, Mississippi, and Wilson Minor, Jackson, Mississippi, also contain useful primary materials.

PUBLIC DOCUMENTS

Government publications, particularly the reports of the state advisory committees on civil rights, are among the more rewarding sources on race relations in the recent South. Among the most helpful are: Arkansas Advisory Committee to the U.S. Commission on Civil Rights, *Report on Arkansas: Education* (Washington, 1963); Louisiana State Advisory Committee on Civil Rights, *The New Orleans School Crisis* (Washington, 1961); Mississippi Advisory Committee to the U.S. Commission on Civil Rights, *Administration of Justice in Mississippi* (Washington, 1963); State Advisory Committees to the U.S. Commission on Civil Rights, *The 50 States Report* (Washington, 1961); U.S. Commission on Civil Rights, *Hearings*, New Orleans, September 27–28, 1960, May 5–6, 1961 (Washington, 1961); U.S. Commission on Civil Rights, *Report, 1959* (Washington, 1959); U.S. Commission on Civil Rights, *Civil Rights U.S.A. Public Schools, Southern States, 1962* (Washington, n.d.); U.S. Commission on Civil Rights, *Survey of School Desegration in the Southern and Border States, 1965–66* (Washington, 1961); U.S. Congress, Senate, *Hearings before the Subcommittee on Constitutional Rights of the Committee on the Judiciary*, 85 Cong., 1957; Harry K. Wright, *Civil Rights U.S.A. Public Schools, Southern States, 1963: Texas* (Washington, 1964).

AUTOBIOGRAPHIES AND MEMOIRS

Although the flow of autobiographical writing has hardly begun, a number of major participants in the controversies of the first decade of desegregation have already recorded their experiences. Out of the Montgomery bus boycott came a pair of contrasting views by two black ministers: Uriah J. Fields, *The Montgomery Story: The Unhappy Effects of the Montgomery Bus Boycott* (New York, 1950); and Martin Luther King, Jr., *Stride toward Freedom: The Montgomery Story* (New York, 1958). Public school desegregation in Little Rock has been covered from several vantage points, most notably by the superintendent of the city's schools, Virgil Blossom, *It Has Happened Here* (New York, 1959); an Episcopal bishop, Robert R. Brown, *Bigger Than Little Rock* (Greenwich, 1958); and an NAACP leader, Daisy Bates, *The Long Shadow of Little Rock* (New York, 1962). The most memorable political memoirs to date are James F. Byrnes, *All in One Lifetime* (New York, 1958); Brooks Hays, *A Southern Moderate Speaks* (Chapel Hill, 1959); and Frank E. Smith, *Congressman from Mississippi* (New York, 1964). The story of school desegregation in the mountain community of Clinton, Tennessee, has been told by a moderate educator, Margaret Anderson, *The Children of the South* (New York, 1966). P. D. East, *The Magnolia Jungle: The Life, Times, and Education of a Southern Editor* (New York, 1960); and Ira B. Harkey, Jr., *The Smell of Burning Crosses: An Autobiography of a Mississippi Newspaperman* (Jacksonville, Ill., 1967), report on the hazards of liberal journalism in the Deep South. Two Ole Miss professors and a student, Russell H. Barrett, *Integration at Ole Miss* (Chicago, 1965), James W. Silver, *Mississippi: The Closed Society*, 3rd ed. (New York, 1966), and James H. Meredith, *Three Years in Mississippi* (Bloomington, 1966), have published their reflections on life inside a university and a state caught in the vortex of social change.

CITIZENS' COUNCIL AND OTHER PROSEGREGATION BOOKS AND PAMPHLETS

(Among the items omitted from this list are dozens of articles reprinted from *The Citizen.* Other omissions include a mass of repetitious material used for recruitment purposes by local Councils.)

Alford, Dale, and L'Moore Alford. *The Case of the Sleeping People (Finally Awakened by Little Rock School Frustrations).* Little Rock: Pioneer Press, 1959.

Annual Report: August, 1955. Winona: Association of Citizens' Councils of Mississippi, 1955.

2nd Annual Report: August, 1956. Greenwood: Association of Citizens' Councils of Mississippi, 1956.

4th Annual Report: August, 1958. Greenwood: Association of Citizens' Councils of Mississippi, 1958.

[Association of Citizens' Councils]. *School Tomorrow.* Greenwood: Greenwood-Leflore Educational Foundation, n.d.

Barnett, Ross R. *Strength through Unity! An Address to Citizens' Council Rally, New Orleans, March 7, 1960.* Greenwood: Association of Citizens' Councils of Mississippi, n.d.

Barrett, J. Paul. *The Church and Segregation.* Augusta: States' Rights Council of Georgia, n.d.

Bilbo, Theodore G. *Take Your Choice: Separation or Mongrelization.* Poplarville, Miss.: Dream House Publishing Co., 1947.

Bodenhamer, William T. *The Aims and Purposes of the States' Rights Council of Georgia, Inc.* Atlanta: States' Rights Council of Georgia, n.d.

———. *Who Started Segregated Schools in Georgia?* Atlanta: States' Rights Council of Georgia, n.d.

Bloch, Charles J. *The Need for States' Rights Councils and Citizens' Councils.* Atlanta: States' Rights Council of Georgia, 1957.

———. *States' Rights: The Law of the Land.* Atlanta: Harrison County, 1958.

———. *We Need Not Integrate to Educate.* Atlanta: States' Rights Council of Georgia, n.d.

Brady, Tom P. *Black Monday.* Winona: Association of Citizens' Councils of Mississippi, 1955.

———. *Impending Educational Crisis: Address to Mississippi Secondary Principals, Jackson, Mississippi, March 20, 1958.* N.p., n.d.

———. *A Review of Black Monday.* Greenwood: Association of Citizens' Councils of Mississippi, [1955].

———. *Segregation and the South: An Address to the Commonwealth Club of California, San Francisco, October 4, 1957.* Greenwood: Association of Citizens' Councils of Mississippi, n.d.

A Brief History of the States' Rights Council of Georgia, Inc. Atlanta: States' Rights Council of Georgia, n.d.

Byrnes, James F. *The Supreme Court Must Be Curbed.* Greenwood: Association of Citizens' Councils of Mississippi, n.d.

Casky, W. M. *The South's Just Cause.* Clinton, Miss.: published by author, n.d.

Cheek, George W., Sr. *The Pending Tragedy in the South,* N.p. n.d.

Cincere, James (pseud.). *Operation Ole Mississippi.* Jackson: Jackson Citizens' Council, 1962.

Citizens' Council of Alabama. *The Undeniable Facts about the NAACP.* Montgomery: Citizens' Councils of Alabama, n.d.

Citizens' Council of America. *Annual Leadership Conference: How Can We Educate Our Children.* N.p., n.d.

Citizens' Councils in Louisiana. Homer: Association of Citizens' Councils of Louisiana, n.d.

Citizens' Council Survey: "Freedom of Choice." Jackson: Jackson Citizens' Council, n.d.

The Citizens' Council: The South's Only Answer. Montgomery: Citizens' Councils of Alabama, n.d.

The Citizens' Councils: Their Platform. Homer: Association of Citizens' Councils of Louisiana, n.d.

The Citizens' Council—What It Is. Dallas: Association of Citizens' Councils of Texas, n.d.

Community Plan to Counteract Racial Agitators. Greenwood: Association of Citizens' Councils of Mississippi, n.d.

Conflicting Views on Segregation: Reprint of a Series of Letters between Doctor D. M. Nelson, President of Mississippi College, Clinton, Mississippi, and an Unnamed Alumnus. Winona: Association of Citizens' Councils of Mississippi, n.d.

Congressional Committee Report on What Happened When Schools Were Integrated in Washington, D.C. Greenwood: Association of Citizens' Councils of Mississippi, n.d.

Cook, Eugene. *The Ugly Truth about the NAACP: An Address before the 55th Annual Convention of the Peace Officers Association of Georgia.* Greenwood: Association of Citizens' Councils of Mississippi, n.d.

Cox, Earnest Sevier. *White America.* Richmond: n.p., 1923.

Criswell, W. A. *Christianity and Segregation: An Address by Dr. W. A. Criswell, Pastor, First Baptist Church, Dallas, Texas, to the Joint Assembly of the Sovereign State of South Carolina.* N.p., n.d.

Cunningham, Morris. *Red Espionage Increase Warned by FBI's Hoover.* Jackson: Tennessee Federation for Constitutional Government, n.d.

Daniel, Carey. *God, the Original Segregationist.* Dallas: published by author, 1957.

Davidson, Donald. *Report of the State Chairman, Tennessee Federation for Constitutional Government.* Nashville: Tennessee Federation for Constitutional Government, 1957.

———. *Tyranny at Oak Ridge.* Nashville: Tennessee Federation for Constitutional Government, 1956.

The Disorders at the District of Columbia High School Championship Football Game. Greenwood: Association of Citizens' Councils of Mississippi, n.d.

Eastland, James O. *Is the Supreme Court Pro-Communist?* Richmond: Patrick Henry Press, n.d.

———. *We've Reached Era of Judicial Tyranny: An Address before the State-Wide Convention of the Association of Citizens' Councils of Mississippi, Jackson, December 1, 1955.* Greenwood: Association of Citizens' Councils of Mississippi, n.d.

Educational Fund of the Citizens' Councils. Greenwood: Association of Citizens' Councils of Mississippi, n.d.

Evans, Medford. *Civil Rights Myths and Communist Realities.* New Orleans: Conservative Society of America, 1965.

The Evers Opinion. Washington: National Putnam Letters Committee, n.d.

Garrett, Henry. *How Classroom Desegregation Will Work.* Richmond: Patrick Henry Press, n.d.

———. *Race: 11 Questions and 11 Answers.* Washington: National Putnam Letter Committee, n.d.

———. *The South and the Second Reconstruction.* N.p., 1963.

George, W. C. *The Biology of the Race Problem.* Richmond: Patrick Henry Press, n.d.

———. *Human Progress and the Race Problem.* Atlanta: Georgia Commission on Education, n.d.

———. *Race Heredity and Civilization: Human Progress and the Race Problem.* New York: Alliance, 1963.

———. *The Race Problem from the Standpoint of One Who Is Con-*

cerned about the Evils of Miscegenation. Birmingham: American States' Rights Association, Inc., 1955.

Gibson, Edmund A. *The Shocking Truth about Northern Virginia's Parent-Teacher Groups.* Arlington: Fairfax County Citizens' Council, n.d.

Gillespie, G. T. *A Christian View on Segregation.* Greenwood: Association of Citizens' Councils of Mississippi, 1955.

Hargis, Billy James. *Integration by Force Is Not a Christian Crusade.* Jackson, Tenn.: Tennessee Federation for Constitutional Government, n.d.

Harris, Roy V. *To the School Teachers and School Officials of Georgia.* Atlanta: States' Rights Council of Georgia, n.d.

Hollis, Louis W. *Integrity, an Address to the Annual Leadership Conference of the Citizens' Councils of America, Montgomery, Alabama, January 16, 1965.* Jackson: Citizens' Councils of America, n.d.

———. *John H. Wisdom, the Man Who Saved Rome* [*Georgia*]*: An Address to the Jackson Civil War Round Table, Jackson, Mississippi, October 18, 1963.* N.p., n.d.

How to Save Our Public Schools. Greenwood: Association of Citizens' Councils of Mississippi, n.d.

Ingram, T. Robert, ed. *Essays on Segregation.* Houston: St. Thomas Press, 1960.

Integration Today Means Racial and National Suicide Tomorrow. New Orleans: Greater New Orleans Citizens' Council, n.d.

Is Segregation Unchristian? Montgomery: Citizens' Councils of Alabama, n.d.

A Jewish View on Segregation. Greenwood: Association of Citizens' Councils of Mississippi, n.d.

Lawrence, Ellett. *Help Save America.* Greenwood: Association of Citizens' Councils of Mississippi, 1955.

Leatherbury, John R. *The National Council of Churches of Christ—Activities Revealed.* Atlanta: States' Rights Council of Georgia, n.d.

The Little Rock School Board's Plans for Your Child. Little Rock: Capital Citizens' Council, n.d.

Manual for Organization of Membership Drives. Homer: Association of Citizens' Councils of Louisiana, 1958.

A Message to the People of Tennessee from the Tennessee Federation for Constitutional Government. Nashville: Tennessee Federation for Constitutional Government, n.d.

Migration, the Only Reasonable Answer. Greenwood: Association of Citizens' Councils of Mississippi, n.d.

Morphew, Richard D. *Ole Miss and the Constitution: An Address to Associated Students of the California Institute of Technology, Pasadena, October 17, 1962*. N.p., n.d.

———. *The Citizens' Councils and the Negro Revolution: An Address to a Convocation at Beloit College, Beloit, Wisconsin* [February 25, 1964]. N.p., n.d.

The NAACP Legislative Scoreboard: The Civil Rights Crisis and the 84th Congress. Greenwood: Association of Citizens' Councils of Mississippi, n.d.

Norfleet, Marvin Brooks. *Forced Racial Integration.* Jackson, Tenn.: Tennessee Federation for Constitutional Government, n.d.

Over Dues: A Dialogue by and for Concerned Citizens. Jackson: Citizens' Councils of America, n.d.

Oxford: A Warning for Americans. Jackson: Mississippi State Junior Chamber of Commerce, 1962.

Patriotic American Youth. *Statewide College Scholarship Essay Contest.* N.p., n.d.

[Patterson, Robert B.] *The Citizens' Council.* Greenwood: Association of Citizens' Councils of Mississippi, [1955].

Patterson, Robert B. *The Citizens' Council: A History, an Address to the Annual Leadership Conference of the Citizens' Councils of America, Jackson, Mississippi, October 26, 1963.* Jackson: Citizens' Councils of America, n.d.

———. *The Road Ahead: An Address to Annual Leadership Conference of the Citizens' Councils of America, Montgomery, January 15, 1965.* Greenwood: Association of Citizens' Councils of Mississippi, n.d.

———. *The Truth Cries Out: An Address to Annual Leadership Conference of the Citizens' Councils of America, Chattanooga, Tennessee, January 8, 1966.* Greenwood: Association of Citizens' Councils of Mississippi, 1966.

Perez, Leander H. *The Challenge to the South and How It Must Be Met: An Address by L. H. Perez.* Belle Chasse: Sendker Printing Co., n.d.

Pittman, R. Carter. *The County Unit System Prevents City Political Machines Controlling the State of Georgia: Address to the Associated Industries of Georgia at Rome, Georgia, August 5, 1959.* Atlanta: States' Rights Council of Georgia, n.d.

———. *Is Integration by Default Planned for Georgia?* Atlanta: States' Rights Council of Georgia, n.d.

———. *The Supreme Court, the Broken Constitution, and the Shattered Bill of Rights.* Atlanta: States' Rights Council of Georgia, n.d.

A Plan for Virginia, Presented to the People of the Commonwealth by the Defenders of State Sovereignty and Individual Liberties. Richmond: Defenders of State Sovereignty and Individual Liberties, 1955.

Putnam, Carleton. *Framework for Love: A Study in Racial Realities, an Address to the Student Forum of the University of California at Davis, December 17, 1964.* Washington: National Putnam Letters Committee, n.d.

———. *Race and Reality: A Search for Solutions,* Washington: Public Affairs Press, 1967.

———. *Race and Reason: A Yankee View.* Washington: Public Affairs Press, 1961.

———. *The Road to Reversal: An Address Delivered before the Fifth Annual Attorney General's Conference for District Attorneys, State of Louisiana, New Orleans, February 16, 1962.* Washington: National Putnam Letters Committee, n.d.

———. *These Are the Guilty: Address Delivered before the Washington Putnam Letters Club, February 12, 1963.* Richmond: National Putnam Letters Committee, n.d.

Racial Facts. Greenwood: Association of Citizens' Councils, 1964.

[Rainach, William M., and William M. Shaw]. *Voter Qualification Laws in Louisiana: A Manual of Procedure for Registrars of Voters, Police Jurors and Citizens' Councils.* Homer: Association of Citizens' Councils of Louisiana, n.d.

Ricau, Jackson. *The Tragic Truth about the Catholic Race-Mixing Program in New Orleans: Address to Parents and Friends of Catholic Children, New Orleans, Louisiana, July 25, 1962.* Jackson: Citizens' Council of America, 1962.

Rogers, S. Emory. *Christian Love and Segregation.* Summerton: Association of Citizens' Councils of South Carolina, n.d.

Sanborn, Herbert C. *Dr. W. C. George's "The Biology of the Race Problem": A Review.* Nashville: Nashville Citizens' Councils, 1962.

Sass, Herbert R. *Mixed Schools and Mixed Blood.* Atlanta: States' Rights Council of Georgia, n.d.

Shearer, William K. *The Majority Consensus: An Address to the Los Angeles Citizens' Council, Los Angeles, California, March 4, 1965.* Jackson: Citizens' Councils of America, n.d.

Sickle Cell Anemia. N.p., n.d.

Simmons, William J. *Civil Rights and the Second Reconstruction: An Address to the Jefferson Society, University of Virginia, Charlottesville, March 22, 1963.* N.p., n.d.

———. *Civil Rights and the Oil Industry: An Address to the Desk and Derrick Club, Fort Worth, Texas, October 2, 1963.* N.p., n.d.

———. *A Comparison of Attitudes during Reconstruction I and II: Address to Jefferson Davis Camp No. 635 Sons of Confederate Veterans, Jackson, Mississippi, April 5, 1962.* N.p., n.d.

———. *The Mid-West Hears the South's Story: An Address before the Oakland Farmers-Merchants Annual Banquet, Oakland, Iowa, February 3, 1958.* Greenwood: Association of Citizens' Councils of Mississippi, n.d.

———. *Race Relations and Civil Rights: An Address to the Yale Political Union, New Haven, Connecticut, February 28, 1963.* N.p., n.d.

———. *The Road to Victory: An Address to the Organizational Meeting of the Atlanta Citizens' Council, May 14, 1963.* N.p., n.d.

———. *Why California Is Organizing: An Address to the Organizational Meeting of the Greater Los Angeles Citizens' Council, Los Angeles, June 30, 1964.* N.p., n.d.

———. *Why Segregation Is Right: An Address Presented at Notre Dame University, South Bend, March 7, 1963.* N.p., n.d.

States' Rights Council of Georgia, Inc. Augusta: States' Rights Council of Georgia, n.d.

Stone, Alfred H. *Civil Rights, States' Rights and the Reconstruction Background.* Greenwood: Association of Citizens' Councils of Mississippi, n.d.

The Story of the NAACP as Told by One of Its Founders. Greenwood: Association of Citizens' Councils of Mississippi, n.d.

Talmadge, Herman E. *Great Masses of People Leaderless, Confused by Slogans of Highly Organized Minorities.* Atlanta: States' Rights Council of Georgia, n.d.

———. *Southern Democrats Tired of Being Party's Whipping Boy!* Atlanta: States' Rights Council of Georgia, n.d.

———. *You and Segregation.* Birmingham: Vulcan Press, 1955.

Texas Citizens' Council. *The Citizens' Council—What It Is.* Dallas: Texas Citizens' Council, n.d.

The Undeniable Facts about the NAACP. Montgomery: Citizens' Council of Alabama, n.d.

Virginia Defenders of State Sovereignty and Individual Liberties. *Principles for Which We Stand.* Richmond: Virginia Defenders, 1958.

Williams, John Bell. *The Supreme Court Must Be Curbed: Reprint of Speech in the United States House of Representatives, January 25, 1956.* New Orleans: Federation for Constitutional Government, n.d.

———. *Where Is the Reign of Terror?* Greenwood: Association of Citizens' Councils of Mississippi, n.d.

What Integration Has Done to Your Nation's Capital. Montgomery: Citizens' Council of Alabama, n.d.

What Is the Citizens' Council Doing? Jackson: Citizens' Councils of America, n.d.

Why Segregation? Jackson: Tennessee Federation for Constitutional Government, n.d.

Why Should I Join the Council School Corporation? Jackson: Jackson Citizens' Council, n.d.

Winning Essays in the 1960 Contest. Greenwood: Association of Citizens' Councils of Mississippi, 1960.

CITIZENS' COUNCIL PERIODICALS

From the outset, state Council and Council-like associations endeavored to publish newspapers for their members. Among the first of these were the crudely mimeographed *Arkansas Faith,* published during 1955 by the White Citizens' Councils of Arkansas, and a more sophisticated tabloid, *The Citizens' Council* (1955–61), first published by the Association of Citizens' Councils of Mississippi and later adopted by the Citizens' Councils of America. In 1966 the CCA abandoned *The Citizens' Council* in favor of *The Citizen,* a monthly journal still published today. Other ventures in Council newspaper publishing were *The Alabamian* (1956–57) and its successor, *The [Montgomery] States' Rights Advocate* (1958–61); *The California Councilman* (n.d.); the *Councilor Newsletter* (1960), published by the Association of Citizens' Councils of Louisiana; *The Councilor* (1966–68), published by the Citizens' Councils of Louisiana; the Virginia *Defenders News and Views* (1956–58); *The Southerner: News of the [North Alabama] Citizens' Council* (1956); and *The [Houston] Texas Councilor* (n.d.). Many local Council organizations also published newsletters at more or less regular intervals. Among those are to be found *Aspect* (Jackson, Miss., 1964–67); *The Bulletin* (Association of Citizens' Councils of Georgia, 1964–65); *The Citizens' Report* (South Louisiana Citizens' Councils, 1961); *Greater Los Angeles Citizens' Council Action* (1966); *Montgomery County [Md.] Citizens' Council Bulletin* (n.d.); *Orangeburg [S.C.] Citizens' Council* (1956); the Georgetown County, South Carolina, *Phoenix* (1956); the Pearl, Mississippi, *Rankin Heritage* (1965); the Atmore, Alabama, *Southern Defender* (1965); and the Ruleville, Mississippi, *Spartan* (1966–67).

Enclosed dates indicate the years in which issues were examined, not necessarily the life of the publication.

OTHER CONTEMPORARY PERIODICALS OF CONTROVERSY

The most complete periodical coverage of both school desegregation and the Citizens' Council was provided by *Southern School News* (1954–65), a forthright and reliable monthly publication of the Southern Education Reporting Service. *New South* (1946–), the monthly journal of the Southern Regional Council, was more subjective but still very useful. The periodical which most nearly reflected the Council's point of view was *South: The Dixie News Magazine* (1936–), an illustrated monthly journal published in Birmingham.

Contemporary articles related to desegregation, and thus the resistance movement, number in the hundreds. Below are listed only those that pertain directly to the Citizens' Councils.

Anthony, Paul. "Pro-Segregation Groups' History and Trends," *New South,* 12 (January, 1957), 4–10.

———. "Resistance," *Research in Action,* Louisiana Council on Human Relations (November, 1956), 1–6.

"Asa Carter and the KKK," *The New Republic,* 136 (February 4, 1957), 6.

Carter, Hodding. "The South and I," *Look,* 19 (June 28, 1955), 74–80.

———. "A Wave of Terror Threatens the South," *Look,* 19 (March 22, 1955), 32–34.

Carter, Hodding, III. "Citadel of the Citizens' Council," *New York Times Magazine* (November 12, 1961), 22, 125.

———. "Mississippi: Deluded and Still Defiant," *The Nation,* 195 (October 13, 1962), 214–16.

Cater, Douglas. "The Bitter Fruits of Southern Bitter-Endism," *The Reporter,* 20 (January 22, 1959), 27–31.

———. "Civil War in Alabama's Citizens' Councils," *The Reporter,* 14 (May 17, 1956), 19–21.

"The Citizen," *Group Research Report,* Sec 3-PUB (April 21, 1965), 1–5.

"The Citizens' Councils and Anti-Semitism," *Facts,* 11 (January, 1956), 67–70.

"Citizens (White) Unite!" *Time,* 64 (September 20, 1954), 57.

Cleghorn, Reese. "The Segs," *Esquire,* 61 (January, 1964), 71–76.

Gamarekian, Edward. "The Ugly Battle of Orangeburg," *The Reporter,* 16 (January 24, 1957), 32–34.

Geyer, Elizabeth. "The New Ku Klux Klan," *Crisis* (March, 1956), 139–48.

Gordon, William. "Boycotts Can Cut Two Ways," *New South*, 11 (April, 1956), 5–10.

Halberstam, David. "A County Divided against Itself," *The Reporter*, 13 (December 15, 1955), 30–32.

———. "The White Citizens' Councils: Respectable Means for Unrespectable Ends," *Commentary*, 22 (October, 1956), 293–302.

"How White Citizens' Councils Came to Alabama," *New South*, 11 (December, 1955), 9–11.

Kelly, Tom. "Catch a Bigot by the Toe," *The Nation*, 200 (February 15, 1965), 169–70.

"Klans and Councils," *The New Republic*, 137 (September 23, 1957), 6.

Lapidary, Charles J. "Belzoni, Mississippi," *The New Republic*, 134 (May 7, 1956), 12–13.

Luce, Phillip Abbott. "Down in Mississippi—The White Citizens' Council," *Chicago Jewish Forum*, 18 (Summer, 1960), 323–27.

Maund, Alfred. "Grass-Roots Racism: White Councils at Work," *The Nation*, 181 (July 23, 1955), 70–72.

Miller, William Lee. "Trial by Tape Recorder," *The Reporter*, 13 (December 15, 1955), 27–30.

Powledge, Fred. "How to Set up a White Citizens' Council," *The New Republic*, 146 (June 11, 1962), 13.

"Pro-Segregation Group Trends," *Alabama Council [on Human Relations] Newsletter*, 3 (June, 1957), 1–5.

Raymond, Shepherd. "Lincoln and the White Supremacists," *Fact*, 10 (May–June, 1964), 49-52.

Rivers, Caryl. "Reporters Help to Turn Racial Group into Farce," *Editor and Publisher*, 98 (February 6, 1965), 55.

Robinson, Glen. "Crusaders for Segregation," *Nation's Schools*, 58 (December, 1956), 54–55.

Routh, Frederick B., and Paul Anthony. "Southern Resistance Forces," *Phylon Quarterly*, 18 (First Quarter, 1957), 50–58.

Scheer, Julian, "The White Folks Fight Back," *The New Republic*, 133 (October 31, 1955), 9–12.

"Segregation and the New Hate Groups," *Facts*, 9 (September, 1954), 21–26.

"Segregation and Southern Politics," *Facts*, 10 (October–November, 1955), 59–62.

Stein, W. "White Citizens' Councils," *Negro History Bulletin*, 20 (October, 1956), 2.

"Tornado Weather in Dixie," *The Christian Century,* 73 (February 29, 1956), 263–65.

Wakefield, Dan. "Respectable Racism: Dixie's Citizens Councils," *The Nation,* 181 (October 22, 1955), 339–41.

"William James Simmons," *Group Research Reports,* Sec 2-IND (May 13, 1964).

Woffard, John G. "The Ballot Box and the Grocery List," *The Reporter,* 17 (October 31, 1957), 23–26.

NEWSPAPERS

The basic source for Council history, like that of Klan history, is the daily and weekly press. Extremist weekly tabloids like the Birmingham *Dixie-American* ("Voice of the Anglo Saxon South") and the Augusta *Courier,* as well as such staunchly pro-Council dailies as the Charleston *News and Courier* and the Jackson *Daily News,* provided coverage not only of resistance group attitudes and policies but activities as well. Moderate and liberal southern papers—the Arkansas *Gazette,* the Atlanta *Constitution,* the Nashville *Tennessean,* the Greenville *Delta Democrat-Times,* the Louisville *Courier Journal,* the St. Louis *Post-Dispatch,* to name only the more prominent ones—provided both a running commentary on the action along the region's troubled racial front and a record of Council excesses. Among northern newspapers, the coverage given by the New York *Times* was by far the most complete; but other newspapers outside the South ran lengthy series of articles on the Council. The best of these were by James Desmond in the New York *Daily News,* November 22–26, 1955 (later reprinted by the NAACP under the title *New Cross Afire in Dixie,* n.d.) and Stan Opotowsky in the New York *Post,* January 7–20, 1957 (reprinted by the NAACP under the title *Dixie Dynamite: The Inside Story of the White Citizens' Council,* n.d.). The black press, most notably the Baltimore *Afro-America,* the Birmingham *World,* the Chicago *Defender,* the Norfolk *Journal and Guide,* the Oklahoma *Black Dispatch,* and the Pittsburgh *Courier,* waged a persistent war of words against militant white segregationists. Also useful were small circulation newspapers, such as the Jackson (Tenn.) *Sun,* the Santa Ana (Calif.) *Register,* and the Yazoo City (Miss.) *Herald,* which reported on the affairs of local Councils.

Altogether some one hundred newspapers were used in the course of this project, most of them conveniently located in the clipping files of the Anti-Defamation League, the Southern Education Reporting Service, and the Southern Regional Council. Although the newspaper files of each of these agencies were sizeable, those of SERS were by far the most extensive. The Eugene Cox Materials at Mississippi State also contain a valuable collection of clippings pertaining to the Citizens' Council in Mississippi, some of which unfortunately are unidentified. The personal scrapbook of Alabama Council leader Samuel M. Engelhardt also proved very useful, as did Meredith Crown's personal file of newspaper clippings on Council activity in California.

PAMPHLETS AND REPORTS OF COUNCIL CRITICS

The most systematic contemporary analysis of Council thought and action was provided by the Southern Regional Council. Although occasionally marred by error, its reports, published and unpublished, provide a wealth of information for the discerning researcher. Its *Special Report: Pro-Segregation Groups in the South,* November 19, 1956, and the revised edition of May 23, 1957, offer a state-by-state analysis of the resistance movement. Paul Anthony, "A Survey of the Resistance Groups of Alabama" (1956), "Patriots of North Carolina, Inc." (n.d.), and "The Resistance Groups of South Carolina" (n.d.) are Southern Regional Council field reports which explore in detail the character of organized segregation groups in three states. Three unpublished "confidential" reports to the Southern Regional Council by H. L. Mitchell chronicle Council growth and activity, particularly in regard to organized labor: "A Report on the Rise of the White Citizens' Council in the South," "On the Rise of the White Citizens' Council and Its Ties with Anti-Labor Forces in the South," and "The White Citizens' Council vs. Southern Trade Unions." Paul Anthony, "An Analysis of the Hate Literature of Resistance Groups of the South" (interoffice memorandum, Southern Regional Council, n.d.), and "Partial Description of Anti-Semitic Activities and of Literature Recommended and Distributed by White Citizens' Councils and Other Groups in the South" (manuscript, Southern Regional Council, February 27, 1956) are highly critical reports on Council propaganda.

The movement's endeavors to organize beyond Dixie's borders are the subject of several brief unpublished reports by Norman Kilpatrick. Copies of these undated manuscripts ("California to Maryland with the White Citizens' Council," "Report on D.C., Virginia, and Maryland Work Given by Joe Mitchell," "Short History of the Citizens' Council in Maryland," "The White Citizens' Councils Move North") are located at the Southern Regional Council.

The field reports of the A-DL offer detailed and remarkably objective accounts of desegregation in several cities. Especially useful are Warren

Breed, *Beaumont, Texas: College Desegregation without Popular Support* (New York, n.d.); John Howard Griffin and Theodore Freedman, *Mansfield, Texas: A Report on the Crisis Situation Resulting from Efforts to Desegregate the School System* (New York, 1957); Anna Halden, Bonita Valien, Preston Valien, and Francis Manis, *Clinton, Tennessee: A Tentative Description and Analysis of the School Desegregation Crisis* (New York, n.d.); Lewis Jones and Stanley Smith, *Tuskegee, Alabama: Voting Rights and Economic Pressure* (New York, 1958).

For the NAACP's assessment of racial crises and the Council's role in them, the *Annual Reports* are indispensable, as are such occasional NAACP publications as Alfred Baker Lewis, *Convict the Killers for a Change* (New York, 1968); *M Is for Mississippi and Murder* (New York, n.d.); and *"We Never Claimed It to Be Authentic"* (New York, 1956).

SECONDARY SOURCES

Except for studies bearing directly on either the Second Reconstruction or the Citizens' Council no attempt will be made here to include secondary works either used or cited in this study. Major bibliographies which describe such tangential sources are Arthur S. Link and Rembert W. Patrick, eds., *Writing Southern History: Essays in Historiography in Honor of Fletcher M. Green* (Baton Rouge, 1965); Elizabeth W. Miller, *The Negro in America: A Bibliography*, 2nd ed. (Cambridge, Mass., 1970); and Meyer Weinberg, *School Integration: A Comprehensive Classified Bibliography of 3,100 References* (New York, 1968). By far the most useful bibliography for the post-*Brown* South, however, is the "Critical Essay on Authorities" in Numan V. Bartley, *The Rise of Massive Resistance: Race and Politics in the South during the 1950's* (Baton Rouge, 1969).

Bartley's *Massive Resistance* is also the best point of departure for any study of the South during the first decade of desegregation. A sprightly and penetrating analysis, it supersedes Reed Sarratt, *The Ordeal of Desegregation: The First Decade* (New York, 1966) and Benjamin Muse, *Ten Years of Prelude: The Story of Integration since the Supreme Court's 1954 Decision* (New York, 1964) as the best survey of white southern resistance to social change. Other noteworthy general accounts of the period since the public school desegregation decision are: Wilma Dykeman and James Stokely, *Neither Black nor White* (New York, 1957); Anthony Lewis and the New York *Times*, *Portrait of a Decade: The Second American Revolution* (New York, 1964); Don Shoemaker, ed., *With All Deliberate Speed: Segregation-Desegregation in Southern Schools* (New York, 1957); James W. Vander Zanden, *Race*

Relations in Transition: The Segregation Crisis in the South (New York, 1965); and Dan Wakefield, *Revolt in the South* (New York, 1960).

Scholarly articles on particular aspects of the post-*Brown* South are numerous, but the most perceptive interpretations are to be found in two popularly written pieces by C. Vann Woodward, "From the First Reconstruction to the Second," *Harper's*, 230 (April, 1965), 127–33, and "The 'New Reconstruction' in the South," *Commentary*, 21 (June, 1956), 501–8.

Accounts of massive resistance at the state level are fairly numerous. Virginia's truculent stand has been ably examined by Robbins L. Gates, *The Making of Massive Resistance: Virginia's Politics of Public School Desegregation, 1954–56* (Chapel Hill, 1962); and Benjamin Muse, *Virginia's Massive Resistance* (Bloomington, 1961). The politics of resistance at the local level and its effects on the children of one Old Dominion county are portrayed in Robert Smith, *They Closed Their Schools: Prince Edward County, Virginia, 1951–1964* (Chapel Hill, 1965). Other works covering the segregation controversy from the vantage point of a single state include Patrick Earl McCauley, "Political Implications in Alabama of the School Segregation Decisions" (unpublished M.A. thesis, Vanderbilt University, 1957); Earlean Mary McCarrick, "Louisiana's Official Resistance to Desegregation" (unpublished Ph.D. dissertation, Vanderbilt University, 1964); Howard H. Quint, *Profile in Black and White: A Frank Portrait of South Carolina* (Washington, 1958); and James W. Silver, *Mississippi: The Closed Society.*

The first scholarly effort to write a history of organized segregation on a regional scale was a broadly based study by a political scientist, James W. Vander Zanden, "The Southern White Resistance Movement to Integration" (unpublished Ph.D. dissertation, University of North Carolina, 1958). It is useful but dull and should be supplemented by two commendable journalistic accounts: John Bartlow Martin, *The Deep South Says "Never"* (New York, 1957) and James Graham Cook, *The Segregationists* (New York, 1962). Both of these works are lively and based primarily on personal interviews with Deep South segregation leaders. On the state level only the Association of Citizens' Councils of Mississippi has been the subject of careful scrutiny. *The South Strikes Back* (Garden City, 1959), by Hodding Carter III, is a well-written and thoughtful book by a young Mississippi liberal who knows his state well. It is vastly superior to Phillip Abbott Luce, "The Mississippi White Citizens' Council: 1954–1959" (unpublished M.A. thesis, Ohio State University, 1960). Something of an itinerant ideologue who has migrated from New Left to Far Right, Luce studied the organization from within, as secretary to

Robert Patterson. But his work is marred by occasional error and frequent invective. Yet another study of the Council in Mississippi is Wilson Minor, "The Citizens' Council: A Decade of Incredible Defiance," an unpublished, unfinished manuscript by one of the region's most perceptive journalists. Although brief, Minor's work is highly suggestive of the Council's political impact on one Deep South state.

Other valuable contributions of a secondary nature include Samuel DuBois Cook, "Political Movements and Organizations," *Journal of Politics,* 26 (February, 1964), 130–53; Harold C. Fleming, "Resistance Movements and Racial Desegregation," *The Annals of the American Academy of Political and Social Science* (March, 1956), 44–52; James W. Vander Zanden, "The Citizens' Council," *Alpha Kappa Deltan,* 29 (Spring, 1959), 3–9, and "A Note on the Theory of Social Movements," *Sociology and Social Research,* 44 (September-October, 1959), 3–7.

Index

A Note on the Author

A hitherto unpublished student of the New South, Neil R. McMillen is assistant professor of history and Dean of the Basic College at his undergraduate alma mater, the University of Southern Mississippi. A high school football star, former marine, one-time welder, ditch-digger, and Dun & Bradstreet credit reporter, this Woodrow Wilson Fellow received his doctorate from Vanderbilt in 1969.

Mr. McMillen was born in 1939. Although a native of Michigan, he has spent most of his adult life in the South. He now lives with his wife and two children in the heart of the south-central Mississippi pine belt.